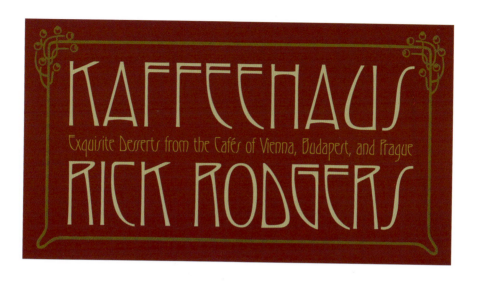

KAFFEEHAUS

Exquisite Desserts from the Cafés of Vienna, Budapest, and Prague

RICK RODGERS

Photographs by Kelly Bugden

Clarkson Potter/Publishers
New York

Published by Clarkson Potter/Publishers, New York,
New York. Member of the Crown Publishing Group.

Random House, Inc.
New York, Toronto, London, Sydney, Auckland
www.randomhouse.com

CLARKSON N. POTTER is a trademark and POTTER and
colophon are registered trademarks of Random House, Inc.

Printed in China

Design by Skouras Design

Library of Congress Cataloging-in-Publication Data
Rodgers, Rick, 1953-
Kaffeehaus: exquisite desserts from the classic cafes of
Vienna, Budapest, and Prague / Rick Rodgers.
Includes bibliographical references and index.
1. Desserts. I. Title.
TX773.R625   2002
641.8′6—dc21

ISBN 0-609-60453-8

10 9 8 7 6 5 4 3 2 1

First Edition

This book is dedicated to Karitas Sigurdsson-Mitrogogos, who took me under her wing in Vienna and enthusiastically guided me through an incredible itinerary of coffeehouses and bakeries. Karitas became my guide, translator, concierge, and "matchmaker" as she introduced me to Viennese who knew the coffeehouse business inside out. Karitas and her husband, Alexander, now feel like family, and I will always be grateful for their friendship.

My research trips to Vienna, Budapest, and Prague were made pleasurable thanks to the efforts of many, many people who took time out of their busy lives.

In Vienna: Irene Jenkins, who started the project as an invaluable researcher and liaison with the great cafés of Vienna, and became a cherished friend; Vinzenz Bäuerle, for showing me the backstage operations at Oberlaa Kurkonditorei; the Bleuel family, owners of the Tulbingerkogel Hotel and Restaurant in the Vienna Woods, for a charming and informative

In Budapest, I never would have gotten my foot in the door without the enormously generous assistance of one of the great men of the international restaurant business, George Lang, owner of two of Budapest's best restaurants, Gundel and Bagolyvár, as well as New York City's Café des Artistes. Once that door was open, Krisztina Péter, Gundel's public relations manager, kindly put out the word about the American writer who was in town looking for recipes from the great cafés. András Hûvös Récsi, pastry chef of Gundel, and Andrea Németh, chef of Bagolyvár, demonstrated their specialties for me. Mária Ágoston Reichné, manager of Lukács, also helped introduce me to the world of Hungarian baking. At Gerbeaud, executive chef Sándor Kovács and Manager Andrea Szappanos gave me a behind-the-scenes look at the kitchens of that great institution, and Krisztina Bacsi guided me through the equally renowned Café New York. My translator in Budapest, Péter Koltai,

ACKNOWLEDGMENTS

evening of talk about Viennese cuisine and a fine dinner showcasing three traditional desserts; Christian Bär of the Hotel Sacher; Dietmar Furthmayr, for a guided tour of the main bakery for Aida; Hans Diglas of Café Diglas, for a long discussion of the day-to-day operations of a coffeehouse; Gert Gerersdorfer of Café Dommayer, for many courtesies; Gerda Hofer, the personification of Gemütlichkeit, for a lovely Jause (afternoon tea) and her insights into Viennese home baking; Raimund Höflinger for a jovial and engrossing visit to the illustrious Café Central; Walter Leschanz and his assistant, Fujiwara, for their hands-on demonstrations of strudel and Sachertorte; Joerg Nairz, architect for the renovation of Café Sperl, for an in-depth discussion of the interior design of classic Viennese cafés; Paul Skop, director of the Berufsschule für den Lebensmittel-Textilbereich, Technische Zeichner und Zahntechniker, for a tour of the school's professional baking program; Frans-Jan Soede of Demel for many favors, from providing recipes, books, and historical information to a tour of Demel's operation from top to bottom, and manager Steffi Kren; Evelyn Petros-Gumpel and Audrey Stotler, respectively, for their melodious companionship; and Ken Balbon de Mapayo, for sharing his table at Café Hawelka and introducing me to the Hawelka family.

smoothed the bumpy road of meeting the Hungarian language head-on.

Before I got to Prague, I had to make initial contacts, which were provided by the resourceful Berta Ledecky of New York City. When Berta got my call for help, she went into action—a very impressive sight indeed. She set me up with her old friend Dr. Karl Zeman, who not only escorted me in Prague from café to café, but provided a healthy serving of his city's fascinating history, as well. Thanks also to Milan Kousal, who also proved to be a fine guide in Prague.

In America: In my career as a food professional, I have been lucky to have the friendship of some of the best bakers in America. I can always depend on them to take an anxious phone call with an urgent question. Beth Hensperger sent along her favorite recipes from the Danube region; Sarabeth Levine spent a day making strudel after strudel with me; Nick Malgieri gave suggestions on resource material; Adrienne Welch, one of my first mentors, continues to inspire me with her attention to detail and unerring sense of taste. Ella Szabo of Perfect Pastries/Hungarian Tortes in Greenwich, Connecticut, and her husband, Arto, shared recipes and their reminiscences of Hungarian life. Thanks also to Flo Braker, Rose Levy Beranbaum, and Carole Walter.

Carin Crowe translated many German language works for me and probably now feels as if she's read every word on cafés ever written. Thanks also to Chris Leone, for introducing me to Carin; fellow food writer Michael Krondl for sharing his family recipes for Czech baking specialties; Johanna Schreiner of the Austrian firm Gmundner Keramik, for donating tabletop products for photography; Gail DeGracia of Austrian Airlines: Hannalore Zolle at the Austrian Trade Council; Andrea Szakál of the Hungarian Tourist Board; Katerina Patilovita of the Czech Tourist Office; Friederike Zeitlhofer at the Austrian Cultural Institute; Abby Rivers; and Erna Zahn.

From the beginning, my editor Roy Finamore appreciated what I hoped to accomplish with this work, and he was generous with his talent for producing beautiful books. Working in four languages was a challenge that I could not have faced without the amazingly meticulous work of Janet McDonald, my copy editor. Thanks to Angela Skouras for supplying the evocative design of the book, and Potter art director Marysarah Quinn for making the match. Also, my gratitude to Martin Patmos, Lance Troxel, Jane Searle, Mark McCauslin, and Leigh Ann Ambrosi.

And, as always, an incalculable amount of gratitude to my longtime friend and agent, Susan Ginsburg; her assistant, Annie Leuenberger; my "home team" of invaluable assistants and irreplaceable buddies, Diane Kniss and Steven Evasew; and my ever-supportive partner, Patrick Fisher.

INTRODUCTION XI

BASIC BATTERS, DOUGHS, ICINGS & GLAZES 1

A Demitasse of History 2

WARM-METHOD SPONGE CAKE 5

COLD-METHOD SPONGE CAKE 7

CHOCOLATE SPONGE CAKE 8

VIENNESE SWEET YEAST DOUGH 8

Demel: Sugar Baker to the Empire 9

The Story Behind Viennese Sweet Yeast Dough 10

PUFF PASTRY 13

CREAM PUFF DOUGH 14

SHORT CRUST DOUGH 15

FAUX FONDANT ICING 15

CHOCOLATE GLAZE 16

APRICOT GLAZE 16

WARM CHOCOLATE SAUCE 18

VANILLA SAUCE 18

MERINGUE CREAM 18

SWEETENED WHIPPPED CREAM 19

SIMPLE CAKES 21

Coffee: Common Man's Gold 22

FARMER'S CHEESECAKE 24

APRICOT TART 26

APRICOT COFFEE CAKE 26

CHERRY-ALMOND COFFEE CAKE 27

CHOCOLATE "SADDLE OF VENISON" CAKE 28

The Story Behind Burgtheatertorte 30

CHOCOLATE-ORANGE CAKE 31

POPPY SEED GUGELHUPF 33

BANANA GUGELHUPF 33

MARBLE GUGELHUPF 34

CHESTNUT SLICES 35

BISHOP'S FRUIT-AND-CHOCOLATE TEA CAKE 36

VIENNESE POUND CAKE 38

PLUM SQUARES 38

FLOURLESS POPPY SEED CAKE 39

BLUEBERRY CREAM ROULADE 40

Café Slavia 41

CHOCOLATE-CHERRY ROULADE 42

Café Dommayer 43

HAZELNUT ROULADE WITH MOCHA CREAM 44

WALNUT CROWN CAKE 46

ZUCCHINI SLICES WITH CHOCOLATE GLAZE 47

FANCY CAKES 49

The Classic Kaffeehaus 51

BROWN LINZERTORTE 52

The Story Behind Linzertorte 54

LADYFINGER TORTE WITH RUM CREAM 54

PUNCH CAKE 56

ORANGE TORTE WITH ORANGE CREAM FROSTING 57

LESCHANZ'S CHOCOLATE MOUSSE CAKE 58

SACHERTORTE 59

The Story Behind Sachertorte 60

LESCHANZ'S SACHERTORTE 62

MERINGUE SHELL WITH STRAWBERRIES AND CREAM 64

The Story Behind Spanische Windtorte 64

WALNUT TORTE WITH WALNUT-CUSTARD BUTTERCREAM 66

STRAWBERRY CREAM TORTE 67

CHOCOLATE-ALMOND TORTE 69

RASPBERRY YOGURT TORTE 70

The Story Behind Dobos Torte 71

DOBOS TORTE 73

CHOCOLATE-CHERRY MOUSSE CAKE 74

STRUDELS 77

STRUDEL DOUGH 78

APPLE STRUDEL 80

SOUR CHERRY STRUDEL 82

GRAPE STRUDEL WITH WEINCHAUDEAU 82

Filo Facts 83

WARM "MILK-CREAM" STRUDEL WITH VANILLA SAUCE 84

PEAR STRUDEL WITH PUFF PASTRY 86

CONTENTS

FARMER'S CHEESE AND RAISIN FILO
   STRUDEL 86

JWEET YEAJT BREADJ 89

Coffee in Three-Quarter Time 91

BRIOCHE BRAID 92

CHEESE-FILLED SWEET ROLLS 94

VIENNESE JAM ROLLS 95

VIENNESE CRESCENT ROLLS 96

The Story Behind Kipferln 97

CURRANT AND HAZELNUT SNAILS 98

GOLDEN DUMPLINGS 99

DALMATIAN FOUR-FLAVOR KOLACKY 100

YEAST GUGELHUPF 102

The Story Behind Gugelhupf 103

YEAST PLUM SQUARES 104

The Municipal House 104

Oberlaa: The Whipped Cream Diet 107

CHRISTMAS SWEET BREAD 108

HUNGARIAN WALNUT ROULADES 110

"JLICEJ" & OTHER INDIVIDUAL DEJJERTJ 113

The Rise of the Kaffeehaus 114

APPLE, WALNUT, AND POPPY SEED
   BARS 116

Tokaji 118

APPLE SQUARES 118

APPLES IN PASTRY ROBES 119

BERRY MERINGUE SLICES 121

HUNGARIAN CHOCOLATE MOUSSE
   SQUARES 122

The Story Behind Rigó Jancsi 123

COFFEE ECLAIRS 123

CHOCOLATE-BANANA SLICES 124

PUFF PASTRY CORNETS WITH WHIPPED
   CREAM 126

The Story Behind Indianerkrapfen 127

CHOCOLATE-COVERED "INDIAN"
   CUPCAKES 127

The Café New York 129

The Story Behind Esterházyschnitten 130

NUT MERINGUE SLICES 130

The Story Behind Gerbeaud Slices 132

GERBEAUD SLICES 133

PUFF PASTRY CREAM SLICES WITH COFFEE
   ICING 134

MERINGUE AND LADYFINGER SLICES 136

HUNGARIAN FLAKY SCONES 138

COOKIEJ & DOUGHNUTJ 141

ISCHL TARTLETS 142

When a Coffeehouse Is Not a Coffeehouse 143

CHOCOLATE-ALMOND MACAROONS 145

COCONUT MACAROONS 146

Aida 146

CHESTNUT "POTATOES" 147

LINZER "EYES" 148

VANILLA CRESCENTS 149

WALNUT CRESCENT COOKIES FROM
   POZSONY 150

THUMBPRINT COOKIES 151

MARDIS GRAS DOUGHNUTS 152

The Story Behind Faschingkrapfen 154

CRULLERS WITH RUM GLAZE 155

PANCAKEJ & JWEET OMELETJ 157

The Fall and Rebirth of the Kaffeehaus 158

BASIC CRÊPES 160

GUNDEL-STYLE CRÊPES 160

JAM-FILLED CRÊPES 161

THE EMPEROR'S PANCAKE 162

The Story Behind Kaiserschmarren 162

CHEESE-FILLED CRÊPES 163

SOUR CREAM MINI-PANCAKES 164

SALZBURG DESSERT SOUFFLÉ 166

SWEET FRUIT OMELET 166

> The Story Behind Stefánia-Omelette 167

SWEET DUMPLINGS & NOODLES 169

> Flour or Sugar? Hot or Cold? 171

FARMER'S CHEESE AND STRAWBERRY
DUMPLINGS 172

FARMER'S CHEESE DUMPLINGS WITH
"ROASTED" PLUMS 174

POTATO NOODLES WITH SWEET POPPY
SEEDS 174

PRUNE POCKETS 175

HOT & COLD PUDDINGS 177

CROISSANT AND APPLE PUDDING 178

> Coffee, Vienna-Style 179

CHOCOLATE-CREAM "DUMPLINGS" 180

MOLDED RICE PUDDING WITH
RASPBERRIES 182

> The Story Behind Reis Trauttmansdorff 183

STEAMED CHOCOLATE PUDDING 183

WARM RICE PUDDING WITH CHERRIES 185

WARM WALNUT PUDDINGS 186

VIENNESE-STYLE ZABAGLIONE WITH
RASPBERRIES 187

HOT & COLD BEVERAGES 189

> The Story Behind Maria Theresia 192

HOT COFFEE WITH ORANGE LIQUEUR 192

> Coffee, Tea, and Chocolate 194

HOT RUM PUNCH 195

MULLED "GLOW" WINE 195

FRUIT AND WINE PUNCH 197

REAL HOT CHOCOLATE 197

HOT SPICED TEA 197

> The Coffee Menu 198

GLOSSARY OF INGREDIENTS, EQUIPMENT &
TECHNIQUES 200

A PERSONAL COFFEEHOUSE GUIDE 217

MAIL-ORDER SOURCES 225

BIBLIOGRAPHY 227

INDEX 228

The old Austro-Hungarian empire has been gone since 1918, but in the empire's capitals of Vienna, Budapest, and Prague, its most beloved and delicious tradition—the coffeehouse—lives on.

An Austro-Hungarian café (known as a *Kaffeehaus* in Austrian, *kávéház* in Hungarian, and *kavárna* in Czech) is living history. It was from the Café Dommayer that the lilting music of Strauss, inseparable from central European culture, first caressed Viennese ears. The violent 1848 Revolution erupted from Budapest's Café Pilvax. The compeers of Václav Havel and his compatriots organized Czechoslovakia's Velvet Revolution over coffee at the Café Slavia. The intelligentsia of all three cities used the cafés as their living rooms, occasionally laying down their pens to argue the latest developments in literary, art, and music circles. Historical and geographical names jump out from the menu—Malakoff, Sacher, Dobos, Maria Theresia, Linz, Rigó Jancsi, Pozsony—and they continue.

Today's coffeehouses, after an admittedly shaky period following World War Two, are now as vital and vibrant as they have ever been. Strolling through Vienna, Budapest, and Prague, the three main cities of the empire, you'll see countless cafés, each with its own style and personality. They may remind you of your own favorite coffeehouse back home, where locals sit and sip, slowly flipping through newspapers and magazines or gossiping with their friends. An Austro-Hungarian coffeehouse may have a familiar feel, but there are tangible differences between our homegrown version and the real thing.

First, the coffeehouse tradition is well over three hundred years old, with customs so entrenched they are almost choreographed. At a true *Kaffeehaus*, there is no such thing as a quick cup of coffee; coffeehouse habitués never rush through their cup. Your coffee comes in a china cup on a gleaming metal tray, always with a glass of cold water that your waiter refills from time to time. If you need a fast coffee to go (a condition that is met with the utmost sympathy), you must search out an espresso bar, an entirely different venue.

The desserts served at a *Kaffeehaus* set it apart from its peers throughout the world. The dessert display can be a modest selection of a few specialties of the house, or it can be an impressively dramatic exposition of towering *Torten*. Your choice of dessert could

INTRODUCTION

be the hardest decision you have to make all day. Should it be a thick, intensely chocolate slice of Sachertorte, one of the world's most beloved cakes? Perhaps freshly baked apple strudel (or grape or cherry or cheese)? Or the sugar-dusted Gugelhupf? A chocolate-glazed "Indian" puff, a wedge of jam-filled Linzertorte, a slice of vanilla-scented cheesecake, or a square of rustic but satisfying plum cake? They are all there in their tempting glory. Austro-Hungarian pastry shares few of its masterpieces with French pâtisserie. It stands proud and independent, and it could be argued that the French picked up plenty of baking secrets from the skilled Viennese bakers.

If the Viennese had a food pyramid, desserts would be the main category. They are a way of life, not just a treat at the end of meal. The Austrians have the equivalent of British teatime, the *Jause* (pronounced YOW-sah, from the Czech word *jouzina,* or lunch). Every afternoon at four o'clock, the city's coffeehouses and bakeries (which always seem to be bustling and filled to the brim regardless of the hour) get a fresh infusion of customers. While British teatime will include savory snacks, *Jause* is always sweet, stemming from the period when filling cheese- or fruit-based meals were served for dinner on meatless Fridays. Adherence to the Catholic rules of abstinence and fast was paramount, as the emperor of Austria was also the emperor of the Holy Roman Empire, a title conferred by the pope himself.

This book is Vienna-centric for many reasons. Vienna was the seat of the royal Hapsburgs, who controlled Austria, Hungary, and what is now the Czech and Slovak Republic (but was called Bohemia and Moravia during the days of the empire). The court influenced everything that happened in Prague and Budapest. There was a healthy exchange of recipes among these cities—the sweet noodles of Bohemia, the tortes of Vienna, and the strudels of Hungary are staples in all three cities. The range of desserts is enormous in Vienna, still impressive in Budapest, but not as expansive in Prague. (Unfortunately, during the Communist era, desserts were considered the food of the bourgeoisie, and, to be frank, many of the Hungarian and Czech bakeries lost their flair for fine baking. But the best, such as Budapest's Gerbeaud, have been restored to their former glory.) Because you will be able to find every one of these desserts in Vienna,

I have chosen to give the Austrian translation of the title for most of them. If a dish is clearly from Hungary or old Bohemia, I use the Hungarian or Czech name.

Finally, Vienna had an enormous influence on world thought, especially in the late nineteenth and early twentieth centuries. Some of this influence is waning as new schools of thought develop. But there is no discounting the importance of the Viennese in modern international culture. The practice of psychiatry was started by Sigmund Freud and Victor Adler. Constantly feuding over the superiority of the subconscious versus the superiority complex, the two did not speak to each other when they ran into each other at Café Landtmann. Trotsky played chess and drank coffee at Café Central. Hollywood would have been less stimulating without movies directed by Billy Wilder, Otto Preminger, and George Cukor. Gustav Mahler, Alban Berg, and Anton Bruckner changed twentieth-century music. Theodor Herzl developed the idea of the Zionist state. The plays of Hugo von Hofmannsthal don't show up on many stages, but his words are regularly sung whenever Richard Strauss's operas are performed. The operettas of Johann Strauss the younger, Franz Lehár, and Oscar Straus were not only European favorites, but hits on Broadway, as well, and were made into movies, in some cases three or four times.

This cookbook is about the classic *Kaffeehäuser.* Yes, there are contemporary cafés, but they are the children of the old guard. Even if the trappings of the new cafés are sleek and modern, the menu will still have apple strudel and not lemongrass sorbet. It should be said here that not every place that serves dessert and coffee is considered a *Kaffeehaus.* There are many categories, including pastry shops, bread bakeries, espresso bars, and café–restaurants. These distinctions are very important to the Europeans if not to Americans or other visitors. Also, this is not meant to be a complete cookbook on the home-baked desserts of the three countries, but a collection of recipes for the desserts you are most likely to find at coffeehouses and bakeries. Recipes contributed by home bakers have been included only if they can be found on coffeehouse menus.

Austro-Hungarian desserts are a part of my heritage. My grandmother was born in Liechtenstein, the tiny principality nestled between Austria and Switzerland. Even though Liechtenstein is independent and managed to stay neutral throughout the world wars of the last century, it has always been influenced by the politics and culture of nearby Vienna. In fact, the principality was formed in 1719 when the emperor rewarded the Liechtenstein family with their very own fiefdom for their services to the empire.

My great-aunts were wonderful bakers in the Viennese style. Relatives still argue over who was the better baker: Auntie Gisela, Auntie Trudy, or Auntie Erna? Auntie Gisela's specialties would have made any bakery jealous. She always made puff-pastry horns filled with whipped cream (*Schaumrollen*) and homemade *Kipferln* (Viennese croissants), and she occasionally graced the table with a tall, light Gugelhupf. They were all accompanied by strong coffee topped with a generous spoonful of whipped cream. I recently learned, however, that my great-aunts really weren't great bakers in the old country. Once they were here, they baked regularly for two reasons. First, it gave them a connection to their past. The second, less romantic, reason was that a couple of my aunties became domestics. Their employers obviously assumed that they would know how to bake Viennese pastries, so they had to learn, and fast!

When I decided to write this book, I initially wanted to expand upon my family's recipe files. On my many research trips to central Europe, happily working at some of the world's best bakeries, I realized that I had opened a sugar-coated Pandora's box. This couldn't just be a collection of dessert recipes. When I interviewed professional and home bakers, they always talked in the context of a recipe's history and its place in their lives. When I went to a coffeehouse, even though they were all different, the experience was almost a recurring ritual, from the floor plan to the menu. Everything was about tradition. There was no need to add fancy new creations to the menu. Who doesn't love a good Sachertorte?

The broad term encompassing all Viennese desserts in *Süßspeisen,* literally "food or meals made from sugar," but can also mean a dessert that incorporates little or no flour. Within *Süßspeisen* is *Mehlspeisen,* "food or meals made from flour." Austro-Hungarian cookbooks often separate the desserts into two distinct categories, warm and cold. While there may be a few overlaps, the chapters in this book generally follow the Viennese categorization, concentrating on the *Mehlspeisen* that are most often served in the classic coffeehouse.

The recipes start with the basic batters, doughs, and icings. The "cold" flour-based desserts start with simple cakes, then move on to fancy tortes, working their way through the *Mehlspeisen* family, offering strudels, sweet breads, cookies, and doughnuts along the way. "Warm" desserts are represented by dishes that may be uncharted territory for many American bakers: pancakes (crêpes), sweet omelets (which are actually more like warm, fluffy cakes than the French egg dish), sweet dumplings and noodles (much beloved by the Czech), puddings, and beverages.

One day I was baking with my friend Walter Leschanz, who had worked at both Demel and Sacher (which is like a star baseball pitcher who has played for both the Yankees and the Mets). We were talking, of course, of the importance of tradition in the Austro-Hungarian pastry kitchen, and of how many recipes are hundreds of years old.

"As one of my master bakers used to say," Walter remarked, "If you keep the flame burning, you won't have to worry about cleaning up the ashes."

The coffeehouses of Vienna, Budapest, and Prague are keeping the fire alive.

PHOTOGRAPHS

FRONTISPIECE   Gerbeaud, Budapest.

vi   Newspapers, Café Dommayer, Vienna.

viii   Silver coffee urns, Café Dommayer.

ix   The main room, Gerbeaud, Budapest.

x   Clockwise, from left: Dobos Torte, Chocolate-Cherry Mousse Cake, Linzertorte.

xiii   Café Slavia, Prague, with a partial view of *The Absinthe Drinker.*

xvi   Clockwise, from top: Warm-Method Sponge Cake, Apricot Glaze, Chocolate Sponge Cake.

12   K. u. K. Hofzuckerbäckerei Demel, Vienna.

17   The café, Municipal House, Prague.

20   View of the main dining room from the central staircase, Café New York, Budapest.

25   Café Dommayer, Vienna.

29   Chocolate "Saddle of Venison" Cake.

32   Poppy Seed Gugelhupf.

37   Café Imperial, Prague.

40   Café Slavia, Prague.

45   The afternoon crowd at Café Dommayer.

48   Chocolate-Cherry Mousse Cake.

53   Brown Linzertorte.

56   Night owls at Café Hawelka, Vienna.

60   Sachertorte, served at the Sacher Hotel, Vienna.

68   Strawberry Cream Torte.

72   Dobos Torte.

76   Warm "Milk-Cream" Strudel with Vanilla Sauce.

81   Grape Strudel with Weinchaudeau.

85   Warm "Milk-Cream" Strudel with Vanilla Sauce.

87   Café Im KunstHausWien, Vienna, a "new style" café.

88   Currant and Hazelnut Snails.

91   Café Dommayer.

93   Statue of Peter Altenberg, Café Central, Vienna.

97   The front salon of Demel.

101   Dalmatian Four-Flavor Kolacky.

105   The café at the Municipal House, Prague.

106   Mellis, Budapest.

109   Main dining room, Municipal House café, Prague.

112   Hungarian Flaky Scones.

117   Apple, Walnut, and Poppy Seed Bar.

120   Berry Meringue Slice.

125   Chocolate-Banana Slice.

128   Chocolate-Covered "Indian" Cupcakes.

132   Gerbeaud Slices.

137   Meringue and Ladyfinger Slices.

140   Walnut Crescent Cookie from Pozsony.

144   Ischl Tartlet.

148   Linzer "Eye."

149   Vanilla Crescents.

152   Mardi Gras Doughnuts, cooking.

153   Mardi Gras Doughnuts.

156   The Emperor's Pancake with Roasted Plums.

165   The Staubs, proprietors, Café Sperl, Vienna.

168   Farmer's Cheese and Strawberry Dumplings being tossed in bread crumbs.

170   The Art Deco clock at Café Slavia.

173   Farmer's Cheese and Strawberry Dumplings with Strawberry Sauce.

174   Café Dommayer.

176   Molded Rice Pudding with Raspberries.

180   Chocolate-Cream "Dumplings."

184   Café Savoy, Vienna.

188   Clockwise, from top: Eiskaffee, Maria Theresia, Großer Brauner, Turkish coffee.

191   Café Dommayer.

193   Classic Viennese coffee service.

196   Eiskaffee.

216   Café Central.

BASIC BATTERS, DOUGHS, ICINGS & GLAZES

Any compendium of Austro-Hungarian desserts is like a family tree. The batters and doughs (sponge cake, puff pastry, sweet yeast dough, and so on) are the heads of the family, the glazes and icings are the spouses, and the desserts themselves are the offspring. Comparisons to the French pastry lexicon are unavoidable, perhaps because Americans are more familiar with the French terms and our culinary students are trained to learn French pâtisserie terminology. In the culinary schools of central Europe a dry sponge cake is called by the German *Biskuittorten,* not by the French *genoise* or *biscuit,* as I was taught when I studied for my culinary degree.

A Demitasse of History

You can sometimes glean history from a country's dishes. France, for example, has many familiar dishes named after aristocrats and cultural figures. America has recipes named for patriots, such as Jefferson Davis pie and Robert E. Lee cake. However, these recipes are usually dishes from the culinary past and only show up in old cookbooks. (When was the last time you saw Tournedos Rossini on a menu?)

In Vienna, Budapest, and Prague, patriotism is kept alive through the old dishes and traditions. Desserts are named for composers, operas and operettas, politicians, emperors, empresses, princes and princesses, counts and countesses, generals, battles, bakers, chefs, canals, hoteliers, countries, states, towns, cities, and villages. It is impossible to really appreciate the desserts of the old Austro-Hungarian empire without understanding a little about its history. The boundaries of the Czech Republic, Austria, and Hungary may have changed many times, but the food remains a constant touchstone to the past. Also, a grasp of the history explains how recipes migrated back and forth among the three capitals, with Vienna dictating fashion. Of course, volumes have been written about the histories of these countries, so this is only a thumbnail sketch to help the baker put the desserts into historical context.

Before World War I, the Austro-Hungarian Empire reached out from Austria to include Bohemia, Moravia, Slovakia, Croatia, Slovenia, Bosnia, Dalmatia, Hungary, and parts of Italy, Romania, Russia, Poland, and the Ukraine. In all, there were over fifty-one million people with a dozen nationalities, sixteen languages, and countless dialects, all ruled by the Hapsburgs.

The first Hapsburg, Rudolf, was elected king of the Romans in 1273, beginning the family's 640-year grip on central European politics. The Hapsburgs cultivated their influence through well-placed marriages, extending into Spain, which meant that for a short time they controlled parts of the New World as well as the Old. When Charles of Spain ceded Austria to his brother Ferdinand in 1521, the Hapsburg rule of central Europe was sealed.

The Hapsburgs were not just the ruling dynasty of Austria and the surrounding regions, but also emperors of the Holy Roman Empire, a mostly honorific title that was granted to the primary Catholic ruler of central Europe. Almost to a man (not to ignore Maria Theresia, one of the empire's greatest rulers), the emperor took his role as his people's religious leader very seriously. In 1806, when Napoleon's power threatened to extinguish the Hapsburgs, Francis II renounced his title as Holy Roman Emperor and refashioned himself as Francis I, emperor of Austria.

Austria had very shaky relationships with Bohemia (now part of the Czech Republic) to the north and Hungary to the south. In 1526, the emperor Ferdinand was elected the king of Bohemia. When Rudolf II ascended the throne fifty years later, he made Prague the center of the Holy Roman Empire, leading to many of the buildings that give the city its present beauty. Clashes between the Catholics and Protestants led to the Thirty Years' War of 1618–48. With a Catholic victory, Hapsburg influence over Prague was complete. In spite of occasional fits of nationalistic fervor, the Czechs would have to wait until 1918 for independence.

The Hapsburgs gained control over Hungary in 1686, mainly as a result of routing the Turks from Buda and Pest (it wasn't until 1873 that the two towns were united with a third, Óbuda, to create Budapest). From the outset, the Hungarians were not pleased to have new rulers, a situation that was to fester for almost three hundred years.

In 1814–15, after the fall of Napoleon, the Congress of Vienna was held to divide the spoils and redefine Europe's national boundaries. Vienna, a city that always knew how to throw a party, was at its best, and many a diplomat returned home with memories of fabulous food, especially the desserts. The competition between the French and Viennese master bakers was fierce. The French representative to the congress, Charles-Maurice de Talleyrand, knew that votes could be won at the dining table. When his king, Louis XVIII, tried to give him guidance for the congress, Talleyrand snapped, "I need saucepans rather than instructions!"

Talleyrand knew whereof he spoke, as his personal chef for many years was none other than Marie-Antoine Carême, one of the greatest chefs who ever lived. In 1823, Carême became the chef to Prince Pál Antal Esterházy, the Austrian ambassador in Paris, in whose service he directly influenced the cuisine of Vienna (and probably picked up a few tricks in the dessert department, too).

The Austrian representative to the congress was Klemens, Prince von Metternich, a politician both revered and reviled. Metternich continued to gather power after the congress concluded, implementing a police state complete with spies who eavesdropped on the public. Even though the middle class was exploding in number and expanding with affluence, they were kept out of politics. They chose to stay home, where they spent their money to cultivate cultured lives. The era was eventually called the Biedermeier period after a smug character in a newspaper column. The art of the baker blossomed, both at home and in the professional sphere. The concurrent Industrial Revolution improved the quality of both sugar and flour and lowered their price, making fine desserts available to the masses. Improved transportation kept a steady supply of coffee coming into the three capital cities.

But the undercurrent of dissatisfaction with Metternich's iron hand exploded in 1848. Rebels ousted Metternich, and the feeble-minded emperor Ferdinand would have to go. He was persuaded to abdicate, turning the throne over to his eighteen-year-old nephew, Franz Joseph. Ferdinand shuffled off to Prague, where he lived in exile until 1875.

With the Hapsburgs seemingly weakened, a Hungarian revolution against the monarchy took place, but the Austrian army smothered the revolt. By 1867, a confederacy between the countries was formed, and the empire became officially known as Austria-Hungary, personified by Franz Joseph, who was crowned king of Hungary.

When Franz Joseph came to power, his reaction to the revolutionary chaos was to establish autocracy. His lavish court was an opulent facade, for the emperor was austere and cold. Nonetheless, the convoluted etiquette of his court was so complex that a new phrase had to be invented to describe it. Everything regarding Hungary alone was called "K," for *Königlich* (royal). Matters pertaining to Austria were called "K.K." for *Kaiserlich-Königlich* (imperial-royal). When a designation was shared by both entities, it was called "K.u.K." for *Kaiserlich und Königlich* (meaning both imperial and royal). Keeping face was everything. When Franz Joseph's thirty-year-old son and his eighteen-year-old-mistress died mysteriously at Mayerling (all facts point to a murder-suicide, but as the Hapsburgs destroyed all physical evidence, questions remain), the cracks of the aged Empire began to show.

During Franz Joseph's rule, Vienna became an enormous metropolis, jammed with emigrants from the surrounding areas. The women of Bohemia, in particular, became sought after as cooks for upper-class households. They brought with them many of their country's humble dishes, and Bohemian sweet noodles, dumplings, and yeast breads became favorites of the rich as well as the peasantry. Coffeehouses became a refuge from intolerably crowded housing, giving people from all walks of life a place to sit down and warm up.

In 1914, the assassination of Archduke Franz Ferdinand, the heir to the Hapsburg throne, sparked the beginning of World War I. When the war was over, the old emperor was dead, and the last Hapsburg, Charles, was forced to abdicate to make way for the first Austrian republic. The old Austro-Hungarian Empire was systematically dismantled, breaking up the empire into the nations of Austria, Hungary, Poland, Yugoslavia, and Czechoslovakia. Of course, recent history has divided up some of these nations even more.

Although most of the following components have Hungarian and Czech names, I will use the more common Austrian terms.

· BISKUITMASSE ·

This sponge cake batter is the cornerstone for most of the famous tortes. Sponge cakes (*Biskuittorten*) are made from beaten eggs without any chemical leavening. Most American cakes depend on creamed butter and sugar for flavor and structure and get an extra lift from baking powder and/or baking soda. However, butter cakes harden when chilled, making the layers unpleasantly firm. Chilled sponge cakes stay soft, an important consideration as refrigeration is imperative for the many tortes with cream fillings. While butter-based cake batters do exist (Sachertorte comes to mind), there is no basic recipe that is used as often as Biskuitmasse.

There are two methods of making sponge cake batter. The "warm" method, by which whole eggs and sugar are heated together before beating to allow better incorporation of air, makes a soft, spongy cake that is best for recipes that use a sugar syrup to flavor and moisten the cake. In fact, "warm" sponge cakes are so soft that they can be baked in a jelly-roll pan to curl into the roulade cakes that the Viennese love so much (butter cakes would crumble). The "cold" method beats the yolks and whites separately, and the resulting cake is firmer and a bit moister.

The German word *Biskuit* comes from the French *biscuit*, a similar whipped-egg cake made by the cold method. In the French pastry kitchen, the warm-method cake is called *genoise*. To the Austrians, they're both Biskuittorten.

· BUTTERTEIG ·

While puff pastry (*Butterteig*, literally "butter dough") isn't used as prodigiously in the Viennese kitchen as the French, it is essential for such Austro-Hungarian favorites as *Cremeschnitten* and *Schaumrollen*. Many Austro-Hungarian bakers insist on a splash of rum in the dough, which they believe crisps and separates the flaky layers. Because of postwar restrictions on butter, some older cookbooks recommend margarine for puff pastry, in which case it was called *Blätterteig* ("leaf dough"), a term that can still be found in today's cookbooks. Margarine does make a flaky pastry, but the flavor is greasy and unappetizing. Don't use any substitutes for high-quality grade AA butter.

· GERMTEIG ·

Literally "yeast dough" (*Germ* is the Austrian word for yeast, which is called *Hefe* in other German-speaking countries), with butter, sugar, eggs, and flavorings added to create a wide range of sweet breads. Many bakeries use one basic *Germteig* for all of their sweet breads, but in this book, I have chosen to use a slightly different dough as needed to allow for the different requirements of each recipe.

· PLUNDERTEIG ·

Even though it is a Viennese invention, this dough is known in America as Danish pastry. (In Paris, however, it is called *pâte viennoise*, and pastries made from it are referred to as *Viennoiserie*.) It combines characteristics of puff pastry and sweet yeast dough to make a very flaky baked product. Literally translated, *Plunderteig* would mean "stacked lumber dough." Doughs created from the artful layering of butter and dough are called laminated doughs, as in laminated wood, so from laminated to lumber isn't really a far stretch. There is also a German phrase, *der ganze Plunder*, or "the whole bag of tricks," and Plunderteig certainly calls for the baker's whole bag of tricks to make it well. It is the basis for Viennese *Kipferln* (crescent rolls, otherwise known as croissants, another Austrian invention that has been unjustly appropriated by another country) and other breakfast pastries.

· MÜRBTEIG ·

This short-crust dough is used to make a crisp, crumbly, but sweet crust (*mürb* means "tender" or "soft"). It is known to many bakers as "3-2-1 dough" because its basic proportions (by weight) are three parts flour, two parts butter, and one part sugar.

The paper-thin dough used to make strudel is discussed in the strudel chapter.

WARM-METHOD SPONGE CAKE
WARME BISKUITTORTE
Makes one 9-inch cake

Many fancy tortes start with classic sponge cake. For a soft, flexible cake that will be flavored with a soaking liquid or can be baked in a jelly-roll pan to make a roulade, the whole eggs and sugar are heated over hot water until very hot. Most recipes use a six-egg batter, but some require the four- or eight-egg recipes, which follow.

Some sponge cake recipes skip butter altogether, but I use a small amount to add flavor and a bit of extra firmness (but not so much that it hardens when refrigerated). To give the butter more flavor, allow it to brown slightly during melting, and leave the milk solids behind in the saucepan when pouring it out.

Take care when folding the flour into the beaten eggs; the flour should be completely incorporated without lumping. The best folding utensil for sponge cake is a large balloon whisk with thin wires, used just like a spatula, allowing the batter and flour to flow through the wires. If you are using a heavy-duty mixer to beat the eggs (by far the best method), the whisk attachment can be detached and held to manually fold in the flour. A large rubber spatula is another option, but a whisk works best.

It is not always necessary to trim off the top crust of the cake. In some tortes, when the cake layers are going to be soaked with syrup, this crust can act as insulation to keep the syrup from seeping out. In this case, place the top cake layer, crust side down, in the pan being used for molding the torte.

The batter works equally well with either cake or all-purpose flour. Cake flour makes a slightly more tender cake.

■ ■ ■

3 tablespoons unsalted butter
1 teaspoon vanilla extract
6 large eggs, at room temperature
2/3 cup sugar
1 cup sifted flour (see note above)
1/8 teaspoon salt

■ ■ ■

1. To make the cake, position a rack in the center of the oven and heat to 350°F. Butter a 9-inch springform pan, and line the bottom with a round of parchment or wax paper. Sprinkle the inside of the pan with flour, coating evenly and tapping out the excess flour.

2. In a small saucepan, bring the butter to a boil over medium heat. Cook for about 1 minute, just until the specks of milk solids in the butter are lighty browned. Remove from the heat and let stand for 5 minutes. Skim the foam from the top, and then pour into a medium bowl, leaving the browned bits behind in the pan. Stir in the vanilla.

3. Meanwhile, combine the eggs and sugar in the bowl of a standing heavy-duty electric mixer (or large heatproof bowl). Place the bowl over a pot of simmering water (the water should not touch the bowl; see photograph 1, page 6). Using a large balloon whisk, stir the mixture until the eggs are very warm to the touch and the sugar is dissolved (rub a bit of the egg mixture between your fingers to check for grains of sugar). Attach the bowl to the mixer and fit with the whisk. Beat on medium-high speed until the mixture is tripled in volume and very light and fluffy, about 3 minutes (see photograph 2). (If using a hand mixer, allow about 5 minutes to reach this consistency.)

4. Combine the flour and salt. Sift half of the flour over the eggs. Using the balloon whisk, fold in the flour, leaving a few visible wisps of flour. Sift the remaining flour over the batter and fold it in. Whisk a large dollop of the batter into the melted butter. Fold this mixture into the batter. Pour into the pan and smooth the top.

5. Bake until the top springs back when pressed in the center and the sides are barely beginning

to shrink from the pan, about 30 minutes. Cool on a wire rack for 5 minutes. Remove the sides of the pan, invert onto the rack, and remove the bottom of the pan and the paper. Reinvert the cake onto another rack, right side up. Cool completely.

SMALL SPONGE CAKE

Use 2 tablespoons (¼ stick) unsalted butter, ½ teaspoon vanilla extract, 4 large eggs, at room temperature, ½ cup sugar, ⅔ cup sifted cake flour, and a pinch of salt. Bake 20 to 25 minutes.

LARGE SPONGE CAKE

This batter requires more gluten in the batter (supplied by all-purpose, not cake, flour) so it won't sag during baking. Bake it in a 9½- to 10-inch cake pan. Use 4 tablespoons (½ stick) unsalted butter, 1 teaspoon vanilla extract, 8 large eggs, at room temperature, ¾ cup sugar, 1¼ cups sifted all-purpose flour, and ¼ teaspoon salt. Bake 35 to 40 minutes.

MAKE AHEAD

The cake can be prepared up to 2 days ahead, covered tightly, and refrigerated, or frozen for up to 1 month.

COLD-METHOD SPONGE CAKE
KALTE BISKUITTORTE

Makes one 9-inch cake

Use this method when you want a firmer cake, which is strictly a matter of personal preference.

■ ■ ■

3 tablespoons unsalted butter
1 teaspoon vanilla extract
6 large eggs, at room temperature
⅔ cup sugar, divided
1 cup sifted cake or all-purpose flour
⅛ teaspoon salt

■ ■ ■

1. To make the cake, position a rack in the center of the oven and heat to 350°F. Butter a 9-inch springform pan, and line the bottom with a round of parchment or wax paper. Sprinkle the inside of the pan with flour, coating evenly and tapping out the excess flour.

2. In a small saucepan, bring the butter to a boil over medium heat. Cook for about 1 minute, just until the milk solids in the butter turn light brown. Remove from the heat and let stand for 5 minutes. Skim the foam from the top, then pour into a medium bowl, leaving the browned bits in the pan. Stir in the vanilla.

3. In a large mixing bowl, using a hand-held electric mixer on high speed, beat the yolks with ⅓ cup of the sugar until the mixture is very pale and forms a thick ribbon that falls back on itself when the beaters are lifted a few inches, about 3 minutes.

4. In another large bowl, using clean beaters, beat the whites on high speed until they form soft peaks. Gradually beat in the remaining ⅓ cup of the sugar until the peaks are shiny and stiff.

5. Stir a large dollop of the whites into the yolks to lighten the mixture, then fold in the remaining whites. Combine the flour and salt. In two additions, sift the flour over the eggs, and use a large balloon whisk or rubber spatula to fold together.

6. Whisk a large dollop of the batter into the melted butter. Fold this mixture back into the batter. Pour into the pan and smooth the top.

7. Bake until the top springs back when pressed in the center and the sides are barely beginning to shrink from the pan, about 30 minutes. Cool on a wire rack for 5 minutes. Remove the sides of the pan, invert onto the rack, and remove the bottom of the pan and the paper. Reinvert the cake onto another rack, right side up. Cool completely.

SMALL SPONGE CAKE

Use 2 tablespoons (¼ stick) unsalted butter, ½ teaspoon vanilla extract, 4 large eggs, at room temperature, ½ cup sugar, ⅔ cup sifted cake flour, and a pinch of salt. Bake 20 to 25 minutes.

LARGE SPONGE CAKE

This batter requires a stronger flour so the larger amount of batter will bake without falling. Use a 9½- to 10-inch pan. Use 4 tablespoons (½ stick) unsalted butter, 1 teaspoon vanilla extract, 8 large eggs, at room temperature, ¾ cup sugar, 1¼ cups sifted all-purpose flour, and ¼ teaspoon salt. Bake 35 to 40 minutes.

MAKE AHEAD

The cake can be prepared up to 2 days ahead, covered tightly, and refrigerated, or frozen for up to 1 month.

CHOCOLATE SPONGE CAKE
SCHOKOLADE BISKUITTORTE
Makes one 9-inch cake

Milk and vegetable oil add moisture to this sponge cake gently flavored with cocoa.

■ ■ ■

4 large eggs, at room temperature
¾ cup sugar
3 tablespoons milk
3 tablespoons vegetable oil
½ teaspoon vanilla extract
⅔ cup sifted cake flour
¼ cup Dutch-processed cocoa powder
(see page 203)
⅛ teaspoon salt

■ ■ ■

1. Position a rack in the center of the oven and heat to 350°F. Butter a 9-inch springform pan, and line the bottom with a round of parchment or wax paper. Dust the inside of the pan with flour, tapping out the excess flour.
2. Combine the eggs and sugar in the bowl of a heavy-duty electric mixer. Place the bowl over a medium saucepan of simmering water over medium heat (the water should not touch the bowl). Whisk until the eggs are very warm to the touch and the sugar is dissolved (rub a bit of

the egg mixture between your fingers to check for grains of sugar). Attach to the mixer and fit with the whisk. Beat on medium-high speed until the mixture is tripled in volume and very light and fluffy, about 3 minutes.
4. Meanwhile, in a small saucepan, heat the milk and vegetable oil until hot to the touch (about 120°F.). Pour into a medium bowl and stir in the vanilla.
5. Sift the cake flour, cocoa, and salt together. Sift half of the cocoa mixture over the egg mixture. Using a large balloon whisk, fold it in. Sift the remaining cocoa mixture over the batter and fold it in. Whisk a large dollop of the batter into the milk mixture. Fold this mixture back into the batter. Pour into the pan and smooth the top.
6. Bake until the top springs back when pressed in the center and the sides are barely beginning to shrink from the pan, about 30 minutes. Cool on a wire rack for 5 minutes. Remove the sides of the pan, invert onto the rack, and remove the bottom of the pan and the paper. Reinvert the cake onto another rack, right side up. Cool completely.

MAKE AHEAD

The cake can be prepared up to 2 days ahead, covered tightly in plastic wrap and refrigerated, or frozen for up to 1 month.

VIENNESE SWEET YEAST DOUGH
PLUNDERTEIG
Makes about 3 pounds

The technique for this dough, used primarily for "Danish" pastries, is similar to the one required by puff pastry, which is also created from layering butter with dough. As with Butterteig, temperature is important: Only after the dough is cut out does it stand in a warm place for its final rise. The same basics about puff pastry on page 13 applies to this dough, so read it as an introduction before you begin.

Demel:
Sugar Baker to the Empire

To pastry lovers, it is impossible to visit Vienna without a pilgrimage to Demel, the doyenne of Vienna's *Kaffeehäuser.*

Ludwig Dehne opened his Burgtheater Zuckerbäckerei in 1786, just around the corner from the old Burgtheater (court theater). When Dehne died, his widow kept the company going, which became the "Imperial Sugar Bakery," or Hofzuckerbäckerei. For a time, Franz Sacher, the inventor of the Sacher-torte, worked at Dehne, but when he moved on, his famous recipe stayed in Dehne's kitchen, a proprietary situation that was to simmer for more than one hundred years and had to be settled in Viennese courts (see page 60).

In 1857, Dehne was sold to one of its bakers, Christoph Demel, and thirty years later, he moved the shop to Kohlmarkt, where it still stands. His wife, Anna, set even higher standards. But she believed that each cake should have personality and look like a human had made it. The Annatorte is a perfect illustration of this philosophy, as the folds of gianduja (a hazelnut-flavored chocolate) fall casually over the top of the cake at the baker's whim, and not in the perfect, hermetic seal of some other cakes (I am thinking of the Sachertorte).

I spent a morning on a personal tour of the Demel factory in the industrial area of Vienna. Here, old traditions are still maintained, but with new equipment. For example, although not without some grousing from older bakers, the wooden tables were replaced by stainless steel. Even though machine decorating is becoming the norm elsewhere, I saw the bakers finishing hundreds of cakes by hand. Instead of combining all-purpose recipes, almost every dessert is created from components unique to the dish. Convection ovens are eschewed. Demel also blends, roasts, and grinds cocoa beans for their own proprietary blend of chocolate. The packaging is exquisite, some of the papers based on decades-old designs.

Fine pastries are never cheap to produce, and Demel's quality is high. When I asked about the cost structure at Demel, the managing director, Frans-Jan Soede, explained it in sobering terms. The labor cost for Austrian pastry chefs is about four times higher than in the United States. There are about 140 people working every day in the shops, in one day shift (the concept of the graveyard shift isn't popular in Austria). The bakers make at least twenty types of cakes every day and about seventy types of cookies at Christmas. There are cheaper, quicker ways to make their products, but if the flavor of the desserts will be affected, Demel just is not interested. So they continue to make their Demeltorten, Annatorten, Guglehupf, Burgtheatertorten, and other delights in the same way they have been made for generations, and anyone who has ever indulged in dessert at Demel will never forget it.

SPONGE
1½ ounces (¾ cube) compressed yeast or 4½ teaspoons (2 envelopes) active dry yeast
½ cup milk (heated to 105° to 115°F. if using dry yeast)
½ cup unbleached flour
1 teaspoon sugar

DOUGH
½ cup milk

½ cup confectioners' sugar
4 tablespoons (½ stick) unsalted butter, melted
3 large egg yolks
1 teaspoon vanilla extract
½ teaspoon salt
2⅔ cups unbleached flour, as needed

BUTTER MIXTURE
1¾ cups (3½ sticks) unsalted butter, chilled, cut into ½-inch cubes
¼ cup unbleached flour

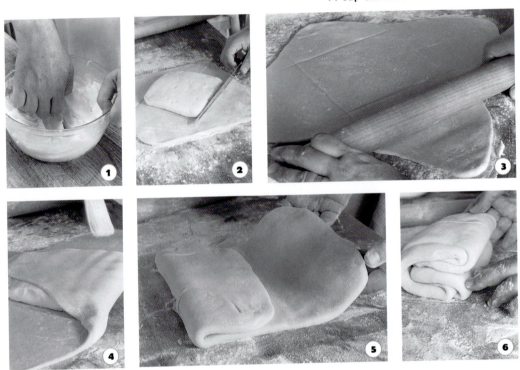

▪ THE STORY BEHIND ▪
VIENNESE SWEET YEAST DOUGH

Plunderteig helped establish Viennese bakers as masters of their art. We think of sweet yeast dough layered with butter as "Danish" pastry. The truth is, it hails from Vienna, not Copenhagen.

In the mid-nineteenth century, Danish bakers went on strike and were replaced by Viennese workers, who brought with them their special sweet dough. The Danes developed a liking for the new pastries, and when their countrymen finally returned to their jobs, the customers demanded the Viennese version. The recipe for the dough traveled with Danish immigrants to America, where it became known as Danish pastry. However, in bakeries of Paris, where the last word on culinary matters is usually dictated, flaky pastries made from layered dough (including croissants) are still called *Viennoiserie,* to acknowledge their city of origin.

• • •

1. To make the sponge: Crumble the compressed yeast over the milk (or sprinkle in the dry) in a small bowl. Let stand 2 minutes, then whisk to dissolve. Add the flour and sugar and whisk for 100 strokes. Cover tightly with plastic wrap and let stand in a warm place until doubled in volume, about 30 minutes.

2. To make the dough: Whisk the milk, confectioners' sugar, melted butter, yolks, vanilla, and salt in the bowl of a heavy-duty standing mixer. Add the sponge. Attach the bowl to the mixer and fit with the paddle blade. On low speed, gradually add enough of the flour to make a very sticky dough that cleans the sides of the bowl. Increase the speed to medium and mix until smooth, about 3 minutes. Transfer the dough to a lightly floured surface and pat into an 8-inch square. Wrap loosely in plastic wrap and refrigerate for 30 minutes.

3. To make the butter mixture (photograph 1): Combine the butter and flour in a medium bowl and use your knuckles to work them together until the butter is smooth and malleable, but still cool. (An instant-read thermometer will read 60°F.) Scrape onto a piece of plastic wrap and wrap loosely in the plastic. Using a rolling pin as an aide, roll and shape into a 6-inch square. If the temperature isn't 60°F., refrigerate or let stand at room temperature until it reaches that point.

4. On a lightly floured work surface, roll out the dough to a 10-inch square. Unwrap the butter square and place in the center of the dough, with the corners of the butter square pointing north, south, east, and west. Using the back of a knife (2), lightly mark the perimeter of the butter square on the dough, and remove the butter square. Using a rolling pin, roll out the dough from each mark to make four 4-inch long "petals" (3). Replace the butter square in the center of the dough. Brushing off the flour as you work, fold each petal over to enclose the dough (4).

5. Dust the work surface and the top of the dough with flour. Roll out the dough into a 14 × 7-inch rectangle. Brush off the flour on the dough. As if folding a business letter, stretching the corners of the dough as well as possible to keep them at right angles, fold the top third of the dough down, then the bottom third of the dough up (5), making a three-layer rectangle about 4½ × 7 inches. This is called a single turn. Reposition the dough so the open side faces left. Dust the top of the dough with flour, and roll again into a 14 × 7-inch rectangle. Brush off the flour. Fold the top quarter of the dough down, then the bottom quarter of the dough up to meet the center. Fold the dough in half at the center crease to make a four-layer rectangle about 3½ × 7 inches (6). This is called a double turn. Flatten the dough slightly by tapping it with the rolling pin lengthwise and crosswise. Wrap in plastic wrap and refrigerate for 30 minutes.

6. Unwrap the dough and return it to a lightly floured work surface. Repeat step five, giving the dough another single turn, then another double turn. Wrap in plastic wrap and refrigerate for at least 4 hours.

MAKE AHEAD

The dough can be prepared up to 2 days ahead, tightly wrapped in plastic wrap, and refrigerated.

While the unbaked dough can be frozen, some of the yeast could die during the freezing process. It is best to bake the leftover dough within a day or two, and freeze the extra baked goods instead.

PUFF PASTRY
BUTTERTEIG

Makes about 1 pound 13 ounces

Nothing compares to the flavor of buttery puff pastry created from rolled layers of butter and dough, so crisp it shatters in your mouth. During baking, the butter melts in the oven and creates steam, separating the layers and making the dough extra-flaky. The addition of rum is a hallmark of Austro-Hungarian bakers.

You can substitute an equal weight of store-bought pastry for homemade but be sure it is made from butter, not shortening. Here are a few pointers:

• If the dough softens in a hot kitchen, refrigerate it until it is cool and firm enough to work with.
• For proper layering of butter and dough, they must be near the same cool temperature. The optimum temperature for the mixture is 60°F. (thanks to Bernard Clayton, who identified the proper temperature in his *New Complete Book of Breads*). If too warm, the butter will soak into the dough; if too cold, it will break through. The 60°F. butter temperature is easy to attain in a cool kitchen by working the butter in a bowl with your knuckles. Don't use your palms too much as they are warmer and could melt the butter.
• If any butter does peek through the dough during rolling, generously sprinkle the offending spot with flour to seal it, then proceed.
• Keep the dough as evenly shaped as possible, stretching the corners as needed to keep them at right angles.
• Brush off excess flour from the top of the dough before rolling the layers; too much flour will toughen the pastry.
• Even when the recipe calls for a half-batch of dough, make the full recipe and freeze the remainder. It is difficult to make puff pastry with amounts smaller than recommended here.

■ ■ ■

DOUGH
1½ cups plus 2 tablespoons unbleached flour
½ teaspoon salt
⅔ cup cold water
1 tablespoon golden rum

BUTTER MIXTURE
1⅓ cups (2¼ sticks plus 1 tablespoon)
unsalted butter, cut into ½-inch cubes, chilled
6 tablespoons unbleached flour

■ ■ ■

1. To make the dough: Measure the flour and salt into a medium bowl and make a well in the center. Mix the water and rum and stir into the flour to make a sticky dough (add droplets of water if needed). Gather up the dough and transfer to a lightly floured work surface. Knead a few times, just until the dough smoothes out a bit (it will still be slightly sticky and rough looking). Wrap the dough loosely in plastic wrap and shape into a 6-inch square. Refrigerate for about 20 minutes or up to 1 hour.

2. To make the butter mixture: Combine the butter and flour in a medium bowl. Using your knuckles and fingertips, work the two together until the butter is smooth and malleable, but still cool. (An instant-read thermometer will read 60°F.) Scrape onto a piece of plastic wrap and wrap loosely in the plastic. Using a rolling pin as an aide, roll and shape into a 5½-inch square. If the temperature isn't 60°F., refrigerate or let stand at room temperature until it reaches that point.

3. On a lightly floured work surface, roll out the dough into an 8-inch square. Unwrap the butter square and place in the center of the dough, with the corners of the butter square pointing north, south, east, and west. Using the back of a knife, lightly mark the perimeter of the butter square on the dough, and remove the butter square. Using a rolling pin, roll out the dough from each mark to make four 4-inch long "petals." Replace the butter square in the center of the dough. Brushing off the flour as you work, fold each petal over to enclose the dough.

4. Dust the work surface and the top of the dough with flour. Roll out the dough into a

14 × 7-inch rectangle. Brush off the flour on the dough. As if folding a business letter, stretching the corners of the dough as well as possible to keep them at right angles, fold the top third of the dough down, then the bottom third of the dough up, making a three-layer rectangle about 4½ × 7 inches. This is called a single turn. Reposition the dough so the open side faces left. Dust the top of the dough with flour, and roll again into a 14 × 7-inch rectangle. Brush off the flour. Fold the top quarter of the dough down, then the bottom quarter of the dough up to meet in the center. Fold the dough in half at the center crease to make a four-layer rectangle about 3½ × 7 inches. This is called a double turn. Gently roll the dough to slightly flatten it, then wrap in plastic wrap. Refrigerate for 20 to 30 minutes.

5. Return the dough to a lightly floured work surface. Repeat step four, giving the dough another single turn, then another double turn. Wrap in plastic and refrigerate for at least 4 hours.

MAKE AHEAD

The dough can be prepared up to 2 days ahead, tightly wrapped in plastic wrap, and refrigerated. It can also be frozen for up to 1 month, and thawed overnight in the refrigerator before using.

CREAM PUFF DOUGH
BRANDTEIG

Makes about sixteen 5-inch eclairs or twelve 4-inch doughnuts

While many doughs require cool ingredients, cream puff dough is cooked before using. Depending on the humidity and relative moisture in the flour, you may not need all of the fourth egg, so add it gradually to judge the dough's consistency. As soon as the water and butter come to a boil, stir in the flour. Don't delay, because if any water evaporates, the measurements will be inaccurate.

■ ■ ■

I cup water
½ cup (I stick) unsalted butter,
cut into ½-inch cubes
I teaspoon sugar
Pinch of salt
I cup unbleached flour
4 large eggs (3 whole and I beaten), at room temperature

■ ■ ■

1. Bring the water, butter, sugar, and salt to a full boil in a heavy-bottomed medium saucepan over medium-high heat, stirring occasionally so the butter is melted by the time the water boils. All at once, add the flour, and stir with a wooden spoon until it forms a ball. Reduce the heat to medium-low and stir until the dough films the bottom of the pan, about 1½ minutes. Adjust the heat as needed to keep the dough from scorching, as the dough needs to cook for at least 1 minute to evaporate excess moisture.

2. Transfer the dough to a medium bowl. Using a handheld electric mixer, beat in the whole eggs, one at a time, being sure the first egg is absorbed before adding another. Beat in enough of the beaten egg to make a thick, shiny dough that holds its shape. If you have egg left over, it can be used to brush over the dough as a glaze before baking. Use the dough while it is warm.

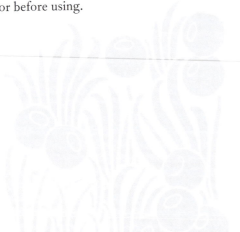

SHORT CRUST DOUGH
MÜRBTEIG
Makes about 1½ pounds

In European kitchens, this dough is memorized by most cooks. They use it when they need a sweet, crumbly butter dough for cookies or tarts. In the metric system, it's easy to recall. In fact, some people call it "3-2-1 dough" because it consists of three parts flour, two parts butter, and one part sugar (here, 300, 200, and 100 grams) with an egg yolk or a bit of water to hold it together. Be sure to keep the butter cool while working it into the flour. If it softens (Viennese call this "burning the butter"), the crust will not be crisp.

■ ■ ■

2 cups plus 2 tablespoons all-purpose flour
½ cup granulated sugar
Pinch of salt
**14 tablespoons (1¾ sticks) unsalted butter,
cut into ½-inch cubes, chilled**
1 large egg, beaten

■ ■ ■

Mix the flour, sugar, and salt in a medium bowl. Add the butter. Using a pastry blender, cut in the butter until the mixture resembles coarse crumbs. Using a fork, stir in the egg and mix well until the dough is moistened and holds together when pressed between your fingers. If necessary, add water, 1 teaspoon at a time, to moisten the dough. Gather up the dough into a flat disk. Wrap in plastic wrap and refrigerate for 30 minutes before using.

MAKE AHEAD
The dough can be prepared up to 2 days ahead, tightly wrapped in plastic wrap, and refrigerated. It can also be frozen for up to 1 month, and thawed overnight in the refrigerator before using.

FAUX FONDANT ICING
WASSERGLASUR
Makes about 1 cup

Fondant is the traditional finish for some classic Austro-Hungarian tortes. Even many professional bakers find handmade fondant a bother, and buy theirs from a supplier. For the home cook, this easy version, based on one from Susan Purdy's *A Piece of Cake*, does very nicely. Like the classic, it must used while barely warm.

■ ■ ■

3¾ cups confectioners' sugar, sifted
⅓ cup water, more if needed
2 tablespoons light corn syrup

■ ■ ■

In a medium saucepan, stir the sugar, water, and syrup until smooth. Stir over very low heat just until the glaze is barely warm, 92° to 95°F. If the temperature rises above 95°F., you will have to start over. If necessary, add warm water to thin to a heavy creamlike consistency. Use immediately.

SMALL-BATCH FAUX FONDANT ICING
Use 1 cup confectioners' sugar, sifted, 1 tablespoon plus 2 teaspoons water, and 2 teaspoons light corn syrup. Make the icing in a small saucepan.

COFFEE FAUX FONDANT ICING
Instead of ⅓ cup water, substitute ¼ cup water and 2 teaspoons instant espresso coffee powder dissolved in 1 tablespoon boiling water.

PINK FAUX FONDANT ICING
Add 1 tablespoon red raspberry liqueur (Chambord) or crème de cassis to the mixture before mixing.

BASIC BATTERS, DOUGHS, ICINGS & GLAZES

CHOCOLATE GLAZE
SCHOKOLADEGLASUR
Makes about 2 cups

This ebony-dark, shiny, intensely sweet choco-late glaze was originally invented to coat Sacher-torte, but it's a great icing to use for many other baked goods. The authentic icing must be cooked into syrup that hardens to a fudge-like consistency (some bakers also temper the syrup, a difficult optional step). Schokoladeglasur stays glossy at any temperature, as long as the cake has an undercoat of preserves. Be sure to allow the undercoat to cool and set before applying the chocolate glaze, and use the chocolate glaze *immediately* after making it, while it is still warm and fluid.

What to do with the leftover glaze that inevitably drips off the pastries and ends up underneath the cooling rack? It makes great hot chocolate! Scrape it up and store it in a covered container in the refrigerator. When you want a cup of hot chocolate, place milk and a few table-spoons of the chocolate glaze to taste in a small saucepan. Heat over low heat, whisking often, to warm the milk and melt the glaze.

■ ■ ■
1½ cups sugar
¾ cup water
**6 ounces high-quality bittersweet chocolate,
coarsely chopped**
■ ■ ■

1. In a heavy-bottomed medium saucepan (no larger than 2 quarts, or the mixture will reduce too rapidly and burn before it reaches the cor-rect temperature) over high heat, bring the sugar, water, and chocolate to a boil over medium-high heat, stirring occasionally. Attach a candy thermometer to the pan. Reduce the heat to medium and cook, uncovered, stirring, until the mixture reaches 234°F., about 5 minutes.
2. Remove from the heat and stir to cool and thicken slightly, about 1 minute. Use imme-diately. When pouring, do not scrape the pan.

SMALL BATCH CHOCOLATE GLAZE
Use 1 cup sugar, ½ cup water, and 4 ounces bittersweet chocolate. Make the glaze in a small saucepan.

APRICOT GLAZE
MARILLENGLASUR
Makes about 1 cup

Fruit glazes—easily prepared from preserves—add flavor, protect crisp crusts from getting soft in contact with moist fillings, and provide a slick undercoat that adds an extra sheen when another glaze is poured over the dessert. Apricot and red currant are the most versatile, as their acidity balances the sweetness of the dessert, but you can use another favorite flavor, if you wish. Just be sure to use preserves, and not jam or jelly, which have different fruit–sugar ratios. The preserves must be simmered for a few minutes to evaporate excess liquid and give a firm, slick finish to the glazed desserts. It's best to turn an entire 12-ounce jar of preserves into glaze, stor-ing the glaze in the empty preserves jar, so you have small amounts ready when needed.

■ ■ ■
1¼ cups apricot preserves
2 tablespoons golden rum or water
■ ■ ■

Bring the preserves and rum to a boil in a small saucepan over medium heat, stirring often. Cook, stirring often, until the last drops that cling to the spoon are very sticky and reluctant to leave the spoon, 2 to 3 minutes. Strain through a wire sieve into a small bowl, pressing hard on the solids. Use warm.

RED CURRANT GLAZE
Substitute red currant preserves for the apricot preserves.

WARM CHOCOLATE SAUCE
SCHOKOLADESAUCE
Makes about 1½ cups

Here's a smooth and seductive chocolate sauce that can embellish many desserts.

■ ■ ■

I cup water
6 ounces high-quality bittersweet chocolate, finely chopped
¾ cup sugar

■ ■ ■

In a small saucepan, bring the water, chocolate, and sugar to a boil over medium heat, stirring often. Cook at a brisk simmer, stirring often, until slightly thickened, about 5 minutes. Cool slightly and serve warm.

RUM CHOCOLATE SAUCE
Substitute 2 tablespoons golden rum for an equal amount of the water.

MAKE AHEAD
The sauce can be prepared up to 2 days ahead, cooled, covered, and refrigerated. Warm carefully over low heat in a saucepan, just until heated through; do not boil.

■ ■ ■

2 tablespoons cornstarch
2½ cups milk, divided
½ cup sugar
2 large egg yolks
One vanilla bean, split lengthwise, or
I teaspoon vanilla extract

■ ■ ■

1. Sprinkle the cornstarch over ½ cup of the milk in a small bowl and whisk to dissolve. Add the sugar and egg yolks and whisk well.
2. Bring the remaining 2 cups of the milk and the vanilla bean just to a simmer in a heavy-bottomed medium saucepan over low heat. Remove the bean, scrape the vanilla seeds into the milk, and discard the bean. Gradually whisk the egg yolk mixture into the milk.
3. Cook, whisking often, until the sauce comes to a full boil, about 3 minutes. If using vanilla extract, stir it in now. Strain through a wire sieve into a bowl. Serve warm.

MAKE AHEAD
The sauce can be prepared up to 1 day ahead, cooled, covered, and refrigerated. Reheat in the top part of a double boiler over simmering water.

VANILLA SAUCE
VANILLESAUCE
Makes about 2¾ cups

A cousin to French *crème anglaise*, this pale yellow dessert sauce is called *Kanarienmilch*, or "canary milk," in some old cookbooks. The Viennese version is boiled, as the egg yolks are protected from curdling by the cornstarch. This makes a slightly thicker, less egg-rich sauce that beautifully offsets Austro-Hungarian desserts. Because it takes less watching, I now use Vanillesauce whenever I need a vanilla dessert sauce.

MERINGUE CREAM
SCHAUMOBERS
Makes about 2½ cups

Why combine meringue with whipped cream? You'll find out when you spoon it over a hot dessert: The egg whites insulate the cream and keep it from melting so quickly. The meringue also lightens the texture of the cream and enhances its whiteness.

■ ■ ■

½ cup sugar
2 large egg whites, at room temperature
I cup heavy cream, chilled
I teaspoon vanilla extract

• • •

1. Whisk the sugar and egg whites in a medium stainless-steel bowl to combine. Place over a medium saucepan of simmering water (the water should not touch the bottom of the bowl). Whisk until the eggs are very warm to the touch and the sugar is dissolved (rub a dab between your fingers to check for any grains of sugar).

2. Beat with a handheld electric mixer on high speed until the whites form stiff, shiny peaks. The meringue must be completely cool before adding the whipped cream. Let the bowl stand briefly in a bowl of cold (not iced) water, if necessary.

3. In a chilled medium bowl, beat the heavy cream and vanilla until quite stiff (it will be softened by the addition of the meringue, so beat it a bit more than usual). Fold a large dollop of the whipped cream into the meringue, then fold the meringue into the remaining cream. Cover and refrigerate until ready to serve.

MAKE AHEAD

The cream can be prepared up to 1 day ahead, covered, and refrigerated.

SWEETENED WHIPPED CREAM
SCHLAGOBERS
Makes 2 cups

Throughout the rest of the German-speaking world, whipped cream is called *Schlagsahne*, but the Viennese call it *Schlagobers*, which translates into something like "very-well whipped." Whipped cream is a very important ingredient in the daily life of a Viennese; a dab goes on top of coffee or tea, or alongside the afternoon snack, or, unsweetened, as a garnish for soup.

First, use high-quality cream (pasteurized, rather than ultra-pasteurized) with a high butterfat content (36 to 40 percent), which whips up thick and fluffy and has better flavor. Your natural food stores might carry such a cream, or look at old-fashioned dairies.

Room-temperature cream won't incorporate air, so use well-chilled cream straight from the refrigerator. Use a chilled metal bowl or place the bowl in a larger bowl of iced water.

For sweetening, confectioners' sugar is preferred to granulated sugar because the small amount of cornstarch in the former discourages the weeping that occurs when whipped cream stands for longer than a few hours. A hint of vanilla is imperative.

Learn to distinguish between the stages of whipped cream; it doesn't always have to be stiff. As a garnish for a dessert, the goal is softly beaten Schlagobers that barely mounds. When used for piping, cream should be whipped to the stiff stage. Of course there is an in-between stage, too, used for when the cream is the base for a torte filling. Take care not to overwhip the cream, at which point it has a coarse, grainy texture and is well on its way to becoming butter.

A balloon whisk will give you the most control over the whipping process, but most people prefer an electric mixer. A hand mixer is best, because the strong motor of a standing mixer makes it difficult to gauge the whipping progress and can quickly overwhip the cream.

■ ■ ■

1 cup heavy cream
2 tablespoons confectioners' sugar
½ teaspoon vanilla extract

■ ■ ■

Pour the cream into a well-chilled bowl and add the sugar and vanilla. Using an electric hand mixer or balloon whisk, beat the cream to the desired consistency. For soft peaks, the cream will be just thick enough to hold its shape in soft billows. For stiffly beaten cream, the beaters or whisk wires will leave distinct traces in the cream and stand in firm peaks when the beaters are lifted.

MAKE AHEAD

The cream can be whipped up to 1 day ahead, covered tightly with plastic wrap, and refrigerated. If liquid separates from the cream, whip it again to incorporate the liquid.

SIMPLE CAKES

Not every Kaffeehaus is a temple to Torten, those complex creations of the pastry chef. Many cafés pride themselves on their simple but tasty "homemade" desserts, more along the lines of what *Oma* (Grandma) would have made. These cakes can be whipped up in a small back kitchen and displayed for perusal on a counter, often right in their baking pans. They are also in the repertoire of many home cooks, who will make them at a moment's notice for an afternoon Jause.

Coffee: Common Man's Gold

Coffee is the common man's gold, and like gold, it brings to every man the feeling of luxury and nobility.

—Abd al-Kadir

Coffee's origins are appropriately dark and murky. The coffee bush has been traced to the province of Kaffa in Ethiopia. Ironically, Kaffa has nothing to do with how coffee got its name, which derives from the Arabic *qahwah*, meaning wine. The Ethiopians knew how to brew the beans into a thick, dark beverage, but it took some time for it to reach other places.

The most common legend of how coffee's invigorating qualities were discovered was first written down in 1671 by a Maronite Christian monk, Faustus Nironus Banesius. Banesius tells how the goatherd at a monastery in Yemen noticed his goats jumping around at all hours of the night. Deducing that their strange behavior must be related to their fodder, he followed them until they reached their grazing ground. There they nibbled on an unfamiliar bush with small red berries and white flowers. The goatherd took branches back for the monks to experiment with, and when they turned it into a beverage that keep them awake all night, they realized that their assumptions were correct. Knowledge of the miraculous new beverage flowed from the monastery throughout the Arab world.

Actually, the "goatherd story" was well established in Arabic and Turkish oral histories, and the beverage itself was quite popular. One version is even included in *A Thousand and One Nights*. As Muslims are not allowed to drink beer or wine, it makes sense that the Prophet would provide them with a substitute.

The first coffeehouse (*kahvehane*) opened in Constantinople in 1554. From the beginning, coffeehouses were gathering places for well-read citizens like poets, who found their imaginations stimulated by the lively atmosphere and intense conversations, not to mention the caffeine. By the late 1500s, coffee began making appearances in Europe. Pope Clement III sipped his first cup of coffee in 1598 and proclaimed it "a truly Christian beverage," taking the onus away from this most Muslim of drinks. His benediction cleared the way for Christians to drink coffee without guilt, and coffeehouses sprang up in Venice (about 1645, exact date disputed), Hamburg (1671), and Paris (1672). London's first coffeehouse was opened by Jacob, a Jew, in 1652. A few years later, Edward Lloyd opened a café where he printed a newsletter with shipping industry news. This practice was the start of Lloyd's of London insurance company.

But coffee had not yet been embraced by the Viennese. The matchmaker, according to legend, was a Polish solider named Georg Franz Kolschitzky. However, recent research has shown that "legend" is the operative word, even though Kolschitzky's story is rousing.

During the terrible 1683 siege of Vienna, things were looking pretty bleak. Vienna had been weakened by the Black Plague and the Thirty Years' War, and Mohammed IV saw another opportunity for conquest. The city's 20,000 defenders were trying to hold off 200,000 Turks. The Viennese were desperate to get a message to the European forces gathering for the counterattack. The volunteer was Kolschitzky, who had worked among the Turks for many years and would be able to blend in. He succeeded.

A decisive battle was staged on September 12, and the Turks were routed. In their haste, they left behind many of their provisions, including five hundred bags of a strange bean, which the Viennese assumed were camel fodder. As they began burning the Turkish spoils, Kolschitzky smelled the familiar aroma of roasting coffee, which he had learned to appreciate during his years among the Turks. He quickly saved the coffee from the fire. Vienna's government wanted to reward Kolschitzky for his bravery, expecting to hear the usual request for a sack of gold. Instead, he asked for the bags of "camel fodder," and the imperial right to brew them into a beverage. The city fathers complied, throwing in 200 ducats and a house, too. It was said that Kolschitzky operated the first Viennese coffee business from his house on the Domgasse, where a plaque still commemorates the enterprise. Eventually, he opened another establishment, The House of the Blue Bottle, near the Belvedere Palace, which became the first coffeehouse built for the purpose. A street is even named for him: Kolschitzkygasse.

A nice story with lots of dramatic touches, but debunked in 1980 by Viennese historian Karl Teply, who discovered the old imperial license, dated January 12, 1685, granting the privilege of "sole purveyor of the Turkish beverage for a span of twenty years" to Johannes Diodato, a merchant who had learned how to make coffee in his native Armenia. Teply believes that Kolschitzky was a war hero but that he didn't apply for his coffeehouse license until well after Diodato's. And the Blue Bottle didn't even open until 1703, nine years after Kolschitzky's death.

Further, by the time of the siege, the Viennese were already well acquainted with coffee. In 1665, the Turkish "Grand Ambassador" Kara Mehmed Pasha set up an embassy in the Leopoldstadt section of the city. Soon, the ambassador began taking audiences in his impressively appointed salon, where he served brewed coffee as well as coffee sherbet (iced desserts being another Turkish culinary specialty) and other sweets. So it seems that neither Diodato nor Kolschitzky can lay claim to being Vienna's first coffee brewers; that honor goes to the Pasha's two Turkish *kahveci* (brewers), Mehmed and Ibrahim. When the Pasha set sail nine months later, he had planted the seeds for Vienna's love affair with coffee.

The coffeehouse business really started perking up with the grant of a concession to another Armenian, Isaak de Luca, in 1697. In addition, the Turks returned to Vienna in 1700 on a peace mission, and they offered coffee tastings to the citizens, thereby increasing demand. The Turks' friendly return prompted a fashion for everything and anything Turkish: smoking water pipes, wearing turbans and other Turkish garb, and music in "the Turkish style." Coinciding with this, de Luca and three other Armenians opened other coffeehouses the city. These new coffeehouses were more comfortable and offered better service than their predecessors. When de Luca died in 1729, there were eleven cafés in Vienna.

The proprietors quickly learned that the Viennese didn't like the bitter Turkish-style coffee. They adapted. First, the coffee grounds, a characteristic of traditionally brewed Turkish coffee, were filtered out. Next, the coffee was sweetened with honey, another improvement. But when the filtered, sweetened coffee was mixed with hot milk and cream, the city beamed with approval. This concoction was the first *Wiener Melange*, which to this day remains the coffee of choice for the Viennese. It is the ancestor of the cappuccino, latté, and other milky drinks in the coffee hall of fame.

Budapest fell to the Turks as early as 1541, beginning a 150-year occupation. It seems that the coffee first arrived in Buda in 1579, about a hundred years before Vienna. By the time the "infidels" were finally chased out in 1686, coffee still had not caught on. Hungarians originally called coffee *fekete leves* ("black soup"), perhaps derogatorily because of its Turkish connotations. In the elaborate Turkish dining etiquette, no business could be discussed during the meal. However, when the coffee was served after the meal, unpleasant subjects could be broached. When contemplating possible misfortune, Hungarians may still say, "The black soup is yet to come."

Prague, which had not been invaded by Turks, had to wait for the Viennese fashion to trickle northward, and didn't get its first coffeehouse until 1712. Both cities were under the direct influence of the Viennese court, and as coffee and places to drink it became indispensable in the capital, it grew proportionately in the outposts of the empire as well.

Austro-Hungarian bakers call these cakes *Kuchen*. While there are exceptions, Kuchen are usually made from a creamed butter–sugar base and served without any frosting or icing (as opposed to Torten, which are most often highly decorated sponge cakes). Until recently, baking powder was looked down on by "serious" bakers, and many of these cakes were leavened by eggs alone. That prejudice is changing because the chemically leavened cakes have a lighter texture that today's tastes prefer. On the other hand, as desserts are rarely enjoyed without a cup of coffee in hand or a moistening mound of whipped cream, the dryer, solid consistency of the old-fashioned cakes hardly matters; it all boils down to a matter of taste. When a cake is baked in a rectangular pan, it can also have the suffix "-fleck," or piece, indicating that the cake will be cut into squares for serving, as in *Zwetschkenflecken* ("Plum Squares"). These are not to be confused with *Schnitten* ("slices"), which are quite tall and are addressed in their own chapter.

Rouladen (Roulades) are another favorite cake in the Kuchen family. They are actually a category of Torten, made from a whipped-egg base and filled with some kind of simple whipped cream. The simple garnish of confectioners' sugar distinguishes it from more complex *Torten*.

Gugelhupf's distinctive fluted tube shape puts it in a category of its own. Originally a yeast cake, it is now often baked in the modern method with baking powder. Many variations exist, but *Marmorgugelhupf* (Marble Gugelhupf) is as popular as any cake can be.

FARMER'S CHEESECAKE
TOPFENTORTE
Makes 12 servings

In Vienna, Budapest, and Prague, cheesecakes are made with farmer's cheese (*Topfen*), not cream cheese. Topfentorte is a light, even deli-cate, alternative to the dense American classic. Some bakers consider a cracked cheesecake a disaster, but a few shallow hairline cracks are fine. Deep cracks are caused by overbaking, so don't be tempted to bake longer than necessary, even if the center seems underdone. Residual heat will continue to cook the cake outside of the oven, and it firms up even more when chilled.

■ ■ ■

CRUST
1 cup all-purpose flour
1/4 cup sugar
Pinch of salt
7 tablespoons (1 stick minus 1 tablespoon) unsalted butter, at cool room temperature, thinly sliced
2 large egg yolks (save 1 white for the filling)
Grated zest of 1/2 lemon
1/4 teaspoon vanilla extract

FILLING
1 pound farmer's cheese (see page 207)
1 cup sour cream
3/4 cup sugar, divided
1/4 cup milk
2 tablespoons cornstarch
2 teaspoons vanilla extract
Grated zest of 1/2 lemon
1/4 teaspoon salt
4 large eggs, separated, plus 1 large egg white, at room temperature
1/4 cup golden raisins
1/4 cup sliced blanched almonds

■ ■ ■

1. Position a rack in the center of the oven and heat to 325°F. Lightly butter a 9-inch round springform pan.

2. To make the crust: Combine the flour, sugar, and salt in a medium bowl. Using a pastry blender, cut in the butter until the mixture resembles coarse crumbs. Make a well in the center of the flour mixture. In a small bowl, beat the egg yolks, lemon zest, and vanilla and pour into the well. Stir with a fork until the mixture is well moistened and the crumbs hold together when pressed between your fingers. Gather up the dough. Press it firmly and evenly into the pan,

bringing the dough about ¾ inch up the sides. Pierce the dough all over with a fork and refrigerate for 2 minutes.

3. Bake until the crust is set and barely beginning to color, about 12 minutes. Cool completely on a wire rack. Reduce the oven temperature to 350°F.

4. To make the filling: Rub the farmer's cheese through a wire sieve into a medium bowl. Add the sour cream, ¼ cup of the sugar, the milk, cornstarch, vanilla, lemon zest, and salt and beat with a handheld electric mixer on medium speed until combined. One at a time, beat in the egg yolks.

5. Using clean beaters, beat the 5 egg whites in a medium bowl on high speed until soft peaks form. Gradually add the remaining ½ cup of sugar and beat until the whites form stiff, shiny peaks. Stir about one fourth of the whites into the cheese mixture, then fold in the remainder.

Pour the filling into the cooled crust and spread evenly. Sprinkle the raisins and almonds over the top.

6. Bake until the sides of the filling are gently puffed and barely touched with golden brown, even though the center will seem unset when the pan is given a jiggle, about 40 to 45 minutes.

7. Remove from the oven and immediately run a sharp knife around the inside of the pan to release the cake. Transfer to a wire rack and cool completely. Remove the sides of the pan. Cover the cake with plastic wrap and refrigerate until chilled, at least 2 hours or overnight. Serve chilled, using a hot, wet knife to slice the cake.

MAKE AHEAD

The cheesecake can be made up to 2 days ahead, covered, and refrigerated.

APRICOT TART
MARILLENKUCHEN
Makes 8 servings

APRICOT COFFEE CAKE
MARILLENFLECK
Makes 9 servings

The word *tart* doesn't really have a direct translation in Austrian German, unless you're talking about bite-sized tartlets. In that case, you'll find *Körbchen* (little baskets), *Schifferl* (little boats), and *Schüsserl* (little dishes). So, even though this looks and tastes similar to a French-style apricot tart, it's called a *Kuchen* (cake). It's made from the standard "3-2-1 dough," with some of the dough reserved to create a crumbly topping.

■ ■ ■

I recipe Short Crust Dough (page 15)
1¼ pounds (about 8) ripe apricots,
pitted and cut lengthwise into quarters
3 tablespoons sugar
2 tablespoons heavy cream

■ ■ ■

1. Position a rack in the center of the oven and heat to 400°F. Place a baking sheet on the rack. Lightly butter a 9-inch tart pan with a removable bottom.

2. Press two thirds of the dough evenly into the bottom and sides of the pan. Pierce all over with a fork, and freeze for 10 minutes.

3. Line the tart shell with aluminum foil and fill the foil with pastry weights or dried beans. Bake on the hot baking sheet until the pastry is set, about 12 minutes. Remove the foil with the weights and continue baking until the pastry looks dry but not browned, about 5 minutes.

4. Remove the tart from the oven. Arrange the apricots, skin sides down, in concentric circles in the pastry. Sprinkle with the sugar and drizzle with the cream. Crumble the remaining dough over the apricots.

5. Return the tart on the baking sheet to the oven. Immediately reduce the oven temperature to 350°F. Bake until the topping is lightly browned and the apricot juices are bubbling, about 30 minutes. Cool for 10 minutes on a wire rack. Remove the sides of the tart pan and cool completely.

This is one of the most popular of all coffee-house treats, and almost every baker has the recipe in his or her head. (The proportions are 200 grams each of flour, sugar, and butter, but these don't translate as easily in the American volume method of measuring.) This version comes from my friend Gerda Hofer, who related it by heart. Don't be put off by the use of canned fruit, which is consistently flavorful and sometimes preferable to the bland fresh fruit we get too often these days; but you can use fresh fruit if you are sure it is at its peak of flavor. If using fresh apricots, sprinkle them with 2 tablespoons additional sugar before baking.

■ ■ ■

14 tablespoons (1¾ sticks) unsalted butter,
at cool room temperature
I cup granulated sugar
4 large eggs, at room temperature
I teaspoon vanilla extract
1⅓ cups all-purpose flour
1½ teaspoons baking powder
Pinch of salt
2 tablespoons fresh lemon juice
Grated zest of ½ lemon
I 15¾-ounce can apricots, well drained
Confectioners' sugar, for garnish

■ ■ ■

1. Position a rack in the center of the oven and heat to 350°F. Lightly butter an 11 × 8-inch glass baking dish.

2. Beat the butter in a medium bowl with a handheld electric mixer on high speed until smooth, about 1 minute. Add the sugar and beat until the mixture is light in color and texture, about 2 minutes. Beat in the eggs, one at a time, beating well after each addition (don't be concerned if the mixture looks slightly curdled). Beat in the vanilla. Sift the flour, baking powder, and salt together and stir into the batter, then stir in the lemon juice and zest.

3. Spread evenly in the pan. Arrange the apricots

over the batter, cutting them into halves or quarters if necessary to give the cake a uniform appearance. (There are often apricots of different sizes in the same can.) Bake until the cake is golden brown and a toothpick inserted in the center comes out clean, 25 to 30 minutes. Transfer to a wire rack and cool completely before serving.

4. To serve, sift confectioners' sugar over the cake and cut into squares.

MAKE AHEAD

The cake can be made up to 1 day ahead, covered with plastic wrap, and served at room temperature.

CHERRY-ALMOND COFFEE CAKE
MEGGYES PISKÓTA

Makes 8 to 12 servings

Cherry coffee cakes like this are beloved in Hungary and in the Czech Republic, where they are called *bublanina*. There, the cherries are usually left unpitted so the stones can add their subtle almond-like flavor to the batter; no one seems to mind spitting out the pits. My version, however, uses pitted cherries and ground almonds in the batter.

■ ■ ■

Dried bread crumbs, for the pan
1 1/2 cups all-purpose flour
2/3 cup sliced natural almonds
1 teaspoon baking powder
1/4 teaspoon salt
1 1/4 cups (2 1/2 sticks) unsalted butter,
at cool room temperature
1 1/2 cups granulated sugar
6 large eggs, separated, at room temperature
1 teaspoon vanilla extract
1/2 teaspoon almond extract
1 pound sweet cherries, pitted
Confectioners' sugar, for garnish

■ ■ ■

1. Position a rack in the center of the oven and heat to 375°F. Butter a 13 × 9-inch baking pan, coat with the bread crumbs, and tap out the excess.

2. Process the flour, almonds, baking powder, and salt in a food processor until the almonds are very finely chopped, almost a powder; set aside.

3. Beat the butter with a handheld electric mixer on high speed in a medium bowl until smooth, about 1 minute. Gradually add the sugar and beat until light in color and texture, about 2 minutes. One at a time, beat in the yolks, then the vanilla and almond extracts.

4. Using clean beaters, beat the egg whites on high speed just until they form stiff, shiny peaks. Fold half of the whites into the butter mixture, then fold in half of the almond–flour mixture; repeat with the remaining whites and almond–flour mixture to make a thick batter. Spread evenly in the pan and arrange the cherries in rows in the batter.

5. Bake until the cake is golden brown and the top springs back when lightly pressed in the center, about 35 minutes. Sift confectioners' sugar over the top. Serve warm, or cool completely.

MAKE AHEAD

The cake can be made up to 1 day ahead, covered with plastic wrap, and stored at room temperature.

CHOCOLATE "SADDLE OF VENISON" CAKE
REHRÜCKEN
Makes one 12-inch-long cake

In its savory form, saddle of venison (*Rehrücken* in German) is often threaded with long strips of lard to moisten the lean meat as it roasts. But to dessert lovers, Rehrücken is chocolate cake baked in a long, half-cylinder-shaped pan to resemble the roast saddle of venison. The trompe-l'oeil effect is completed by studs of slivered almonds, which are supposed to look like the lard strips sticking out of the meat. Rehrücken is always made with cake crumbs and almonds, never flour, and is gently spiced. If you have a stash of frozen crumbs in the freezer, use them, or buy unfrosted vanilla- or chocolate-flavored cupcakes to turn into crumbs.

■ ■ ■

3 ounces high-quality bittersweet chocolate, finely chopped
²/₃ cup (2 ounces) cake crumbs (see headnote)
¹/₂ cup (2 ounces) sliced blanched almonds
¹/₄ teaspoon ground cinnamon
Zest of 1 lemon
4 large eggs, separated, at room temperature
¹/₂ cup sugar, divided
2 tablespoons unsalted butter, melted
¹/₃ cup Red Currant Glaze (page 16), warm
Small-Batch Chocolate Glaze (page 16), hot
¹/₂ cup (2 ounces) slivered blanched almonds, as needed, for garnish

■ ■ ■

1. Position a rack in the center of the oven and heat to 350°F. Using a cylinder-shaped pastry brush, butter a 12-inch Rehrücken mold (see Note). Dust with flour and tap out the excess.
2. Melt the chocolate in the top part of a double boiler over hot, not simmering, water, or in a microwave oven at medium power. Cool slightly.
3. In a food processor fitted with the metal blade, process the cake crumbs and almonds until the almonds are very finely ground and almost powdery. Add the cinnamon and lemon zest and pulse to combine.
4. Beat the yolks and ¼ cup of the sugar in a medium bowl, using a handheld electric mixer at high speed, until thick and pale yellow, about 2 minutes. Mix in the melted chocolate and butter, then the almond–crumb mixture.
5. Using clean beaters, beat the egg whites on high speed until they form soft peaks. Gradually beat in the remaining ¼ cup of sugar, until the whites are shiny. Stir one fourth of the whites into the chocolate batter to lighten it, then fold in the remaining whites. Pour into the pan.
6. Bake until a toothpick inserted in the center comes out clean, about 35 minutes. Cool in the pan on a wire rack for 5 minutes. (The cake will fall slightly.) Invert onto the rack and cool completely (the cake will even itself out).
7. Place the cake on the rack on a jelly-roll pan. Brush the cake with the warm red currant glaze. Cool completely to set the glaze.
8. Pour the warm chocolate glaze over the cake, using a metal spatula to smooth it over the sides, coating the cake completely. Stud the cake with the almonds. Don't overdo it or the cake will be too crunchy to eat easily—two parallel rows of almonds, running just above the long sides of the cake, spaced about ½ inch apart, should be enough. Refrigerate the cake to firm the glaze. Serve chilled or at room temperature.

NOTE
Rehrücken pans are available at well-stocked kitchenware shops and by mail order (see Mail-Order Sources, page 000).

MAKE AHEAD
The cake can be made up to 2 days ahead, covered with plastic wrap, and stored at room temperature.

▪ THE STORY BEHIND ▪
BURGTHEATERTORTE

The Burgtheater, near the Hofburg on the Ringstrasse, was Austria's royal theater, and it benefitted from the Emperor's largesse. When the theater was rebuilt in the 1880s, it was decorated with murals by Gustav Klimt, whose sexually frank nymphs became the cause of some acrimony with Vienna's art establishment. The cake was created by Demel, the court bakery, as an intermission snack.

Emperor Franz Joseph was a frequent visitor to the Burgtheater, but his tastes in theater, like his tastes in food, were simple. His favorite actress was the charming soubrette Katharina Schratt, who became confidante to both the emperor and his wife, Elizabeth. In spite of (or perhaps because of) the rumors concerning Katharina's friendship with the emperor, the royal couple did everything possible to show the public and press that there was to be no misunderstanding about Frau Schratt's role in the palace household. The dramatic death (suicide?) of Crown Prince Rudolf and the assassination of Empress Elizabeth brought Katharina and the emperor closer together as soulmates, but there is no evidence of any physical relationship between them. Of course it is possible that they were "just good friends." It is said that their relationship became strained in later years because Katharina took offense when the emperor refused to appoint her to a higher position in court, as he was afraid this would send a signal that they were, in fact, romantically involved. They reconciled at the very end of the emperor's life, which coincided with the demise of the Empire and the way of life they both loved.

Katharina was a talented cook, and the emperor preferred her cooking to all others. She was ready to feed him at the drop of a hat, and many mornings he came by for breakfast. Just in case her home-baked Gugelhupf wasn't up to her high standards, Katharina had a standing order for a backup cake from Zauner, Bad Ischl's premier bakery, where they both had summer homes.

A few years ago, Katharina Schratt's handwritten recipe book was found. The recipes have been printed in *To Set Before the King* (University of Iowa Press), which gives a fascinating look at the inside of an upper-class kitchen in fin de siècle Vienna.

CHOCOLATE-ORANGE CAKE
BURGTHEATERTORTE
Makes 12 to 16 servings

At Vienna's esteemed Demel, those who want a sweet that isn't *too* sweet might choose a slice of Burgtheatertorte. Bakers never let anything go to waste, even cake crumbs, and they are used here to make a moist chocolate-almond cake dotted with candied orange peel. The 4 cups of cake crumbs are easily obtained during a day's work at a bakery, where the tops of countless cakes are routinely trimmed off, but home cooks will need a strategy (unless you are a frequent baker and freeze trimmings until you have reached the quota). You might bake a chocolate cake layer expressly for this recipe (the Chocolate Sponge Cake or Sachertorte batter on pages 8 or 62 are perfect), or buy an unfrosted cake at your favorite bakery. But remember, the better your crumbs, the better the cake.

■ ■ ■

1¾ cups (9 ounces) natural (with skin) sliced
almonds
2 cups confectioners' sugar
2 tablespoons Dutch-processed cocoa powder
1 cup plus 2 tablespoons (2¼ sticks) unsalted
butter, at room temperature
6 large eggs, at room temperature, beaten
1 teaspoon cinnamon
4 cups (14 ounces) chocolate cake crumbs,
processed in a blender or food processor
½ cup diced candied orange peel
⅓ cup Red Currant Glaze (page 16), warm
Confectioners' sugar, for garnish

■ ■ ■

1. Position a rack in the center of the oven and heat to 350°F. Butter the inside of a 9-inch springform pan. Line the bottom with a buttered round of wax paper. Dust the inside of the pan with flour, tapping out the excess.

2. In a food processor fitted with the metal blade, process the almonds, ¼ cup of the confectioners' sugar, and the cocoa until the almonds are very finely ground, almost a flour.

3. In a medium bowl, using an electric mixer on high speed, beat the butter until creamy, about 1 minute. Reduce the speed to low and add the remaining 1¾ cups confectioners' sugar. When combined, return the speed to high and beat until light in color and texture, about 2 minutes. Very slowly, beat in the eggs, then the cinnamon. Stir in the almond mixture, then the cake crumbs and the candied peel. Spread evenly in the pan.

4. Bake until a toothpick inserted in the center of the cake comes out clean, about 1 hour. Cool on a wire rack for 5 minutes. Run a knife around the inside of the pan to release the cake. Remove the sides of the pan. Invert the cake onto the rack, and remove the wax paper. Cool completely.

5. Turn the cake right side up. Using a long serrated knife, cut the cake in half horizontally. Spread the bottom layer with the warm glaze. Replace the top layer. Sift a generous layer of confectioners' sugar over the top of the cake. Using a sharp knife, trace a crosshatch pattern in the sugar. Let stand at room temperature for 1 hour before serving.

MAKE AHEAD
The cake can be prepared up to 3 days ahead, covered tightly with plastic wrap, and stored at room temperature.

POPPY SEED GUGELHUPF
MOHNGUGELHUPF
Makes 10 to 12 servings

When I make this cake for guests, the aromatic flavor stumps them. Could it be cardamom, five-spice powder, or something even more exotic? They are surprised to learn the source is nothing more than fresh, ground poppy seeds.

■ ■ ■

I cup (2 sticks) unsalted butter,
at cool room temperature
I cup confectioners' sugar
4 large eggs, at room temperature
Grated zest of I lemon
2 cups cake flour
2 teaspoons baking powder
Pinch of salt
¾ cup poppy seeds, ground (see page 212)
½ cup milk
2 tablespoons golden rum
I teaspoon vanilla extract

■ ■ ■

1. Position a rack in the center of the oven and heat to 350°F. Using a cylinder-shaped pastry brush, butter the inside of a 9- to 9½-inch Gugelhupf mold or fluted cake pan. Coat with flour, tapping out the excess.
2. Beat the butter in a medium bowl using a handheld electric mixer on high speed until smooth, about 1 minute. On low speed, beat in the confectioners' sugar. Return the speed to high and beat until the mixture is very pale and light in texture, about 3 minutes. One at a time, beat in the eggs, then the lemon zest.
3. Sift the flour, baking powder, and salt together into a bowl, and stir in the poppy seeds. Mix the milk, rum, and vanilla in a glass measuring cup. Stir in half of the flour, then half of the milk, then repeat. Spread evenly in the pan.
4. Bake until a toothpick inserted in the center of the cake comes out clean, 50 to 60 minutes. Cool on a wire rack for 10 minutes. Invert onto the rack to unmold and cool completely.

MAKE AHEAD

The cake is best the day it is made. Cover leftovers tightly in plastic wrap and store at room temperature. To refresh, heat slices in a toaster oven.

BANANA GUGELHUPF
BANANENGUGELHUPF
Makes 12 servings

Banana Gugelhupf is one of the newer additions to the Austro-Hungarian pastry roster. I've made countless American-style banana breads before, but this is a very special recipe, resulting in a beautiful loaf filled with moist banana flavor. Use ripened bananas freckled with brown spots with an intensely sweet aroma, and not ones that are overly ripe and blackened.

■ ■ ■

½ cup (I stick) unsalted butter,
at cool room temperature
I cup confectioners' sugar
4 large eggs, at room temperature
2 cups all-purpose flour
2 teaspoons baking powder
Pinch of salt
I cup mashed ripe bananas
(about 3 medium bananas)
¾ cup packed light brown sugar
⅓ cup heavy cream
I teaspoon vanilla extract
Grated zest of I lemon

■ ■ ■

1. Position a rack in the center of the oven and heat to 350°F. Using a cylinder-shaped pastry brush, butter the inside of a 9- to 9½-inch Gugelhupf mold or fluted tube pan. Coat with flour and tap out the excess.
2. Beat the butter in a medium bowl with a handheld electric mixer on high speed until smooth, about 1 minute. Reduce the speed to low and gradually add the confectioners' sugar. Return the speed to high and beat until very light in

color and texture, about 2 minutes. One at a time, beat in the eggs, beating well after each addition.

3. Sift the flour, baking powder, and salt together and set aside. In another medium bowl, whisk the bananas, brown sugar, cream, vanilla, and lemon zest until the sugar is dissolved. With the mixer on low speed, one third at a time, alternately beat in the flour and banana mixtures, scraping down the sides of the bowl often, until the batter is smooth. Pour into the pan and smooth the top.

4. Bake until the top is golden brown and a toothpick inserted in the center of the cake comes out clean, 50 to 60 minutes. Cool in the pan on a wire rack for 10 minutes. Invert onto the rack and cool completely.

MAKE AHEAD

The cake can be made up to 1 day ahead, covered with plastic wrap, and stored at room temperature.

MARBLE GUGELHUPF
MARMORGUGELHUPF
Makes 10 servings

This tender, buttery cake is based on the marble Gugelhupf at Demel in Vienna, although I've added baking powder to give it the lighter crumb Americans prefer.

■ ■ ■

2 ounces high-quality bittersweet chocolate,
finely chopped
2 cups cake flour
2 teaspoons baking powder
1/4 teaspoon salt
1/2 cup milk
2 teaspoons vanilla extract
1 1/8 cups (2 sticks plus 2 tablespoons)
unsalted butter, at cool room temperature
1 1/4 cups confectioners' sugar
6 large eggs, separated, at room temperature

3/4 cup granulated sugar
Confectioners' sugar, for garnish

■ ■ ■

1. Position a rack in the center of the oven and heat to 350°F. Using a cylinder-shaped pastry brush, butter the inside of a 9- to 9½-inch Gugelhupf mold. Coat with flour, tapping out the excess.

2. Melt the chocolate in the top part of a double boiler over hot, not simmering, water or in a microwave oven. Remove from the heat and cool, stirring occasionally, until tepid.

3. Sift the flour, baking powder, and salt together. Mix the milk and vanilla in a liquid measuring cup.

4. Beat the butter in a large bowl with a hand-held electric mixer on high speed until smooth, about 1 minute. On low speed, beat in the confectioners' sugar, then increase the speed to medium-high and beat until the mixture is very light in color and texture, about 2 minutes. Beat in the egg yolks, one at a time.

5. Using clean beaters, beat the egg whites on high speed until soft peaks form. Gradually beat in the granulated sugar until the whites form shiny, soft peaks. Stir about one fourth of the whites into the batter. Stir in half of the flour, then half of the milk; repeat. Fold in the remaining whites. Transfer about one third of the batter to a medium bowl and stir in the melted chocolate.

6. Spread half of the plain batter in the pan. Spoon in the chocolate batter, then top with the remaining plain batter. Zigzag a knife through the batter.

7. Bake until a toothpick inserted in the center of the cake comes out clean, about 1 hour. Cool in the pan on a wire rack for 10 minutes. Invert onto the rack and cool completely. Before serving, sprinkle with confectioners' sugar.

MAKE AHEAD

The cake can be made up to 1 day ahead, wrapped in plastic wrap, and stored at room temperature.

CHESTNUT SLICES
GESZTENYESZELET
Makes 12 slices

The passion for chestnut-based desserts knows no limits in central Europe. Hungary is especially chestnut-crazy (some of Europe's best chestnuts are grown there). Outside of the occasional holiday stuffing, chestnuts have never really taken off in America, but this recipe could make some converts. I suspect the difficult peeling process is one of the reasons for chestnuts' lack of popularity. Here's a Hungarian recipe that puts a 16-ounce can of chestnut purée to very good use: A bit is used in the cake batter for flavor, then the remainder is turned into a whipped-cream topping.

■ ■ ■

CAKE
6 large eggs, at room temperature
1/3 cup plus 1 tablespoon granulated sugar
3 tablespoons canned unsweetened chestnut purée
1 teaspoon vanilla extract
Pinch of salt
3/4 cup cake flour

BRANDY SYRUP
1/2 cup water
1/4 cup plus 1 tablespoon granulated sugar
1/4 cup brandy

CHESTNUT TOPPING
1 1/2 cups canned unsweetened chestnut purée
1 1/2 cups confectioners' sugar, divided
2 teaspoons vanilla extract
2 cups heavy cream

2 ounces bittersweet chocolate, for garnish

■ ■ ■

1. Position a rack in the center of the oven and heat to 350°F. Lightly butter and flour a 13 × 9-inch baking pan and tap out the excess flour.

2. To make the cake: Combine the eggs and sugar in the bowl of a standing heavy-duty electric mixer. Place over a pot of simmering water (the water should not touch the bottom of the bowl). Whisk constantly until the eggs are very warm to the touch and the sugar is dissolved (rub a bit of the egg mixture between your fingers to check for grains of sugar). Attach to the mixer and fit with the whisk. Beat on high speed until the mixture is tripled in volume and very light and fluffy, about 3 minutes. Beat in the chestnut purée, vanilla, and salt and beat until the chestnut purée is well distributed (the eggs will deflate slightly). Sift half of the flour over the eggs. Using a large balloon whisk or rubber spatula, fold it in. Repeat with the remaining flour. Spread evenly in the pan.

3. Bake until the cake is golden and springs back when pressed in the center, about 20 minutes. Cool completely on a wire rack.

4. To make the syrup: Bring the water and sugar to a boil in a small saucepan over high heat, stirring to dissolve the sugar, then boil for 1 minute. Cool completely. Stir in the brandy.

5. To make the topping: Beat the chestnut purée with 3/4 cup of the confectioners' sugar and the vanilla in a medium bowl with a handheld electric mixer on low speed until smooth. In a chilled medium bowl, beat the cream with the remaining 3/4 cup of confectioners' sugar until stiff. Stir a large spoonful of the whipped cream into the chestnuts to lighten, then fold in the remainder.

6. Brush and drizzle the syrup over the cake. Spread the chestnut cream on top. Grate the chocolate through the large holes in a box grater over the chestnut cream. Cover loosely with plastic wrap and refrigerate until chilled, at least 2 hours.

7. To serve, cut into 12 rectangles and serve from the pan. Serve chilled.

MAKE AHEAD
The cake can be prepared up to 1 day ahead, covered loosely with plastic wrap, and refrigerated.

BISHOP'S FRUIT-AND-CHOCOLATE TEA CAKE
BISCHOFSBROT
Makes 10 to 12 servings

Picture the local Catholic bishop in his rectory serving a simple, tasty cake to his visitors with a cup of hot coffee or perhaps a small glass of schnapps. That's how this delicious almond-scented fruitcake got its name. Some Bischofs-broten are pretty austere, nothing more than sponge cake with a bit of candied fruit tossed in. This recipe, based on one from *Das große Buch der österreichischen Mehlspeisen,* must have come from a rich bishopric: Almond paste, chocolate, rum, and nuts all find their way into the cake along with the required fruit. It's baked in a Rehrücken pan, which gives it an attractive shape. (See the Note at the end of the recipe to bake in an American loaf pan.)

■ ■ ■

FRUIT
½ cup chopped candied mixed fruit
½ cup dried currants
2 tablespoons golden rum
½ cup chopped almonds
2 ounces finely chopped bittersweet chocolate
2 tablespoons all-purpose flour

CAKE
⅔ cup (1 stick plus 2 tablespoons) unsalted butter, at cool room temperature
½ cup (5 ounces) almond paste, crumbled
4 large eggs, separated, at room temperature
1 teaspoon vanilla
⅔ cup sugar
1¼ cups all-purpose flour
2 teaspoons baking powder
Pinch of salt

■ ■ ■

1. To prepare the fruit: Mix the candied fruit, currants, and rum in a small bowl and set aside to plump for 1 hour. Stir in the almonds and chocolate, then toss with the flour.

2. To make the cake: Position a rack in the center of the oven and heat to 350°F. Using a cylinder-shaped pastry brush, butter the inside of a 12-inch nonstick Rehrücken pan. Dust with flour and tap out the excess.

3. Beat the butter and almond paste in the bowl of a standing heavy-duty electric mixer on medium-high speed until smooth and very light in color, about 2 minutes. One at a time, beat in the yolks, then the vanilla.

4. In a medium bowl, beat the egg whites with a whisk or handheld electric mixer on high speed until soft peaks form. Gradually beat in the sugar until the peaks are stiff and shiny. Fold into the butter mixture. Sift the flour, baking powder, and salt together. Sift half of the flour mixture over the batter and fold in. Repeat with the remaining flour. Fold in the fruit and nut mixture. Spread evenly in the pan.

5. Place in the oven and reduce the oven temperature to 325°F. Bake until browned and the top springs back when pressed in the center and a toothpick inserted in the center comes out absolutely clean (this is a sticky batter, so look closely), about 35 minutes. Cool on a wire rack for 10 minutes. Invert and unmold onto the rack and cool completely.

MAKE AHEAD
The cake can be made up to 2 days ahead, wrapped tightly in plastic wrap, and stored at room temperature.

NOTE
To bake in an American loaf pan, butter and flour a 9 × 5-inch loaf pan and line the bottom with parchment paper. Pour in the batter and smooth the top. Place in a preheated 350°F. oven, then immediately reduce the heat to 325°F. Bake about 1¼ hours, testing carefully to be sure the cake is baked through.

VIENNESE POUND CAKE
SANDTORTE
Makes 8 to 10 servings

When a Viennese cake starts with a mixture of creamed butter and sugar, it is called a "sand cake," easily recognizable as a relation of the English pound cake, the batter of which is made from one-pound weights of eggs, flour, butter, and sugar. In this recipe from the revered Hofzuckerbäckerei Demel, the weight of each ingredient is reduced to 250 grams (9 ounces). Notice that Demel has such confidence in the quality of their ingredients that the cake has no added flavorings, but you may add 1 teaspoon vanilla extract or the grated zest of 1 lemon or orange, if you wish. The cornstarch is important, as it cuts the amount of gluten in the batter and does a good job of reducing the cracked top of flour-only pound cakes. It bakes best in an 8-inch Gugelhupf pan, rather than the larger pan used in other recipes in this book.

■ ■ ■

1¼ cups (2 sticks plus 2 tablespoons)
unsalted butter,
at cool room temperature
1¼ cups sugar, divided
5 large eggs, separated
1⅓ cups all-purpose flour
⅓ cup cornstarch
Pinch of salt

■ ■ ■

1. Position a rack in the center of the oven and heat to 350°F. Using a cylinder-shaped pastry brush, butter the inside of an 8-inch Gugelhupf pan. Coat with flour and tap out the excess.
2. Beat the butter in the bowl of a heavy-duty standing mixer at high speed until smooth, about 1 minute. Add ¾ cup of the sugar and beat, occasionally scraping down the bowl, until very light in color and texture, about 4 minutes. One at a time, beat in the egg yolks, beating well after each addition.
3. Beat the egg whites in a medium bowl until they form soft peaks. Gradually beat in the remaining ½ cup sugar and beat until the whites form stiff, shiny peaks. Fold the egg whites into the butter mixture. Sift the flour, cornstarch, and salt together. In two additions, fold the flour into the batter. Spoon into the cake pan and smooth the top.
4. Bake until a toothpick inserted in the center of the cake comes out clean, about 50 minutes. Cool on a wire rack for 10 minutes. Invert and unmold onto the rack and cool completely.

MAKE AHEAD
The cake can be baked up to 1 day ahead, wrapped tightly in plastic wrap, and stored at room temperature.

PLUM SQUARES
ZWETSCHKENFLECKEN
Makes 12 to 16 servings

In late summer and early fall, when the blue-purple prune plums are in season, almost every coffeehouse will have plum cake sitting front and center in the display case. This version is based on the one served at Café Sperl, one of Vienna's protected landmark coffeehouses. With its easy-to-make short crust dough, it can be prepared in no time and disappears as quickly as homebaked apple pie in an American diner in October.

■ ■ ■

2¾ cups all-purpose flour
1¾ cups confectioners' sugar
Pinch of salt
1⅓ cups (2½ sticks plus 1 tablespoon)
unsalted butter, at cool room temperature,
cut into thin slices
1 large egg
1 teaspoon vanilla extract
1¼ pounds Italian prune plums (about 16
plums), cut in half lengthwise and pitted
1 tablespoon granulated sugar
½ cup Apricot Glaze (page 16), warm

■ ■ ■

1. Mix the flour, confectioners' sugar, and salt in a large bowl. Add the butter. Using a pastry blender, cut in the butter until the mixture resembles coarse meal. Mix the egg and vanilla with a fork in a small bowl. Pour over the flour mixture and use your fingers to mix together into a dough. Gather into a thick disk, wrap in plastic wrap, and refrigerate for 30 to 60 minutes.

2. Position a rack in the center of the oven and heat to 350°F. Lightly butter a 17 × 12 × 1-inch jelly-roll pan.

3. Press the dough firmly and evenly into the pan. Arrange the plums in rows on the crust, cut sides up, and sprinkle with the granulated sugar.

4. Bake until the crust is golden brown, about 45 minutes. Cool completely.

5. Brush the top of the cake with the warm apricot glaze; cool. To serve, cut into large squares.

MAKE AHEAD

The cake can be prepared a day or two ahead, covered with plastic wrap, and stored at room temperature.

FLOURLESS POPPY SEED CAKE
MOHNKUCHEN
Makes 8 servings

When I was first served this cake at a Jause by the charming Gerda Hofer, I was surprised by its almost black color. Dense with poppy seeds, without flour or starch of any kind, it's a moist treat for poppy seed lovers.

■ ■ ■

10 tablespoons (1¼ sticks) unsalted butter, at cool room temperature
5 large eggs, separated, at room temperature
1 cup granulated sugar
1¾ cups (9 ounces) poppy seeds, ground (see page 212)
½ cup heavy cream
Confectioners' sugar, for garnish
Sweetened Whipped Cream (page 19)

■ ■ ■

1. Position a rack in the center of the oven and heat to 350°F. Lightly butter an 11 × 8-inch baking dish.

2. Beat the butter in a medium bowl with a hand-held electric mixer at high speed until smooth, about 1 minute. One at a time, beat in the egg yolks and continue beating until the mixture is light and fluffy, about 2 minutes. Beat in the sugar.

3. Using clean beaters, beat the egg whites in another medium bowl on high speed until they form soft peaks. Stir about one fourth of the beaten whites into the butter mixture, then fold in the remainder, stopping before all of the whites are completely incorporated. Fold in the poppy seeds, then the cream. Spread the batter evenly in the pan.

4. Bake until the top of the cake is lightly browned and the center springs back when pressed gently in the center, about 45 minutes. Transfer to a wire rack and cool completely. Just before serving, sift with confectioners' sugar. Serve with a dollop of whipped cream.

MAKE AHEAD

The cake can be made up to 1 day ahead, covered with plastic wrap, and stored at room temperature.

BLUEBERRY CREAM ROULADE
HEIDELBEERROULADE
Makes 8 to 10 servings

Sponge cake batter is often baked in a jelly-roll pan to make a flexible cake that can be rolled into a cream-filled roulade. Here's one of my favorites: vanilla cake with a blueberry cream. You can substitute 2 cups of your favorite berry, but if you use strawberries, they should be sliced before measuring.

■ ■ ■

CAKE
**Batter for Warm-Method Sponge Cake
(page 5)
Confectioners' sugar, for sprinkling and
garnish**

BLUEBERRY CREAM
**2 tablespoons orange-flavored liqueur,
such as Cointreau
1 tablespoon water**

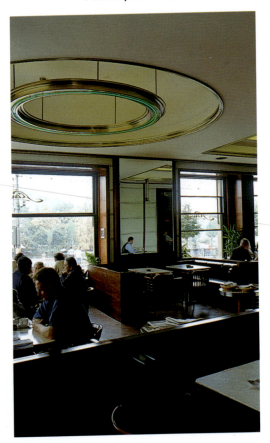

**1 envelope (2½ teaspoons) unflavored gelatin
1 pint fresh blueberries, divided
¼ cup confectioners' sugar
Grated zest of 1 lemon
1 cup heavy cream**

■ ■ ■

1. To make the cake: Position a rack in the center of the oven and heat to 350°F. Lightly butter a 15½ × 10½-inch jelly-roll pan. Line the bottom of the pan with parchment paper. Flour the buttered sides, tapping out the excess.

2. Spread the batter for the sponge cake evenly in the pan with an offset metal spatula, being sure to fill the corners. Bake until the center of the cake springs back when pressed, about 15 minutes. Dust a light coating of confectioners' sugar through a sieve over the top of the cake. Place a clean kitchen towel over the cake. Invert the cake onto a large wire rack or baking sheet to unmold. Carefully peel off the parchment. Using the towel as an aide, starting at a long end, roll up the cake into a thick cylinder. Wrap the cake in the towel and cool completely on the rack.

3. To make the blueberry cream: Combine the liqueur and water in a small bowl and sprinkle the gelatin on top. Let stand until the gelatin absorbs the liquid, about 2 minutes. Place the bowl in a small saucepan filled with about ½ inch of simmering water and stir until the gelatin is completely dissolved. Remove the bowl from the water. (Or microwave on medium at 10-second intervals, stirring well after each interval, until the gelatin dissolves.) Cool until tepid.

4. Purée 1 cup of the blueberries with the confectioners' sugar and lemon zest in a blender. Beat the cream in a medium bowl with a hand-held electric mixer on high speed just until soft peaks form. Still beating, pour the dissolved gelatin into the beaters and whip until the cream is stiff. Fold in the blueberry purée.

5. Unroll the cooled cake. Spread with the blueberry cream, leaving a ½-inch border around all sides. Sprinkle with the remaining blueberries. Roll up the cake into its original shape. Wrap the roulade in plastic wrap and refrigerate until the blueberry cream is chilled and set, at least 1 hour.

Café Slavia

The Café Slavia is the heart of Czech culture. Built on one of the busiest corners in Prague, across from the National Theater complex, the café has seen much history pass by its windows, from state funeral processions to marching columns of Nazis and Communists. After a long real-estate battle that closed the café, the Slavia has been lovingly restored. Instead of the fin-de-siècle trappings of other classic cafés, sleek Art Deco surroundings set the scene for your meal.

The café was originally built in 1884 along the traditional coffeehouse lines. In the 1920s, it emerged as a meeting place for the pioneers of modern Czech art, called "The Stubborn Ones" for their firm beliefs. Nobel prize-winning poet Jaroslav Seifert wrote a poem celebrating the Slavia. During Communist occupation, opposition intellectuals like Václav Havel gathered to share dreams of democracy and plant the seeds for the Velvet Revolution.

Victory for democracy came in 1989. But privatization proved a disaster for the Slavia. In 1991, the café's state-owned management sold the business to a Boston firm, which promised renovation. A year later, a "Closed for Renovations" sign went up. After three years, with no work being done to the café, Praguers were becoming sad and angry at seeing their beloved Slavia wasting away. A sit-in was held, with trespassers occupying the café under placards that read, WE WON'T GIVE THE SLAVIA UP! Havel himself announced a petition for the reopening of the café. Finally, because the American firm had not, in fact, done any renovation work, the Czech Republic declared the sale of the Slavia null and void, and the café was finally reopened in 1997.

The interior of the Slavia dates back to the 1930s, when the old Jugendstil decorations were razed in favor of a slick Art Deco design. Where once an old-fashioned triptych representative of Mother Slavia stood, *The Absinthe Drinker,* by Viktor Oliva, was hung. This painting, with a café client looking emptily into the eyes of his ghostly, liquor-induced muse, reflects the debilitating effects of absinthe on its drinkers. Distilled from wormwood, absinthe is psychedelic and addictive. It is outlawed in many countries, including the United States, but not in the Czech Republic, where it is for sale at the Slavia. While a drink or two won't drive you insane, it will give you one heck of a hangover if you're not cautious. The flavor isn't delicious (it reminded me of salty cough syrup), so you won't have much trouble turning down a second glass.

6. To serve, sprinkle confectioners' sugar through a sieve over the top of the roulade. Using a serrated knife, cut on a slight diagonal into thick slices. Serve chilled.

MAKE AHEAD

The roulade can be prepared up to 2 days ahead, wrapped tightly in plastic, and refrigerated.

CHOCOLATE-CHERRY ROULADE
SCHOKOLADE-KIRSCHENROULADE
Makes 8 to 10 servings

The farms in the hills of the Danube are famous for their cherries. Tucked into kirsch-scented whipped cream for a chocolate roulade, they are put to very good use. A plunge-handled cherry pitter (page 201) makes short work of the tedious job of stoning the cherries. In Europe, cooks use a few drops of bitter almond oil to heighten the flavor of the cherries. It's hard to locate here, but a bit of almond extract has a similar effect.

■ ■ ■

3/4 cup cake flour
1/3 cup Dutch-processed cocoa powder
1/8 teaspoon salt
5 large eggs, at room temperature
3/4 cup granulated sugar
3 tablespoons unsalted butter
1/4 cup milk
1/2 teaspoon vanilla extract
Confectioners' sugar, for sprinkling

CHERRY CREAM
2 tablespoons kirsch or cherry schnapps
1 tablespoon water
1 1/2 teaspoons unflavored gelatin
1 1/2 cups heavy cream
1/4 cup confectioners' sugar
1/2 teaspoon vanilla extract
1/4 teaspoon almond extract
12 ounces fresh sweet cherries, pitted and cut into halves

Confectioners' sugar and Dutch-processed cocoa, for garnish

■ ■ ■

1. To make the cake: Position a rack in the center of the oven and heat to 350°F. Lightly butter a 15½ × 10½ × 1-inch jelly-roll pan. Line the bottom of the pan with parchment paper. Coat with flour and tap out the excess.
2. Sift the flour, cocoa, and salt together. Whisk the eggs and sugar in the work bowl of a heavy-duty standing mixer. Place over a saucepan of simmering water (the water should not touch the bottom of the bowl). Whisk until the eggs are very warm to the touch and the sugar is completely dissolved (rub a bit of the mixture between your fingers to check). Attach to the mixer and fit with the whisk. Beat on medium-high speed until the mixture is light and tripled in volume, about 3 minutes. In two additions, sift the cocoa mixture over the eggs and use a balloon whisk or large rubber spatula to fold in.
3. Melt the butter in a small saucepan over medium heat. Add the milk and heat until hot. Pour into a medium bowl and add the vanilla. Whisk in a large dollop of the batter, and fold this mixture back into the batter. Using an offset spatula, spread the batter evenly in the pan, being sure to fill the corners.
4. Bake until the cake springs back when gently pressed in the center, about 15 minutes. Sift a light coating of confectioners' sugar through a sieve over the top of the cake. Place a clean kitchen towel over the cake. Invert the cake onto a large wire rack or baking sheet to unmold. Carefully peel off the parchment. Using the towel as an aide, starting at a long end, roll up the cake into a thick cylinder. Wrap the cake in the towel and cool completely on the rack.
5. To make the cherry cream: Combine the kirsch and water in a small bowl and sprinkle the gelatin on top. Let stand until the gelatin absorbs the liquid, about 2 minutes. Place the bowl in a small saucepan filled with about ½ inch of simmering water and stir until the gelatin is completely dissolved. (Or microwave on medium at 10-second intervals, stirring well after each interval until the gelatin dissolves.) Remove the bowl from the water; cool slightly.
6. Using a handheld electric mixer, beat the cream, confectioners' sugar, vanilla, and almond extract in a medium bowl just until soft peaks form. Still beating, pour the dissolved gelatin into the beaters and whip until the cream is stiff.
7. Unroll the cooled cake. Spread with the whipped cream, leaving a ½-inch border around all sides. Arrange the cherries in rows over the cream. Roll up the cake into its original shape. Wrap the roulade in plastic wrap and refrigerate until the cream is chilled and set, at least 1 hour.

Café Dommayer

Johann Strauss junior and senior are forever linked with the Dommayer Konzert-Café (a designation given to coffeehouses with regularly scheduled music), and, by extension, with all Viennese cafés. The owners, the Gerersdorfer family, pride themselves on promoting the oldest traditions of the café culture, at the same time being attuned to such contemporary concerns as using organic foods whenever possible.

The Dommayer was originally a small coffeehouse in the village of Hietzing, built in 1787 (the village was eventually incorporated into Vienna). By 1823, it had become a large, richly decorated casino with twenty-four columns holding up the roof of the dance hall. Public transportation had been introduced in 1815, which made the village easier to get to, and people came to escape the crowded inner city. Ten years later, Johann Strauss the elder opened the summer season of the casino with his orchestra, to immediate success. Dommayer became Vienna's most famous concert hall and a popular venue for carnival balls. Joseph Lanner, too, played at the Dommayer. When the eighteen-year-old Johann Strauss the younger and his orchestra played for the first time in 1844, there was no stopping the waltz.

After a long run, the original Dommayer shut its doors in 1907 and was replaced by the Schönbrunner Parkhotel. The hotel housed Thomas Edison while he was hired to install electricity in the nearby Schönbrunn Palace, but he ended up staying much longer than he wanted. The Hapsburgs were not accustomed to paying on demand, and Edison refused to budge until he got all of his money. It is said that Vienna's city council paid the bill to get rid of the American and keep their royalty's poor disbursement habits under wraps.

A new Dommayer was built not far from the original in 1924. It went through a few owners until 1963, when the present proprietors, the Gerersdorfer family, took over. The family studied the traditions of the old coffeehouses, then started to bring them back. One of the first innovations was to return live music to the café, and now a summer garden offers a large selection of musical and theatrical entertainment in addition to the chamber music played inside during the cooler months. In 1984, an extensive renovation brought back the café to its full splendor.

8. To serve, sprinkle confectioners' sugar through a sieve over the top of the roulade, then dust with cocoa powder. Using a serrated knife, cut on a slight diagonal into thick slices. Serve chilled.

MAKE AHEAD

The roulade can be prepared up to 2 days ahead, wrapped tightly in plastic, and then refrigerated.

HAZELNUT ROULADE
WITH MOCHA CREAM
HASELNUßROULADE MIT MOKKACREME
Makes 8 to 10 servings

Hazelnuts, chocolate, and coffee are orchestrated into this superb roulade. For an extra boost of nut flavor, I substitute hazelnut or walnut oil for the usual melted butter in the cake batter. Even though the pan is lined with parchment, this cake has a tendency to stick, so butter and flour the parchment as insurance.

■ ■ ■

CAKE
½ cup toasted and peeled hazelnuts or
coarsely chopped walnuts
½ cup cake flour
Pinch of salt
6 large eggs, at room temperature
⅔ cup sugar
3 tablespoons hazelnut, walnut,
or vegetable oil
Confectioners' sugar, for sprinkling and
garnish

MOCHA CREAM
1½ cups heavy cream
2 teaspoons instant espresso coffee powder
dissolved in 1 tablespoon boiling water
2 tablespoons confectioners' sugar
6 ounces bittersweet chocolate,
finely chopped

Toasted and peeled whole hazelnuts,
for garnish

■ ■ ■

1. To make the cake: Position a rack in the center of the oven and heat to 350°F. Lightly butter a 15½ × 10½ × 1-inch jelly-roll pan. Line the bottom of the pan with parchment paper. Butter the paper. Coat the pan with flour, tapping out the excess.

2. In a food processor fitted with the metal blade, process the hazelnuts, flour, and salt until the nuts are finely ground, almost into a powder; set aside.

3. Whisk the eggs and sugar in the bowl of a heavy-duty standing mixer. Place over a saucepan of simmering water (the water should not touch the bottom of the bowl). Whisk until the eggs are very warm to the touch and the sugar is completely dissolved (rub a bit of the mixture between your fingers to check). Attach to the mixer and fit with the whisk. Beat on medium-high speed until the mixture is very light and tripled in volume, about 3 minutes. In two additions, using a balloon whisk or large rubber spatula, fold in the nut mixture. Transfer a large dollop of the batter to a medium bowl and whisk in the oil. Fold this mixture into the batter. Pour into the pan. Using an offset metal spatula, spread evenly, being sure to fill the corners.

4. Bake until the cake springs back when gently pressed in the center, about 15 minutes. Run a knife around the edges of the cake to release it from the pan. Sift confectioners' sugar over the top of the cake. Place a clean kitchen towel over the cake. Invert the cake onto a large wire rack or baking sheet to unmold. Carefully peel off the parchment. Using the towel as an aide, starting at a long end, roll up the cake into a thick cylinder. Wrap the cake in the towel and cool completely on the rack.

5. To make the mocha cream: Bring the cream to a simmer in a medium saucepan over medium heat. Remove from the heat and whisk in the dissolved coffee and the confectioners' sugar. Place the chocolate in a medium bowl and pour the hot cream mixture on top. Let stand for 3 minutes, then whisk until the chocolate is melted and smooth.

6. Place the mocha cream in a larger bowl of ice water. Let stand, whisking often, until cold but not set. Using a handheld electric mixer, with the bowl still in the ice, beat the mocha cream on medium speed just until fluffy and stiff enough to spread. Do not overbeat or the cream will separate. (If this happens, melt the cream over simmering water, chill in the ice water, and beat again.)

7. Transfer ⅔ cup of the mocha cream to a pastry bag fitted with a ⁹⁄₁₆-inch open star tip, such as Ateco Number 825. Unroll the cake. Spread the

cake with the remaining mocha cream, leaving a ½-inch border on all sides. Roll up the cake. If there are visible cracks, give the roulade a generous sifting of confectioners' sugar. Rotating your hand in a tight circle as you move down the center of the roulade, pipe a spiral of mocha cream to make connecting rosettes. Insert whole hazelnuts in the rosettes. Refrigerate until the mocha cream sets, at least 1 hour.

8. Using a serrated knife, cut the roulade on a slight diagonal into thick slices. Serve chilled.

MAKE AHEAD

The cake can be prepared up to 2 days ahead, covered with plastic wrap, and refrigerated. To wrap, chill the uncovered cake until the mocha cream decoration on the top of the cake is firm, then wrap in plastic.

WALNUT CROWN CAKE
BABKA
Makes 12 servings

One afternoon at Prague's Café Slavia, over a glass of the infamously narcotic turquoise-green absinthe, the manager shared the recipe for this simple coffee cake, a perfect example of how Czech recipes have evolved over the years. Babka has roots in the cooking of Russia and Poland and, along with some ugly architecture, is one of the few remnants of the Russian years in Prague. While old recipes for babka certainly used butter, this one uses vegetable oil, a reminder of the Communist era, when butter was looked down on as a capitalist extravagance. It doesn't suffer from the substitution, and the cake is moist and filled with chunks of nuts and raisins.

■ ■ ■

CAKE
2¼ cups all-purpose flour
2 teaspoons baking powder
Pinch of salt

5 large eggs, separated, at room temperature
1½ cups sugar
¾ cup vegetable oil
1 teaspoon vanilla extract
Grated zest of 1 lemon
⅔ cup milk
½ cup coarsely chopped walnuts
½ cup raisins

RUM GLAZE
2 cups confectioners' sugar, sifted
2 tablespoons golden rum, or more if needed
1 tablespoon water, or more if needed

■ ■ ■

1. To make the cake: Position a rack in the center of the oven and heat to 350°F. Using a cylinder-shaped pastry brush, butter the inside of a 10-inch Gugelhupf mold or fluted cake pan. Coat with flour and tap out the excess.

2. Sift the flour, baking powder, and salt together. Beat the egg yolks, sugar, oil, vanilla, and lemon zest in a medium bowl with a hand-held electric mixer on high speed until well combined. Beat in half of the milk, then half of the flour; repeat with the remaining milk and flour.

3. In a medium bowl, using clean beaters, beat the egg whites just until they form stiff peaks. Stir about one fourth of the whites into the batter, then fold in the remaining whites.

4. Combine the walnuts and raisins. Spread about one third of the batter in the pan. Sprinkle with half of the walnut mixture, leaving about ½ inch of batter visible around the edges of the pan (if the walnuts and raisins touch the edge of the pan, they could burn during baking). Cover with half of the remaining batter, then sprinkle with the remaining walnut mixture. Spread with the remaining batter.

5. Bake until the cake is golden brown and a toothpick inserted in the center comes out clean, 50 to 60 minutes. Cool in the pan on a wire rack for 10 minutes. Turn out onto the rack and cool completely.

6. To make the glaze: In a medium bowl, whisk the confectioners' sugar, rum, and water until it is the consistency of heavy cream, adding more water if needed. Place the cake on a wire rack set over a jelly-roll pan. Slowly pour the glaze over the cake to coat it completely, using a metal spatula to help spread and coax the glaze. Let stand until the glaze sets.

MAKE AHEAD

The cake can be made up to 1 day ahead, covered with plastic wrap, and stored at room temperature.

ZUCCHINI SLICES WITH CHOCOLATE GLAZE
DOMMAYERSCHNITTEN
Makes 12 servings

Café Dommayer prides itself on being the only café in Austria with a certificate from the government's ecological department, and they bake their desserts with organic flour, butter, cream, and fruits. If you are expecting a crunchy-granola zucchini cake, think again; the apricot and chocolate glazes give this a distinctly Viennese flair.

■ ■ ■

CAKE
Bread crumbs, for dusting the pan
3/4 cup sugar
2 large eggs
I tablespoon golden rum
I tablespoon wildflower or clover honey
I teaspoon vanilla extract
1/2 cup vegetable oil
1 1/3 cups all-purpose flour
1/2 cup (2 ounces) coarsely chopped walnuts
I teaspoon baking powder
I teaspoon baking soda
I teaspoon ground cinnamon
Pinch of salt
Scant 2 cups (9 ounces) shredded zucchini
(2 small zucchini)

1/2 cup Apricot Glaze (page 16), warm
1/3 cup plus I tablespoon heavy cream
3 ounces high-quality bittersweet chocolate, finely chopped

■ ■ ■

1. To make the cake: Position a rack in the center of the oven and heat to 350°F. Lightly butter an 11 × 8-inch glass baking dish, dust with bread crumbs, and tap out the excess.

2. In a medium bowl, whisk the sugar, eggs, rum, honey, and vanilla until well combined. Gradually whisk in the oil.

3. In a food processor fitted with the metal blade, process the flour, walnuts, baking powder, baking soda, cinnamon, and salt until the nuts are very finely chopped. Stir into the oil mixture. Stir in the zucchini. Pour into the pan and spread evenly.

4. Bake until a toothpick inserted in the center comes out clean, 25 to 30 minutes. Cool for 5 minutes on a wire rack. Invert and unmold the cake onto the rack, leaving the cake upside down. Cool completely.

5. Brush the warm glaze over the top and sides of the cake. Cool completely.

6. In a small saucepan, bring the cream to a boil over high heat. Remove from the heat and add the chocolate. Let stand 1 minute, then whisk until completely melted. Place the cake on the rack on a jelly-roll pan. Pour all of the chocolate mixture on top of the cake. Using an offset spatula, spread the icing evenly over the top of the cake, letting any excess drip down the sides. Refrigerate until the chocolate glaze sets, about 20 minutes.

MAKE AHEAD

The cake can be prepared up to 1 day ahead, covered with plastic wrap, and stored at room temperature.

FANCY CAKES

An Austro-Hungarian Torte is the edible equivalent of a Mozart symphony combined with the frivolity of a Strauss waltz. Just as the finest conductors find levels of sophistication in the simplest tunes, master bakers create masterpieces of flavor and beauty from Torten. For it is not enough for a Torte to just taste good—it must be impressively gorgeous as well. Some of these classics became legends.

In common American usage, a torte means a cake that is made from crumbs or ground nuts instead of flour. In the Austro-Hungarian kitchen, many Torten still use these ingredients, but they aren't a requirement, and even a cake with flour can be called a Torte. The word *Torte* comes from the Italian *torta*, which means "fine cake" and first appeared in print in 1418. (*Torta* could have derived from the Latin *tortum*, which can mean "bread" or to "twist.") The first Torten were savory, and filled with meat, fish, herbs, or vegetables. To this day, a French *tourte* is always made from meat—and is usually a covered pastry—and even though there are savory *tartes*, most are sweet.

Originally, Torten often used ground nuts in their batters because they were abundant and less expensive than flour, and stale crumbs were put to use because nothing edible was wasted. Sugar was an extremely costly rarity (twenty pounds of sugar cost the equivalent of one of today's automobiles), and the secret of how to process it from cane was held tight by the Arabs. Honey was used as a sweetener, making cakes that were on the heavy side. In fact, the dough was so heavy it was often pressed into decorative wooden molds, a technique that is still used in some gingerbread recipes.

As the milling of flour improved, and as sugar became more available to the middle classes, cakes became lighter and more delicate. Master bakers strove to take their culinary art to higher levels, and Torten became more and more baroque, reflecting the lavish, full-blown visual art of the period. One cookbook from 1719 already included ninety-six recipes for Torten.

When the technique of extracting sugar from beets was finally perfected in 1802, making sugar even less expensive, bakers were inspired to create more and more Torten to keep up with the demand.

From then on, the Austro-Hungarian citizenry would no sooner give up their Torten than their Kaffee. Torten are traditionally named for their main ingredients (as in *Nußtorte*, or Walnut Torte), for their inventor (Sachertorte or Dobostorte being two famous examples), or in honor of a place or event (Panamatorte or Malakofftorte). Bakers and their public know the components of each of these cakes by heart. There is no need to explain to them that a Panamatorte has chocolate and almond flavors. Even if the eater knows nothing about Austrian military history or the Battle of Malakoff, he or she is sure that a Malakofftorte will be made from ladyfingers (or some other light cake) with a creamy filling. It will *never* contain chocolate, even if the baker is dying to stretch his or her imagination.

At a Kaffeehaus, cream-filled Torten are usually displayed in a refrigerated dessert case, where the desserts don't have to be covered. (The cut surfaces are protected from drying by small pieces of clear plastic pressed against them.) In your home refrigerator, use a plastic cake dome to cover the cake, which will keep out unwanted flavors from other foods in the refrigerator and won't touch and mar the surface of glazed cakes. You'll be surprised at the shelf life of these fancy cakes. They'll last at least a couple of days, *if* everyone who opens the refrigerator has the willpower of a saint.

The Classic Kaffeehaus

What are the characteristics of a classic Austro-Hungarian Kaffeehaus? Even from a distance you can spot it, solidly claiming the corner real estate at the intersection of two streets. The windows are as large as possible, all the better to let in the light. Entering, you'll feel a calming, quiet atmosphere, suitable for intense concentration or intimate conversation. (There are bustling coffeehouses with higher volume levels, but don't expect the waiter to hurry in syncopation.) The L-shaped room might be separated into two portions—one for serving coffee, and the other for playing billiards. Newspapers hanging on bamboo reading racks are waiting to be chosen; the most literate *Stammgäste* (the coffeehouse's regular customers) will rate a café not just by the quality of its drink, but by the breadth of its reading material. Some even have an encyclopedia set handy to solve disputes and supply hints to the answers for crossword puzzles. And no one will complain when a customer hoards a pile of favorite newspapers, reading them one by one in his or her good time.

Thonet bentwood chairs at marble-topped tables, and cushy booths await. Some banquettes may be past their prime, the springs long sprung from decades of use, but they are still prime seating. If you need to hang your coat, a very heavy wrought-iron rack stands at attention; it will hold the heaviest coats without tipping over. The coffee and dessert menus (and the absolute absence of a "to-go" menu) are comforting in their predictability. If you are a *Stammgast*, you won't need to order anyway, as your tuxedoed waiter will automatically bring your regular beverage. Cold meals or desserts are the extent of most coffeehouses' food menus, unless you are visiting a café–restaurant with more extensive fare.

When your coffee arrives, it is always served on a metal tray (silver, nickel, or aluminum, depending on the coffeehouse's pedigree) with a glass of water on the side. The water is a leftover custom from the Turks, who wanted to show the guest that they were in no hurry for him to leave. They also knew that strong coffee can use a water chaser. The best waiters will continually refill your water glass as it is emptied. Some coffeehouses will give a single customer two glasses of water, a tradition that is supposed to suggest that the next time you should bring a friend (but I suspect it means less refilling for the waiter). As a final flourish and indication of your waiter's motor skills, the coffee spoon may be balanced on top of the water glass.

You are not expected to rush the time you spend as the guest of the Kaffeehaus. In fact, hurrying is somewhat of an insult. Sip, chat, stir, read, sniff, ponder. When you're ready to leave, call over the waiter with a friendly "Herr Ober!" (If you have a waitress, you may try "Frau/Fraulein Ober!") Usually he'll scribble your bill on a scrap of paper, and you'll pay him on the spot. Regardless of how long you've lingered, he really doesn't expect more than a fifteen percent tip. But if you're generous, the next time you come in, chances are good that he'll have memorized your coffee order.

Cafés often play a lively part in the history of a city, usually by offering a convival place for intellectuals to foment new ideas. The ideas of French literati from Voltaire to Simone de Beauvoir were fueled in Paris cafés, and where would the San Francisco and New York Beat Generation have gone to give their poetry readings if not for the bohemian dives of North Beach and Greenwich Village? The coffeehouses in the capitals of the old Austro-Hungarian empire have remained indispensable as a proving ground for forward thinkers for well over three hundred years.

BROWN LINZERTORTE
LINZERTORTE BRAUN
Makes 8 servings

A high proportion of nuts and a dash of cocoa make this a "brown" Linzertorte. In Europe, bakers use a 9 × 1-inch ring form to make the cake, but as the forms are very difficult to find here, I use the familiar 9 × 3-inch springform pan instead.

European bakers also use rice paper (Oblaten) on the bottom crust to protect it from the preserves, which would make it soggy. I solve the problem by brushing the crust with egg white (a major ingredient in Oblaten), and prebaking it first. The choice of preserves is up to you, but I vote for black currant.

∎ ∎ ∎

LINZER DOUGH
1½ cups all-purpose flour
1¼ cups (7 ounces) hazelnuts, toasted and peeled
1 cup sugar
1 tablespoon cocoa powder, preferably Dutch-processed
Grated zest of 1 lemon
½ teaspoon ground cinnamon
⅛ teaspoon ground cloves
¼ teaspoon salt
14 tablespoons (1¾ sticks) unsalted butter, at cool room temperature
2 large egg yolks
1 tablespoon fresh lemon juice

1 large egg, separated
Pinch of salt
1 cup black currant, red currant, or seedless raspberry preserves
1 tablespoon milk

3 tablespoons sliced almonds, for garnish
Confectioners' sugar, for garnish

∎ ∎ ∎

1. To make the dough: In a food processor fitted with the metal blade, process the flour and hazelnuts until the nuts are ground into a fine powder.

Pour the mixture into a large bowl. Stir in the sugar, cocoa, lemon zest, cinnamon, cloves, and salt. Using a pastry blender, cut in the butter until the mixture is crumbly. In a small bowl, mix the yolks and lemon juice. Using a fork, stir into the flour mixture until it clumps together. Press the dough into a ball, and divide equally into two thick disks. Wrap each in plastic wrap and refrigerate until firm, at least 60 minutes and up to overnight.

2. Position a rack in the center of the oven and heat to 350°F. Butter the sides and bottom of a 9-inch springform pan. Line the bottom of the pan with a round of parchment paper and butter the paper.

3. Crumble one of the dough disks into the pan. Press firmly and evenly into the pan, bringing the dough 1 inch up the sides. (If the dough is very cold and cracks while using, the heat of your hands will eventually soften it.) The dough will be quite thick, about ¼ inch at the sides. Prick the dough with a fork and freeze for 10 minutes. In a small bowl, beat the egg white with a pinch of salt until foamy. Lightly brush the inside of the shell with some of the beaten white. Place the springform on a baking sheet and bake just until the dough is set, about 15 minutes. Cool completely on a wire rack.

4. Let the other disk of dough stand at room temperature for 5 minutes. Spread the preserves in the shell. Roll out the remaining dough on a lightly floured work surface into a ¼-inch-thick circle. Using a fluted pastry wheel, cut the dough into ¾-inch-wide strips. Arrange the strips over the jam in a lattice pattern, trimming as needed, pressing the ends of the strips to the side crust. If the strips crack, piece them back together. Gather up any odd strips and trimmings and press a thin layer of dough all around the edge of the crust, securing the ends of the strips. (Discard any leftover dough.) In a small bowl, beat the egg yolk with the milk. Brush the strips lightly with the egg-yolk mixture and sprinkle the top with the almonds. Bake on the baking sheet until the preserves are bubbling, about 45 minutes.

5. Cool for 10 minutes on a wire rack. Run a knife around the inside of the pan to loosen the torte, then cool completely in the pan on the rack, at least 3 hours. Remove the sides of the pan. Invert the torte onto a plate and peel off the parchment paper (it may tear off in pieces, but keep at it). Invert again onto a serving plate. Sift the confectioners' sugar over the torte and serve.

MAKE AHEAD

The dough can be made up to 2 days ahead, wrapped tightly in plastic wrap, and refrigerated. Let stand for 10 minutes before using. The tart can be baked up to 2 days ahead, wrapped in plastic wrap, and stored at room temperature.

▪ THE STORY BEHIND ▪
LINZERTORTE

Along with the Sachertorte, Linzertorte is Austria's most famous dessert, named for the city of Linz. Its distinctive lattice, preserves filling, and spicy crust make it immediately recognizable.

The exact origin of the Torte is not known. The spicy, nutty flavors in Linzertorte are clues that the recipe is quite old. Spices were rare and costly, and would be used by finer bakeries as a sign of distinction. The first printed recipe dates to 1719, and it contains the flour, almonds, sugar, egg yolks, and lemon zest that can still be found in today's version. During the Biedermeier period, the Linzertorte was popularized by the Linz baker Johann Konrad Vogel, who boasted unconvincingly that he was its inventor.

Variations on the Linzertorte theme are many, but there are essentially three types. The first two are based on a short crust dough, in which the butter is cut into the dry ingredients. "White" Linzertorte is made from blanched almonds. Cocoa (or chocolate) and toasted hazelnuts (or unskinned almonds) give "Brown" Linzertorte a darker color and deeper flavor. "Creamed" Linzertorte, called *Gerührte Linzertorte,* uses the same ingredients, but the butter is creamed, making the dough soft enough to pipe the lattice pattern on the torte, sometimes almost completely covering the preserves. Every Austrian cook must have a reliable family favorite on file, because it is also used to make cookies, such as Linzer "Eyes" (Linzer Augen; page 148). The dough is usually filled with black currant preserves (raspberry preserves are used only in other countries like America, where they are cheaper than currant), but even that isn't a constant and changes from baker to baker.

LADYFINGER TORTE WITH RUM CREAM
MALAKOFFTORTE
Makes 12 servings

When choosing a pastry from the coffeehouse display case, whipped-cream lovers usually gravitate toward Malakofftorte, named for a decisive battle of the Crimean War of the 1850s. (This was this war where Florence Nightingale served so bravely, and which inspired Alfred Lord Tennyson's epic poem "The Charge of the Light Brigade.") There are a few variations on the theme—some feature almond buttercream instead of rum cream, or use Cointreau rather than rum, or favor cake layers over ladyfingers —but the torte is usually constructed of liquor-soaked ladyfingers with lots of spiked Bavarian cream. Home-baked ladyfingers are best, but if you prefer, feel free to substitute store-bought ladyfingers, either the sponge cake ones or dry

Italian savoiardi, trimmed to fit as needed. Don't let the ladyfingers soak in the rum syrup; the quickest of dips will do.

▪ ▪ ▪

RUM SYRUP
⅓ cup granulated sugar
⅓ cup water
⅓ cup golden rum

LADYFINGERS
¾ cup all-purpose flour
Pinch of salt
4 large eggs, separated, at room temperature
⅔ cup granulated sugar, divided
¼ teaspoon vanilla extract
Confectioners' sugar, for sifting

RUM CREAM
1 cup milk, divided
1 envelope unflavored powdered gelatin
2 large egg yolks
¼ cup sugar

1¼ cups heavy cream, chilled
2 tablespoons golden rum

ASSEMBLY
1 cup heavy cream
2 tablespoons confectioners' sugar
½ teaspoon vanilla extract
¼ cup sliced blanched almonds, toasted
(see page 211), optional

■ ■ ■

1. To make the rum syrup: Bring the sugar and water to a full boil in a small saucepan over high heat, stirring to help dissolve the sugar. Pour into a small bowl and stir in the rum. Cool completely.

2. To make the ladyfingers: Position racks in the center and top third of the oven and heat to 400°F. Line two large baking sheets with parchment paper. Fit a large pastry bag with a ⁷⁄₁₆-inch-wide plain tip, such as Ateco Number 805.

3. Sift the flour and salt together into a small bowl. In a large bowl, beat the egg yolks and ⅓ cup of the sugar with a handheld electric mixer on high speed until the mixture is thick and tripled in volume, about 3 minutes. Beat in the vanilla.

4. Using clean beaters, beat the egg whites in a medium bowl until soft peaks form. Gradually beat in the remaining ⅓ cup of sugar and beat until the peaks are stiff and shiny. Stir about one fourth of the whites into the yolk mixture to lighten it. Using a large balloon whisk or rubber spatula, fold in the remaining whites, leaving a few wisps of whites visible. Sift half of the flour over the eggs and fold in. Repeat with the remaining flour.

5. In batches, transfer the batter to the pastry bag. Pipe out strips of the batter, about 3 inches long and about 1 inch apart, onto the baking sheets. You should have about 30 ladyfingers. Sift confectioners' sugar over the ladyfingers. Bake until golden brown, 8 to 10 minutes. Transfer the ladyfingers to a wire rack and cool completely. Choose 6 of the thinnest ladyfingers for garnishing the torte and set aside.

6. To make the rum cream: Pour ¼ cup of the milk into a small bowl and sprinkle the gelatin on

top. Let stand 5 minutes to moisten the gelatin, then stir. Meanwhile, in a small saucepan or the microwave oven, heat the remaining milk until very hot.

7. In a medium saucepan, whisk the egg yolks and sugar to combine, and gradually whisk in the hot milk. Add the softened gelatin. Stirring constantly over medium-low heat with a heat-proof rubber or wooden spatula (this scrapes the bottom of the saucepan better than a spoon and gets into the corners, too), cook until the mixture is thick enough to coat the spatula, about 3 minutes. Do not boil; an instant-read thermometer inserted in the custard will read 185°F. Immediately strain the custard into a medium stainless-steel bowl set in a larger bowl of ice water. Stir often until the custard is cool, but not set. Remove the custard from the ice water.

8. Beat the cream in a chilled medium bowl with a handheld electric mixer at high speed until stiff peaks form. Beat in the rum. (Beat the cream a little stiffer than usual.) Stir about one fourth of the whipped cream into the custard, then fold in the rest. The rum cream should hold its shape. If necessary, chill in a larger bowl of ice water until lightly set.

9. To assemble the torte: Lightly oil the inside and bottom of a 8-inch springform pan. First dipping the ladyfingers briefly in the rum syrup, arrange a layer of 6 to 8 ladyfingers in the pan, fitting as closely as possible, trimming to fit. Don't worry about any open spaces. Add about one third of the rum cream to the pan and spread it. Repeat with another layer of ladyfingers, and top with half of the remaining cream. Dip and layer the remaining ladyfingers, and spread with the remaining cream. Discard any remaining syrup. Cover tightly with plastic wrap and refrigerate until the rum cream is set, about 4 hours or overnight.

10. Rinse a thin knife in hot water and run it along the inside of the pan. Remove the sides of the pan. In a chilled medium bowl, beat the heavy cream with the confectioners' sugar and vanilla until stiff peaks form. Transfer about half of the whipped cream to a large pastry bag fitted with a ⁹⁄₁₆-inch-wide open star tip, such as Ateco

Number 825. Using a metal spatula, frost the top and sides of the cake with the remaining whipped cream. Using a decorating comb, mark the sides of the cake. Pipe 12 rosettes on top of the cake. Cut the 6 reserved ladyfingers in half crosswise. Insert the cut side of each ladyfinger into each rosette, placing the cookies at a jaunty 45-degree angle. If desired, sprinkle the toasted almonds in the center of the cake. Refrigerate, uncovered, until ready to serve.

MAKE AHEAD

The ladyfingers can be prepared up to 1 day ahead, stored in an airtight container at room temperature. The syrup can be prepared up to 3 days ahead, stored in a jar at room temperature. The cake can be made up to 1 day ahead, stored under a cake dome in the refrigerator.

PUNCH CAKE
PUNSCHTORTE
Makes 10 to 12 servings

This sweetly aromatic cake seems to be unique to Austro-Hungarian baking. There are many variations, with the constants being a filling of punch-soaked cake crumbs and a pink glaze. Each bakery has its own method for coloring the center layer (some use melted chocolate or chocolate cake crumbs) and the pink glaze. The best choice is Chambord or crème de cassis which will impart flavor as well as color.

■ ■ ■

PUNCH
1 medium orange
1 medium lemon
1/4 cup golden rum
1/4 cup sugar
2 tablespoons apricot preserves
2 tablespoons black-raspberry liqueur
(Chambord) or crème de cassis

Large Warm-Method Sponge Cake
(page 7)
1 cup Apricot Glaze (page 16), warm
2 ounces high-quality bittersweet chocolate,
finely chopped
Pink Faux Fondant Icing (page 15)

■ ■ ■

1. To make the punch: Grate the zests from the orange and the lemon. Juice the orange and lemon, straining the juice. Measure out 1/4 cup orange juice and 3 tablespoons lemon juice and save the rest for another use.

2. Bring the orange juice, lemon juice, both zests, rum, sugar, apricot preserves, and liqueur to a boil in a small saucepan over medium heat, stirring often. Cook for 2 minutes to reduce slightly. Pour the punch into a medium bowl.

3. Using a long serrated knife, trim off the top skin from the cake. Process the trimmings in a food processor to make crumbs; set aside to decorate the cake later. Cut the cake crosswise into 3 equal layers; the bottom layer, which is smooth, will be turned upside-down to become the top of the cake.

4. Place the top cake layer on a 9-inch cardboard round. Cut a round from the center of the middle layer, starting about 1 inch from the edge. Cut the center section into 1-inch cubes. (You'll use the cake ring later.) Mix the cake cubes with the warm punch, soaking them well. Brush the bottom cake layer with some of the apricot glaze. Top with the cake ring. Fill the ring with the soaked crumbs, spreading them evenly with your fingers. Brush the cut side of the remaining layer with some more glaze. Place, cut side down, on the cake and press firmly to adhere the layers. If there are any crumbs in the glaze, reheat it over low heat and strain them out. Brush the top and sides of the cake with the remaining glaze to make a smooth surface. Refrigerate until the glaze is set, about 10 minutes.

5. Meanwhile, melt the chocolate in the top part of a double boiler or in the microwave on medium heat. Transfer to a paper cone (see page 204) and cool slightly.

6. Place the cake on a wire rack set over a jelly-roll pan. Make the fondant icing (it must be freshly prepared). Pour all of the warm icing over the top of the cake, smoothing it over the top and down the sides with an offset metal spatula. Immediately pipe vertical lines of the melted chocolate on the top of the cake, spacing them 1 inch apart. Starting 1 inch from the bottom edge of the top layer, lightly draw the tip of a small sharp knife from left to right through the chocolate and icing, creating a feather effect. Wipe the knife clean. Moving 1 inch up, and going from right to left, repeat the motion. Continue up the cake, 1 inch at a time, alternating the direction of the drawing motion, until you reach the top of the cake. If desired, press the cake crumbs on the sides of the cake. Refrigerate the cake to set the glaze. Cover with a cake dome and refrigerate for at least 4 hours to meld the flavors. Serve chilled.

MAKE AHEAD

The cake can be prepared up to 2 days before serving, stored under a cake dome in the refrigerator.

ORANGE TORTE WITH ORANGE CREAM FROSTING
ORANGENTORTE
Makes 10 servings

Orangentore dates back to the Congress of Vienna of 1815, when the desserts of the various diplomats found their way into the hearts and stomachs of the Viennese. A specialty of Dalmatia, a province along the Adriatic coast, it is made with bread crumbs, not flour. This lack of flour (and baking powder) results in a dense, moist torte that may look a little forlorn compared to other high-rising cakes. Don't be concerned, because the delicious frosting of orange curd and whipped cream disguises any visual flaws. Refreshing and full of citrus flavor, this torte deserves every second of its long-lived popularity.

■ ■ ■

TORTE
⅔ cup plain dried bread crumbs,
plus more for the pan
1⅔ cups (5¾ ounces) sliced blanched
almonds
6 large eggs, separated, at room temperature
¾ cup sugar, divided
Grated zest of ½ orange
¼ cup fresh orange juice

ORANGE ICING
¾ cup sugar
Grated zest of 1 orange
½ cup fresh orange juice
4 tablespoons fresh lemon juice
4 tablespoons unsalted butter
3 large egg yolks
1 tablespoon cornstarch
1 cup heavy cream

ASSEMBLY
Two seedless navel oranges, for garnish

■ ■ ■

1. Position a rack in the center of the oven and heat to 350°F. Lightly butter a 9-inch springform pan and line the bottom with a round of parchment or wax paper. Dust with the bread crumbs, tilt to coat, and tap out the excess crumbs.

2. To make the torte: In a food processor fitted with the metal blade, process the ⅔ cup of bread crumbs and the almonds until the almonds are very finely ground, almost to a powder. Set aside.

3. Beat the yolks and ¼ cup of the sugar in a medium bowl with a mixer on high speed until they are very thick and light in color, about 3 minutes. Beat in the orange zest and juice.

4. Using clean beaters, beat the egg whites on high speed until they form soft peaks. Gradually beat in the remaining ½ cup of sugar and beat until the whites are stiff and shiny. Fold about one fourth of the beaten whites into the yolk mixture. Add the almond–crumb mixture and fold a few times, just to moisten. Add the remaining whites and fold until the batter is combined. Spread evenly in the pan.

5. Bake until the top springs back when gently pressed in the center, about 35 minutes. Transfer to a wire rack and cool for 5 minutes. Run a sharp knife around the inside of the pan to release the cake, then remove the sides of the pan. Invert onto the rack and lift off the bottom of the pan. Peel off the paper and turn the cake right side up. Cool the cake completely on the rack.

6. To make the icing: Whisk the sugar, orange zest and juice, lemon juice, butter, egg yolks, and cornstarch in a medium saucepan. Cook, stirring constantly, until the mixture comes to a full boil. Transfer to a medium bowl set in a larger bowl of ice water. Let stand, stirring occasionally, until the curd has cooled and thickened.

7. In a chilled medium bowl, beat the heavy cream until quite stiff (it will soften with the addition of the curd, so beat it a little more stiffly than usual). Fold in half of the chilled curd.

8. To assemble: Using a long serrated knife, cut the torte into two layers. Slip the bottom of the springform pan between the layers. Invert the top layer onto an 8½-inch cardboard round.

Spread with the remaining orange curd. Top with the other layer (a wide spatula helps the transfer), cut side down. Frost the top of the torte with the icing, then frost the sides. Chill, uncovered, until the icing sets, about 1 hour. Cover loosely with a cake dome and chill at least 4 hours or overnight.

9. Cut the thick skin off each orange where it meets the flesh. Cut between the membranes to release the segments. Arrange the segments around the edge of the torte in a spoke pattern, and serve chilled.

MAKE AHEAD

The cake can be made up to 2 days ahead, without the orange garnish, and can be stored under a cake dome in the refrigerator.

LESCHANZ'S CHOCOLATE MOUSSE CAKE
LESCHANZTORTE
Makes 12 to 16 servings

Walter Leschanz, an extraordinary baker who has worked at both Sacher and Demel, spent an afternoon with me demonstrating his specialties. This two-tone chocolate cake is deceptively easy for all its richness. Look at the ingredients: Both the filling and the cream topping are practically identical in ingredients and proportions, but they are manipulated to give amazingly different results. The first mixture is baked and cools into a thin, fudgy cake that falls in the center. It's supposed to do that—all the better for spreading with the chocolate mousse filling.

■ ■ ■

CAKE

5½ ounces high-quality bittersweet chocolate,
finely chopped
¾ cup (1½ sticks) unsalted butter, at room
temperature, cut into 12 pieces
7 large eggs, separated, at room temperature
1 cup plus 2 tablespoons sugar

MOUSSE TOPPING

5½ ounces high-quality bittersweet chocolate,
finely chopped
¾ cup (1½ sticks) unsalted butter, at room
temperature, cut into 12 pieces
1¼ cups confectioners' sugar
6 large eggs (see page 207)
About 2 ounces chocolate curls
(see page 204), for garnish

■ ■ ■

1. To make the cake: Position a rack in the center of the oven and heat to 350°F. Lightly butter the inside of a 9-inch springform pan. Dust with flour and tap out the excess.

2. In a large metal bowl set over a pot of hot, not simmering, water, melt the chocolate. Remove from the heat. Whisk in the butter, one piece at a time. Whisk in the egg yolks.

3. In a large bowl, using a handheld electric mixer on low speed, beat the egg whites until they form soft peaks. Gradually beat in the sugar and beat until they form stiff, shiny peaks. Stir one fourth of the beaten whites into the chocolate mixture, then fold in the remainder. Spread evenly in the pan.

4. Bake until the top is puffed, cracked, and crisp, and a toothpick inserted in the center comes out clean, about 30 minutes. Remove from the oven and run a sharp knife around the inside of the pan to release the cake from the sides. Transfer to a wire rack and cool completely in the pan. Don't worry if the cake sinks.

5. To make the topping: Melt the chocolate in the top part of a double boiler over hot, not simmering, water, or in a microwave on medium power. Remove from the heat. Cool, stirring often, until the chocolate is tepid.

6. In a large bowl, using a handheld electric mixer at low speed, beat the butter and confectioners' sugar until combined. Increase the speed

to high and beat until light and fluffy, about 2 minutes. Beat in the cooled chocolate. One at a time, beat in the eggs.

7. Spread the topping evenly over the cake in the pan. Cover the pan tightly with plastic wrap. Refrigerate until the topping is set, at least 4 hours or overnight.

8. To serve, rinse a thin sharp knife under hot water and run it inside the pan to release the cake. Remove the sides of the pan. Garnish the top of the cake with the chocolate curls. Using a thin, sharp knife rinsed under hot water, slice the cake. Serve chilled.

MAKE AHEAD

The cake should be served within 24 hours.

SACHERTORTE
SACHERTORTE
Makes 12 to 16 servings

In the past few years, bakers have been upping the ante with chocolate desserts (think of your local American bistro's "warm chocolate cakes with gooey chocolate centers"). The Sachertorte is a refined, elegant combination of chocolate flavors, complemented by a compulsory mound of Schlag. The whipped cream is an important part of the picture, as it moistens the frankly firm cake layers. Every bite of Sachertorte is supposed to be dipped in the whipped cream. This version is based on the recipe in *Das Große Sacher Backbuch* ("The Big Sacher Baking Book"), which should be a reliable source.

Don't expect the cake layer to look perfect; sometimes the air bubbles are large and make holes in the top of the cake. If that happens, take some cake trimmings and mash them with a little of the apricot glaze to make a paste, and use a metal icing spatula to "spackle" the holes with the mixture.

■ ■ ■

▪ THE STORY BEHIND ▪
SACHERTORTE

Sachertorte is the culinary symbol of Vienna, as recognizable as "The Blue Danube." Even though you can find the chocolate-glazed cake at every shop in town, the right to use the name "The *Original* Sacher Torte" has been hotly contested. In fact, it was the subject of a seven-year court case between Demel and Sacher that had all of Vienna watching every move.

The story begins in 1832 with Klemens, Prince von Metternich, one of the masterminds of the Congress of Vienna and no slouch in the party department. Here was a man who knew what he liked, and got it. He had a big party coming up and he ordered his personal chef to create a new dessert. The prince wanted to make a splash, so he instructed the chef to come up with the opposite of the light, fluffy, creamy "feminine" Torten popular at the time, and to surprise his guests with a dryer, more compact "masculine" cake.

The chef never was able to fulfill the prince's request, because he fell ill. The kitchen's sixteen-year-old second apprentice, Franz Sacher, would have to take over in the master's absence. Chocolate, one of the most aggressive and "masculine" flavors in the kitchen, would be his cake's motif, tempered by the tart tang of apricot preserves. (More than one hundred years later, just where young Sacher spread the preserves on the cake would become the crux of the argument between the two master bakeries.) The recipe for the chocolate cake layer was nothing new, but the glossy chocolate topping was a true innovation.

The dessert was a sensation, and Franz was quickly catapulted out of the prince's employ into the Hungarian court of Prince Pál Antal Esterházy. It was actually in Budapest that the cake made its biggest splash, whence it traveled back to Vienna. Sacher returned to Vienna to assume a high position at Dehne (precursor to Demel), the royal bakery to the emperor. From there he offered the

Sachertorte to the willing lips of the masses. It is interesting, if not revealing, to note that in the Hotel Sacher's press material on the history of the cake, Franz's stint at Dehne is omitted.

With his earnings, Franz opened his own fancy grocery near St. Stephen's Cathedral, of course taking his recipe with him. Dehne, understandably, continued to sell the cake as their top moneymaker, even after Christoph Demel purchased the bakery and renamed it in 1857. Franz's son, Eduard, followed his father in the food business, training in London and Paris. Upon his return, he eventually opened a restaurant not far from the newly constructed Ringstrasse. It was an immediate success, perhaps due to its private dining rooms, which allowed for extremely intimate, very discreet dinners. In 1876, Eduard moved his operation to a premier location behind the new opera house, where he established a full-scale hotel on the upper floors.

Under the autocratic control of Eduard Sacher's cigar-smoking widow, Anna, Hotel Sacher flourished and became one of the most famous hotels in the world. Waltzes, songs, movies, and operettas have been written about it, attempting to evoke its unsurpassable elegance.

After World War II, Viennese businesses had to fight hard for their piece of the Austrian economy. Anything that would help give brand identification to a product was welcome. So it happened that the owners of the Sacher, the Gürtler and Siller families, decided to sue Demel over which establishment had the right to call its cake the "original."

Seven long years of court depositions and the dragging out of ancient recipes awarded the Sacher the exclusive rights to the phrase, "The Original Sacher Torte," allowing them to place an official chocolate seal on each cake. The court concluded that Franz Sacher's original recipe split the cake horizontally with apricot preserves between the layers and glazing the top and sides of the cake. The Demel version does not split the cake. So now the capitalized "Sacher Torte" means the certified cake, sold only by the hotel's bakery, whereas a "Sachertorte" indicates a cake made in the Sacher style.

The official recipe for the Hotel Sacher's torte remains a secret, locked away in a steel safe. The alleged recipe did leak, however, when some former employees of the hotel printed it in the lean postwar years. Now many different incarnations of the Sachertorte exist, and most of them are excellent.

While there are many "authentic" Sachertorte recipes out there (and I have probably tested them all), many of them are victims of faulty translation from German to English and metric to volume measurements. To mention just two examples I discovered in my latest research: The "original" recipe calls for 110 grams of confectioners' sugar, which weighs 4 ounces and measures 1 cup by volume. It also calls for 110 grams granulated sugar, which may weigh the same 4 ounces, but measures only about ½ cup by volume. Many translations mistakenly convert this to 1 cup. This mistake makes a very heavy cake. Also, some versions call for "kneading" the "dough," an obvious mistranslation for "stirring the batter," and call for keeping the oven door propped open with a wooden spoon—an obvious throwback to the days when wood-burning ovens, which run hot, were used to bake the cake.

I shared a Sacher Torte in the Blaue Bar (Blue Bar) of the Hotel Sacher with Christian Bär, the hotel's food and beverage manager, and learned some interesting statistics about Sacher Torte production. The Sacher bakes about 300,000 cakes a year, approximately 800 a day, with peak production at Christmas, when many Sacher Tortes are ordered by mail. The fourteen bakers use more than 1.2 million eggs a year and mix three different chocolates to make the glaze. Not all Sacher Tortes are sold at the hotel; a brisk business is done in the airport gift shops and other locations off premises.

For the true Sachertorte/Sacher Torte experience, visits to the hallowed rooms of both Hotel Sacher and Demel are required pilgrimages for the serious dessert lover. You must taste both and make your own choice. You may not agree with the court, but it will be heavenly trying to decide.

TORTE

4½ ounces high-quality bittersweet
chocolate, finely chopped
9 tablespoons (1 stick plus 1 tablespoon)
unsalted butter,
at cool room temperature
1 cup confectioners' sugar
6 large eggs, separated, at room temperature
1 teaspoon vanilla extract
½ cup granulated sugar
1 cup all-purpose flour (for this recipe,
spoon gently into cup and level top)

ASSEMBLY

1 cup Apricot Glaze (page 16), warm
Small Batch Chocolate Glaze (page 16)
Sweetened Whipped Cream (page 19),
for serving

■ ■ ■

1. To make the torte: Position a rack in the center of the oven and heat to 400°F. Lightly butter a 9-inch springform pan and line the bottom with a round of parchment or wax paper. Dust the sides of the pan with flour and tap out the excess.
2. In the top part of a double boiler over very hot, but not simmering, water, or in a microwave at medium power, melt the chocolate. Remove from the heat or the oven, and let stand, stirring often, until cool.
3. Beat the butter in the bowl of a heavy-duty standing mixer fitted with the paddle blade on medium-high speed until smooth, about 1 minute. On low speed, beat in the confectioners' sugar. Return the speed to medium-high and beat until light in color and texture, about 2 minutes. Beat in the egg yolks, one at a time, scraping down the sides of the bowl. Beat in the chocolate and vanilla.
4. Beat the egg whites and granulated sugar in a large bowl with a handheld electric mixer on high speed just until they form soft, shiny peaks. Do not overbeat. Stir about one fourth of the beaten whites into the chocolate mixture to lighten it, then fold in the remaining whites, leaving a few visible wisps of whites. Sift half of the flour over the chocolate mixture, and fold in with a large balloon whisk or rubber spatula. Repeat with the remaining flour.

5. Spread evenly in the pan. Bake until a toothpick inserted in the center comes out clean, about 45 minutes. (The cake will dome in the center.) Cool on a wire rack for 10 minutes. Remove the sides of the pan, and invert the cake onto the rack. Remove the paper and reinvert on another rack to turn right side up. Cool completely.
6. To assemble: Using a long serrated knife, trim the top of the cake to make it level. Cut the cake horizontally into two equal layers. Place one cake layer on an 8-inch cardboard round. Brush the top of the cake layer with the apricot glaze. Place the second cake layer on top and brush again. Brush the top and sides of the cake with the remaining glaze. Transfer the cake to a wire rack placed over a jelly-roll pan lined with wax paper. Let cool until the glaze is set.
7. Make the chocolate glaze (it must be freshly made and warm). Pour all of the warm chocolate glaze on top of the cake. Using a metal offset spatula, gently smooth the glaze over the cake, allowing it to run down the sides, being sure that the glaze completely coats the cake (patch any bare spots with the spatula and the icing that has dripped). Cool until the glaze is barely set, then transfer the cake to a serving plate. Refrigerate until the glaze is completely set, at least 1 hour. Remove the cake from the refrigerator about 1 hour before serving.
8. To serve, slice with a sharp knife dipped into hot water. Serve with a large dollop of whipped cream on the side.

MAKE AHEAD

The cake can be prepared up to 2 days ahead and stored in an airtight cake container at room temperature.

LESCHANZ'S SACHERTORTE
LESCHANZ-SACHERTORTE
Makes 12 to 14 servings

Two Sachertorte recipes? An embarassment of riches? Because for many years the Sachertorte was a guarded secret, most Viennese bakers were forced to come up with their own versions, so most cookbooks include at least two, if not three, recipes for this, perhaps the most Viennese of all cakes. One Viennese acquaintance says she has seven different Sachertortes in her recipe box.

Leschanz provides baked goods and chocolates to some of the best cafés and hotels in Vienna (not every establishment makes its own pastries, although they prefer to keep the fact under wraps). Walter Leschanz, the owner, baked both at Demel and Sacher. He makes a tall cake to cut into three layers (as opposed to Demel's one layer and Sacher's two), allowing for more glaze, which also increases the moisture and shelf life of the cake. While the authentic Sachertorte is always made with apricot glaze, feel free to substitute your own favorite preserve for apricot in the glaze. I like raspberry, my friend Karitas loves peach, and another friend likes strawberry. Use 1½ cups of preserves to make enough glaze for this cake.

■ ■ ■

CAKE
5½ ounces high-quality bittersweet chocolate, finely chopped
¾ cup (1½ sticks) unsalted butter, at room temperature
7 large eggs, separated, at room temperature
1 cup plus 2 tablespoons granulated sugar
1 cup plus 1 tablespoon all-purpose flour, sifted

ASSEMBLY
1¼ cups Apricot Glaze (page 16), or glaze made with 1½ cups of your favorite preserves, warm
Small Batch Chocolate Glaze (page 16)
Sweetened Whipped Cream (page 19), for serving

■ ■ ■

1. To make the cake: Position a rack in the center of the oven and heat to 400°F. Lightly butter a 9-inch springform pan and line the bottom with a round of parchment or wax paper. Dust the sides of the pan with flour and tap out the excess.

2. In the top part of a double boiler over very hot, but not simmering, water, or in a microwave oven at medium power, melt the chocolate. Remove from the heat or the oven, and let stand, stirring often, until tepid.

3. Beat the butter in a large bowl with a hand-held electric mixer on high speed until the butter is smooth, about 1 minute. Add the chocolate and beat for another minute. Beat in the egg yolks, one at a time.

4. Using clean beaters, beat the egg whites and sugar at high speed until they form soft, shiny peaks. Do not overbeat. Stir about one fourth of the beaten whites into the chocolate mixture to lighten, then fold in the remaining whites, leaving a few visible wisps of whites. In two additions, sift the flour over the mixture, and fold.

5. Spread evenly in the cake pan. Bake until a toothpick comes out clean, about 50 minutes. (The cake will dome in the center.) Cool on a wire rack for 10 minutes. Remove the sides of the pan, and invert the cake onto the rack. Remove the paper and reinvert on another rack to turn right side up. Cool completely.

6. To assemble: Using a long serrated knife, trim the top of the cake to make it level. Cut the cake horizontally into three equal layers. Place one cake layer on an 8½-inch cardboard round. Brush the top of the cake layer with the apricot glaze. Place the second cake layer on top and brush again. Top with the remaining cake layer. Brush the top and sides of the cake with the remaining glaze. Let cool until the glaze is set.

7. Transfer the cake to a wire rack placed over a jelly-roll pan lined with wax paper. Make the chocolate glaze (it must be freshly made and warm). Pour all of the warm chocolate glaze on top of the cake. Using a metal icing spatula, gently smooth the glaze over the cake, allowing it to run down the sides, being sure that it completely coats the cake (patch any bare spots with the spatula and the icing that has dripped into the pan). Cool until the glaze is barely set, then transfer to a serving plate. Cool completely.

8. To serve, slice with a sharp knife dipped into hot water. Serve with a large dollop of whipped cream on the side.

▪ THE STORY BEHIND ▪
SPANISCHE WINDTORTE

In her classic *Gourmet's Old Vienna Cookbook*, Lillian Langseth-Christensen speaks at length about this dessert, which at one time was the true mark of an accomplished home baker. You can still special-order a Windtorte from some Konditorein (pastry shop) for a party, but it is rarely found in a display case with the daily fare. Nonetheless, it deserves to be included in this book because it always makes an enormous impression on dinner guests, and meringue desserts (such as the Australian Pavlova and French *vacherin*) have made a recent comeback with the low-fat-cooking crowd. In typical Viennese fashion, the low-fat attributes of the meringue are obliterated by the indulgent fruit and Schlagobers filling. But it can also be filled with a plain fruit salad with great success.

So why is it called Spanische Windtorte? Sugar arrived in Europe from the Middle East via North Africa and Spain. The Spanish court were the first Europeans to popularize sugar, at least among the upper classes. While no one is sure of the source of the first meringue, the name of this dessert acknowledges the Spanish love for sugary egg-based sweets. And the meringue's airy texture explains the "wind" part.

MERINGUE SHELL WITH STRAWBERRIES AND CREAM
SPANISCHE WINDTORTE
Makes 8 to 10 servings

One of the most spectacular desserts in any cuisine, the Spanische Windtorte is a rococo meringue drum filled with berries and cream.

The keys to a successful Windtorte are a bit of organization and long, slow baking. On paper, it looks like the torte will take four hours to prepare but almost all of that time is spent in the oven. The first rule is never make meringue on a rainy or humid day. The meringue attracts the moisture in the air and will never dry properly.

Use an oven thermometer to ensure the proper low temperature. It is better to have the oven too low than too high. Do not be tempted to raise the oven temperature to speed things along or the meringue will crack and color beyond the correct very pale beige. To be sure the oven temperature remains low, open the oven door a few times during baking for 30 seconds, being careful not to slam the door. If you insist on a pristine, white Windtorte, you must have a very well calibrated oven that will maintain a steady 170°F., but most ovens don't go that low. If you go this route, increase the baking times by one fourth. Read all of the information about egg whites on page 206 before you proceed.

To construct the meringue bases, you will need pastry tips with 7/16- to 1/2-inch openings (one plain and one open-star), a large pastry bag (at least 14 inches long), two 17 × 11-inch or larger baking sheets, and parchment paper. The meringue cake can be prepared one day ahead, but fill it just before serving so the shell remains nice and crisp.

Other berries can be used in addition to, or in place of, the strawberries. During berry season, a combination of red and golden raspberries, blackberries, and blueberries is especially luxurious. Maraschino liqueur has a unique flavor that elevates the filling to the same level as the meringue. Kirschwasser, a stronger cherry liqueur, would also be appropriate, as would Cognac or Grand Marnier.

▪ ▪ ▪

FIRST MERINGUE
6 large egg whites, at room temperature
1/4 teaspoon cream of tartar
1 1/2 cups superfine sugar

SECOND MERINGUE
8 large egg whites, at room temperature
½ teaspoon cream of tartar
2 cups superfine sugar

STRAWBERRY FILLING
1 cup heavy cream, chilled
3 tablespoons confectioners' sugar
2 tablespoons maraschino or kirschwasser
2 pints fresh strawberries, hulled and sliced

■ ■ ■

1. Position two racks in the center and bottom third of the oven and heat to 200°F. Line two 17 × 11-inch baking sheets with parchment paper. Using an 8- to 8½-inch round springform pan bottom or cake pan as a guide, and a thick, dark pen, draw 4 circles on the paper, spacing them as far apart as possible. Turn the papers over and fit them into the baking sheets; the circles should be visible from the other side.

2. To make the first meringue: In a large, grease-free bowl, using an electric mixer at low speed, beat the egg whites until foamy. Add the cream of tartar and beat until soft peaks begin to form. Still beating, gradually add the sugar 1 tablespoon at a time and beat until stiff, shiny peaks form. Transfer to a large pastry bag fitted with a ⁷⁄₁₆-inch-wide plain tip, such as Ateco Number 805.

3. Pipe a ½- to ¾-inch ring of meringue just inside one of the circles, and continue in a spiral until it finishes in the center of the ring. Use a metal spatula to smooth the surface. (This disk will be the bottom of the torte.) Pipe 3 plain rings just inside each of the remaining circles. These will become the sides of the torte.

4. Bake on separate racks until the meringues are pale beige and firm, and release easily from the parchment, about 50 minutes for the plain rings, and 1¼ hours for the disk. Occasionally open the oven door for 30 seconds or so to ensure that the oven temperature remains low. After 30 minutes of baking, switch the positions of the baking sheets from top to bottom and front to back. Carefully remove the meringues from the paper. Cool completely.

5. To make the second meringue, line a baking sheet with parchment paper. Following the instructions in Step 1, mark the paper with an 8- to 8½-inch circle, turn the paper over, and line the sheet. Line the second sheet with parchment paper, but do not mark the paper.

6. Make the second batch of meringue according to the instructions in Step 2. Transfer half of the meringue to a large pastry bag fitted with a ⁷⁄₁₆-inch-wide open star tip, such as Ateco Number 825. On the marked parchment paper, pipe another spiral of meringue just inside the circle and smooth it with a metal spatula. Pipe rosettes on top to completely cover the disk. (This will be the lid to the meringue shell.)

7. Transfer about two thirds of the remaining meringue to the pastry bag. Place the baked meringue disk on a lined baking sheet. Using some of the meringue in the bag as cement, stack the three rings on the disk. Using a metal spatula and the meringue in the bowl, spread a smooth wall of meringue over the sides of the stacked rings to make a large "drum." Transfer any remaining meringue in the bowl to the pastry bag. Pipe rosettes or shells around the top and bottom of the meringue "drum."

8. Bake the drum and the lid on separate racks until the meringues are pale beige, firm, and release easily from the paper, 1¼ to 1½ hours. After 45 minutes of baking, switch the positions of the baking sheets from top to bottom and front to back. Turn off the oven and prop the door ajar. Let the meringues stand in the oven for at least 1 and up to 3 hours to dry completely.

9. To make the strawberry filling: Just before serving, in a chilled large bowl, beat the cream and confectioners' sugar until stiff. Fold in the maraschino, then the strawberries.

10. To serve, transfer the meringue shell to a serving dish. Spoon the filling into the meringue and top with the lid. Use a serrated knife to cut into wedges, and serve immediately.

MAKE AHEAD

The meringue shell can be prepared up to 1 day ahead and stored uncovered at cool room temperature.

WALNUT TORTE WITH WALNUT-CUSTARD BUTTERCREAM
DIOSTORTE
Makes 12 servings

Ground walnuts give this Hungarian cake the dense texture that Americans think of when they hear the word "torte." The catch is that the nuts *must* be ground by hand with a rotary nut grinder. Don't use a food processor, as it doesn't give the nuts the requisite fluffiness. The frosting is based on a custard, which gives it a rich creaminess that is hard to duplicate or surpass with other methods. Thanks to Ella Szabo for her fine recipe.

■ ■ ■

CAKE
1/3 cup dried unflavored bread crumbs, for the pan
1 cup walnuts (4 1/2 ounces)
1 cup all-purpose flour
7 large eggs, at room temperature
3/4 cup granulated sugar

ICING
2 cups (8 ounces) chopped walnuts
1 1/4 cups confectioners' sugar
1 cup milk
2 tablespoons cornstarch
2 large egg yolks
2 tablespoons golden rum
1 teaspoon vanilla extract
1 1/2 cups (3 sticks) unsalted butter, at cool room temperature

ASSEMBLY
1/2 cup (2 ounces) finely chopped walnuts, for garnish
12 walnut halves, for garnish

■ ■ ■

1. To make the cake: Position a rack in the center of the oven and heat to 350°F. Lightly butter a 9-inch springform pan. Dust with bread crumbs and tap out the excess crumbs. Line the bottom of the pan with a round of parchment or wax paper.

2. Grind the nuts in a rotary nut grinder fitted with the fine grating drum. Transfer to a bowl and mix with the flour.

3. Beat the eggs in the bowl of a heavy-duty electric mixer at high speed until the mixture is very thick and forms a slowly dissolving ribbon when the beaters are lifted a few inches, about 15 minutes.

4. In two additions, fold in the walnut mixture with a large balloon whisk or rubber spatula. Spread evenly in the pan.

5. Bake until a toothpick inserted in the center of the cake comes out clean, about 35 minutes. Cool in the pan on a wire rack for 5 minutes. Remove the sides of the pan, and invert the cake onto the rack. Remove the paper. Reverse onto another rack and cool completely.

6. To make the icing: Process the walnuts and confectioners' sugar in a food processor fitted with the metal blade until the walnuts are very finely chopped, almost a powder.

7. Pour the milk into a medium saucepan. Sprinkle in the cornstarch, and whisk to dissolve. Whisk in the yolks. Cook over medium-low heat, whisking constantly, until the sauce is boiling and as thick as pudding. The sauce must come to a full boil; the cornstarch will prevent the yolks from curdling. Strain the custard into a medium bowl set in a larger bowl of ice water. Stir in the rum and vanilla. Let stand until cool, stirring occasionally.

8. Transfer the custard to the bowl of a heavy-duty standing mixer with the whisk attached and beat until smooth, about 1 minute. On medium speed, one tablespoon at a time, beat in the butter, occasionally increasing the speed to high for about 10 seconds to ensure smooth blending. Beat in the walnut–confectioners' sugar mixture. If the icing is too warm to spread, place the bowl in a larger bowl of ice water and let stand, stirring occasionally, until chilled and spreadable.

9. To assemble: Transfer about 3/4 cup of the icing to a pastry bag fitted with a 9/16-inch-wide French star tip, such as Ateco Number 865. Using a long serrated knife, horizontally slice the cake into 2 equal layers. Place the bottom layer on an 8-inch cardboard round or a serving plate. Spread with about 1 cup of the remaining icing. Top with the other layer, and frost the top and sides of the cake with the remaining icing. Press the chopped walnuts onto the side of the cake. Pipe twelve rosettes on top of the cake and place a walnut half on each. Refrigerate under a cake dome until 1 hour before serving.

MAKE AHEAD

The cake can be prepared up to 2 days before serving and stored under a cake dome in the refrigerator.

STRAWBERRY CREAM TORTE
ERDBEEROBERSTORTE
Makes 10 servings

This is the epitome of the *Oberstorte*, the kind of torte that is constructed with as much (or more) whipped cream as cake. In its season, strawberry cream torte is ubiquitous in European cafés, not unlike the strawberry shortcake found in our Southern diners. Choose smallish berries for the garnish, or the cake will look out of balance.

■ ■ ■

ORANGE SYRUP
⅓ cup water
3 tablespoons sugar
6 tablespoons Grand Marnier, Triple Sec, or orange juice

FILLING
1 envelope unflavored powdered gelatin
⅓ cup water
2 pints fresh strawberries, hulled, divided
¾ cup sugar
1 tablespoon fresh lemon juice
2 drops red food coloring, optional
2 cups heavy cream, chilled

ASSEMBLY
Small Sponge Cake (page 7)
Vegetable oil cooking spray, for the wax paper
10 perfect strawberries (on the small side), unhulled
½ cup Red Currant Glaze (page 16), warm
½ cup heavy cream, chilled
2 teaspoons confectioners' sugar
½ teaspoon vanilla extract

■ ■ ■

1. To make the syrup: Bring the water and sugar to a full boil in a small saucepan, stirring to dissolve the sugar. Remove from the heat and add the Grand Marnier. Pour into a small bowl and cool completely.

2. To make the filling: Sprinkle the gelatin on top of the water in a small bowl. Let stand until the gelatin absorbs the water, about 5 minutes.

3. Meanwhile, purée 1 pint of the strawberries in a food processor or blender. (This works best by dropping the hulled berries through the feed tube or lid with the machine running.) You should have 1 cup of purée. Transfer the purée to a medium-size, nonreactive saucepan and stir in the softened gelatin, the sugar, and lemon juice. Cook over medium-low heat, stirring constantly, just until the gelatin is dissolved, about 2 minutes. Do not simmer. Stir in the food coloring, if using. Transfer to a large bowl set in a larger bowl of ice water. Let stand, stirring often, until cool and thickened, but not set. Remove from the ice water.

4. Beat the cream in a chilled medium bowl until very stiff. Stir about one fourth of the cream into the strawberry purée, then fold in the remaining cream.

5. To assemble: Using a long serrated knife, cut the cake horizontally into 2 equal layers (do not trim off the top crust). Using an 8-inch-diameter plate or cake pan as a guide, trim each layer into an 8-inch round. Grind the trimmings in a food processor or blender to make cake crumbs. Transfer to a bowl and cover with plastic wrap.

6. Lightly oil a 9-inch springform pan. Place the top layer, top crust down, in the pan. Drizzle and brush with half of the orange syrup. Spread half of the filling over the cake, being sure it flows

around the sides of the cake. Slice the remaining pint of strawberries and arrange over the filling. Top with the second layer, and drizzle with the remaining syrup. Spread with the remaining filling. Cover tightly with plastic wrap and refrigerate until the filling is chilled and set, at least 4 hours or overnight.

7. To garnish the cake, make glazed strawberries: Line a jelly-roll pan with wax paper and spray with oil. Quickly rinse the strawberries and pat completely dry with paper towels. Holding each berry by the hull, dip in the glaze, let the excess glaze drip off, and place on the wax paper. Let stand until the glaze sets, about 15 minutes.

8. Run a sharp knife around the inside of the springform pan and remove the sides. Press the reserved cake crumbs onto the sides of the cake. In a chilled medium bowl, beat the cream with the confectioners' sugar and vanilla until stiff. Transfer to a pastry bag fitted with a ⅜₆-inch-wide open star tip such as Ateco Number 825. Pipe 10 large rosettes around the top circumference of the cake. Top each rosette with a glazed strawberry. Serve chilled.

MAKE AHEAD

The cake can be made up to 2 days before serving and stored under a cake dome in the refrigerator.

CHOCOLATE-ALMOND TORTE
PANAMATORTE
Makes 12 servings

This cake was invented to commemorate the opening of the Panama Canal in 1914. The chocolate–almond cake layers are wonderful, but this chocolate icing has become one of my particular favorites. Be sure to cool the egg mixture completely before incorporating the butter. And soften the butter just to the point where it is cool, but maleable and not shiny.

■ ■ ■

PANAMA CAKE
3 ounces high-quality bittersweet chocolate, finely chopped
1¼ cups (5 ounces) sliced natural or blanched almonds
⅓ cup dried bread crumbs
7 large eggs, separated, at room temperature
½ cup sugar, divided
1 teaspoon vanilla extract
½ teaspoon almond extract

CHOCOLATE–ALMOND ICING
3 ounces high-quality bittersweet chocolate, finely chopped
2 large eggs, at room temperature
¾ cup sugar
1 cup (2 sticks) unsalted butter, at cool room temperature
½ teaspoon vanilla extract
¼ teaspoon almond extract
2 tablespoons heavy cream, optional

ASSEMBLY
½ cup sliced natural or blanched almonds, toasted (see page 211)

■ ■ ■

1. To make the cake: Position a rack in the center of the oven and heat to 350°F. Lightly butter the inside of a 9-inch springform pan. Line the bottom of the pan with parchment or wax paper. Dust with flour and tap out the excess.
2. Melt the chocolate in the top part of a double boiler over hot, not simmering, water, or in a microwave at medium power. Cool slightly.

3. In a food processor fitted with the metal blade, process the almonds and bread crumbs until the almonds are chopped into a fine powder, but not oily.
4. Beat the yolks and ¼ cup of the sugar in a large bowl with a handheld electric mixer on high speed until thick and pale yellow, about 3 minutes. Beat in the chocolate, vanilla, and almond extract.
5. Using clean beaters, beat the whites in a large bowl until they form soft peaks. Gradually beat in the remaining ¼ cup of sugar until the peaks are stiff and shiny. Stir about one fourth of the whites into the chocolate batter to lighten, then fold in the remaining whites, using a large balloon whisk or a rubber spatula. In two additions, fold in the nuts. Spread evenly in the pan.
6. Bake until a toothpick inserted in the center of the cake comes out clean and the cake is beginning to shrink from the pan, about 35 minutes. Cool on a wire rack for 10 minutes. Run a knife around the inside of the pan to release the cake, then remove the sides of the pan. Invert onto the rack, and remove the paper. Cool completely.
7. To make the icing: Melt the chocolate in the top part of a double boiler or in a microwave at medium power.
8. Whisk the eggs and sugar in a medium heatproof bowl. Place over a saucepan of barely simmering water (the water should not touch the bottom of the bowl). Whisk gently until the eggs are very hot (an instant-read thermometer will read 170°F.). Remove from the heat. Stir in the chocolate. Using a handheld electric mixer on high speed, beat until completely cooled, about 5 minutes. One tablespoon at a time, beat in the butter, incorporating the first addition before adding another. Add the vanilla and almond extract. If the icing seems thick, beat in the heavy cream.
9. To assemble: Using a long serrated knife, trim the top of the cake to level it. Cut the cake horizontally into 2 equal layers. Dab a tablespoon of the icing in the center of an 8-inch cardboard round. Place the bottom layer on the round. Spread with ½ cup of the icing, then top with the other layer. Spread the top of the cake with a

generous ½ cup of icing. Use the remaining icing to frost the sides of the cake, then smooth the top. Lift the cake with one hand, and use your other hand to press the almonds onto the sides of the cake. Refrigerate at least 1 hour before serving.

MAKE AHEAD
The cake can be made up to 1 day before serving and stored under a cake dome in the refrigerator.

RASPBERRY YOGURT TORTE
HIMBEERJOGHURTTORTE
Makes 12 to 16 servings

Yogurt tortes represent one of the few "new" tortes to enter the Austro-Hungarian dessert lexicon in the past twenty years, and this raspberry version is one of the tastiest renditions. In America, yogurt in a dessert usually suggests a reduced-calorie or low-fat treat. Not so in central Europe, where yogurt is appreciated for its tang and creaminess and is combined with a good amount of whipped cream for lightness. Whole-milk yogurt has more body and flavor than the low-fat or non-fat varieties, so don't make any substitutions.

■ ■ ■

RASPBERRY SYRUP
⅓ cup water
3 tablespoons sugar
6 tablespoons framboise
(raspberrry eau-de-vie)

FILLING
⅓ cup water
4 teaspoons (2 envelopes) unflavored
powdered gelatin
4 6-ounce containers fresh raspberries or
4 cups frozen raspberries without syrup,
divided
1¾ cups sugar
2 tablespoons fresh lemon juice

2 cups plain whole-milk yogurt
1 cup heavy cream, chilled
1 or 2 drops red food coloring, optional
Small Sponge Cake (page 7)

GLAZE
1¼ teaspoons unflavored
powdered gelatin
¼ cup water
1 tablespoon finely chopped pistachios,
for garnish

■ ■ ■

1. To make the syrup: Bring the water and sugar to a full boil in a small saucepan, stirring to dissolve the sugar. Remove from the heat and add the framboise. Pour into a small bowl and cool completely.

2. To make the filling: Pour the water into a small bowl and sprinkle the gelatin on top. Let stand until the gelatin absorbs the water, about 5 minutes.

3. Meanwhile, purée 3 containers of the fresh raspberries, the sugar, and lemon juice in a food processor or blender. Strain. Measure 1 cup raspberry purée, cover, and refrigerate. Transfer the remaining purée to a medium non-reactive saucepan and stir in the softened gelatin. Heat over medium-low heat, stirring constantly, just until the gelatin dissolves, about 2 minutes. Do not simmer. Transfer a large bowl set in a larger bowl of ice water. Let stand, stirring often, until cool and thickened, but not set. Remove from the ice water.

4. Whisk the yogurt into the raspberry mixture. In a chilled medium bowl, beat the cream just until stiff. Stir about one fourth of the cream into the yogurt mixture, then fold in the remaining cream. Stir in the food coloring, if using.

5. Using a long serrated knife, cut the cake horizontally into 2 equal layers (do not trim the top crust). Using an 8-inch-round plate or cake pan as a guide, trim each layer into an 8-inch round, reserving the trimmings. In a blender or food processor, process the trimmings into crumbs; transfer to a bowl and cover with plastic wrap.

6. Lightly oil a 9-inch springform pan. Place the top layer, "skin" side down, in the pan. Drizzle

and brush with half of the syrup. Spread half of the filling over the cake, being sure it flows around the sides of the cake. Press the remaining raspberries into the filling. Top with the second layer, and drizzle with the remaining syrup. Spread with the remaining filling. Cover tightly with plastic wrap and refrigerate until the filling is chilled and set, at least 2 hours or overnight.

7. To make the glaze: Sprinkle the gelatin over the water in a small bowl and let stand until the gelatin absorbs the water, about 5 minutes. In a small saucepan, stir the reserved 1 cup of raspberry purée and the soaked gelatin. Stir over medium heat just until the gelatin dissolves. Do not simmer. Transfer to a small bowl set in a larger bowl of ice water. Let stand, stirring often, until cooled but not set.

8. Pour the glaze on the top of the torte and tilt the pan so it spreads evenly. Refrigerate uncovered to set the glaze, about 30 minutes.

9. Run a sharp knife around the inside of the springform pan and remove the sides. Press the reserved crumbs onto the sides of the cake. Sprinkle the pistachios in a ring around the top of the cake. Serve chilled.

▪ THE STORY BEHIND ▪
DOBOS TORTE

Jószef Dobos was the Auguste Escoffier of Hungary, creating his culinary extravaganzas during the same period as the French master. And like Escoffier, his name became known well beyond his country's borders.

Dobos came from a family of cooks. He prided himself on the quality and variety of the offerings at his fancy-food shop, which catered to the well heeled. In a time when shipping was expensive and unreliable, he offered more than sixty cheeses and twenty-two champagnes. Budapest loved big World's Fair–like exhibitions, which, of course, gave the citizens ample opportunity to sample their other favorite indulgences, food and wine. In 1885, at the first General National Exhibition, Dobos had a pavilion selling his delicacies. His most famous customers were the emperor and empress themselves (also styled king and queen of Hungary), who heartily approved of their meal. Elizabeth was unpopular in Vienna for promoting Hungarian independence, which, of course, made her a heroine in Budapest, so her endorsement of Dobos's products ensured his position as a super-chef.

A few years later, Dobos introduced his most famous invention, the Dobos torta. The amazingly thin cake layers and caramel crown were impressive indeed, but it was the cake's profuse use of chocolate buttercream—a recipe only recently imported from France—that literally put Dobos torta on everyone's lips. Dobos devised a special package that allowed the cake to be shipped, and soon the cake appeared in other European capitals. Of course, other Budapest bakeries wanted the recipe so they could sell their own version, but Dobos shrewdly kept it a secret—for a time. During the 1896 Millennium Exposition, celebrating one thousand years of Hungarian nationality, Dobos opened another pavilion, selling thousands and thousands of his cakes. Dobos torta mania had taken hold.

When Dobos finally retired in 1906, he made a well-publicized gift of the recipe to the Budapest Trade Association, preserving it (and his name) for prosperity. The legend was further enhanced by an operetta detailing Dobos's intrigues.

By coincidence, *dob* in Hungarian means "drum." As the caramel-glazed top of a Dobos torte looks somewhat like the stretched skin of a drum, some sources mistakenly believe that the name of the cake is derived from *dob.* Could his choice of a hard caramel topping have been intentional? After all, could his surname come from *dob,* as well?

DOBOS TORTE
DOBOS TORTA
Makes 12 servings

Five thin layers (no more, no less) of vanilla sponge cake, each slathered with chocolate buttercream icing, and topped with wedges of caramel-glazed cake—this is the famous Dobos. It's one of the few Austro-Hungarian creations that is never literally translated, as any Hungarian can tell you that the Dobos is a national institution, and much more than just a layer cake.

There are no shortcuts to a perfect Dobos Torte. The layers must be baked individually—*never* sliced from one thick cake—to give them their characteristic dryness, all the better to spread with the chocolate buttercream. Luckily the batter bakes very quickly and the process can be speeded up by using two or more baking sheets—and a kitchen timer to keep track of baking times. Get yourself in an assembly-line frame of mind, and you'll be finished in no time.

■ ■ ■

BATTER
6 large eggs, separated, at room temperature
1 1/3 cups confectioners' sugar, divided
1 teaspoon vanilla extract
1 cup plus 2 tablespoons sifted cake flour
Pinch of salt

CHOCOLATE ICING
4 ounces bittersweet chocolate, finely chopped
1 1/2 cups (3 sticks) unsalted butter, at cool room temperature
2 tablespoons Dutch-processed cocoa powder
1 1/4 cups confectioners' sugar, sifted
1 teaspoon vanilla extract

CARAMEL TOPPING
3/4 cup sugar
3 tablespoons water
2 teaspoons fresh lemon juice

12 whole hazelnuts, toasted and peeled, for garnish
1/2 cup toasted, peeled, and finely chopped hazelnuts, for garnish

■ ■ ■

1. Position the racks in the center and top third of the oven and heat to 400°F.

2. Cut six pieces of parchment paper to fit the baking sheets. Using the bottom of a 9-inch springform pan as a template and a dark pencil or pen, trace a circle on each of the papers, and turn them over (the circle should be visible from the other side, so the graphite or ink doesn't touch the cake batter).

3. To make the batter: Beat the egg yolks, 2/3 cup of the confectioners' sugar, and the vanilla in a medium bowl with a mixer at high speed until the mixture is thick, pale yellow, and forms a thick ribbon when the beaters are lifted a few inches above the batter, about 3 minutes.

4. In another bowl, using clean beaters, beat the egg whites until soft peaks form. Gradually beat in the remaining 2/3 cup of the confectioners' sugar until the whites form stiff, shiny peaks. Using a large rubber spatula, stir about one fourth of the beaten whites into the egg yolk mixture, then fold in the remainder, leaving a few wisps of whites visible. Combine the flour and salt. Sift half of the flour over the eggs, and fold in; repeat with the remaining flour.

5. Line one of the baking sheets with a circle-marked paper. Using a small offset spatula, spread about 3/4 cup of the batter in an even layer, filling in the traced circle on one baking sheet. Bake on the top rack for 5 minutes, until the cake springs back when pressed gently in the center and the edges are lightly browned. While this cake bakes, repeat the procedure on the other baking sheet, placing it on the center rack. When the first cake is done, move the second cake to the top rack. Invert the first cake onto a flat surface and carefully peel off the paper. Slide the cake layer back onto the paper and let stand until cool. Rinse the baking sheet under cold running water to cool, and dry it before lining with another parchment. Continue with the remaining papers and batter to make a total of six layers. Completely cool the layers. Using an 8-inch round springform pan bottom or plate as a template, trim each cake layer into a neat round.

6. To make the chocolate icing: Melt the chocolate in the top part of a double boiler over hot water or in a microwave at medium powder. Cool until tepid.

7. Beat the butter with a handheld electric mixer on high speed in a medium bowl until smooth. On low speed, beat in the cocoa, then the confectioners' sugar. Beat in the cooled chocolate, then the vanilla.

8. Set aside the best-looking layer for the caramel top. Place a dab of the icing in the center of a 7½-inch cardboard round and top with one cake layer. Spread the layer with about N cup of the chocolate icing. Repeat with 4 more cake layers. Spread the remaining icing on the sides of the cake. Refrigerate uncovered while making the caramel top.

9. To make the caramel topping: Line a jelly-roll pan with parchment paper and butter the paper. Place the reserved cake layer on the paper. Score the cake into 12 equal wedges. Lightly butter a thin, sharp knife and an offset metal spatula.

10. Stir the sugar, water, and lemon juice in a small saucepan. Bring to a boil over medium-high heat, stirring often to dissolve the sugar. Boil without stirring, swirling the pan by the handle occasionally and washing down any sugar crystals on the sides of the pan with a wet brush, until the syrup has turned into an amber-colored caramel.

11. Immediately pour all of the hot caramel over the cake layer. Using the spatula, quickly spread the caramel evenly to the edge of the cake layer. Let cool until beginning to set, about 30 seconds. Using the tip of the knife, cut through the scored marks to divide the caramel layer into 12 equal wedges. Cool another minute or so, then use the edge of the knife to completely cut and separate the wedges. Cool completely.

12. Propping a hazelnut under each wedge so it sits at an angle, arrange the wedges on top of the cake in a spoke pattern. Refrigerate the cake under a cake dome until the icing is set, about 2 hours. Serve chilled.

MAKE AHEAD

The cake can be made up to 2 days ahead, stored under a cake dome, and refrigerated.

CHOCOLATE-CHERRY MOUSSE CAKE
LÚDLÁBTORTA (HUNGARIAN)
Makes 12 servings

Lúdláb means "goose leg," and the only connection between this cake and a goose would be that both are very rich. A specialty of the finest cafés in Budapest, Lúdlábtorta is the true test of the pastry maker's art. It's like eating a chocolate–cherry truffle, as the glaze comes in direct contact with the mousse filling. To keep the mousse from melting, be sure that the cake is well chilled and the glaze is as cool as it can be while still fluid.

■ ■ ■

Chocolate Sponge Cake (page 8)

CHOCOLATE MOUSSE
1½ cups milk, divided
⅓ cup Dutch-processed cocoa powder
½ cup sugar
2 egg yolks
2 tablespoons cornstarch
3 ounces bittersweet chocolate, finely chopped
1 tablespoon kirsch, optional
1½ cups (3 sticks) unsalted butter, at cool room temperature
½ cup cherry preserves
12 ounces sweet cherries, pitted (about 2 cups) or thawed frozen sweet cherries

GLAZE
½ cup heavy cream
4 ounces bittersweet chocolate, finely chopped

12 fresh sweet cherries, with stems attached, for garnish

■ ■ ■

1. Cut the cake in half horizontally. Reserve one half for another use.

2. To make the mousse: Heat ½ cup of the milk in a small saucepan or the microwave. Combine the cocoa and sugar in a heavy-bottomed medium saucepan. Gradually whisk in the hot milk to dissolve the cocoa (a paddle-shaped "sauce" whisk works best). Add the yolks and whisk well.

3. Sprinkle the cornstarch over the remaining 1 cup of the milk and whisk to dissolve. Add to the saucepan. Whisking often (a flat "roux" whisk works best), and being sure to reach the corners of the saucepan, bring to a full boil over medium heat; the mixture will be very thick. Remove from the heat and add the chopped chocolate. Let stand 1 minute, then whisk until the chocolate melts. Rub through a wire strainer into a medium bowl set in a larger bowl of ice water. Stir in the kirsch, if using. Cool completely, whisking often.

4. Transfer the cooled chocolate mixture to a heavy-duty electric mixer fitted with the whisk. On medium-high speed, add the butter, one tablespoon at a time, occasionally increasing the speed to high for about 10 seconds to ensure smooth blending, until the mixture is smooth and fluffy.

5. Place the cake on an 8-inch cardboard cake round. Bring the cherry preserves to a boil in a small saucepan over medium heat. Strain though a wire sieve into a small bowl, rubbing the cherries through the sieve. Spread the warm preserves over the cake. Spread a thin layer of the mousse over the preserves. Arrange the cherries in concentric circles over the mousse. Spread almost all of the mousse in a thick layer to completely cover the cherries. Using the remaining mousse, frost the sides of the cake and make the top as level as possible. (Don't worry about making the cake look perfect at this step, as it will be easier to smooth later.) Refrigerate, uncovered, until chilled and firm, at least 4 hours or overnight.

5. To make the glaze: Bring the cream to a simmer in a small saucepan over high heat. Place the chocolate in a medium bowl. Add the hot cream, let stand 1 minute, then whisk until smooth. Let stand until cooled but still pourable, about 5 minutes.

6. Smooth the filling mousse with a metal spatula that has been rinsed under hot water, giving it an even shape. Place the cake on a wire rack over a jelly-roll pan. Pour all of the glaze over the cake. Using an offset metal spatula, smooth and coax the glaze over the top of the cake, letting the glaze run down the sides. Use the spatula to gather the glaze on the sheet, and touch up any bare spots. Arrange the cherries around the top edge of the cake as a garnish. Refrigerate until the glaze is set, at least 20 minutes.

7. To serve, slice with a sharp knife dipped in a glass of hot water. Serve chilled.

MAKE AHEAD

The cake can be made up to 2 days ahead, stored under a cake dome in the refrigerator.

·STRUDELS·

During one trip to central Europe, I was on a strudel-making mission. Everywhere I went, I saw bakers take flour, oil, and water and make a dough that was effortlessly stretched to edible gossamer. In Vienna, the master baker Walter Leschanz and his assistant spent all morning patiently teaching an American man how to make apple strudel. In Budapest, I spend another morning in the kitchen of Bagolyvár Restaurant, near the city park, where the chefs are women. I was assured by these chefs that my case wasn't hopeless, and that it was merely a matter of practice. The ladies of Bagolyvár were right.

When I returned home to the States, strudel-stretching skills aching to be tested, my friend Sarabeth Levine and I stretched strudel after strudel, testing different recipes. We learned a lot of things that afternoon. First, freshly sautéed bread crumbs sprinkled on the dough not only add flavor, but help separate the layers and encourage flakiness. Don't cut corners and use packaged bread crumbs. Also, most cookbooks give unrealistic instructions on how to really pull the dough, assuming that two people will do the job. We decided that this book should assume only one baker (although the job *is* easier if you enlist a friend to help). We also realized that these recipes should be for one strudel making eight to ten servings. Some European recipes yield enough for two to three strudels.

The thin, parchment-like pastry that surrounds the apples in an Austro-Hungarian strudel is really filo dough, another culinary inheritance from the Turks. The major difference is that most filo recipes from the Middle East layer the dough with the filling in a pan, but most strudels are wound around their fillings (*Strudel* means "whirlpool" or "vortex"). As the Turks occupied Hungary for more than a hundred years before they tried to conquer Vienna, strudel is even more established in the coffeehouses of Budapest, where it is called *rétes*. In fact, every Hungarian supermarket carries a coarsely ground, semolina-like flour specifically for making strudel dough.

In this country, no one will complain if you don't make your strudel dough by hand and you use store-bought filo. But, with that all-important practice, strudel dough is actually very easy to make. My European hostesses think nothing of whipping up a strudel. This is a throwback to the days when people ate what they raised. The ingredients for the dough were always at hand, and the filling was chosen depending on what was in season or how much cheese was on hand. Cheese strudel was one of the most popular *Mehlspeisen*, or flour meals, served as a filling repast on meatless Fridays in Catholic households. The seasonal approach to strudel still holds today. Autumn's apples and summer's sour cherries are great reasons for learning how to make strudel by hand.

Strudel is always best when served warm from the oven, or at room temperature a few hours after baking. Refrigerated strudel gets stodgy. If necessary, reheat the unwrapped strudel in a preheated 350°F. oven for about 10 minutes before serving, but don't use the microwave, which will make the crust soggy.

To make strudel, you need three things. First, the right flour (our unbleached flour is a fine stand-in for Hungarian *réteslisz̧t*, or strudel flour). Second, a place to pull the strudel from all sides, like a kitchen table. And finally, the willingness to learn and the acceptance that your first attempt at strudel pulling may not be perfect.

STRUDEL DOUGH
STRUDELTEIG (GERMAN)
Makes 1 strudel

Strudel dough just looks difficult to prepare. The biggest stumbling block for American cooks was finding the right flour. Now that unbleached flour is in every market, the next step is to find the right space to pull it—a space that allows access to the dough on all sides. I pull my strudel dough on the 23 × 49-inch wooden pastry worktop in my kitchen. You can use your kitchen or dining-room table of a similar size, or even a card table. Some bakers recommend a circular table, but I don't see the advantage of that, because you want a rectangular shape. Whether it's pulled into a square, rectangle, oblong, or circle, however, the dough will still work.

■ ■ ■

1 1/3 cups unbleached flour
1/8 teaspoon salt
7 tablespoons water, plus more if needed
2 tablespoons vegetable oil, plus additional
for coating the dough
1/2 teaspoon cider vinegar

■ ■ ■

1. Measure the flour and salt into the bowl of a heavy-duty electric mixer fitted with the paddle blade. Mix the water, oil, and vinegar in a glass measuring cup. With the machine on low speed, add the liquid to the flour and mix to form a soft dough (remember the dough must be soft enough to pull and stretch, so add a bit more water if needed). Gather the dough into a ball. Change to the dough hook. Knead the dough on medium-low speed to make a soft ball of dough with a somewhat rough surface.

2. Transfer the dough to an unfloured work surface. Knead by hand, occasionally picking up the dough and throwing it down hard onto the surface, for 1 to 2 minutes. Gather the dough into a ball. Place the dough on a plate. Lightly oil the top of the dough. Cover tightly with plastic wrap and let stand for at least 30 and up to 90 minutes, the longer the better.

3. Choose a work area that you can walk around on all sides (such as a 36-inch round table or a rectangular table or work surface about 23 × 48 inches) and cover with a tablecloth. Dust well with flour and rub the flour into the tablecloth. Place the dough in the center of the cloth and roll out as much as you can (photograph 1). Hold the dough by an edge and pick it up. Letting gravity and the weight of the dough help stretch the dough as it hangs, use the backs of your hands to gently pull and stretch the dough. As the dough stretches, use your forearms to support it (2).

4. When the dough becomes too large to hold, place it on the work surface, leaving the thicker edge of the dough to hang over one edge of the table. Slip your hands underneath the dough and use the backs of your hands to stretch and pull the dough even thinner (3); anchor the edge of the dough hanging over the table with your hip to give the dough additional tension. Continue pulling and stretching (you don't have to use the backs of your hands, as long as you are careful not to pull too hard), until it is tissue-thin and about 2 feet wide and 3 feet long. For additional anchorage, pull the edge of the tablecloth up to cover the dough, and weigh it down with a heavy can or other object. Don't worry about a few

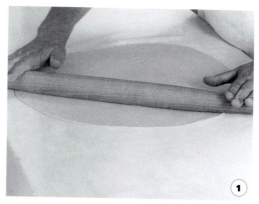

 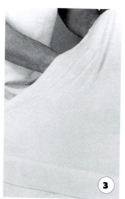

small holes, as they will disappear when the strudel is rolled. Using scissors, trim away and discard the thick dough around the edges. The dough is now ready to fill.

Here are some other tips for strudel dough.

• The first (or second or third) time you make strudel, make two batches of dough; the ingredients are inexpensive. This way if your first dough is less than perfect, you have a backup to try again. Strudel makers and Carnegie Hall aspirants have something in common: practice, practice, practice.

• The fabric for the tablecloth isn't important, cotton or polyester will do. But it helps if it is patterned, for if you can clearly see the pattern underneath the dough, it's been pulled thin enough.

• When kneading the dough, give it a few hard throws against the work surface to help develop the gluten. Get aggressive, and really throw! It will make the dough easier to stretch.

• Most bakeries use two people to pull the dough, with one person anchoring the dough as the other person stretches it, or with both people gently stretching the dough in opposite directions. The instructions above assume that only one person will be pulling the dough. If you have a friend to help you, so much the better.

• Don't be daunted by the surface area of the pulled dough.

• Before pulling the dough, remove all of your jewelry (large rings, watch, bracelets) and wear a short-sleeved shirt (sleeve buttons can catch and tear the dough). You will be using not just your hands, but your forearms.

• Use your hip to anchor the dough against the edge of the table so you can pull more easily.

• Let gravity do some of the work for you. A thick rope of unpulled dough will remain on all four sides of the rectangle, and its extra weight will help stretch the dough. The rope will be trimmed off before baking.

APPLE STRUDEL
APFELSTRUDEL
Makes 1 strudel, 8 servings

Truly one of the glories of the Austro-Hungarian kitchen, apple strudel deserves its place of honor. Use the hardest, tartest apples you can find—the farmers' market may hold some unknown treasures. My strudel mentors told me "the uglier the apple, the better the strudel." At any rate, choose apples that will hold their shape during baking, such as Golden Delicious or Pippin, and avoid those that fall apart when cooked, such as Jonathan and McIntosh. This is Walter Leschanz's recipe.

■ ■ ■

3 tablespoons raisins
2 tablespoons golden rum
1/3 cup plus 1 tablespoon sugar
1/4 teaspoon ground cinnamon
1/2 cup (1 stick) unsalted butter, melted, divided
11/2 cups fresh bread crumbs

Strudel Dough (page 78)
1/2 cup coarsely chopped walnuts
2 pounds tart cooking apples, peeled, cored, and cut into 1/4-inch-thick slices

■ ■ ■

1. Mix the raisins and rum in a small bowl. Mix the sugar and cinnamon in another bowl.

2. Heat 3 tablespoons of the melted butter in a large skillet over medium-high heat. Add the bread crumbs and cook, stirring often, until golden and toasted, about 3 minutes. Transfer to a plate and set aside to cool completely.

3. Position a rack in the upper third of the oven and heat to 400°F. Line a large baking sheet with parchment paper. Stretch and trim the strudel dough as described on page 79. Using your hands or a feather pastry brush (a bristle brush could tear the dough), spread about 3 tablespoons of the remaining melted butter over the dough. Sprinkle the bread crumbs over the dough. Spread the walnuts in a 6-inch-wide strip about 3 inches from the short edge of the dough. Toss the apples, the raisins with their rum, and the cinnamon sugar, and spread over the walnuts.

4. Fold the short end of the dough onto the filling. Pick up the end of the tablecloth at the short end of the strudel, and lift the tablecloth to roll the strudel on itself. Lift the strudel (be brave—it's sturdier than you think) and transfer to the baking sheet, curving it into a horseshoe to fit. Tuck the ends under the strudel. Brush the top of the strudel with the remaining melted butter, leaving any milk solids in the bottom of the saucepan or bowl.

5. Bake until the strudel is deep golden brown, about 30 minutes. Cool for at least 30 minutes. Using a serrated knife, cut into thick slices, and serve warm or at room temperature.

MAKE AHEAD
The strudel is best the day it is baked.

SOUR CHERRY STRUDEL
KIRSCHSTRUDEL
Makes 1 strudel, 8 servings

Make this strudel in the summer, when sour cherries enjoy their short season. Frozen cherries give off too much water when baked and make a soggy strudel, so fresh are a must. Sweet Bing cherries will work, but once you've tasted the sour ones, you'll never go back.

■ ■ ■

1/2 cup (1 stick) unsalted butter, melted, divided
1 1/2 cups fresh bread crumbs
Strudel Dough (page 78)
1/2 cup finely chopped sliced almonds
2 pounds sour or sweet cherries, pitted (4 cups)
3/4 cup sugar
2 tablespoons fresh lemon juice, if using sweet cherries

■ ■ ■

1. Heat 3 tablespoons of the melted butter in a large skillet over medium-high heat. Add the bread crumbs and cook, stirring often, until golden and toasted, about 3 minutes. Transfer to a plate and set aside to cool completely.
2. Position a rack in the upper third of the oven and heat to 400°F. Line a large baking sheet with parchment paper. Stretch and trim the strudel dough as described on page 79. Using your hands or a feather pastry brush (a bristle brush could tear the dough), spread about 3 tablespoons of the remaining melted butter over the dough. Sprinkle the bread crumbs over the dough, with most of them concentrated in a 6-inch-wide strip about 3 inches in from the short end of the dough. Sprinkle the almonds over the thick strip of bread crumbs. Toss the cherries with the sugar (and lemon juice, if using sweet cherries), and spread over the almonds.
3. Fold the short end of the dough onto the filling. Pick up the end of the tablecloth at the short end of the strudel, and lift the tablecloth to roll the strudel on itself. Lift the strudel (it is sturdier than you think) and transfer to the baking sheet, curv-

ing it into a horseshoe to fit. Tuck the ends under the strudel. Brush the top of the strudel with the remaining melted butter, leaving any milk solids behind in the bottom of the saucepan or bowl.
4. Bake until the strudel is deep golden brown, about 30 minutes. Cool for at least 30 minutes. Using a serrated knife, cut into thick slices and serve warm or at room temperature.

GRAPE STRUDEL WITH WEINCHAUDEAU
WEINTRAUBENSTRUDEL MIT WEINCHAUDEAU
Makes 8 servings

This recipe sounds so cutting-edge that my American baker friends don't believe it's an old classic from Styria, the region south of Vienna. The Weinchaudeau, a Viennese-style zabaglione, is a wonderful extravagance and part of the traditional presentation. This strudel is one of my favorites to show the range of Austro-Hungarian desserts (photograph, page 81).

■ ■ ■

1/2 cup (1 stick) unsalted butter, melted, divided
1 cup fresh bread crumbs
1/2 cup toasted, peeled, and coarsely chopped hazelnuts
3 tablespoons sugar
Pinch of ground cinnamon
Strudel Dough (page 78)
1 1/4 pounds seedless green grapes
Weinchaudeau (page 187)

■ ■ ■

1. Heat 3 tablespoons of the melted butter in a large skillet over medium-high heat. Add the bread crumbs and cook, stirring often, until golden and toasted, about 3 minutes. Transfer to a plate and set aside to cool completely.
2. Process the hazelnuts, sugar, and cinnamon in a food processor fitted with the metal blade until the nuts are very finely chopped.

3. Position a rack in the upper third of the oven and heat to 400°F. Line a large baking sheet with parchment paper. Stretch and trim the strudel dough as described on page 79. Using your hands or a feather pastry brush, spread about 3 tablespoons of the remaining melted butter over the dough. Sprinkle the bread crumbs over the dough. Spread the hazelnuts in a 6-inch-wide strip about 3 inches from the short end of the dough. Spread the grapes over the hazelnuts.

4. Fold the short end of the dough onto the filling. Pick up the end of the tablecloth at the short end of the strudel, and lift the tablecloth to roll the strudel on itself. Lift the strudel (be brave) and transfer to the baking sheet, curving it into a horseshoe to fit. Tuck the ends under the strudel. Brush the top of the strudel with the remaining melted butter, leaving any milk solids behind in the bottom of the saucepan or bowl.

5. Bake until the strudel is deep golden brown, about 30 minutes. Cool for at least 30 minutes. Using a serrated knife, cut into thick slices and serve warm or at room temperature, with a spoonful of Weinchaudeau on the side.

Filo Facts

Store-bought filo sheets are supposed to be the pastry chef's friend. However, they can be temperamental. Frozen filo dough needs to be approached with care. Too often I have purchased frozen dough and gotten home to find that it had been poorly stored by the market. If you have defrosted the filo carefully and it still sticks together, or if the baked dough has an off taste, then it shows that the filo was defrosted and refrozen, and it's the grocer's fault. If you simply pay attention to a few rules, you'll sidestep the problems.

- Buy frozen filo from a reliable source with a brisk turnover. If possible, purchase it from a Greek or Middle Eastern delicatessen or the best supermarket in town (the one where all the foodies shop). The fresher the filo, the less chance you have of it picking up any unwanted flavors from other foods in the freezer case.
- Filo is numbered from the thickest (Number 7) to the thinnest (1). Finicky cooks choose the proper thickness for each recipe. Number 4 is a common supermarket thickness and a good all-purpose choice.
- Filo defrosted at room temperature will stick together. Always defrost filo in the refrigerator overnight. Let chilled filo stand at room temperature for one hour before unfolding.
- While working with filo, keep the unused portion well covered with a large sheet of plastic wrap, which works better than the moist kitchen towels that are often recommended.
- Rewrap any unused filo tightly in plastic wrap and refrigerate for up to one week. Never refreeze filo dough—it will be impossible to separate the thawed sheets.
- To substitute filo dough for homemade, you overlap. Start by covering a work surface with a tablecloth, and dust with flour. Overlap sheets of defrosted dough by 1 inch, trimming with scissors as needed, to cover an area 2 × 3 feet long on the tablecloth.

There are still a few pastry shops in ethnic neighborhoods that make handmade dough. These treasures are few and far between, but if you live near one, it is always worth the trip to buy their fresh product. If necessary, cut handmade filo into 12 × 17-inch rectangles (the same size as the frozen sheets used to test the recipes). Two great sources are: Poseidon Greek Bakery, 629 Ninth Avenue, New York, NY 10036 (212) 757-6173; and The Fillo Factory, P.O. Box 155, Dumont, NJ 07628, (800) OKFILLO, www.fillofactory.com. The Fillo Factory will mail order.

WARM "MILK-CREAM" STRUDEL WITH VANILLA SAUCE
MILCHRAHMSTRUDEL
Makes 2 strudels, 12 servings

Here is one of the most typically Viennese of all strudels. It lends new meaning to the phrase "comfort food." With minor variations, Milch-rahmstrudel always starts with farmer's-cheese-filled strudels baked briefly to set the pastry. A *Royale* (custard) is then poured around the strudels to create a warm dessert with an incredible interplay of crisp and creamy textures. Mrs. Bleuel of the Berghotel Tulbingerkogel in Mauerbach bei Wien, nestled in the Vienna Woods, shared her recipe with me. She stirs milk into a portion of the cheese filling to create the royale, and serves a vanilla sauce on the side.

This wonderful dessert doesn't easily lend itself to today's "make-ahead" mentality, as it was originally a hearty supper dish. I make it for good friends who love to watch me fill and roll the strudels in front of them just before we sit down to dinner. For that reason, I make this with store-bought filo.

■ ■ ■

CHEESE FILLING
1¼ cups sugar
10 tablespoons (1¼ sticks) unsalted butter,
at room temperature
6 large eggs, separated, at room temperature
½ cup all-purpose flour
⅓ cup golden raisins
2 tablespoons chopped candied citron,
optional
1⅔ cups sour cream
1 pound farmer's cheese, rubbed through a
wire sieve

CUSTARD (ROYALE)
2 cups milk
2 large eggs

8 12 × 17-inch sheets of filo dough,
thawed or fresh
4 tablespoons unsalted butter, melted
Vanilla Sauce (page 18), for serving

■ ■ ■

1. Position a rack in the center of the oven and heat to 375°F. Lightly butter a 10 × 15-inch glass baking dish.

2. To make the cheese filling: In a large bowl, using a handheld electric mixer on high speed, beat the sugar and butter until light in color and texture, about 2 minutes. One at a time, beat in the egg yolks. Beat in the flour, raisins, and citron, if using. Stir in the sour cream, then the farmer's cheese.

3. In a medium bowl, using very clean beaters, beat the egg whites until the whites form soft peaks. Stir about one fourth of the whites into the cheese mixture, then fold in the rest.

4. To make the custard, transfer 2 cups of the cheese filling to a medium bowl and beat in the milk and eggs.

5. You will be making two strudels, placing them side by side in the dish. To make the first strudel, place one filo sheet on a large kitchen towel (at least 24 inches square), with the long side of the filo running horizontally. Using a soft pastry brush, drizzle and spread with some of the melted butter. Overlap with three sheets, buttering each sheet as it is laid down, to make a 17-inch square. About 1 inch from the bottom, spread half of the cheese filling in a thick log, leaving a 1-inch border at the sides. Using the towel as an aide, roll up the strudel. (The next step requires some nerve, but you will be surprised at the strudel's strength and flexibility.) Lift the strudel and transfer to the dish, placing the strudel about 1 inch from the edge of the dish. Tuck in the ends of the dough to fit the dish. Brush with the melted butter. Repeat with the remaining four filo sheets, filling, and melted butter, positioning the second strudel about 1 inch from the other side of the dish.

6. Bake for 10 minutes. Pour the reserved royale around (not over) the strudels. Bake until the strudel dough is golden brown, 30 to 40 minutes.

7. Remove from the oven and cool slightly (or up to 1 hour). Serve warm, with the custard clinging to the strudel, and a bit of vanilla sauce spooned on the side.

The filling and the custard (without the egg whites) can be prepared, covered, and refrigerated for up to 4 hours. Just before filling the strudel, beat the whites, fold them into the filling, and proceed. The strudel should be served warm, without reheating, although leftovers are delicious.

FARMER'S CHEESE AND RAISIN FILO STRUDEL
TOPFENSTRUDEL
Makes 12 servings

Not every café has a full-time baker. At many, it's just Mama in the kitchen, and often Mama doesn't feel like (or doesn't have enough counter space for) hand-pulling strudel dough. This classic recipe layers store-bought filo dough with a *Topfen* filling in a pan to make a deep-dish dessert. Thanks to Gerda Hofer for this recipe.

■ ■ ■

6 tablespoons (3/4 stick) unsalted butter, melted
20 ounces farmer's cheese
2 1/3 cups fresh bread crumbs
1 cup milk
10 tablespoons (1 1/4 sticks) unsalted butter, at cool room temperature
3/4 cup granulated sugar
Grated zest of 1 lemon
1 teaspoon vanilla extract
6 large eggs, separated, at room temperature
1 cup sour cream
1 cup golden raisins
12 12 × 17-inch sheets of fresh or thawed frozen filo
Confectioners' sugar, for garnish
Vanilla Sauce (page 18), optional

■ ■ ■

1. Position a rack in the center of the oven and heat to 350°F. Lightly brush a 13 × 9-inch glass baking dish with a little of the melted butter.
2. Using a rubber spatula, work the cheese through a medium-meshed wire sieve into a medium bowl. Stir the bread crumbs and milk in another medium bowl.

3. Beat the room-temperature butter in a large bowl with a handheld mixer on high speed until creamy. Add the sugar, lemon zest, and vanilla and beat until light in color and texture, about 2 minutes. Beat in the egg yolks, one at a time. Mix in the farmer's cheese, soaked bread crumbs, and sour cream.

4. In another medium bowl, using very clean beaters, beat the egg whites at high speed until they form stiff peaks. Stir about one fourth of the whites into the cheese mixture, then fold in the remaining whites. Fold in the raisins.

5. Place a filo sheet in the prepared pan, letting the excess dough hang over the sides. Using a soft brush, lightly brush the filo as best as you can with melted butter. Layer 5 more filo sheets, buttering each layer. Pour in the cheese mixture and spread evenly. Layer with 6 more filo sheets, buttering each layer and the top. Tuck the excess filo into the baking pan.

6. Bake until the top is golden brown, about 1 hour. Cool for 30 minutes. Dust the top of the strudel with confectioners' sugar. Serve warm or cooled, with the vanilla sauce, if you wish.

MAKE AHEAD
The strudel is best the day it is baked.

PEAR STRUDEL WITH PUFF PASTRY
BIRNENSTRUDEL AUS BUTTERTEIG
Makes 6 to 8 servings

When people say strudel, they mean the kind with the thin pastry. But many bakers also make it with puff pastry as a delicious alternative. Bosc pears are a good choice for this strudel as they hold their shape when baked and don't give off as much juice as other varieties, such as Comice or Anjou. A dusting of crumbs under the filling keeps the dough from getting soggy.

■ ■ ■
3 firm-ripe Bosc pears, peeled, cored,
and cut into ½-inch cubes
1 tablespoon golden rum
1 tablespoon fresh lemon juice
Grated zest of ½ lemon
⅓ cup sugar
⅓ cup raisins
⅛ teaspoon ground cinnamon
½ batch Puff Pastry (page 13)
½ cup cookie, cake, or dried bread crumbs
1 large egg, beaten, for brushing
■ ■ ■

1. Position a rack in the center of the oven and heat to 375°F. Line a large baking sheet with parchment paper.

2. Toss the pears, rum, lemon juice, and zest in a medium bowl. Mix in the sugar, raisins, and cinnamon.

3. Roll out the dough to a 16 × 10- inch rectangle on a lightly floured surface, with the long side facing you. Sprinkle the crumbs in a lengthwise, 3-inch-wide strip down the center of the dough. Heap the pear mixture over the crumbs, leaving a ¾-inch border at the short ends. Fold the top and bottom of the pastry over to cover the pears with a ½-inch overlap, brushing the area under the overlap with beaten egg, and pressing the edges of the dough together to seal. Transfer the roll to the baking sheet, seam side down, curving the roll into a gentle horseshoe shape. Fold the ends under the roll. Freeze for 15 minutes.

4. Brush the top of the roll with the egg. Bake until crisp and golden brown, about 40 minutes. Serve warm or cool to room temperature.

MAKE AHEAD
The strudel is best the day it is baked.

SWEET YEAST BREADS

Stuffed with cheese, nuts, poppy seeds, dried fruit, or preserves, twisted into braids or crescents, rolled into disks and topped with streusel or baked into fluted loaves, sweet breads are beloved by Austro-Hungarians from Prague to Budapest and beyond.

A heavy-duty standing mixer with a dough hook has become standard equipment in many kitchens, and the recipes in this chapter use it. Note that the ingredients for the doughs are first mixed together into a mass with the paddle blade (the dough hook is not designed for mixing), gathered by hand into a ball, and then kneaded with the dough hook. However, all of these breads can be made by hand. Simply mix all of the liquid ingredients and flavorings into a large bowl, and gradually stir in enough of the flour to make a soft, sticky dough. Turn out the dough onto a well-floured surface and knead, adding more flour as needed, until the dough is smooth.

Except when using very small amounts where it's easier to measure dry yeast, I use fresh compressed yeast for these breads. Every professional baker I've ever met prefers it, because they feel more "oomph" and a milder flavor than dried yeast. However, because it isn't reliably available in every supermarket, I also give measurements for active dry yeast. Unlike dry yeast, fresh yeast doesn't require warm liquid for dissolving. If using dry yeast, warm the milk to lukewarm (105° to 115°F.), as the tiny capsules of yeast need the tepid temperature to dissolve properly.

Most yeasted breads call for rising in an unspecified "warm place." This is never a problem in a professional bakery because hot ovens provide the perfect ambient temperature (about 78°F.). If your kitchen is cooler, that's fine. Your dough will simply take longer to rise. However, as all ovens should be well heated before baking, why not utilize its heat? Turn on the oven to the baking temperature, opening the door occasionally so the hot air can be released into the kitchen (but close the oven during the final fifteen minutes before baking). Sure, the oven is on for an hour or two, but it's money well spent if it gives the dough a comfortable place to rise. Place the bread in a spot near the oven, watching out for any hot exhaust. It's now in a place where you can keep an eye on its progress.

Many of these doughs are divided into buns, which should all be the same size so they bake at the same rate. One of the most efficient uses of a kitchen scale is to make uniformly sized rolls or buns. Weigh the entire batch of dough, then divide by the number of pieces you want. For example, if your dough weighs 2½ pounds (40 ounces or 1120 grams) and you want a dozen rolls, divide the total dough weight by 12. You should cut and weigh 3½-ounce or 90- to 95-gram portions.

Most professional bakeries are equipped with proofing boxes, enclosed cabinets that maintain just the right temperature and humidity for rising dough. Occasionally, when a dough might stick to a covering of plastic wrap, you can create your own mini-proofing box. Just slip the baking sheet with the formed bread into a "tall" kitchen garbage bag, and close the bag with a rubber band. If the dough seems sticky and likely to cling to the plastic, place a tall glass of hot water in the bag to keep the plastic from touching the bread (this adds humidity, too).

Unbaked sweet doughs don't freeze especially well because there is the chance that some yeast will die. If you know you are going to freeze the dough to bake later, increase the yeast by one fourth as a safeguard. But if you want to have fresh-baked sweet bread for a morning meal, there are two better options.

The best way is to bake and freeze the bread ahead of time, then defrost it overnight at room temperature, and warm it in an oven for serving. Remember that even frozen breads have a shelf life, and don't freeze them for longer than one month. The other option is to make the dough in the evening, and allow it to rise overnight in the refrigerator (don't forget to coat the dough well with softened butter and cover the bowl tightly with plastic wrap). The next morning, put the dough in a warm place for an hour or two so it can lose its chill. The dough is now ready to shape and rise again as the recipe directs. The disadvantage here is that the dough can sometimes develop a yeasty flavor, so keep the final rising time as short as you can.

Store sweet breads wrapped in aluminum foil at room temperature; plastic encourages the bread to get soggy. If the breads do get stale, they can usually be revived with a quick trip to the oven or toaster.

Coffee in Three-Quarter Time

If you are in a traditional café that offers live music, the chances are very good that the tunes will be in three-quarter time. From Austria, the waltz swept through the world like wildfire in the early 1800s.

While we look at the waltz as a quaint dance of restraint, it was considered scandalous when it was introduced to the Viennese aristocracy. It was one of the first dances that traveled from the lower classes up to the court instead of the other way around. Instead of the regimental, stately court dances, the waltz called for the partners to hold each other close, sexily face to face. The twirling and swirling made the dancers' hearts beat faster, and women were allowed to show a glow of perspiration. All of these factors made the waltz a notorious dance, and then, as now, notoriety sold tickets.

Most peasant communities had someone who could play the violin, an instrument that was easily transported from town to town to play music for the dances at social affairs like weddings. Many of these folk dances were in the now-familiar three-quarter time. When these songs were expanded for the big-city waltz orchestra, the violin became the primary instrument.

The senior Johann Strauss and Joseph Lanner were the two band leaders who brought the waltz into the urban arena. Their first successes were at the Dommayer, then a large casino in the village of Hietzing. Lanner formed his own band, an unusual step in a city whose orchestras were usually "pick-up" groups of free-agent musicians. Strauss played the violin while he conducted his orchestra. Strauss's son Johann turned the waltz into a worldwide phenomenon, using operettas as another way to carry his music to faraway places.

Today, many cafés offer live music, mostly during the weekends, free or with a very minimal charge. For a complete listing of the café concerts, get a brochure at a tourist board outlet in Vienna, or look in the local newspapers.

BRIOCHE BRAID
BRIOCHESTRIEZEL
Makes 1 very large braid

One morning, I sat in on baking classes at the prestigious technical school Berufsschule für den Lebensmittel-Textilbereich, Technische Zeichner und Zahntechniker, where they include textile design and dental technology along with culinary studies. I had already met some of the students because they were the apprentices at some of the best bakeries in Vienna. I recognized a young woman whom I had seen stretching strudel dough at Demel just the day before, and I was able to compliment her professionalism in front of her professor/chef. This put me in very good stead with the teachers, who responded by sharing some of their favorite recipes with me.

Here's a recipe for an outstanding sweet bread from Paul Skop, director of the BS LTZ. It is an old family favorite; the recipe he wrote down for me is entitled *Briochestriezel von Opa*, or "Grandpa's Brioche Braid." It makes a very large braid, one that just might last an entire weekend with lots of guests. Under normal circumstances, cut the loaf in half and freeze one piece for another time. Even stale, this bread can be revived in the toaster, and it also makes incredible French toast.

■ ■ ■

SPONGE
I ounce (¹/₂ cube) fresh compressed yeast or
3³/₄ teaspoons (about 1¹/₂ envelopes) active
dry yeast
¹/₂ cup milk (heated to 105° to 115°F.
if using dry yeast)
¹/₄ teaspoon sugar
¹/₂ cup unbleached flour

DOUGH
¹/₂ cup plus 2 tablespoons milk
³/₄ cup sugar
I large egg yolk
I tablespoon golden rum
I tablespoon fresh lemon juice
1¹/₄ teaspoons salt
3¹/₂ cups unbleached flour, as needed
7 tablespoons (¹/₂ stick plus 3 tablespoons)
unsalted butter, at room temperature
¹/₂ cup golden raisins

I large egg, well beaten, for glaze
3 tablespoons pearl sugar, optional (see Note)

■ ■ ■

1. To make the sponge: Crumble the yeast into the milk in a small bowl and add the sugar. Let stand for 3 minutes. Add the flour and whisk until smooth. Cover with plastic wrap and let stand in a warm place until bubbly and doubled in volume, about 30 minutes.

2. To make the dough: Mix the sponge, milk, sugar, egg yolk, rum, lemon juice, and salt in the bowl of a heavy-duty standing mixer. Attach to the mixer and fit with the paddle blade. On low speed, add enough of the flour (about 3¹/₂ cups) to make a sticky dough. One tablespoon at a time, beat in the butter, allowing each addition to be absorbed before adding more. The dough will look somewhat shaggy at this point.

3. Stop the machine and gather the dough in the bowl into a ball. Change to the dough hook. Knead the dough on medium-low speed, gradually adding about ¹/₄ cup flour, until the dough is smooth and glossy, about 6 minutes. During the last minute of kneading, add the raisins.

4. Transfer the dough to a lightly floured work surface and knead to check the texture; if the dough doesn't stick to the work surface, it has enough flour. Form into a ball and place in a large, well-buttered bowl. Turn the dough to coat with butter. Cover tightly with plastic wrap. Let stand in a warm place until doubled in volume, about 1¹/₂ hours.

5. Transfer the dough to a clean, flourless work surface and knead briefly. Cut the dough into three equal portions. Working with one piece of

dough at a time, loosely covering the other pieces with plastic wrap, roll the dough back and forth on the work surface, pressing down on the dough at the same time, slowly moving your hands apart until the dough is stretched into a 17-inch-long rope. As the ropes are formed, cover loosely with plastic wrap.

6. Line up the three ropes next to each other and perpendicular to yourself. Begin the braid from the center to one bottom end, dropping the ropes loosely into place without stretching them. When you have finished half of the braid, pinch the ends together. Flip the dough over with the unbraided ropes facing you. Braid from the center to the other end, and pinch the ends together.

7. Line a large baking sheet with parchment paper. Place the braid on the baking sheet and slip the sheet into a "tall" kitchen plastic bag. Close the bag and let stand in a warm spot until the braid is doubled in volume, 45 to 60 minutes.

8. Meanwhile, position a rack in the center of the oven and heat to 350°F. Remove the baking sheet from the plastic bag. Brush the braid with some of the beaten egg. Sprinkle with the pearl sugar, if using.

9. Bake until the braid is golden brown, 35 to 40 minutes. During the last 10 minutes of baking, if the braid seems to be browning too deeply, cover it loosely with aluminum foil. Transfer to a wire rack and cool completely.

MAKE AHEAD

The braid is best the same day it is baked, but it will keep for 1 or 2 days, wrapped in aluminum foil, stored at room temperature. It can also be frozen, wrapped in aluminum foil, for up to 1 month. To refresh the braid, reheat it, wrapped in foil, in a 350°F. oven for 10 to 15 minutes.

NOTE

Pearl sugar consists of large, round white crystals that do not dissolve when baked and are used as a decoration for sweet breads. It is available at specialty grocers and by mail order from La Cuisine and The Baker's Catalogue (see Mail-Order Sources, page 225).

CHEESE-FILLED SWEET ROLLS
BUCHTY
Makes 12 rolls

There's a Czech fairy tale about a hero who sustained himself during his adventures with these filling sweet rolls. This recipe came with the Bohemian bakers who emigrated to work for the elite in Vienna, where it eventually became *Buchteln* (see following recipe) They can be stuffed with the typical ingredients of the Austro-Hungarian baking world, (prune butter, apricot preserves, walnuts, or poppy seeds), but the farmer's cheese is especially popular.

■ ■ ■

SPONGE
1 ounce (½ cube) fresh compressed yeast or
3¾ teaspoons (about 1½ envelopes) active
dry yeast
½ cup milk (heated to 105° to 115°F.
if using dry yeast)
¼ teaspoon sugar
½ cup unbleached flour

DOUGH
2¾ cups unbleached flour, as needed
½ cup sugar
½ teaspoon salt
½ cup (1 stick) unsalted butter, chilled,
cut into ½-inch cubes
6 tablesoons milk
1 large egg
2 large egg yolks
1 teaspoon vanilla extract
½ teaspoon almond extract
Grated zest of 1 lemon

CHEESE FILLING
3 tablespoons confectioners' sugar
1½ tablespoons unsalted butter,
at cool room temperature
8 ounces farmer's cheese, rubbed through a
coarse wire sieve
1 large egg, separated, at room temperature
⅓ cup golden raisins

3 tablespoons unsalted butter, melted

■ ■ ■

1. To make the sponge: Crumble the yeast over the milk in a small bowl and add the sugar. Let stand for 3 minutes. Add the flour and whisk until smooth. Cover tightly with plastic wrap and let stand in a warm place until the mixture is bubbly and almost doubled in volume, about 30 minutes.

2. To make the dough: Stir the flour, the sugar, and the salt in the bowl of a heavy-duty standing mixer. Add the butter. Attach to the mixer and fit with the paddle blade. With the machine on low speed, mix until the mixture resembles coarse cornmeal. Add the sponge, milk, egg, yolks, vanilla, almond extract, and lemon zest and mix on low speed. Mix in additional flour as needed to make a somewhat sticky dough that pulls away from the sides of the bowl. Gather up the dough and transfer to a lightly floured work surface. Knead by hand just until the dough is smooth, about 2 minutes.

3. Gather the dough into a ball and place in a large buttered bowl. Turn to coat the dough with butter, then cover tightly. Let stand in a warm place until doubled in volume, about 1¼ hours.

4. Meanwhile, make the filling: Mash the sugar and butter together with a rubber spatula to combine. Beat in the cheese, then the egg yolk and raisins. Whisk the egg white in a small bowl until stiff, and fold into the cheese mixture.

5. Punch down the dough. Turn out onto a work surface and knead briefly. Using a sharp knife, cut the dough into twelve pieces and form each into a taut ball. Cover with plastic wrap and let stand for 10 minutes.

6. Butter a 13 × 9-inch baking pan. On the work surface, pat and stretch a ball of dough into a 4½-inch round. Place a generous tablespoon of the filling in the center of the dough. Bring up the edges of the circle to enclose the filling, and pinch closed. Place smooth side up in the pan. Repeat with the remaining dough and filling. Cover loosely with plastic wrap and let stand in a warm place until almost doubled, about 45 minutes.

7. Position a rack in the center of the oven and heat to 350°F. Brush the tops of the rolls with half of the melted butter. Bake until golden brown, 30 to 35 minutes. Remove from the oven and brush with the remaining butter (which may have solidified, but will melt in contact with the hot rolls). Cool for at least 20 minutes before serving warm or at room temperature.

MAKE AHEAD

The rolls are best the same day they are baked, but they will keep for 1 day, wrapped in aluminum foil, stored at room temperature. They can also be frozen, wrapped individually in foil, for up to 1 month. To refresh the rolls, reheat them, wrapped in foil, in a 350°F. oven for 10 to 15 minutes.

VIENNESE JAM ROLLS
BUCHTELN
Makes 15 rolls

At the venerable Café Hawelka, the witching hour is ten P.M., not midnight, for that is when the pastry chef's *Buchteln* hit the tables. In a matter of minutes, they magically disappear. Sure, you can enjoy these sweet rolls filled with preserves at room temperature at any time of the day, but served warm from the oven late at night, they are unsurpassable. They use a good amount of butter—in fact, many recipes say they should swim in the butter during baking. Thanks to Herr Schrammel at the Berufsschule für Bäcker und Konditoren for his recipe.

■ ■ ■

SPONGE
1 ounce (1/2 cube) compressed yeast or
3³/₄ teaspoons (about 1¹/₂ envelopes) active dry yeast
1/2 cup milk (heated to 105° to 115°F. if using dry yeast)
1/4 teaspoon sugar
1/2 cup unbleached flour

DOUGH
1/2 cup cold milk
1/3 cup sugar
1 large egg, beaten
1 teaspoon vanilla
1/2 teaspoon salt
2¹/₂ cups unbleached flour, as needed
5 tablespoons (1/2 stick plus 1 tablespoon) unsalted butter, at room temperature
2 tablespoons finely chopped candied citron, orange peel, or lemon peel (optional)

6 tablespoons (3/4 stick) unsalted butter, melted

1/3 cup prune butter (lekvar) or apricot preserves, approximately
Confectioners' sugar, for serving

■ ■ ■

1. To make the sponge: Crumble the yeast over the milk in a small bowl and add the sugar. Let stand for 3 minutes. Add the flour and whisk until smooth. Cover with plastic wrap and let stand in a warm place until bubbly and doubled in volume, about 30 minutes.

2. To make the dough: Mix the sponge, milk, sugar, egg, vanilla, and salt in the bowl of a heavy-duty electric mixer. Attach the bowl to the machine and fit with the paddle blade. With the machine on low speed, add enough of the flour to make a soft dough that cleans the sides of the bowl. One tablespoon at a time, beat in the butter. Add 3 or 4 more tablespoons flour until the dough cleans the sides of the bowl again. Gather the dough into a ball. Switch from the paddle blade to the dough hook. Return the dough to the bowl and knead on medium-low speed until the dough is smooth and slightly sticky, adding a little more flour if necessary, about 5 minutes. During the last minute, add the chopped citron, if desired.

3. Transfer the dough to a lightly floured work surface and knead to check the texture: If the dough doesn't stick to the work surface, it has enough flour. Form into a ball and place in a large, well-buttered bowl. Turn the dough to

coat with butter. Cover tightly with plastic wrap. Let stand in a warm place until doubled in volume, about 1¼ hours.

4. Tightly wrap the bottom of a 10-inch spring-form pan with aluminum foil (to prevent leaking butter). Pour the melted butter into a small bowl; it should be cooled but still liquid. Brush the pan generously with some of the butter.

5. Turn out the dough onto a clean surface and knead a few times. Stretch and pat out the dough into a 9 × 6-inch rectangle. Cover with a large sheet of plastic wrap and let rest for 5 minutes. Using a rolling pin, and keeping the plastic wrap on the dough, roll out to a 15 × 9-inch rectangle. Cut the dough into fifteen 3-inch squares.

6. Working with one square at a time, pat and stretch into a 4-inch square. Place a scant teaspoon of the lekvar in the center of the square. Bring up the corners of the dough to enclose the preserves and pinch closed. Pull the resulting four corners of dough up to the top and pinch closed, stretching the dough into a round bun. Turn the bun pinched-side down, dip in the melted butter, and place in the pan. Repeat with the remaining dough and preserves, placing the buns comfortably in the pan but allowing for some expansion. Slather the remaining butter over the buns. Cover with plastic wrap and let stand in a warm place until doubled in volume, 20 to 30 minutes.

7. Position a rack in the center of the oven and heat to 350°F. Bake until the rolls are golden brown, about 10 minutes. Cool the buns in the pan for 10 minutes. Remove the sides of the pan. To serve, break the buns apart and serve warm, sprinkled with the confectioners' sugar.

MAKE AHEAD

The rolls are best the same day they are baked, but they will keep for 1 day, wrapped in aluminum foil, stored at room temperature. They can also be frozen, wrapped individually in foil, for up to 1 month. To refresh the rolls, reheat them, wrapped in foil, in a 350°F. oven for 10 to 15 minutes.

VIENNESE CRESCENT ROLLS
KIPFERLN
Makes 12 crescents

Here are the authentic Viennese crescent rolls, based on the "Danish" sweet dough. Granted, with less sugar and no egg yolks in the dough, French croissants are flakier, but the jury is out as to which country's crescents are the most delicious.

If you are serving these for a brunch, make the dough the night before and roll it out the next morning. Allow 2 hours for the rolls to rise and another 20 minutes for them to bake.

■ ■ ■

½ batch Viennese Sweet Yeast Dough
(page 8)
1 large egg
⅛ teaspoon salt

■ ■ ■

1. On a lightly floured surface, roll out the dough into a 12-inch square. Cover the dough with plastic and let rest for 5 minutes. Line two baking sheets with parchment paper.

2. Using a pastry wheel or very sharp knife (you want clean cuts so the layers are not compressed), cut the dough in half lengthwise, making two 6 × 12-inch strips. Working with one strip at a time, stretch and pull out the upper right corner to bring the right side to an approximate 45-degree angle. Pull the lower left corner out to bring the left side to a 45-degree angle. Starting at the lower left corner, mark 4 inches in on the bottom of the strip. From this point, cut up diagonally to the upper left corner to make a 6-inch triangle with a 4-inch base. Make a mark 4 inches in on the top edge of the strip, and cut diagonally from the left corner to make another triangle. Continue in this manner to cut out four more triangles. Repeat with the other strip. If the dough has softened, refrigerate the triangles until they are chilled and firmer.

3. Roll out a triangle on a lightly floured surface to make it wider (about 5½ inches) and longer (about 7 inches). Starting at the base of the tri-

▪ THE STORY BEHIND ▪
KIPFERLN

The French may have refined the croissant, but they certainly didn't invent it. The flaky, buttery, crescent-shaped Kipferln had been a specialty of Viennese bakers for years before the Austrian princess Marie-Antoinette took them with her to her adopted country.

There is a distinction between the Kipfel, which is an everyday roll made from a simple yeast dough (Germteig), and the Kipferl, a fine, high-quality roll made from layered butter dough (Plunderteig, the so-called Danish pastry). In Viennese dialect, the addition of a "r" toward the end of certain words elevates their status. Kipfeln are plain rolls, but Kipferln are more special.

It would be nice to believe the stories that connect the crescent roll to the half-moon on the Turkish flag. These tales relate how the Viennese invented the roll to snub their hated Ottoman enemies: By eating a crescent roll you would be figuratively killing a Turk. Some sources cite the inventor as baker Peter Wendler, and some historians even say it was the wife of Georg Kolschitzky (who supposedly introduced coffee to the Viennese) who served them at the Blue Bottle coffeehouse. But Peter Wendler died three years before the Turkish siege, and it is questionable whether Kolschitzky had anything concrete to do with coffee at all.

Kipfel is related to the High German word for goat horns, *kipfa*. Well before the seventeenth century, horn-shaped rolls were baked in the cloisters for Easter, when animal imagery is common. Whatever the origin of the word, the crescent roll became the favorite bread of any self-respecting Viennese; it is said that Frau Constanze Mozart was especially fond of her breakfast Kipfel.

angle, roll up the triangle. Place it point side up or down, depending on your preference, on the baking sheet, and curve it into a crescent. Repeat with the remaining triangles, placing them 1½ inches apart. Cover loosely with plastic wrap. Let stand in a warm place until the crescents look puffed (they won't double in volume), about 2 hours. Be patient; it takes time for the chilled dough to rise.

4. Position the racks in the center and top third of the oven and heat to 400°F. Beat the egg and salt in a small bowl. Brush the tops of the crescents with the egg glaze. Bake, switching the sheets from top to bottom and front to back after 10 minutes, until the crescents are golden brown, about 20 minutes. (The crescents will seem a bit underdone inside at this point, but they will cook further as they cool.) Let cool completely on the sheets.

NUT-FILLED CRESCENTS

These are a specialty of Zauner Bakery in Bad Ischl, and are sometimes called Zaunerkipferln. Make the walnut filling for Apples in Pastry Robes on page 119. Before rolling up the crescent rolls, spread a scant tablespoon of filling on the base of the triangle.

MAKE AHEAD

The rolls are best the same day they are baked, but they will keep for 1 day, wrapped in aluminum foil, stored at room temperature. They can also be frozen, wrapped individually in foil, for up to 1 month. To refresh the rolls, reheat them, wrapped in foil, in a 350°F. oven for 10 to 15 minutes.

CURRANT AND HAZELNUT SNAILS
SCHNECKEN
Makes 16 rolls

These are a far cry from garden-variety cinnamon snails. With just a hint of spice, but lots of currants and ground hazelnuts, they have a distinctly European flair.

■ ■ ■

½ cup (2 ounces) toasted, peeled, and coarsely chopped hazelnuts
¼ cup sugar
¼ teaspoon ground cinnamon
Viennese Sweet Yeast Dough (page 8)
2 tablespoons unsalted butter, melted
½ cup dried currants
⅔ cup Apricot Glaze (page 16), warm

■ ■ ■

1. Position racks in the center and top third of the oven and heat to 375°F. Line two large baking sheets with parchment paper.

2. Process the hazelnuts, sugar, and cinnamon in a food processor fitted with the metal blade until the nuts are very finely chopped. Transfer to a bowl.

3. Cut the dough into two pieces. On a lightly floured work surface, roll out half of the dough into a 12 × 8-inch rectangle. Brush the dough with half of the melted butter. Sprinkle with half of the hazelnut sugar, then sprinkle with ¼ cup of the currants. Starting at a short end, roll up the dough into a tight cylinder, pinching the long seam closed as best as possible. Using a sharp knife, without compressing the layers, cut the dough into eight 1-inch-wide slices. Place the slices 1½ inches apart on the sheets. Repeat with the remaining dough, butter, hazelnut sugar, and currants. Cover the sheets with plastic wrap and let stand for 30 minutes.

4. Bake, switching the positions of the sheets from top to bottom and front to back halfway through baking, until the snails are golden brown, about 20 minutes. Transfer to wire racks and cool.

5. Brush the warm glaze over the snails and cool until the glaze sets.

MAKE AHEAD

The snails are best the day they are made. Or, bake, cool, and freeze the unglazed snails for up to 3 months. Glaze the snails before serving.

GOLDEN DUMPLINGS
ARANYGALUSKA
Makes 8 to 12 servings

One day at a very modest café in Budapest, I tasted this amazingly beautiful and delicious cake that reminded me of American "monkey bread," layers of round balls held together by a golden sugar-walnut crust. When I returned to the States and described it to my Hungarian friends, they knew exactly what I had enjoyed: Golden Dumplings. This is one of those recipes that every family has in its repertoire, perhaps because the dough doesn't require heavy kneading. The dumplings look very homey when layered in a baking dish or springform mold, but using a Gugelhupf pan makes a spectacular presentation.

■ ■ ■

SPONGE
²/₃ ounce (¹/₃ cube) compressed yeast or
2¹/₄ teaspoons (1 envelope) active dry yeast
¹/₂ cup milk (heated to 105° to 115°F.
if using dry yeast)
¹/₄ teaspoon sugar
¹/₂ cup unbleached flour

DOUGH
¹/₂ cup milk
4 tablespoons unsalted butter, melted
¹/₄ cup sugar
¹/₄ teaspoon salt
4 large egg yolks
2¹/₂ cups unbleached flour, as needed

2 tablespoons dried bread crumbs, for the pan
²/₃ cup sugar
³/₄ cup walnut pieces
Grated zest of 1 lemon
¹/₂ cup (1 stick) unsalted butter, melted and
cooled to lukewarm

■ ■ ■

1. To make the sponge: Crumble the yeast over the milk in a small bowl and add the sugar. Let stand for 3 minutes. Add the flour and whisk until smooth. Cover tightly with plastic wrap and let stand in a warm place until the mixture is bubbly and doubled in volume, about 30 minutes.

2. To make the dough: Stir the milk, melted butter, sugar, and salt in the bowl of a heavy-duty standing mixer. Add the egg yolks and the sponge. Attach the bowl to the mixer and fit with the paddle blade. With the machine on low speed, add enough of the flour to make a very stiff, somewhat sticky dough that pulls away from the sides of the bowl. Gather up the dough and transfer to a lightly floured work surface. Briefly knead by hand just until the dough is smooth.

3. Gather the dough into a ball and place in a large buttered bowl. Turn to coat the dough with butter, then cover tightly. Let stand in a warm place until doubled in volume, about 1¼ hours.

4. Punch down the dough and knead briefly. Using a sharp knife, cut the dough into 30 equal pieces. Rolling the dough between your palms, form it into balls. Place the balls on the work surface and cover loosely with plastic wrap.

5. Using a cylinder-shaped pastry brush, generously brush the inside of a 10-inch Gugelhupf or fluted tube pan with softened butter, sprinkle with the bread crumbs, and tap out the excess. Process the sugar, walnuts, and lemon zest in a food processor until the walnuts are very finely chopped, and pour into a medium bowl. Pour the melted butter into another bowl. One at a time, keeping the remaining balls covered, dip the balls in the melted butter to coat completely, then roll in the walnut mixture. Reserve any remaining butter. Arrange the balls in layers in the pan (don't worry if the layers are not exactly even). Cover with plastic wrap and let stand in a warm place until the dough is almost doubled in volume, about 45 minutes.

6. Position a rack in the center of the oven and heat to 350°F. Bake for 20 minutes. Cover the pan loosely with aluminum foil and continue baking until the dumplings are golden brown (an instant-read thermometer inserted in the dumplings will read 200°F.). Brush the crusty parts on the exposed top of the dumplings with the reserved butter. Cool in the pan for 5 minutes, then invert onto a plate and cool until warm or room temperature. To serve, break apart the dumplings.

MAKE AHEAD

The rolls are best the same day they are baked, but they will keep for 1 day, wrapped in aluminum foil, stored at room temperature. They can also be frozen, wrapped in aluminum foil, for up to 1 month. To refresh the rolls, reheat them, wrapped in foil, in a 350°F. oven for about 15 minutes.

DALMATIAN FOUR-FLAVOR KOLACKY
DOMAŽLICÉ KOLAČE
Makes 12 kolacky

In Czech, *kolače* literally means any round pastry, but it has come to specify those made with a sweet yeast dough. There are many, many ways to shape and fill kolacky (as we call them here), but every Prague bakery seems to make *Domažlicé kolače*, or Dalmatian-style kolacky, which are like small sweet pizzas with poppy seed, farmer's cheese, apricot, and prune butter toppings.

■ ■ ■

SPONGE
1 ounce (½ cube) fresh compressed yeast or
3¾ teaspoons (about 1½ envelopes) active dry yeast
½ cup milk (heat to 105° to 115°F.
if using dry yeast)
½ cup unbleached flour
¼ teaspoon sugar

DOUGH
⅔ cup (1 stick plus 2 tablespoons) unsalted butter, at cool room temperature
⅓ cup sugar
3 large egg yolks
½ cup milk
1 teaspoon vanilla extract
¼ teaspoon salt
Grated zest of ½ lemon

3½ cups unbleached flour, as needed

Farmer's Cheese Filling (recipe follows)
Poppy Seed Filling (recipe follows)
¼ cup prune butter (lekvar)
¼ cup apricot preserves

STREUSEL
2 tablespoons unbleached flour
1 tablespoon sugar
1 tablespoon unsalted butter,
at cool room temperature

1 large egg yolk beaten with 1 teaspoon milk, for glazing

■ ■ ■

1. To make the sponge: Crumble the yeast over the milk in a small bowl. Let stand for 3 minutes. Add the flour and the sugar and whisk until smooth. Cover tightly with plastic wrap and let stand in a warm place until the mixture is bubbly and doubled in volume, about 30 minutes.

2. To make the dough: Beat the butter in a heavy-duty standing mixer fitted with the paddle blade on high speed until creamy, about 1 minute. Beat in the sugar and mix until light in color and texture, about 2 minutes. Add the sponge. On low speed, add the yolks, one at a time, then the milk, vanilla, salt, and lemon zest. Gradually mix in enough of the flour to make a soft, sticky dough. Gather up the dough into a ball. Change to the dough hook. Knead the dough on medium-low speed until the dough is smooth and supple, but slightly sticky, about 6 minutes.

3. Form the dough into a ball and place in a well-buttered medium bowl. Turn to coat the dough with butter, and cover tightly with plastic wrap. Let stand in a warm place until doubled in volume, about 1¼ hours.

4. Turn out the dough onto an unfloured work surface and knead briefly. Cut into 12 pieces, then form each piece into a ball. Cover with plastic wrap and let stand for 5 minutes.

5. Line two large baking sheets with parchment paper. Working with one ball at a time, on an unfloured work surface, roll out into a 4-inch round. In each quadrant of the round, about 1

inch from the edge of the round, place a heaping teaspoon of one of each of the fillings. (Each pastry will contain all four fillings.) Transfer to the baking sheet. Repeat with the remaining dough and fillings, placing the rounds about 1½ inches apart on the sheets. Cover loosely with plastic wrap and let stand in a warm place until puffed, about 40 minutes.

6. Meanwhile, make the streusel. Using your fingertips, combine the flour, sugar and butter until crumbly; set aside.

7. Position racks in the top third and center of the oven and heat to 350°F. Brush the edges of the dough with the egg mixture. Sprinkle the tops of the kolacky with the streusel.

8. Bake until golden brown, switching the positions of the sheets from top to bottom and front to back halfway through baking, about 20 minutes. Serve warm or cooled to room temperature.

FARMER'S CHEESE FILLING

Cream 1 tablespoon softened butter with 1 tablespoon sugar in a small bowl. Add a heaping ⅓ cup farmer's cheese, 2 teaspoons beaten egg yolk, 1 tablespoon raisins, and a few gratings of lemon zest.

POPPY SEED FILLING

Grind ⅓ cup poppy seeds in an electric coffee grinder. Pour into a small saucepan and add 3 tablespoons milk, 1 tablespoon black currant preserves, 1½ teaspoons sugar, and ¼ teaspoon Dutch-processed cocoa powder. Bring to a boil over low heat, stirring often, and cook until thickened, about 1 minute. Cool completely.

MAKE AHEAD

The rolls are best the same day they are baked, but they will keep for 1 day, wrapped in aluminum foil, stored at room temperature. They can also be frozen, wrapped individually in foil, for up to 1 month. To refresh the rolls, reheat them, wrapped in foil, in a 350°F. oven for 10 to 15 minutes.

YEAST GUGELHUPF
GERMGUGELHUPF
Makes 8 to 12 servings

Gugelhupf is a versatile Viennese specialty that can be made by many methods in different sizes and flavors. The original version is a sweet yeast dough, but when baking powder became available, some (but not all) cooks embraced the new, easy-to-use leavening. This classic version uses yeast, but it is more of a beaten batter than a kneaded dough, and it makes a very moist and rich cake, perfect for an afternoon Jause. The egg whites give this dough a lovely light texture.

■ ■ ■

SPONGE
1 ounce (½ cube) fresh compressed yeast or
3¾ teaspoons (about 1½ envelopes) active
dry yeast
1 cup milk (heated to 110° to 115°F.
if using dry yeast)
½ teaspoon sugar
1 cup unbleached flour

DOUGH
12 tablespoons (1½ sticks) unsalted butter,
at cool room temperature
½ cup sugar
4 large eggs, separated, at room temperature
1 tablespoon golden rum
1 teaspoon vanilla extract
Grated zest of 1 lemon
½ teaspoon salt
3 cups unbleached flour, as needed
1 cup golden raisins

¼ cup sliced almonds
Confectioners' sugar, for serving

■ ■ ■

1. For the sponge: Crumble the yeast into the milk in a medium bowl and add the sugar. Let stand 3 minutes. Add the flour and whisk until smooth. Cover with plastic wrap and let stand in a warm place until bubbly and doubled in volume, about 30 minutes.

2. For the dough: Beat the butter and sugar in the bowl of a heavy-duty standing mixer fitted with the paddle blade on high speed, until light in color and texture, about 2 minutes. Add the sponge, and then beat on low speed. Add the egg yolks, one at a time, then the rum, vanilla, lemon zest, and salt. Gradually mix in enough of the flour to make a soft dough that barely leaves the sides of the bowl. Let the dough mix for a minute or two before deciding to add more flour —it takes time to come together. Beat with the paddle blade until smooth, occasionally scraping the dough off the blade, about 5 minutes.

3. Beat the egg whites in a grease-free medium bowl with a handheld electric mixer on high speed until stiff peaks form. Before adding the whites to the batter, scrape all of the batter off the paddle blade. On low speed, gradually beat the whites into the dough until they are incorporated. The whites will deflate, and the dough will become a batter. Mix in the raisins.

4. Generously butter a 9- to 9½-inch Gugelhupf or fluted tube pan. Sprinkle the almonds in the pan, pressing them to adhere to the sides. Spread the batter evenly in the pan. Place the pan in a large plastic bag. Put a tall glass of hot water in the bag next to the pan so the plastic doesn't touch the top of the pan, and close the bag. Let stand in a warm place until the dough fills the pan by three quarters, about 1 hour.

5. Position a rack in the center of the oven and heat to 350°F. Bake for 30 minutes. Cover the top of the pan loosely with aluminum foil to prevent overbrowning. Continue baking until the top is golden brown and an instant-read thermometer inserted in the loaf reads 200°F., about 30 minutes more. Cool on a wire rack for 10 minutes. Unmold onto the rack and cool completely. Sift generously with confectioners' sugar before serving.

MAKE AHEAD

The Gugelhupf is best the same day it is baked, but it will keep for 1 or 2 days, wrapped in aluminum foil, stored at room temperature. It can also be frozen, double wrapped in plastic wrap and aluminum foil, for up to 1 month. To refresh the bread, reheat it, wrapped in foil, in a 350°F. oven for 10 to 15 minutes, or cut it into slices and toast.

▪ THE STORY BEHIND ▪
GUGELHUPF

Keeping up the tradition of quaint Viennese culinary tales, some sources say that the Gugelhupf's design was modeled after the folds in a Turk's turban; thus eating a turban-shaped cake showed hatred for the enemy.

Actually, the wavy design in a Gugelhupf mold dates back to Roman times—bronze molds have been found throughout the Roman Empire in almost the same pattern—and it is assumed that the markings are meant to symbolize the rays of the sun. There are a few ways that the word could have derived. In Austrian dialect, *Gugl* means "bandanna" and *Kopf* means "head," and the mold does look like something a worker would tie around his head. In German *Kogel* means "peak," another reference that is easy to see. Germans spell the cake *Kugelhopf*, as do the French. (The cake arrived in France via Alsace and the Austrian members of the French court.)

Gugelhupf acquired its revered status in Austrian history as one of the favorite dishes of Emperor Franz Joseph. During the summer, when his court was ensconced in Bad Ischl, it was his habit to end his morning walk at the villa of his great friend, the actress Katharina Schratt, where she always had homemade, freshly baked Gugelhupf waiting for him. In case there was an unforeseen accident in her kitchen, she always had a backup, ordered from Zauner, the town's premier bakery.

YEAST PLUM SQUARES
GERMZWETSCHKENFLECK
Makes 1 large cake, 12 to 15 servings

Every good Austrian baker has two recipes for plum squares on file—one with yeast, and one without. This yeast version gilds the lily with a streusel topping. Dark purple Italian plums (often called prune plums) are best because they don't give off as much juice as other varieties (the juice can make the dough soggy). See page 38 for a version without yeast.

■ ■ ■

SPONGE
1½ ounces (¾ cube) fresh compressed yeast or 3¾ teaspoons (1½ envelopes) active dry yeast
½ cup milk (heated to 105° to 115°F. if using dry yeast)
½ cup unbleached flour
¼ teaspoon sugar

DOUGH
½ cup milk
⅓ cup sugar
1 tablespoon golden rum
1 teaspoon vanilla extract
½ teaspoon salt
4 tablespoons unsalted butter, melted
1 large egg, beaten
2¾ cups unbleached flour, as needed

1½ pounds (about 20) Italian plums, cut in half lengthwise and pitted

STREUSEL
⅔ cup unbleached flour
⅓ cup sugar
⅓ cup (½ stick plus 1 tablespoon) unsalted butter, cut into ½-inch cubes, chilled
¼ teaspoon vanilla extract
Pinch of ground cinnamon

1 tablespoon unsalted butter, melted, for brushing

■ ■ ■

The Municipal House

Next to the twelfth-century Powder House tower in Prague's old town stands a pastel yellow edifice with intricate, colorful decorations from top to bottom. The Municipal House opened in 1912 as the finishing touch to a huge modernization project that was meant to bring Prague up to the standards of other European capitals. The building houses a concert hall, many reception rooms, a series of restaurants and bars, and one of the most beautiful cafés in the world.

The Municipal House Café (Kavárna Obecní dům) is often called Café Nouveau, because it is such a perfect representative of the Czech Art Nouveau style. Art Nouveau ("New Art" in French) and its Viennese offshoot, Jugendstil ("Youth Style"), had undulating lines and repetitive forms that were inspired by nature, such as flowering vines. In Vienna, the leading proponent was Gustav Klimt. Prague's Alfons Mucha took his art to Paris, where his influence was felt in the commerical and theatrical posters of the time. It has remained in the collective consciousness of graphic art ever since (many a 1960s college dorm room was decorated with a Mucha print). Mucha was just one of the Czech artists called upon to help embellish the Municipal House with its countless mosaics, murals, frescoes, gargoyles, columns, portals, and other decorative architectural touches.

The renovation of the café was finished in 1997. What you now see is a long gallery with leather-covered booths, mahogany trimming, magnificent chandeliers, and an unusual altar-like marble fountain at the end of the room. It is guaranteed to be one of the most beautiful places in which you'll ever drink a cup of coffee.

Oberlaa: The Whipped Cream Diet

One morning, my friend Karitas and I took the tram out to the flagship bakery and main kitchen of Oberlaa. There are four Oberlaa café–restaurants now throughout Vienna, but the original was built to house a garden show in the 1970s. When the garden show left the premises, Oberlaa was transformed into a spa, complete with all the sports equipment and beauty treatments required, and then some. Somewhat perversely, it is also known as being one of the best bakeries in town.

After a tour of the kitchen, where we observed cakes being baked and finished and the hand-dipping of mountains of chocolates, the head chef, Vinzenz Bäuerle, took us into the gleaming café. (It should be noted that the young chef is as slim as a pastry chef could ever be, perhaps a testament to the spa's treatments.) The dessert case was filled with row after row of some of the most picture-perfect pastries imaginable. At Vinzenz's invitation, we took a modest selection (of about six pastries for the two of us) and went into our tasting mode, in which we promised ourselves to take only a bite, but actually cleaned the plates. These desserts tasted even better than they looked.

I asked Vinzenz why a spa, where people come to lose weight, would pose so many temptations to its guests. He looked puzzled.

"One comes to a spa to make one feel good about oneself. And what makes you feel better than a piece of good cake?"

Sounds like perfect reasoning to me.

1. To make the sponge: Crumble the yeast over the milk in a medium bowl. Let stand for 3 minutes. Add the flour and sugar and whisk until smooth. Cover tightly with plastic wrap. Let stand in a warm place until bubbly and doubled in volume, about 30 minutes.

2. To make the dough: Mix the sponge, milk, sugar, rum, vanilla, and salt in the bowl of a heavy-duty standing mixer. Stir in the melted butter and the egg. Attach to the machine and fit with the paddle blade. On low speed, add enough of the flour to make a soft, sticky dough. Gather the dough into a ball and return to the bowl. Change to the dough hook. Knead the dough on medium speed until smooth, about 5 minutes.

3. Transfer the dough to a large buttered bowl and turn to coat with the butter. Cover tightly with plastic wrap and let stand in a warm place until doubled in volume, about 1 hour.

4. Punch down the dough. Butter a 17 × 12 × 1-inch pan. Stretch and pat the dough into the pan. Cover with plastic wrap and let stand for 5 minutes. If the dough shrinks, pull it back into the pan's corners. Top the dough with rows of the plums, skin sides down. Cover again with plastic wrap and let stand in a warm place until the dough looks puffy, about 30 minutes.

5. Meanwhile, position a rack in the center of the oven and heat to 350°F.

6. To make the streusel: Mix the flour, sugar, butter, vanilla, and cinnamon in a small bowl. Using your fingertips, blend the ingredients until crumbly. Sprinkle the streusel over the plums.

7. Bake until the crust is golden brown, 30 to 35 minutes. Brush the crust with the melted butter. Serve warm or cooled to room temperature.

MAKE AHEAD

The cake is best served the day it is baked. It will also keep for 1 day, wrapped in aluminum foil and stored at room temperature. To refresh the cake, reheat, wrapped in foil, in a 350°F. oven for 10 to 15 minutes.

CHRISTMAS SWEET BREAD
STOLLEN
Makes 2 loaves

Stollen is the traditional Christmas bread in German-speaking countries. It gets its name from its shape, which resembles a stole, or more specifically, the Christ Child's swaddling clothes. Some people think that stollen is best when aged for at least a day or two before serving. If it seems dry, toast slices and serve them buttered. This recipe is based on one from my friend Beth Hensperger, one of America's great bakers, who is of Hungarian heritage. European bakers would use candied fruit peels in their stollen, but Beth's selection of dried fruits is colorful and more tasty, and her use of the soaking liquid to add flavor to the dough is inspired. The addition of almond paste was a suggestion from the bakers at Oberlaa, one of the newest and best of Vienna's Konditorein.

■ ■ ■

SOAKED FRUITS
3/4 cup dried tart cherries
1/2 cup coarsely chopped dried apricots
1/4 cup dried currants
1/4 cup golden raisins
3 tablespoons golden rum
1/2 cup hot water, as needed
2 tablespoons unbleached flour

SPONGE
1/2 cup milk
1 ounce (1/2 cube) fresh compressed yeast or
3 3/4 teaspoons (about 1 1/2 envelopes) active
dry yeast
3/4 cup unbleached flour

DOUGH
2 1/2 cups unbleached flour, divided
1 cup sliced natural almonds
1/2 cup (1 stick) unsalted butter,
at room temperature
1/3 cup granulated sugar
1 large egg
1 large egg yolk
1/2 teaspoon almond extract
Grated zest of 1 lemon
1 teaspoon salt

2 tablespoons unsalted butter, melted,
for brushing
2 tablespoons granulated sugar mixed with
1/2 teaspoon grated nutmeg, for sprinkling
2 ounces almond paste, cut into
1/2-inch cubes (about 1/3 cup)
3/4 cup confectioners' sugar, for dredging

■ ■ ■

1. To prepare the soaked fruits: Combine the cherries, apricots, currants, and raisins in a small bowl. Add the rum and enough hot water to barely cover the fruits. Stir well and cover. Let stand until the fruits are plumped, at least 1 hour or overnight. Drain the fruits well, reserving 1/4 cup of the soaking liquid. Pat the fruits dry with paper towels.

2. To make the sponge: Add the milk to the 1/4 cup of the fruit soaking liquid in a medium bowl. (If using dry yeast, heat the liquids to 105° to 115°F.) Crumble the yeast into the mixture. Let stand for 3 minutes. Add the 3/4 cup of flour and whisk until smooth. Cover with plastic wrap and let stand in a warm place until bubbly and doubled in volume, about 30 minutes.

3. To make the dough: Process 1 cup of the flour and the almonds in a food processor fitted with the metal blade until the almonds are very finely ground. Add the remaining flour and pulse until combined.

4. In the bowl of a heavy-duty standing mixer fitted with the paddle blade, beat the butter and sugar on high speed until light in color and texture, about 2 minutes. Remove the bowl from the stand and add the sponge, egg, yolk, almond extract, lemon zest, and salt. On low speed, add enough of the almond-flour to make a soft, sticky dough that cleans the side of the bowl. Gather up the dough into a ball. Switch to the dough hook and knead the dough on medium speed until the dough is soft and supple, but still quite sticky, about 7 minutes.

5. Toss the soaked fruits with the 2 tablespoons of flour to coat. Transfer the dough to a lightly floured work surface, press the dough into a thick disk, sprinkle with some of the fruit, fold, and knead briefly. Repeat until all of the fruit has been added. If necessary, work in a bit more

flour during kneading, but do not add too much —the dough should be soft and sticky, but not so moist that it sticks to the work surface. Gather the dough into a ball and place in a large buttered bowl. Turn to coat the ball with butter. Cover tightly with plastic wrap and let stand until doubled in volume, about 1½ hours.

6. Without kneading the dough, cut it in half. On a lightly floured surface, pat and stretch one half of the dough into a 12 × 7-inch oval with rounded points. Brush the oval with some of the butter and sprinkle with half of the nutmeg-sugar. Sprinkle half of the almond paste cubes down the center of the oval. Without stretching the dough, fold the stollen in half lengthwise to ¾ inch from the opposite side (it will be slightly off center), enclosing the almond paste. Lightly press the top edge to seal. Repeat with the other half of dough.

7. Line a large baking sheet with parchment paper. Place the stollen 4 inches apart on the sheet. Cover loosely with plastic wrap and let stand in a warm place until puffy but not doubled in volume, about 30 minutes.

8. Position a rack in the center of the oven and heat to 350°F. Brush the tops of the stollen with the remaining melted butter. Bake until lightly browned, about 40 minutes. During the last 15 minutes, tent the loaves with aluminum foil. Do not overbake. Cool on the baking sheet for 10 minutes.

9. Sift about half of the confectioners' sugar onto a work surface. Place the warm stollen in the pan, and sift with a heavy coating of more sugar. Let cool in the sugar. Wrap in aluminum foil to store. Coat again in confectioners' sugar before serving.

MAKE AHEAD

The stollen will keep for up to 2 weeks, wrapped in aluminum foil and stored at room temperature. It can also be frozen, wrapped in aluminum foil, for up to 1 month. To refresh the bread, reheat it, wrapped in foil, in a 350°F. oven for 10 to 15 minutes, or cut it into slices and toast in a toaster oven (the sugar will melt and drip in a regular toaster).

HUNGARIAN WALNUT ROULADES
BEIGLI
Makes two 9-inch rolls

Christmas is the time for beigli; the nut-filled roulades are sold in every bakery in Budapest. Like Vienna's Faschingkrapfen, what used to be a holiday treat can now be found year-round, but they are still considered a special treat. And like our fruitcake, there are very good ones and not so good ones, and some fresh or not so fresh, so they can be the butt of Hungarian jokes. But a first-class beigli, with its firm but tender crust, crackled exterior, and moist filling, is a delight. The crumb should be tight, so the rising is carefully modulated with refrigeration (which makes sense because in the old days the weather would have been cold during beigli-making season, and finding a warm place for rising would have been harder than it is today). This recipe for walnut beigli, with dried fruit in the filling to give it extra moistness, is from one of the oldest bakeries in the world in continuous operation, Budapest's Ruszwurm Cukrászda.

■ ■ ■

WALNUT FILLING
2¼ cups coarsely chopped walnuts
½ cup cake or bread crumbs
2 tablespoons raisins
2 pitted prunes, coarsely chopped
2 tablespoons candied orange peel
Pinch of ground cinnamon

²/₃ cup sugar
¹/₄ cup water
2 tablespoons honey
Grated zest of 1 lemon

DOUGH
1 teaspoon active dry yeast
¹/₂ cup milk, heated to 105° to 115°F.
2 cups unbleached flour
3 tablespoons sugar
Pinch of salt
7 tablespoons (³/₄ stick plus 1 tablespoon)
unsalted butter, cut into ¹/₂-inch cubes, chilled

1 large egg, separated, yolk and white
beaten separately

■ ■ ■

1. To make the filling: Process the walnuts, crumbs, raisins, prunes, candied peel, and cinnamon in a food processor fitted with the metal blade until the walnuts and fruits are very finely chopped. Transfer to a medium bowl. Bring the sugar, water, honey, and lemon zest to a boil in a small saucepan over high heat. Pour over the walnut mixture and stir well. Cool completely.

2. To make the dough: Sprinkle the yeast over the milk in a small bowl. Let stand 5 minutes, then stir to dissolve.

3. Stir the flour, sugar, and salt in the large bowl of a heavy-duty standing mixer. Add the butter. Attach to the mixer fitted with the paddle blade. Mix on low speed until the mixture looks crumbly. Add the dissolved yeast and mix to form a soft, sticky dough that cleans the sides of the

bowl. Gather into a ball and return to the bowl. Change to the dough hook and knead the dough on medium speed, adding sprinkles of flour as needed to keep it from sticking, until the dough is smooth, about 5 minutes. Wrap in plastic wrap and refrigerate for 15 minutes.

4. Line a large baking sheet with parchment paper. Cut the dough in half. Roll one piece of the dough on a lightly floured work surface into a 10 × 8-inch rectangle. Spread half of the filling over the dough, leaving a ¹/₂ inch border on all sides. Fold in the short sides. Starting at a long side, roll up the dough into a tight cylinder; pinch seams closed. Transfer to the baking sheet, seam down. Repeat with the remaining dough and filling. Brush the rolls with the beaten egg yolk. Refrigerate, uncovered, until the yolk glaze dries, about 1 hour.

5. Remove the rolls from the refrigerator and brush with the egg white. Let stand in a warm place until the egg white dries, about 45 minutes. (The rolls will barely rise.)

6. Position a rack in the center of the oven and heat to 375°F. Pierce each roll 3 times with a fork. Bake the rolls until golden brown, 25 to 30 minutes. Cool completely. To serve, cut into thin slices, and arrange in an overlapping pattern on a serving platter.

MAKE AHEAD
The rolls will keep for up to 2 weeks, wrapped tightly, stored at cool room temperature.

"SLICES" & OTHER INDIVIDUAL DESSERTS

As far as Austro-Hungarian bakers are concerned, when a pastry is baked free-form, served free-standing, or not cut from a Torte or Kuchen, it belongs to yet another dessert category.

Slices, or *Schnitten*, could be thought of as rectangular Torten, cut into slabs. While they are often only slightly less intricate than their fancy relations, they can feature more straightforward, less sophis-ticated flavor combinations, such as bananas and chocolate.

Stückdessert, literally "Piece Dessert," are individually formed pastries, often created from puff pastry or Viennese sweet yeast dough. It can be argued that some sweet yeast breads, such as Kip-ferln, belong in this category, but there are always gray zones and overlaps in the subject of Austro-Hungarian dessert categorization.

The Rise of the Kaffeehaus

"A place where people want to be alone, but need company to do so."

—Alfred Polgár (speaking of Café Central)

When Viennese coffeehouses came into their own in the early 1700s, the proprietors wanted to do more than serve beverages like a common inn. They needed to make their establishments distinctive. Someone took up the English custom of having free local newspapers available for the perusal of the clientele. By the 1720s, foreign newspapers began to appear in the coffeehouses, playing up to the merchant class who needed to know what was happening in Amsterdam or Berlin.

The new sport of billiards prompted other cafés to open playing rooms adjacent to the dining room. These rooms were necessarily long to hold the rectangular tables. Coffeehouses began being built on corner properties in an "L" shape. This allowed as much sunlight as possible to shine in so people could read more easily. One room was reserved for serving coffee and reading newspapers, and the other was for shooting billiards. At the junction of the two rooms was the cashier, usually a lady, who watched over the proceedings with an eagle eye. By 1736, an imperial decree gave coffeehouses tax-exempt status, an economy-increasing move, as people could drink freely without any additional costs added onto their coffee.

The Congress of Vienna in 1815 showed these refined establishments off to the world. By 1819, there were 150 coffeehouses in Vienna. After the Congress, Metternich suspected that a network of spies had stayed behind in the city to extract political secrets from the Hofburg, and he began a secret police effort to find the offenders. The Viennese began to suffer under the oppression of rumors and accusations.

To avoid being rounded up by the not-so-secret police, the citizens took two tactics. First, they simply stayed at home, running their lives along the straight and narrow and strengthening the rise of the middle class. Entertaining guests in well-appointed (but not ostentatious) homes became an art. Hosts and hostesses invited their guests to enjoy an evening of music; Schubert was a popular figure on the musicale circuit. Fine desserts were an expected part of the package. New cookbooks appeared to teach housewives how to bake, and bakeries were given ample opportunity to practice their art.

Coffeehouses provided the other means of escape. Their crowded atmosphere made it virtually impossible for a spy to overhear any conversation, subversive or not. Coffeehouses added mirrors, plush fabrics, and chandeliers to simulate the cozy interior of the Viennese home, and music to soothe caffeine-jangled nerves. The era from 1814 to 1848, characterized by the rising of the middle class and its expression of culture through home life, became known as the Biedermeier period. "Gottlieb Biedermaier" (which translates to something like "God-loving Goody-two-shoes") was a shy do-gooder in some satirical verses by Ludwig Eichrodt that were published in the 1850s. *Biedermeier* (with an "e") became the accepted spelling later.

The Revolution of 1848 got rid of the elderly Metternich and his puppet, the emperor Ferdinand, replacing the two with the eighteen-year-old Franz Joseph. He was not a popular ruler from the start. The old city ramparts had been barely holding together since the Turkish invasion, and Franz Joseph decreed that they be razed. They were to be replaced with an impressive *grand boulevard*, the Ringstrasse, lined with the important civic buildings of the city and court. These buildings were designed in the heavily ornamented Neoclassic mode, drawing from Gothic, Roman, Greek, and other styles of architecture. In 1873, Vienna held a world exhibition to celebrate Franz Joseph's first twenty-five years of rule, and to show off the Ringstrasse and the other pleasures of the city, including, of course, the coffeehouses.

Now began the golden age of the Kaffeehaus. Entire literary movements were formed around coffeehouse tables. The most famous of all the literary cafés was Café Griensteidl, opened in 1847 and home to "Young Vienna," a group of upstarts who wanted to do away with the stuffy confines of Neoclassicism in favor of the new and untried. Names like Hermann Bahr, Felix Dörmann, and Karl Kraus are best known to devotees of Austrian literature, but some of them made an impact on world culture. Hugo von Hofmannsthal was a wunderkind–poet who became the librettist for Richard Strauss's most enduring operas; Felix Salten wrote *Bambi,* which remains a children's literature classic; the plays of Arthur Schnitzler, particularly *Reigen* (usually called *La Ronde* in English and French productions), are still performed.

Griensteidl was torn down in 1897 (the café that now stands on the spot is a reproduction of the original, built almost one hundred years later). Young Vienna packed up and moved lock, stock, and coffee cup to Café Central, right up the street. The stars here were Egon Friedell and Alfred Polgár, but they were out-classed by Peter Altenberg, the personification of eccentric, sandal-wearing bohemian writers (it is said that his final illness was complicated by his insistence on wearing sandals in the snow). Today, a life-size, painted statue of Altenberg sits at his table at the Central.

A monument to Adolf Loos's minimalist style, Café Museum opened in 1899, shocking the establishment. Instead of the opulent surroundings they had come to expect in a coffeehouse, Loos gave them a room that expounded his philosophy of function dictating form. This place attracted a more theatrical crowd, drawing such regulars as Erich Wolfgang Korngold (remembered best for his Hollywood scores of the 1930s and '40s), Alban Berg (whose music was as atonal as Korngold's was florid), Frank Wedekind (the forerunner of Expressionism, whose plays *Pandora's Box* and *Earth Spirit* were the basis for Berg's opera *Lulu*), and operetta composers Oscar Straus and Franz Léhar. Artists like Oskar Kokoschka and Egon Schiele dipped their Kipferln here.

During this period, the coffeehouse was evolving from a refuge for the middle class to a democratic place where anyone could sit for hours for the price of a coffee. By no means were the celebrity Stammgäste ("regular customers") always rich and famous while they were regulars at their favorite café. Vienna was tragically overpopulated, and housing for the lower classes was dismal. Many people went to the coffeehouse to warm up. Because so many writers could be found sitting at their favorite table hour after hour, cafés began taking phone calls and mail deliveries for their best guests. (Peter Altenberg's calling card gave the Café Central as his address!) The cafés were to flourish until the end of World War I, and the subsequent fall of the Hapsburgs.

APPLE, WALNUT, AND POPPY SEED BARS
FLÓDNI
Makes 12 large bars

Flódni are tall, triple-layer bars—a hearty, delicious snack created by the Jews of Hungary. The same dough and fillings can be rolled into cylinder shapes, in which case they are called *kindli*. To keep the kitchen kosher, many Jewish cooks didn't cook with butter (even though it was allowed under some circumstances), substituting chicken or goose fat (schmalz) in many of their doughs. My version isn't kosher, but it uses vegetable shortening, which gives the crust the crumbly texture you would get from schmalz. The bars are best if made a day before serving so the flavors can blend and the top crust soften.

■ ■ ■

DOUGH
3½ cups all-purpose flour
½ cup confectioners' sugar
Pinch of salt
I cup vegetable shortening, cut into
½-inch cubes
½ cup plus I tablespoon water
2 large egg yolks

APPLE FILLING
6 Golden Delicious apples (about
2½ pounds), peeled
2 tablespoons honey
I tablespoon fresh lemon juice
¼ teaspoon ground cinnamon

WALNUT FILLING
2 cups (8 ounces) coarsely chopped walnuts
I cup sugar
½ cup water

POPPY SEED FILLING
I cup (5 ounces) poppy seeds, ground
(see page 212)
⅓ cup sugar
¼ cup water

I large egg yolk
I teaspoon heavy cream or water

■ ■ ■

1. To make the dough: Stir the flour, sugar, and salt in a large bowl. Using a pastry blender, cut in the shortening until the mixture resembles coarse cornmeal. Stir the water and yolks together in a small bowl. Using a fork, stir into the flour mixture to make a soft dough, adding a bit more water if needed. Gather up into a ball, then divide into four equal portions. Pat each portion into a 5 × 4-inch rectangle (shaping into a rectangle at this point will make it easier to roll it into that shape later), wrap in plastic wrap, and refrigerate to relax the dough, at least 30 minutes and up to 2 hours. (If the dough chills until very firm, let stand at room temperature for 10 minutes before rolling out.)

2. Meanwhile, make the fillings. To make the apple filling: Cut ¼-inch slices from 4 of the apples, turning the apples as you reach the cores to slice from all sides. Grate the other 2 apples on the large holes of a box grater, turning the apples when you reach the cores. Discard the cores. Combine the sliced and grated apples, honey, lemon juice, and cinnamon in a medium saucepan. Cover and place over medium-low heat until the apples give off some juices. Uncover and cook, stirring occasionally, until the sliced apples are barely tender, about 8 minutes. Transfer to a bowl and cool completely.

3. To make the walnut filling: Process the walnuts and sugar in a food processor fitted with the metal blade until the nuts are very finely chopped. Transfer to a medium saucepan and add the water. Bring to a boil over medium heat, stirring constantly. Cook until thickened to a moist paste, about 3 minutes. Transfer to a bowl and cool completely.

4. To make the poppy filling: Cook the poppy seeds, sugar, and water in a small saucepan over medium heat, stirring almost constantly, until the wine is absorbed and the mixture has thickened into a moist paste, about 2 minutes. Transfer to a bowl and cool completely.

5. Position a rack in the center of the oven, place a baking sheet on the rack, and heat the oven to 400°F. Butter the inside of an 11½ × 8-inch glass baking dish.

6. On a lightly floured work surface, roll out a portion of dough into an 11½ × 8-inch rectangle. Transfer to the pan and spread evenly with the apple filling. Roll out a second portion of dough into an 11½ × 8-inch rectangle, and fit over the apples, pressing lightly to make as flat as possible. Spread with the walnut filling. Roll out a third dough rectangle, and fit over the walnuts, pressing lightly. Spread with the poppy seed filling, top with a fourth rectangle, and press lightly. Pierce the top dough in a few places with a fork. Beat the yolk and cream together in a small bowl and brush some of it over the top dough.

7. Place on the baking sheet in the oven. Bake for 10 minutes, then reduce the oven temperature to 350°F. Bake until the top is golden brown, about 50 minutes.

8. Transfer to a wire rack and cool in the pan for 15 minutes. Run a sharp knife around the inside of the pan. Hold a baking sheet over the pan and invert to unmold the dessert in one piece. Hold the rack over the dessert and invert right-side up. Cool completely, at least 2 hours. (If you have the time, wrap in plastic wrap and let stand overnight before cutting.)

9. Using a serrated knife, trim off the edges of the rectangle. Cut in half lengthwise, then crosswise into sixths to make twelve bars.

MAKE AHEAD

The bars can be made up to 3 days ahead, wrapped loosely in plastic wrap, and refrigerated. They are best at room temperature.

Tokaji

Tokaji (not to be confused with imitations with such names as Tokay or Tokai) is one of the great dessert wines of the world. It ranges in sweetness from the extraordinary Aszú Eszencia (often compared to fine aged Sauternes) to the dry Furmint. Many great figures in history loved this wine; Louis XV is supposed to have exclaimed to Madame de Pompadour, "This is the king of wines, and the wine of kings!" Maria Theresia (Queen of Hungary as well as Archduchess of Austria and Queen of Bohemia) was its greatest promoter. She once sent some of the golden elixir to Pope Benedict XIV, who wrote back these words of thanks: "Blessed be the land that produced you; blessed be the woman that sent you; blessed am I that drink you." Maria Theresia's pet parrots also benefited from the wine's qualities: She fed them wine-soaked cake crumbs, which she was convinced kept their feathers bright and glossy.

APPLE SQUARES
ALMÁS PITES
Makes 9 servings

Hungarians have apple pie, too, but there are many differences from the American version. First, almas pités is rarely round, and is always cut into squares. Sour cream in the dough gives it a central European touch, tenderizing the dough in the process. Some recipes use sliced apples, but grating the apples and squeezing out the excess juice is a good alternative. The dough makes a bit more than you will need, and allows for ease of rolling out and fitting into the pan. If you wish, cut the trimmings into decorations, brush with the beaten egg, and place on the glazed top crust.

■ ■ ■

FILLING
6 medium (2¾ pounds) Golden Delicious apples
2 tablespoons fresh lemon juice
¼ cup granulated sugar
⅓ cup raisins
⅓ cup very finely chopped walnuts
2 tablespoons dried bread crumbs
¼ teaspoon ground cinnamon

DOUGH
2 cups all-purpose flour
½ cup granulated sugar
Pinch of salt
14 tablespoons (1¾ sticks) unsalted butter, chilled, cut into ½-inch cubes
¼ cup sour cream
3 large egg yolks
½ teaspoon vanilla extract

1 large egg, beaten, for glazing

■ ■ ■

1. To make the filling: Peel the apples. Working with one apple at a time, grate on the large holes of a box grater, turning the apple when you reach the core. Discard the cores. In a medium bowl, toss the apples with the lemon juice. Press a large piece of plastic wrap directly on the surface of the apples and refrigerate for 1 hour. A handful at a time, squeeze the excess juices from the apples. In a large bowl, mix the apples with the sugar, raisins, walnuts, bread crumbs, and cinnamon.

2. To make the dough: Meanwhile, in a large bowl, combine the flour, sugar, and salt. Using a pastry blender, cut in the butter until the mixture resembles coarse meal with a few pea-size pieces of butter. In a small bowl, combine the sour cream, egg yolks, and vanilla. Add to the dry ingredients and mix with a fork until the mixture begins to clump together. Divide into two por-

tions, one a bit larger than the other. Shape each into a thick, flat square, wrap in plastic wrap, and refrigerate for 1 hour.

3. Position a rack in the center of the oven and heat to 350°F. Lightly butter an 8-inch square baking pan (preferably nonstick).

4. Place the larger portion of dough on a lightly floured work surface and sprinkle the top with flour. Roll out approximately 9½ inches square and ¼ inch thick. Fit into the pan, pressing against the sides of the pan. Brush the dough with the beaten egg and fill with the apples. Roll out the remaining dough into an 8-inch square about ¼ inch thick. Place over the apples, and press the edges of the two layers of pastry together to seal. Trim away any excess pastry to make a tight pastry "box" enclosing the apples. Pierce the top crust in a few places with a fork. Brush the top lightly with the beaten egg.

5. Bake until the crust is golden brown, 40 to 45 minutes. Cool completely in the pan on a wire rack. Hold a baking sheet over the pan, and invert the pastry onto the sheet. Reinvert, right side up, onto a cutting board. Cut the pastry into 9 portions, using a serrated knife. Transfer to a platter and serve.

MAKE AHEAD

The slices can be made 1 day ahead, covered, and stored at room temperature.

APPLES IN PASTRY ROBES
APFEL IM SCHLAFROCK
Makes 4 servings

Nut-filled apples wrapped in puff pastry are a hearty dessert; many coffeehouse customers have them as a lunch or light supper. I have adapted this recipe for less-gargantuan appetites by using typical supermarket-size apples, but trimming them to a more reasonable diameter. Instead of the walnut filling used here, feel free to stuff the core's channel with raisins, apricot preserves, or a combination of the two.

■ ■ ■
WALNUT FILLING
½ cup coarsely chopped walnuts or hazelnuts
2 tablespoons sugar
2 tablespoons milk
2 tablespoons fresh bread crumbs
⅛ teaspoon ground cinnamon
Grated zest of ½ lemon

4 small Golden Delicious apples
1 lemon, cut in half
½ batch Puff Pastry (page 13)
1 large egg, beaten
Vanilla Sauce (page 18), for serving
■ ■ ■

1. To make the filling: Grind the walnuts and sugar in a food processor fitted with the metal blade until finely chopped. Transfer to a medium saucepan and stir in the milk, bread crumbs, cinnamon, and lemon zest. Bring to a boil over medium heat, stirring often. Cook, stirring almost constantly, until thickened, about 3 minutes. Cool.

2. Position a rack in the center of the oven and heat to 375°F. Line a baking sheet with parchment paper.

3. Peel and core the apples, then trim them to a 2½-inch height, rubbing the cut surfaces with the lemon halves. Fill the cored centers with the nut filling.

4. Roll out the dough on a lightly floured surface to a 12-inch square. Using a pastry wheel or a very sharp knife, trim the edges straight, and then cut into four 6-inch squares. Brush a border of beaten egg around the perimeter of each square. Place an apple in the center, and bring up the corners to meet over the top of the apple, pressing the seams closed. Place on the baking sheet. Freeze until the pastry is firm.

5. Brush each pastry with the egg. Bake until golden brown, about 40 minutes. Serve warm, with the vanilla sauce passed on the side.

MAKE AHEAD

The apples can be prepared up to 1 day ahead, cooled, covered, and refrigerated. Reheat in a 350°F. oven, loosely tented with aluminum foil, until heated through, about 20 minutes.

BERRY MERINGUE SLICES
BEERENSCHAUMSCHNITTEN
Makes 12 servings

The Austrian baking repertoire has an entire family of Schnitten topped with seasonal berries crowned with fluffy meringue. Red currant meringue slices are a favorite, but their season is fleeting—when you can find them (usually at a farmer's market). This is based on a blueberry slice I had at Vienna's Café Diglas, and it's a winner.

■ ■ ■

CAKE
1⅓ cups all-purpose flour
1½ teaspoons baking powder
Pinch of salt
14 tablespoons (1¾ sticks) unsalted butter,
at cool room temperature
1 cup granulated sugar
4 large eggs, at room temperature
1 teaspoon vanilla extract
2 tablespoons fresh lemon juice
Grated zest of ½ lemon

TOPPING
6 large egg whites, at room temperature
1 cup plus 2 tablespoons granulated sugar
2 pints fresh blueberries
3 tablespoons confectioners' sugar

■ ■ ■

1. Position a rack in the center of the oven and heat to 350°F. Lightly butter and flour a 13 × 9-inch baking pan, tapping out the excess flour.
2. To make the cake: Stir the flour, baking powder, and salt to combine. Beat the butter in a medium bowl with a handheld electric mixer on high speed until smooth. Add the sugar and beat until light in color and texture, about 3 minutes. One at a time, beat in the eggs, then the vanilla. On low speed, in two additions, beat in the flour mixture. Beat in the lemon juice and zest.
3. Spread evenly in the pan. Bake until golden and the top springs back when pressed in the center, about 25 minutes. Remove from the oven and set on a wire rack while making the meringue. Increase the oven temperature to 450°F.

4. To make the topping: Beat the egg whites in a large bowl until they form soft peaks. Gradually beat in the granulated sugar until the whites are stiff and shiny. Toss the blueberries and confectioners' sugar in a medium bowl. Spread the berries in a single layer over the cake, then spread with the meringue.
5. Bake until the meringue is lightly tipped with brown, 3 to 5 minutes. Cool completely on a wire rack. To serve, cut into 12 rectangles with a sharp knife dipped in hot water and serve from the pan.

RASPBERRY SLICES
Substitute 4 cups fresh raspberries for the blueberries. Increase the confectioners' sugar to 4 tablespoons.

RED CURRANT SLICES
Substitute 4 cups stemmed fresh red currants for the blueberries (to stem currants, strip them from their tiny stems with the tines of a fork). Increase the confectioners' sugar to ½ cup.

MAKE AHEAD
The cake can be prepared up to 1 day ahead, covered loosely with plastic wrap, and refrigerated. Serve at room temperature.

HUNGARIAN CHOCOLATE MOUSSE SQUARES
RIGÓ JANCSI
Makes 9 servings

Rigó Jancsi is Hungary's national chocolate dessert, although Somlói Galuska (see page 180) would probably make a strong showing at the polls. Squares of cocoa mousse sandwiched between chocolate cake are covered with a shiny chocolate glaze. For years, like many other bakers, I used a recipe for mousse that was based on bittersweet chocolate. But when I discussed this dessert with Sándor Kovács, head pastry chef at Budapest's Gerbeaud, he said, "Whatever you do, remember that the *real* Rigó Jancsi always has cocoa, never chocolate." For a contemporary touch, set off the dark chocolate glaze with a candied violet or rose petal, or even fresh, edible, pesticide-free flowers like Johnny-jump-ups or pansies.

■ ■ ■

CAKE
½ cup all-purpose flour
3 tablespoons Dutch-processed cocoa powder
¼ teaspoon salt
3 tablespoons milk
3 tablespoons vegetable oil
½ teaspoon vanilla extract
3 large eggs, at room temperature
⅔ cup sugar

FILLING
2 tablespoons golden rum or water
1½ teaspoons unflavored powdered gelatin
1 teaspoon vanilla extract
½ cup confectioners' sugar
¼ cup Dutch-processed cocoa powder
2 cups heavy cream

GLAZE
¼ cup hot water
3 ounces high-quality semisweet chocolate, finely chopped
1 tablespoon unsalted butter, at room temperature

⅓ cup Apricot Glaze (page 16), warm
■ ■ ■

1. To make the cake: Position a rack in the center of the oven and heat to 350°F. Lightly butter a 15 × 11-inch jelly-roll pan, and line the bottom and sides with parchment or wax paper. (Cut slashes in the corners of the paper to help them fold neatly.) Lightly butter the paper.

2. Sift the flour, cocoa, and salt together into a bowl. Mix the milk, oil, and vanilla in a measuring cup.

3. Crack the eggs into a medium bowl and add the sugar. Using an electric mixer on high speed, beat until very light in color and texture, about 2 minutes. Sift half of the flour mixture over the eggs and fold in. Fold in half of the milk mixture. Repeat with the remaining flour and milk mixtures. Spread evenly in the pan, being sure the batter fills the corners.

4. Bake until the cake springs back when pressed in the center, about 15 minutes. Cool for 5 minutes on a large wire rack. Invert onto the rack and peel off the paper. Cool completely.

5. To make the filling: Pour the rum into a small bowl and sprinkle with the gelatin. Set aside for 5 minutes. Place the bowl in a skillet of gently simmering water. Using a small rubber spatula, stir constantly until the gelatin is completely dissolved, being sure to wipe down any undissolved gelatin on the sides of the bowl. Remove the bowl from the water, stir in the vanilla, and set aside to cool slightly.

6. In a bowl, combine the confectioners' sugar and cocoa. In a chilled medium bowl, beat the cream until it just begins to thicken. Sift the cocoa mixture into the cream and beat until barely stiff. Stir about one third of the whipped cream into the gelatin mixture, then beat back into the cream, beating until the filling is very stiff. (But do not overbeat, or it will separate.)

7. Cut the cake into two 7½-inch-wide pieces. Place one cake on a baking sheet. Spread all of the filling on the cake in a thick layer, smoothing the sides. Refrigerate while making the glaze.

8. To make the glaze: Combine the water and chocolate in a small saucepan. Cook over low heat, stirring constantly with a rubber spatula, until the chocolate is almost melted. Remove from the heat and let stand, stirring occasionally,

RIGÓ JANCSI

His gaze was so soulful, it melted the heart of a millionairess. Their passionate affair scandalized the world and inspired the sinful chocolate dessert that bears his name. He was Johnny Rigó (or, as he is known in Hungary, where surnames come first, Rigó Jancsi).

It was the end of the nineteenth century, and Johnny was playing the violin at a Parisian hotel. In the audience was Baron Chimay, a Belgian, and his beautiful American wife, the former Klara Ward, a millionaire's daughter. Klara was so mesmerized with the good-looking gypsy that she slipped her diamond ring off her finger, and onto the pinky of the violinist! Even in Paris, this was a racy gesture. Klara soon left her husband and two children and joined Johnny on his travels. During the height of the scandal, a Budapest pastry chef named a new sinfully chocolate dessert after Johnny.

Like many superstar marriages, this one didn't last long. Klara and Johnny separated, and Johnny disappeared from public view. No one knows how or where he ended, although some people think he came to New York and found work in a Broadway orchestra. He contributed little to the art of the violin, but he is immortalized in one of the world's most chocolate-intense desserts.

---

until the chocolate is completely melted. Add the butter and stir until melted and combined. Set aside to thicken and cool slightly.

9. Place the remaining cake layer, smooth side up, on a wire rack set over a jelly-roll pan. Spread the apricot glaze over the cake and refrigerate to set. Pour all of the glaze on top of the cake. Using a metal spatula, smooth and coax the glaze over the sides, smoothing the glaze on the sides of the cake. Refrigerate until the glaze is set, about 15 minutes.

10. Using a thin, sharp knife rinsed under hot water between cuts, cut the glazed cake into 9 rectangles. Following their original positions, arrange the rectangles on top of the filling. Refrigerate until the filling is set, about 1 hour. Cut between the rectangles to make individual servings. Serve chilled.

MAKE AHEAD

The mousse squares can be prepared up to 2 days ahead and stored under a cake dome in the refrigerator.

COFFEE ECLAIRS
MOKA ECLAIRS
Makes 14 to 16 eclairs

Cream puff pastry is a versatile batter, ready to bake into pastries or fry into crullers (see page 155). Eclairs are possibly the most exalted of the pastries. A double baking ensures that the pastry stays crisp and light without a soggy interior.

■ ■ ■

Cream Puff Dough (page 14)
1 large egg, beaten, for glazing
Coffee Faux Fondant Icing (page 15)

FILLING
2 tablespoons cornstarch
1½ cups milk, divided
½ cup sugar
2 large egg yolks
1 cup heavy cream
1½ teaspoons instant espresso powder
dissolved in 1 tablespoon boiling water
and cooled

■ ■ ■

1. Position racks in the center and upper third of the oven and heat to 400°F. Line two baking sheets with parchment paper.

2. Fit a large pastry bag with a $^{11}\!/_{16}$-inch-wide plain tip such as Ateco Number 809 and fill with the warm dough. Spacing 1 inch apart, pipe strips of dough, about 4½ inches long and 1 inch wide, onto the sheets. Using a pastry brush, brush the strips with the beaten egg, tamping down any pointed ends of dough at the same time. Do not use so much glaze that it drips onto the parchment, or the puffs won't rise well.

3. Bake until the eclairs are puffed, golden brown, and set, about 20 minutes. Remove from the oven and pierce each eclair on its side with the tip of a small sharp knife to release the steam. Return to the oven, switching the positions of the sheets from top to bottom and front to back, and continue baking until the eclairs are crisp, about 10 minutes. Cool completely.

4. Using a serrated knife, split the eclair strips in half lengthwise, separating the tops from the bottoms, but keeping track of the matching halves. Place the tops on a large rack set over a jelly-roll pan.

5. Make the coffee icing (it must be warm). Pour the warm icing over the eclair tops, letting the excess run off. If you wish, scrape up the icing on the pan and pour over the eclairs to give another coating. Refrigerate until the icing sets, about 10 minutes.

6. To make the filling: Sprinkle the cornstarch over ½ cup of the milk in a medium bowl and whisk to dissolve. Add the sugar and yolks and whisk well. In a heavy-bottomed medium saucepan, bring the remaining 1 cup milk to a simmer over medium heat, stirring to dissolve the sugar. Whisk the yolk mixture into the saucepan. Cook, whisking often, until the pastry cream comes to a full boil. Strain through a wire sieve into a large bowl set in a larger bowl of ice water and let stand, stirring often, until chilled.

7. Whip the cream in a chilled medium bowl with a handheld electric mixer on high speed until stiff. Beat in the dissolved coffee. Stir one fourth of the whipped cream into the pastry cream, and fold in the remaining cream.

8. Fill a large pastry bag fitted with a $^9\!/_{16}$-inch-wide French star tip (such as Ateco Number 865) with the filling. Pipe the filling into the bottom

halves of the pastry. Cover with the glazed tops. Refrigerate uncovered until serving. Serve chilled.

CHOCOLATE-BANANA SLICES
SCHOKOLADE-BANANENSCHNITTEN
Makes 8 servings

Chocolate and bananas are a typically American combination, but they have found their way into this very Viennese dessert. In order to mold the filling, you'll need to create an aluminum foil collar to wrap around the cake—a simple task.

■ ■ ■

CAKE
½ cup sifted cake flour
3 tablespoons Dutch-processed cocoa powder
Pinch of salt
3 large eggs, at room temperature
⅔ cup sugar
2 tablespoons unsalted butter
2 tablespoons milk
¼ teaspoon vanilla extract
Vegetable oil cooking spray, for the foil collar

FILLING
1½ cups heavy cream
6 ounces bittersweet chocolate, finely chopped
1½ tablespoons golden rum
3 ripe bananas, peeled and cut in half lengthwise

GLAZE
¼ cup heavy cream
2 ounces bittersweet chocolate, finely chopped
1 teaspoon corn syrup

■ ■ ■

1. To make the cake: Position a rack in the center of the oven and heat to 350°F. Butter an 11 × 8-inch baking pan and line the bottom with parchment or wax paper. Dust the inside of the pan with flour to coat the sides and tap out the excess.

2. Sift the cake flour, cocoa, and salt together. Whisk the eggs and sugar in the bowl of a heavy-duty standing mixer. Place over a medium saucepan of simmering water (the water should not touch the bottom of the bowl) and whisk constantly until the eggs are hot to the touch and the sugar is dissolved (rub a bit between your fingers to be sure). Attach to the mixer and fit with the whisk. Beat on high speed until the eggs have tripled in volume and are light and fluffy, about 3 minutes. (If you use a handheld electric mixer, allow 5 minutes to reach this consistency.)

3. Meanwhile, melt the butter in a small saucepan over low heat. Add the milk and heat until hot to the touch. Pour into a medium bowl and stir in the vanilla.

4. In two additions, sift the cocoa mixture over the eggs and fold in, using a large balloon whisk or rubber spatula. Transfer a large dollop of the batter into the milk mixture and whisk to combine. Pour into the bowl of batter and fold in. Spread evenly in the pan.

5. Bake until the top springs back when pressed in the center, about 20 minutes. Cool on a wire rack for 5 minutes. Invert and unmold onto the rack, and remove the paper. Cool completely.

6. To make the filling: Bring the cream to a simmer in a small saucepan over medium heat. Remove from the heat and add the chocolate and rum. Let stand for 3 minutes, then whisk until smooth. Transfer to a medium bowl set in a larger bowl of ice water. Let stand, stirring occasionally, until cooled but not set. With the bowl still in the water, whisk until the mixture is thick and spreadable. Do not overbeat.

7. Place 2 of the bananas on the cake, cut sides down, trimming and piecing the remaining banana to fit, discarding (or snacking on) any leftovers. Spoon the chocolate filling over the bananas, and spread evenly to cover the bananas, almost to the edge of the cake.

8. Fold a 40-inch-long piece of aluminum foil in half lengthwise to make a 6-inch-tall strip. Spray the foil with the oil. Oiled side in, wrap the foil strip around the perimeter of the cake to make a collar, and tape it in place. Crimp the foil so it makes a tight fit. Spread the chocolate filling to touch the collar. Place the cake on a serving plate. Refrigerate until the filling is chilled and set, about 2 hours.

9. To make the glaze: Bring the cream to a simmer in a small saucepan over medium heat. Add the chocolate and corn syrup and whisk until smooth. Cool slightly.

10. Remove the foil collar. Pour all of the glaze on top of the filling. Using an offset metal spatula, immediately spread in a thin layer just to the edge (don't worry if some glaze drips down the sides). Refrigerate until the glaze sets, about 30 minutes. To serve, use a hot, wet knife to slice into 8 pieces. Serve chilled.

MAKE AHEAD

The slices can be made 1 day ahead, stored under a cake dome in the refrigerator.

PUFF PASTRY CORNETS WITH WHIPPED CREAM
SCHAUMROLLEN
Makes 12 pastries

During one visit to Vienna, my friend Irene and I were eyeing a bakery window filled with Schaumrollen, and it brought back memories for both of us. I recalled that in my family a party wasn't a party unless my Auntie Gisela made a platter of her Schaumrollen—flaky cream horns prepared from her homemade puff pastry. Irene told me how, in postwar Vienna, her mother used to insist that she eat meringue-filled horns, as it was believed that the eggs made them much more nutritious than the cream-filled version. Not the most solid nutritional advice, but it points out how the Austrians consider desserts to be food, not just a treat. Nonetheless, I take the middle ground and fill my pastry horns with a meringue–whipped cream combination because it keeps the pastry from getting soggy. Cream horn molds (such as Ateco 921), 5½ inches long, with a 1-inch-wide top tapering to a ½-inch-wide bottom (available at well-supplied kitchenware shops or by mail order) will give your pastries a tapered look; or use 5½-inch long cannoli tubes.

■ ■ ■

½ batch (14 ounces) Puff Pastry (page 13)
1 large egg yolk
1 teaspoon heavy cream
Meringue Cream (page 18) or
Sweetened Whipped Cream (page 19)

■ ■ ■

1. Position a rack in the center of the oven and heat to 425°F. Line a large baking sheet with parchment paper.

2. On a lightly floured work surface, roll the chilled pastry into a rectangle 16 inches long, 9 inches wide, and ⅛ inch thick, keeping the corners at sharp right angles as well as you can. Using a pastry wheel, cut the pastry lengthwise into twelve ¾-inch-wide strips. Brush the strips lightly with water.

3. Damp side out, press the end of the first strip onto the small end of a mold, leaving the remainder of the strip resting on the work surface. Turn the mold to wind the strip onto it, slightly overlapping the strip onto itself and winding at a slight diagonal, pressing the end of the strip to the coil with water. Place on the baking sheet, sealed end down. Repeat with the remaining pastry strips and molds. Freeze until chilled and firm, about 15 minutes.

4. In a small bowl, beat the yolk and cream. Brush the tops of the pastries lightly with the yolk mixture, being careful not to let any excess glaze drip onto the parchment. Bake until the pastry is set and lightly browned, about 15 minutes. Remove from the oven. Using kitchen towels to protect your fingers, slip the pastries off the molds and back onto the baking sheet. Continue baking until the horns are crisp and golden brown, about 5 minutes. Cool completely.

5. Just before serving, transfer the meringue cream to a pastry bag fitted with a ⁹⁄₁₆-inch-wide French star tip, such as Ateco Number 865. Pipe the cream filling through the large end into the horns, making a swirl at the finish. Serve chilled.

MAKE AHEAD
The unfilled pastry horns can be baked up to 1 day ahead and stored in an airtight container at room temperature. While they are best filled

just before serving, they can be filled up to 8 hours ahead, covered loosely with plastic wrap, and refrigerated.

CHOCOLATE-COVERED "INDIAN" CUPCAKES
INDIANERKRAPFEN
Makes 14 cakes

"Indianers," chocolate-glazed orbs of sponge cake filled with a swirl of whipped cream, are one of the most scrumptious pastries a café can offer. Indianerkrapfen molds are commonplace in Austria but are not available here. Against the advice of my Viennese friends, and on the recommendation of some otherwise reliable cookbooks, I spent many frustrating hours trying to make free-form globes of cake. Beaten, I consulted my friend Karitas, who suggested that I use a Danish ebelskiver (apple dumpling) pan, which is available at many kitchenware shops and is exactly the right size and shape. In a pinch, fill muffin tins three-fourths full, but you will only get eight or nine cakes, and your Indianer won't have the perfectly round shape that makes these cakes so distinctive.

• • •

CAKES
3 tablespoons all-purpose flour
3 tablespoons cornstarch
Pinch of salt
3 large eggs, separated, at room temperature
3 tablespoons granulated sugar
1/4 teaspoon vanilla extract

CHOCOLATE GLAZE
1/2 cup heavy cream
4 ounces high-quality bittersweet chocolate, finely chopped

WHIPPED CREAM FILLING
1 1/4 cups heavy cream
3 tablespoons confectioners' sugar
1/2 teaspoon vanilla extract

ASSEMBLY
1/2 cup Apricot Glaze (page 16), warm

• • •

1. Position a rack in the center of the oven and heat to 400°F. Lightly butter and flour the cups of an ebelskiver pan, tapping out the excess flour.

2. To make the cakes: Sift the flour, cornstarch, and salt together. Beat the egg whites in a medium bowl with a handheld electric mixer on high speed until soft peaks form. Gradually beat in the sugar and beat until the peaks are stiff and shiny.

3. Place the egg yolks and vanilla in a medium bowl. Sift about half of the flour mixture on top and beat with the mixer on medium speed, just until smooth. Add one fourth of the whites into the yolks and mix. Fold in the remaining whites, just until barely combined. Sift the remaining flour mixture on top, and fold in until smooth. Divide half of the batter evenly (about 3 table-

spoons for each) among the cups, filling almost to the brim. Cover the remaining batter in the bowl with plastic wrap.

4. Bake until golden brown and a toothpick inserted in the centers of the cakes comes out clean, 10 to 12 minutes. Cool in the pan for 3 minutes. Run the tip of a sharp knife around the cakes to release them, then remove from the cups. Cool completely on a wire rack. (The unfilled cakes can be prepared up to 1 day ahead, stored at room temperature in an airtight container.) Rinse the ebelskiver pan (don't use soap or you'll remove the pan's natural nonstick seasoning), then dry, butter, and flour the pan, and repeat with the remaining batter.

5. To make the chocolate glaze: Bring the ½ cup of cream to a boil in a small saucepan over high heat. Remove from the heat and add the chocolate. Let stand for 3 minutes, then whisk until smooth. Let stand until slightly cooled, about 10 minutes.

6. To make the filling: In a chilled medium bowl, beat the cream, confectioners' sugar, and vanilla until stiff peaks form. Cover and refrigerate until ready to use.

7. To assemble the cupcakes using a small serrated knife, slice the tops off the cakes, keeping the bottom slices about ⅛ inch thick. Pull out the insides of the domed tops, leaving ⅛-inch shells.

Brush the insides of the shells and the cut sides of the bottom slices with the warm apricot glaze. Set aside until the glaze is cooled and set.

8. Place the shells, cut sides down, on a wire rack set over a jelly-roll pan lined with wax paper. Spoon the warm chocolate glaze over the top of each, letting the excess glaze run down the sides. If desired, use a metal spatula to scrape up the glaze, and drizzle over the shells to give them a second coat. Refrigerate the shells to set the glaze.

9. Transfer the whipped cream to a pastry bag fitted with a ⁹⁄₁₆-inch-wide open-star tip such as Ateco Number 825. Pipe a tall swirl of cream onto each base. Use a small metal spatula to lift and place a shell over each base and refrigerate until ready to serve.

MAKE AHEAD

The cupcakes can be prepared 1 day ahead, loosely covered with plastic wrap, and refrigerated. They are best the day they are made.

The Café New York

The four-story-high scaffold surrounding the Café New York gives no indication of the luxury within. Marble columns, crystal chandeliers, wrought-iron filigree work, fresco-covered walls, gilt fixtures—are you in Versailles or a Budapest coffeehouse?

This example of pre-Communist conspicuous consumption was built in 1894 as part of the New York Life Insurance Company's new Budapest office. When the insurance company left Budapest, the New York stayed and established itself, with the Budapest's Café Central, as a congregation point for the capital's artists and writers. Ferenc Molnár, who wrote a number of Broadway hits in the 1920s (including *Liliom*, the basis of Rodgers and Hammerstein's *Carousel*), was addicted to the New York. Legend has it that he stole the key and threw it into the Danube, so the owner would never be able to lock the doors.

Budapest had a thriving theater world, and a number of Hollywood's most colorful personalities hung out at the New York. Alexander Korda, who almost singlehandedly established Britain as a major film center, was a mere journalist when a Hungarian movie producer stepped up to his table and asked Korda to help him out by directing a movie. George Cukor, who directed *My Fair Lady* and countless MGM classic movies, and Michael Curtiz, director of *Casablanca*, saw plenty of drama at the New York.

During the Communist years, the New York was called the Hungaria, and it barely hung on to its former reputation (there was even a period when it was converted into a sports equipment store). In the late 1960s, a long renovation took place, and the café reopened in 1973. Finally, in 1990, it was rechristened the Café New York. The future of the New York is in question, as the building that houses it is in dire need of expensive repair and could be condemned at any time.

ESTERHÁZYSCHNITTEN

The Esterházys were an impressively wealthy Hungarian family with enormous castles, palaces, and mansions in both Austria and Hungary. Prince Miklós ("the Splendid") hired Joseph Haydn as his court composer. Even after the Esterházys disbanded the court orchestra, they still remained influential in musical circles, and Beethoven and Schubert premiered some of their works at the family's soirées. Later, Prince Pál Esterházy became a well-known gourmet.

During the Communist years, the state would have nothing to do with dishes that were named after nobility (there is a famous Roast Beef Esterházy, too), and anything "Esterházy" was renamed for Pushkin, the Russian poet. When the Communists lost power, the dishes got their old names back.

NUT MERINGUE SLICES
ESTERHÁZYSCHNITTEN
Makes 8 slices

Rare is the central European coffeehouse or bakery that doesn't serve Esterházyschnitten. The nut layers (always six of them, no more and no less) are sometimes baked into rounds and made into a torte, but the rectangular version is the more popular by far. Sometimes the layers are created from either almond or hazelnut, but I like the resulting depth of flavor when they are combined. You may use one or the other if you prefer. The feathered glazed top is another constant design feature for this multilayered torte. This is a simple technique, but you must work quickly while the glaze and chocolate are wet and unset. Be sure that you have everything ready (warm melted chocolate in a paper cone, just-prepared icing at the proper temperature, clean offset spatula at your side) before you start. In appearance, this might remind you of the classic French Napoleon pastry, but when you taste it, all comparisons will be meaningless. The Esterházy (as famous a historical name in Hungary as the name Bonaparte is in France) is in a class of its own.

■ ■ ■

NUT LAYERS
½ cup (2½ ounces) hazelnuts,
toasted and peeled

½ cup (2 ounces) natural or blanched
sliced almonds
¼ cup confectioners' sugar
5 large egg whites, at room temperature
½ cup granulated sugar

KIRSCH BUTTERCREAM
1 cup milk, divided
2 tablespoons cornstarch
⅔ cup granulated sugar
2 large egg yolks
1 cup (2 sticks) unsalted butter, at cool room
temperature, cut into small pieces
2 tablespoons kirsch, Cognac, or golden rum

ASSEMBLY
¼ cup Apricot Glaze (page 16), warm
1 ounce bittersweet chocolate, melted
(see page 203)
Small-Batch Faux Fondant Icing (page 15),
warm
½ cup sliced almonds, toasted
(see page 211), for garnish

■ ■ ■

1. To make the nut layers: Position a rack in the center of the oven and heat to 350°F. Lightly butter a 17 × 11-inch jelly-roll pan. Line the bottom and sides of the pan with parchment paper. (Cut slashes in the corners of the paper to help them fold neatly.)

2. In a food processor fitted with the metal blade, process the hazelnuts, almonds, and confectioners' sugar until the nuts are very finely chopped, almost a flour. In a large grease-free bowl, using an electric mixer on high speed, beat the egg whites until soft peaks form. Still beating, gradually add the granulated sugar and beat just until stiff, shiny peaks form. Fold in the nuts.

3. Using an offset metal spatula, spread the nut batter evenly into the pan. Bake until golden brown and beginning to crisp around the edges, about 20 minutes. Hold a cutting board or flat platter over the pan, and invert together to unmold the cake. Carefully peel away the parchment and cool completely. Using a serrated knife, trim uneven edges, and cut the cake vertically into six 2¾-inch-wide strips. Don't worry if any of the strips crack, as they can be pieced together when layered with the filling.

4. To make the buttercream: Pour ¼ cup of the milk into a heavy-bottomed medium saucepan, and add the cornstarch. Whisk to dissolve the cornstarch, then whisk in the sugar and yolks until smooth. Whisk in the remaining ¾ cup of the milk. Whisking constantly, being sure to reach into the corners of the saucepan, bring to a full boil over medium heat; the pastry cream will be thick. Remove from the heat and transfer to a bowl set in a larger bowl of ice water. Stirring often, cool the pastry cream.

5. In a medium bowl, using a handheld electric mixer on high speed, beat the butter until smooth, about 1 minute. A tablespoon at a time, beat in the cooled pastry cream. Beat in the kirsch.

6. To assemble: Place the best-looking nut layer, short end facing you, smooth side up, on a wire rack set over a jelly-roll pan. Using an offset metal spatula, spread the top of the layer evenly with the warm apricot glaze. Let stand until the glaze sets, about 15 minutes.

7. Place the warm melted chocolate in a paper cone (see page 204) and snip off the point. Pour the warm fondant icing over the glazed nut layer, and smooth it evenly with a clean offset spatula (photograph 1), letting the excess drip over the sides. Immediately pipe four thin lines of chocolate about ¾ inch apart along the entire length of the glazed nut layer (2). (You will not use all the chocolate, but it is difficult to melt less.) At 1-inch intervals, draw a wooden toothpick in verti-

cal straight lines from right to left across the glaze and chocolate. Then working left to right, draw vertical lines exactly between the first set of lines to make a feathered effect (3). Let stand until the glaze is set. Run a thin, sharp knife under the layer to free it from the rack.

8. Meanwhile, place 1 nut layer on an 11 × 2½-inch cardboard rectangle, securing the layer to the board with a dab of buttercream. Spread the layer with about 3 tablespoons of the buttercream. Repeat with the remaining layers and buttercream, ending with the buttercream. Use the remaining buttercream to spread a thin layer around the sides of the cake. Press the almonds onto the sides. Top with the glazed layer.

9. Refrigerate, uncovered, until the buttercream is firm and chilled, about 1 hour. To serve, use a thin, sharp knife to cut crosswise into 8 slices. Serve chilled.

MAKE AHEAD

The slices can be made up to 2 days ahead, covered loosely with plastic wrap, and refrigerated.

▪ THE STORY BEHIND ▪
GERBEAUD SLICES

In Hungary, the name Gerbeaud is so famous as a sign of quality in baking that it is worth millions. And one of the Gerbeaud family got the check to prove it.

Gerbeaud—one of the world's most beautiful cafés, resplendent in gold leaf and red plush—has meant the best in Budapest's desserts for more than 125 years. The original owner was Henrik Kugler, a man who wanted to introduce to Hungary pastries baked with the same level of sophistication as those he found in Paris and other European capitals. He appropriated a café that stood on Vörösmarty Square to turn into his own temple to pastry, and worshipers have been coming to the shrine ever since.

In 1884 he retired and left the business to his associate, Emil Gerbeaud, from French-speaking Geneva. Emil's dedication raised the standards even higher, and he introduced a line of chocolates that still contribute to Gerbeaud's bottom line. As the middle classes in Hungary thrived, so did Gerbeaud Cukrászda. The interior became more and more palatial, and in the present café you'll still find some of the marble-topped tables that Emil had delivered from the Paris World Fair in 1900.

During World War I, Budapest was hit hard, and for 133 miserable days, Gerbeaud's café was turned into a stable. It bounced back when the war ended, and after Emil died, his wife ran the business for many years. When nationalization occurred in 1948, the family left, and the Gerbeauds died out, except for a daughter, who had emigrated to Brazil. Gerbeaud Cukrászda was renamed the Vörösmarty, until 1984, when its owners decided that the old name would inject a sense of pride into the flagging business. Miss Gerbeaud, then ninety-eight years old, set the price of the name at two million dollars. And she got it.

Gerbeaud has so many specialties that it is impossible to list them all, but they invented two Austro-Hungarian star pastries, Esterházy torta (originally a cake, but often served as a Schnitten) and Gerbeaud slices. Today, Gerbeaud is a large corporation, providing desserts to Malev Airlines as well as to their flagship store.

GERBEAUD SLICES
GERBEAUD·SZELET
Makes 12 slices

The word "Gerbeaud" is never translated. It's assumed that everyone who orders it knows that it is thin, tender layers of sweet yeast dough alternating with apricot jam and ground walnuts, covered with a shiny chocolate glaze. This is an unusual yeast dough; the small amount of yeast and high proportion of sugar keep the dough from rising high, so don't expect this to be a puffy yeast pastry. Thanks to Gerbeaud's executive chef, Sándor Kovács, who shared the prized recipe with me.

■ ■ ■

DOUGH
1 ounce (1/2 cube) fresh compressed yeast or
3 3/4 teaspoons (about 1 3/4 envelopes) active
dry yeast
1/2 cup milk (heated to 105° to 115°F.
if using dry yeast)
3 egg yolks
1 teaspoon vanilla extract
3 1/2 cups unbleached flour
1 cup sugar
1/4 teaspoon salt
14 tablespoons (1 3/4 sticks) unsalted butter,
cut into 1/2-inch cubes, chilled

FILLING
1 cup walnuts
1/2 cup sugar
1 cup apricot preserves, warmed

CHOCOLATE ICING
3 1/2 ounces bittersweet chocolate,
finely chopped
1/3 cup sugar
1/4 cup water
1 tablespoon unsalted butter

■ ■ ■

1. To make the dough: Crumble the yeast into the milk in a glass measuring cup. Let stand 3 minutes, then stir to dissolve. Mix in the egg yolks and vanilla.

2. Measure the flour, the sugar, and the salt into the bowl of a heavy-duty standing mixer fitted with the paddle blade. Add the butter and mix on low speed until the mixture resembles coarse cornmeal. Add the yeast mixture and mix, adding more milk if necessary, to form a very stiff, sticky dough. Transfer to a lightly floured work surface and knead for 2 to 3 minutes. The dough will remain sticky and resemble a sugar cookie dough; do not add more flour to the board. Wrap in plastic wrap and refrigerate for 1 hour.

3. Meanwhile, prepare the filling: Process the walnuts and sugar together in a food processor fitted with the metal blade until very finely chopped.

4. Butter and flour a 13 × 9-inch baking dish and tap out the excess flour. Divide the dough into three equal portions. Roll out one portion of dough into a 13 × 9-inch rectangle and transfer to the pan, pressing it into the corners to fit. Spread with half of the preserves and sprinkle with half of the walnut mixture. Roll out another layer of dough, fit into the pan, and spread with the remaining preserves and walnuts. Top with the third layer of rolled dough. Cover with plastic wrap and let stand in a warm place for 1 hour (the dough's rising will be barely perceptible).

5. Position a rack in the center of the oven and heat to 350°F. Pierce the top layer of dough well with a fork. Bake until the top is golden brown, 30 to 35 minutes. If the top browns too deeply, cover loosely with aluminum foil.

6. Cool on a wire rack for 15 minutes. Run a sharp knife around the edge of the pan. Holding a long rack over the pan, invert and unmold the cake and cool completely, leaving the cake upside down.

7. To make the icing: Bring the chocolate, sugar, and water to a boil in a small saucepan over medium heat, stirring often. Boil until an instant-read thermometer reads 220°F., 3 to 4 minutes. Remove from the heat and stir in the butter to melt. Cool the icing until slightly thickened and lukewarm, but still pourable.

8. Place the cake on the rack over a jelly-roll pan. Pour all the icing over the top of the cake and spread evenly with an offset metal spatula, letting the excess icing drip over the sides. (Don't bother smoothing the sides, as they will be trimmed off.) Refrigerate the cake until the icing sets.

9. Using a thin, sharp knife dipped in hot water, trim the sides of the cake. Cut the cake in half lengthwise, then crosswise into 12 bars. Serve at room temperature.

MAKE AHEAD

The slices can be made up to 2 days ahead, covered tightly with plastic wrap, and stored at room temperature.

PUFF PASTRY CREAM SLICES WITH COFFEE ICING
FRANCIA KRÉMES
Makes 8 to 10 slices

A member of the Napoleon pastry family, this dessert of crisp puff pastry layers sandwiched with a thick strata of cream-based filling is even richer than its French cousin. (By the way, Napoleons were originally Italian, and called Neapolitans, but the recipe was appropriated by French bakers, who changed the name.) Napoleons are usually prepared with classic pastry cream, but the Austro-Hungarian baker can't bear not to add whipped cream, a step that lightens the filling. Some bakers forego the pastry cream altogether and slather a slab of gelatin-stabilized whipped cream between only two layers of pastry. In either case, the Viennese call these Cremeschnitten. But in Budapest, where the dessert is usually topped with a simple coffee icing, it's called Francia krémes.

The trick to making Napoleons, Creme-schnitten, and similar confections is to bake the puff pastry into firm, crisp, but unpuffed layers. This takes some cajoling, as this pastry is *supposed* to puff. The pastry must be pierced well with a fork or pastry docker (this useful tool for evenly perforating puff pastry can be found at professional bakery suppliers and many kitchen-ware shops), weighed down with a heavy pan (a baking sheet is too light), and baked at varying temperatures to dry out the interior.

■ ■ ■

½ batch (14 ounces) Puff Pastry (page 13)

ICING
2 teaspoons instant espresso coffee powder
2 tablespoons plus 1 teaspoon boiling water
1 cup confectioners' sugar

CREAM FILLING
1½ cups milk, divided
2 tablespoons cornstarch
⅔ cup sugar
4 large egg yolks
1 teaspoon vanilla extract
3 tablespoons water
2 tablespoons golden rum
2 envelopes (4 teaspoons) unflavored gelatin
1¼ cups heavy cream

■ ■ ■

1. Turn a 15½ × 10½-inch jelly-roll pan upside down, and cut a piece of parchment paper to fit the underside. On a lightly floured work surface, roll out the pastry slightly larger than the paper, and slide it onto the paper. Transfer to the underside of the pan (the pastry will shrink slightly). Roll out the pastry again on the pan so it fits the paper. Using a fork or a pastry docker, pierce the pastry well. Cover loosely with plastic wrap and freeze for 20 to 30 minutes.

2. Position a rack in the center of the oven and heat to 400°F. Using a pastry wheel or a very sharp knife, trim the pastry to make an even rectangle. Cover with another sheet of parchment paper, and top with a large roasting pan (the pastry must be completely weighed down). Bake until the pastry is set and beginning to brown at the edges, about 20 minutes.

3. Reduce the heat to 350°F., remove the roasting pan and the top parchment paper, and leave the oven door open for about 30 seconds to drop the temperature. Close the door and continue baking until the pastry is golden, about 15 minutes. Remove the pastry from the oven; leave the oven on. Cool the pastry for 10 minutes. Using a serrated knife, cut into three strips, each about 3½ × 15½ inches (the center will still appear slightly uncooked). Return the strips to the oven and bake for 10 minutes, or until the pastry is crisp and golden brown. Turn off the oven, prop the door ajar, and cool the pastry in the oven.

4. To make the icing: Dissolve the coffee in the boiling water in a small bowl. Sift the confectioners' sugar into a medium bowl. Add the coffee and whisk until smooth, adding additional droplets of water if needed to get a pourable icing.

5. Place the center strip, smooth underside up, on a wire rack set over a jelly-roll pan. Pour all of the icing over the strip. Using an offset spatula, spread the icing over the pastry, letting the excess run down the sides. Let stand until the icing sets, about 20 minutes.

6. To make the filling: Pour ½ cup of the milk into a medium saucepan, sprinkle with the cornstarch, and whisk to dissolve. Whisk in the sugar and yolks. Heat the remaining 1 cup of milk in a saucepan or microwave oven. Whisk into the yolk mixture and bring to a full boil over medium heat, whisking constantly. Remove from the heat and whisk in the vanilla. Transfer to a large bowl set in a larger bowl of ice water and let stand, stirring often, until the pastry cream is cooled.

7. Meanwhile, combine the water and rum in a small heat-proof bowl and sprinkle the gelatin on top. Let stand until the rum soaks up the gelatin, about 5 minutes. Place in a skillet with ½ inch of simmering water and stir constantly until the gelatin dissolves. (Or cook in the microwave on medium power at 10-second intervals, scraping down the sides and stirring well with a small rubber spatula after each interval, until the gelatin is completely dissolved.) Let stand until the gelatin is tepid, but still liquid.

8. In a chilled medium bowl, beat the cream with a handheld electric mixer at high speed just until soft peaks form. With the mixer running, pour the gelatin directly into the blades and beat until the cream is stiff. Stir one fourth of the whipped cream into the pastry cream, then fold in the remaining whipped cream. Don't worry if the filling looks slightly lumpy; it will even out during spreading and chilling. Let the filling stand in the ice water bath, folding occasionally, until chilled and firm enough to spread, 10 to 15 minutes.

9. Place one of the un-iced pastry strips on a 15½ × 10½-inch cardboard rectangle. Using an offset spatula, spread with half of the filling. Top with the second strip and the remaining filling, pressing gently to even the filling layers. Top with the iced strip. Refrigerate until the filling is chilled and completely set, at least 1 hour and up to overnight.

10. To serve, use a serrated knife to cut crosswise into 8 to 10 slices. Serve chilled.

WHIPPED-CREAM PUFF PASTRY SLICES

Omit the coffee icing. Omit the milk, cornstarch, sugar, and egg yolks for the pastry cream. Increase the heavy cream to 2¼ cups and beat until stiff. Add the vanilla, then beat in the dissolved gelatin. Let stand in an ice-water bath until chilled and firm enough to spread. Sift confectioners' sugar on top of the finished pastry.

MAKE AHEAD

The slices can be made up to 1 day ahead, covered loosely with plastic wrap, and stored in the refrigerator.

MERINGUE AND LADYFINGER SLICES
KARDINALSCHNITTEN
Makes 10 slices

When the Viennese want to feel that they are eating a less sinful dessert, they order this ethereally light, spectacular-looking confection of alternating ladyfinger batter and meringue strips. It is said that the dessert got its name from the original red-currant filling, as red as a cardinal's robes, but most bakeries now make it with apricot preserves. You will need two large pastry bags (at least 14 inches long) or extra-large plastic storage bags for the meringue and batter, two 7/16-inch-wide plain tips, and two 17-inch-long baking sheets.

■ ■ ■

MERINGUE
8 large egg whites, at room temperature
3/4 cup plus 1 tablespoon granulated sugar

LADYFINGER BATTER
3 large eggs, at room temperature
2 large egg yolks, at room temperature
1/3 cup granulated sugar
1/2 teaspoon vanilla extract
1/2 cup all-purpose flour
Pinch of salt
Confectioners' sugar, for dusting and garnish

**2/3 cup Apricot Glaze or
Red Currant Glaze (page 16), warmed**

■ ■ ■

1. Position two racks in the upper third and center of the oven and heat to 375°F. Line two large baking sheets with parchment paper.

2. To make the meringue: Beat the whites in a large bowl with a handheld mixer on high speed until the whites form soft peaks. Gradually beat in the sugar and beat until the peaks are stiff and shiny.

3. To make the ladyfinger batter: In another large bowl, beat the eggs, yolks, and granulated sugar on high speed until the mixture is very light and fluffy in texture and forms a thick rib-bon that falls back on itself when the beaters are lifted a few inches, about 3 minutes. Beat in the vanilla. Sift the flour and salt over the mixture and fold it in.

4. Fit two large pastry bags with 7/16-inch-wide plain pastry tips (such as Ateco Number 805). Spoon half of the meringue into one bag, and half of the ladyfinger batter into the other. Starting 1/2 inch from a long edge of one baking sheet, pipe a 16-inch-long strip of meringue. Now pipe a strip of ladyfinger batter alongside and touching the meringue. Repeat, alternating meringue and ladyfinger batter, to make a total of 4 meringue and 3 ladyfinger strips, forming a rectangle about 7 inches wide and 16 inches long. Repeat to make another rectangle on the other sheet. Sift confectioners' sugar over the layers.

5. Bake until golden brown and a ladyfinger strip springs back when pressed in the center, 15 to 20 minutes. (The layer on the upper rack may be done before the lower layer.) Cool completely on the sheets.

6. Sift confectioners' sugar over the cooled layers. With the strips running horizontally, place a baking sheet over one layer, invert, and peel away the parchment, leaving the layer upside down. (Don't worry—the cake is pretty flexible.) Using a serrated knife, trim the short ends, and cut the layer in half vertically. Brush one half with 1/4 cup of the warm apricot preserves. Top with the other half, right side up; the two halves are now back to back. Slice vertically into 5 pieces. Repeat the procedure with the other layer and remaining preserves. Cover loosely with plastic wrap and refrigerate until serving.

MAKE AHEAD
The ladyfinger slices can be prepared up to 2 days ahead, covered loosely with plastic wrap, and refrigerated.

HUGARIAN FLAKY SCONES
POGÁCSA
Makes about 12 scones

Almost every subway stop in Budapest has its own bakery (and some have two or three). Piled high in the display cases are many kinds of pogácsa—a round, flaky scone that can be enjoyed at any time of the day. Pogácsa loosely translates into pompom, a reference to their crosshatched tops. Some of them are slightly sweet, sprinkled with sesame or poppy seeds or nuts, but most of them are on the salty, savory side. You'll also find bite-size pogácsa made for nibbling with wine or beer.

Hungarians love pork (tepertös pogácsa, made from pork or goose cracklings, is one of the most popular varieties), and many bakeries' pogácsa have the distinct taste and tender flakiness that comes from lard. Because good lard is hard to come by unless you make it yourself, butter pogácsa is the best choice for the American cook and gives a more subtle flavor that is delicious with morning coffee.

To keep the pogácsa flaky, the dough is folded like puff pastry and not allowed to rise as much as other yeast pastries. If you make round pogácsa, the trimmings can be gathered up and cut into more scones, but the subsequent cuttings are never as attractive as the first ones. (Most bakeries turn the trimmings into the bite-size version, in which the lack of flakiness isn't as noticeable.) You can solve this problem by making rectangular scones, but the round ones are really the prettier.

■ ■ ■

1 ounce (¹⁄₂ cube) fresh compressed yeast or
4 teaspoons active dry yeast
3 tablespoons milk (heated to 105° to 115°F.
if using dry yeast)
Pinch of granulated sugar
¹⁄₃ cup sour cream, or more if needed
2 large egg yolks
2¹⁄₄ cups all-purpose flour
3 tablespoons confectioners' sugar

¹⁄₂ teaspoon salt
¹⁄₂ cup (1 stick) unsalted butter,
cut into ¹⁄₂-inch cubes, chilled

1 large egg, beaten, for glaze
1¹⁄₂ tablespoons poppy seeds or sesame seeds,
for garnish

■ ■ ■

1. Crumble the yeast over the milk in a small bowl and add the pinch of sugar. Let stand for 5 minutes, then stir to dissolve the yeast. Stir in the sour cream, then the yolks.

2. Combine the flour, confectioners' sugar, and salt in the bowl of a heavy-duty standing mixer. Add the butter. Attach to the mixer and fit with the paddle blade. Mix on low speed until the mixture resembles coarse cornmeal, about 2 minutes. Add the yeast mixture and mix to form a soft, sticky dough, adding more sour cream if needed. Gather the dough into a ball. Fit the mixer with the dough hook. Knead the dough on medium speed until smooth and glossy, about 6 minutes. (The dough will look a little rough, but it will smooth out with rolling.)

3. On a lightly floured work surface, roll out the dough into a 12 × 6-inch rectangle. Stretch the corners to give them sharp right angles. Fold the top third down, then the bottom third up, like a business letter, brushing away any excess flour. Turn the dough with the open side to your left. Roll out again into a 12 × 6-inch rectangle with sharp corners. Now fold the top half down to the center of the rectangle, and the bottom half up to meet it. Fold the dough in half at the center, like a book, to make a four-layer rectangle. Rap the dough with the rolling pin, horizontally and vertically, to flatten it slightly and give it an even thickness. Wrap in plastic wrap and refrigerate for 20 to 30 minutes.

4. Repeat the rolling and folding steps described above, first folding the dough into thirds, then into quarters. Wrap in plastic and refrigerate for at least 2 hours or overnight. If the dough is chilled for more than 2 hours, let it stand at room temperature for 15 to 30 minutes before rolling.

5. Position a rack in the center of the oven and

heat to 400°F. Line a baking sheet with parchment paper.

6. Roll out the dough on a lightly floured surface into an 11 × 6-inch rectangle, ½ inch thick. Using a sharp knife, score the dough in a cross-hatch pattern, making the cuts about ¾ inch apart and ¹⁄₁₆ inch deep. To make rectangular pogácsa, cut the dough into twelve rectangles. To make round pogácsa, using a 2½-inch round cutter, cut out 8 or 9 biscuits, cutting them as close as possible. Gather up the scraps, knead very briefly until barely smooth, roll out ½ inch thick, score the top, and cut out 2 or 3 more pogácsa.

7. Place the pogácsa on the baking sheet. Brush the tops with the beaten egg and sprinkle with the seeds. Bake until golden brown, 18 to 20 minutes. Serve warm or at room temperature.

CHEESE POGÁCSA

Reduce the confectioners' sugar to 2 tablespoons. In Step 3, roll out the dough the first time, sprinkle with ¼ cup freshly grated Romano cheese, and fold into thirds. Roll out the dough the second time, sprinkle with another ¼ cup Romano cheese, and fold into quarters. Chill, and roll out again, but without additional cheese. Mix ¼ cup grated Romano cheese, ¼ teaspoon freshly ground black pepper, and ¼ teaspoon sweet Hungarian paprika. Sprinkle the top of each glazed pogácsa with 1 teaspoon of the cheese mixture.

BACON POGÁCSA

Reduce the sugar to 2 tablespoons. Add ½ teaspoon coarsely ground black pepper to the dry ingredients for the dough. Cook 6 ounces sliced bacon in a medium skillet over medium heat until crisp and browned, about 6 minutes. Drain on paper towels, cool, and chop fine. During the last minute or so of kneading, add the bacon to the dough.

MAKE AHEAD

The dough can be prepared up to 1 day ahead, wrapped, and refrigerated. The scones are best the day they are made, but they will keep for 1 or 2 days, stored in an airtight container at room temperature. Wrap in aluminum foil and reheat at 350°F. for 10 minutes to refresh them.

·COOKIES·&· DOUGHNUTS·

Tell Herr Ober (the generic name for a coffeehouse's waiter) that you want "just a little something to go with the coffee," and you're likely to get an assortment of cookies. They are called *Kaffeegebäck* or *Teegebäck,* indicating to anyone with an Austro-Hungarian palate that they are baked goods meant to be paired with coffee or tea. So much for the all-American combination of cookies and milk.

During the Christmas holiday season when gingerbread-like Lebkuchen and Honigkuchen (spiced cookies and honey cake) make their annual appearance, it may seem like the cookie selection is endless. But the rest of the year cookies take a backseat, and *Torten* return to the display windows.

Versatile Mürbteig (or its close relative, Linzerteig) is the base for many favorite cookies. Rolled into disks for Ischl Tartlets, or molded into rounds and imprinted with a finger to fill with jam for thumbprint cookies (or Hussar Cookies to the Austrians), this dough gets a workout. Sometimes part of the flour is replaced with ground nuts to give variety to the dough, as in the Viennese Vanilla Crescents. Macaroons, created from fluffy egg-white meringue, are another beloved cookie group. Unless they're the classic almond version, they're rarely called *Makarons*—that's too prosaic. The Viennese prefer to call them by the much more charming *Busserl* or *Küsse*, both words for "kiss."

Fried desserts, especially fruits dipped in batter and fried, are found on a few café-restaurant menus, but they are usually served at home. Doughnuts are another matter. *Faschingkrapfen* (filled doughnuts) are the traditional food for Fasching (the Carnival season before Lent). You are expected to eat plenty of them from Epiphany to Fat Tuesday to prepare for the coming religious season of Lent, when your eating habits are expected to be more austere. (Remember that Austria remains a seriously Catholic country.) Lately, they are being baked year-round.

The key to successful cookie baking is a good cookie sheet, such as the professional-quality "half-sheet" pan. I was baking for years on the same thin, shoddy sheets that had darkened with age before I realized that the sheets—and not my oven or a bad recipe—were responsible for my cookies' burnt bottoms. Now that I've replaced them with sturdy, shiny, heavy pans (shiny surfaces reflect the oven heat to encourage even baking, while stained, dark sheets absorb the heat and cause burning), my cookies are much better. Parchment paper is another boon. You won't have to wash the sheets between batches (washing a hot baking sheet before it cools completely causes warping), nor worry about buttering and flouring the pans.

Austro-Hungarian cookies are generally too delicate to be stored in a cookie jar. Arrange them carefully in layers in an airtight container, separating the layers with wax paper. Rectangular plastic or hard rubber food storage containers are perfect. Separate the cookies according to type; if you mix them up, they will exchange flavors, and the hard cookies will get soft and the soft cookies will get hard.

ISCHL TARTLETS
ISCHLER TÖRTCHEN
Makes 12 large cookies

Bad Ischl in Upper Austria was the favorite summer spot of Franz Josef, and therefore of the entire blue-blooded population of Vienna. (One of the best bakeries in the world, Zauner, is located in Bad Ischl, and there's nothing like having an emperor as your best customer to ensure quality control.) These large, crisp sandwich cookies, filled with preserves and glazed with chocolate, became popular with vacationers, who took them back home and thereby spread their popularity. The tartlets are now firmly ensconced in the cookie selection of every bakery along the Danube. Sometimes they are filled with a chocolate buttercream, but I love the contrast between the tart preserves and the sweet chocolate glaze.

■ ■ ■

DOUGH
I cup all-purpose flour
2/3 cup (2 1/2 ounces) natural or blanched
sliced almonds
Pinch of salt
10 tablespoons (1 stick plus 2 tablespoons)
unsalted butter, cut into 1/2-inch cubes,
at cool room temperature
2/3 cup confectioners' sugar

When a Coffeehouse
Is Not a Coffeehouse

Not every place that serves coffee is a coffeehouse. In Vienna, coffeehouses are strictly licensed according to what they serve, although there is some blurring of boundaries.

In 1999, there were 2,635 Viennese "coffeehouses" in operation in six categories:

- 564 Kaffeehäuser (coffeehouses), cafés with seating, serving only cold food, especially desserts, which may or may not be baked on the premises. Typical coffeehouse cold plates include sausages and cheese platters.

- 611 Kaffee-Restaurants (café-restaurants), establishments that serve hot food as well as cold. The exact menu varies; but you can usually dig into a bowl of goulash, and hot sandwiches are very popular.

- 911 Espressos, places serving a quick cup of espresso. They usually don't serve liquor, pastry, or food—just espresso, and no other coffee-based beverages. There may be a few stools and counters for basic seating.

- 133 Kaffee-Konditoreien (café-bakeries), which are full-scale bakeries with seating. Some of the most famous names in Viennese pastry, such as Demel, Oberlaa, Heiner, Gerstner, and Lehmann, are actually Konditoreien and not coffeehouses. Even though both words can be translated as "bakery," Konditorei is different from Bäckerei. A Konditorei specializes in sweet baked goods (not necessarily made with yeast) and confections, but a Bäkerei produces yeasted baked goods, especially the household daily bread. A Kurkonditorei is a bakery that has set very high standards.

- 35 Stehkaffee ("standing coffee"), a stall serving coffee and rolls, found at train stations and the like.

- The balance consisted of 381 Nichtbetriebe, places that were holding licenses but not using them.

These figures are very revealing. For all of the nervousness concerning the rise of the impersonal espresso bar, if the figures for classic establishments are added up (including coffeehouses, café-restaurants, and bakeries with seating), they prove that the traditional settings remain to serve their customers in style.

FILLING
1/2 cup raspberry or red currant preserves,
stirred to loosen

GLAZE
5 ounces bittersweet chocolate,
finely chopped
2 tablespoons hot brewed coffee
2 tablespoons hot water
2 tablespoons unsalted butter,
at room temperature

1 tablespoon finely chopped pistachios,
for garnish

■ ■ ■

1. To make the dough: Process the flour, almonds, and salt in a food processor until the nuts are finely ground, almost a flour.

2. Beat the butter in a medium bowl with a hand-held electric mixer on high speed just until smooth. On low speed, beat in the confectioners' sugar, just until combined. Using a spoon, stir in the nut flour to make a stiff dough. Gather into two thick disks and wrap each in plastic wrap. Refrigerate for 30 minutes and up to 2 hours. (If the dough is chilled until firm, let it stand at room temperature for 10 minutes before rolling out.)

3. Position racks in the center and top third of the oven and heat to 350°F. Line two baking sheets with parchment paper.

4. On a lightly floured work surface, roll out one portion of dough into a 1/8-inch-thick round. The dough may seem crumbly at first, but it will eventually come together with rolling. Using a 2½-inch round fluted cookie cutter, cut out cookies, and place on the sheets, about 1 inch apart. Gather up the scraps and set aside. Repeat with the other half of dough. Combine the scraps and knead together until smooth. Roll out and cut out cookies to make a total of 24.

5. Bake until the cookies are golden brown, 12 to 15 minutes, switching the positions of the baking sheets from top to bottom and front to back halfway through baking. Cool slightly on the sheets, then transfer to wire racks to cool completely.

6. Using about 1 teaspoon of preserves for each, sandwich two cookies together, smooth sides facing in. Arrange the cookies 1 inch apart on a wire rack set over a jelly-roll pan.

7. To make the glaze: Place the chocolate, coffee, and water in the top part of a double boiler set over barely simmering water. Stir occasionally until the chocolate melts. Whisk in the butter. Remove from the heat. Cool slightly.

8. Pour the warm glaze over the top of each cookie, using a small offset spatula to smooth it over the top and around the sides. Sprinkle a pinch of chopped pistachios in the center of each glazed cookie. Refrigerate until the glaze sets, about 30 minutes.

MAKE AHEAD
The cookies can be prepared up to 3 days ahead, stored in layers separated by wax paper in an airtight container, and refrigerated.

CHOCOLATE-ALMOND MACAROONS
SCHOKOLADE BUSSERLN
Makes about 36

Viennese macaroons are called kisses (Busserln). This chocolate–almond version is a good representation of this cookie.

■ ■ ■

6 ounces bittersweet chocolate,
finely chopped
2 cups (10 ounces) sliced natural almonds
1⅓ cups confectioners' sugar, divided
4 large egg whites, at room temperature

■ ■ ■

1. Position racks in the center and top third of the oven and heat to 325°F. Line two baking sheets with parchment paper.

2. Melt the chocolate in the top part of a double boiler over barely simmering water or in a microwave oven. Cool until tepid.

3. Process the almonds and ⅔ cup of the confectioners' sugar in a food processor fitted with the metal blade until the almonds are very finely chopped, almost a powder. Beat the egg whites with a handheld electric mixer until soft peaks form, then gradually beat in the remaining ⅔ cup of sugar until stiff, shiny peaks form. Fold in the almond mixture, then the cooled chocolate. Transfer to a pastry bag fitted with a ⅞16-inch-wide plain tip, such as Ateco Number 805.

4. Pipe 1½-inch-wide mounds of the batter, about 1 inch apart, on the sheets. Bake until the edges are firm and the macaroons lift easily from the paper, about 30 minutes (see Note). Cool completely on the sheets.

NOTE

Usually when baking cookies on two racks, the positions of the racks are switched halfway through baking to allow for even baking. Because macaroons are created from a somewhat delicate meringue, and could fall if jostled, this isn't a good idea. If necessary, simply allow extra time for the cookies on the middle rack to finish baking (the top rack cooks more quickly because heat rises).

MAKE AHEAD

The macaroons can be prepared up to 3 days ahead and stored in an airtight container at room temperature.

COCONUT MACAROONS
KOKOBUSSERLN
Makes about 30 macaroons

As in America, coconut is one of the most popular macaroon variations in Austria. However, these have a crisp, meringue-like texture and a hint of lemon that make them much different than our chewy macaroons. Read the Note in the preceeding recipe about baking the macaroons.

■ ■ ■

3 large egg whites, at room temperature
1¼ cups confectioners' sugar
2 cups shredded sweetened coconut
2 tablespoons all-purpose flour
Grated zest of 1 lemon

■ ■ ■

1. Position racks in the center and top third of the oven and heat to 325°F. Line two baking sheets with parchment paper.

2. Beat the egg whites in a medium bowl with a handheld electric mixer on high speed until soft peaks form. Gradually beat in the confectioners' sugar, and beat until stiff, shiny peaks form. Fold in the coconut, flour, and lemon zest. Transfer to a pastry bag fitted with a ⅞16-inch-wide plain tip, such as Ateco Number 805.

3. Pipe out 1½-inch mounds on the sheets, about 1 inch apart. Bake until the edges are firm and the

Aida

A Viennese institution, Aida is everyone's favorite everyday bakery—the place you'd go to pick up a birthday cake for someone at the office, or little cakes for a Jause.

Their desserts are mass-produced (they make more than 1.2 million pieces of more than 200 products a year), but no matter: They have to be excellent to be so popular with the discerning Viennese. With that kind of production (they even provide the Austrian McDonald's with ice cream birthday cakes), their cakes are necessarily machine-finished. However, during a personal tour of their factory at the end of town, I was surprised to find it surrounded by orchards. The apples, apricots, and quinces from these very trees are used to make fillings and preserves for their cakes. Not exactly a cookie-cutter mentality, after all.

macaroons are lightly browned and can be easily lifted from the sheet, about 30 minutes (see Note, page 146). Cool completely on the sheets.

MAKE AHEAD

The macaroons can be prepared up to 3 days ahead and stored in an airtight container at room temperature.

CHESTNUT "POTATOES"
KAŠTANOVÉ BRAMBŮRKY
Makes about 24 truffles

These are really a truffle-like confection, but they appear next to the cookies in many a bakery display case during the Christmas holidays. Like fruit-shaped marzipan, these are supposed to charmingly resemble potatoes. They're made with fresh chestnuts, and they need to dry and firm at room temperature for three days before serving. Thanks to Czech-born food writer Michael Krondl for this recipe.

■ ■ ■

12 ounces fresh chestnuts
½ cup granulated sugar
¼ cup brandy
1 ounce unsweetened chocolate, grated on the large holes of a box grater
Pinch of freshly grated nutmeg
¼ teaspoon vanilla extract
¼ cup Dutch-processed cocoa powder
¼ cup confectioners' sugar

■ ■ ■

1. Using a small serrated knife, cut an "X" on the flat side of each chestnut. Place in a medium saucepan and cover with water. Cover and bring to a boil over high heat. Reduce the heat to medium low and simmer to loosen the skins, about 10 minutes.

2. Drain the chestnuts, transfer to a bowl, and cover to keep as hot as possible. Protecting your hands from the hot chestnuts with a towel, and using a small paring knife, peel the hard outer and thin inner shells. Chop the chestnuts; you should have about 1¾ cups of chestnut pieces.

3. In a small saucepan, bring the granulated sugar and brandy to a boil over medium heat. Reduce the heat to low and simmer for 1 minute. (Take care not to let the brandy catch fire. Have a lid handy to put on the saucepan to extinguish the flames, if necessary.) Add the chestnuts and cover tightly. Simmer, stirring occasionally and adding water if the liquid evaporates too quickly, on medium-low heat until the chestnuts are very tender, 10 to 15 minutes.

4. Transfer the hot chestnuts and syrup to a food processor fitted with the metal blade. Add the chocolate and purée. Add the nutmeg and vanilla and process until very smooth. Transfer to a bowl and cool until easy to handle.

5. Form the chestnut mixture in 1-inch balls. Sift the cocoa and confectioners' sugar together into a small bowl. Roll the balls in the cocoa mixture, then form them into irregularly shaped "potatoes." Store in an airtight container at a cool room temperature for at least 3 days, then refrigerate until serving. Roll again in the cocoa mixture before serving.

MAKE AHEAD

The truffles can be prepared up to 1 week ahead, stored in an airtight container at a cool room temperature.

LINZER "EYES"
LINZER AUGEN
Makes about 30 large cookies

Many bakers use spicy, nutty Linzertorte dough to make preserve-filled ring-shaped cookies that look like big eyes. You'll need two round cookie cutters, 2½ inches and 1 inch, to cut out the cookies.

■ ■ ■

Linzer Dough (page 52)
½ cup raspberry or black currant preserves
Confectioners' sugar, for garnish

■ ■ ■

1. Position racks in the top third and center of the oven and heat to 350°F. Line two large cookie sheets with parchment paper.
2. Place one half of the dough on a well-floured surface and dust the top with flour. Roll out into a ¼-inch-thick sheet, being sure the dough doesn't stick to the surface (slide a long metal spatula under the dough to check, dusting the work surface and top of the dough with additional flour as needed). Using a 2½-inch round fluted cookie cutter, cut out rounds of dough and place ½ inch apart on a cookie sheet. Knead

the scraps together, and roll out more cookies until the dough is used up. Repeat the procedure with the other portion of dough. Using a 1-inch round fluted cookie cutter, cut holes from the centers of half the rounds. If the dough softens, making it difficult to cut out the holes, refrigerate it briefly.
3. Bake, switching the positions of the cookie sheets from top to bottom and front to back halfway through baking, until the cookies are barely beginning to brown on the edges, about 12 minutes. Cool completely on the sheets.
4. Stir the preserves to loosen them. For each cookie, spoon about ½ teaspoon of preserves into the center of an uncut cookie round and top with a ring-shaped round. Sift confectioners' sugar over the cookies.

MAKE AHEAD
The dough can be prepared up to 2 days ahead, covered tightly with plastic wrap, and refrigerated. The cookies can be prepared up to 3 days ahead and stored in layers separated by wax paper in an airtight container at room temperature.

VANILLA CRESCENTS
VANILLEN KIPFERLN
Makes about 42 cookies

These crescents are *the* Austro-Hungarian Christmas cookie, and during the holidays you will find mountains of the little vanilla-sugar-coated treats in Konditorei windows. Crisp yet tender at the same time, they are at their very best when made with a vanilla bean instead of extract. Vanilla sugar is a staple European grocery item, but it's not so easy to find here. One way to make it is to bury a vanilla bean in confectioners' or granulated sugar (depending on its final use) for a couple of weeks, allowing the bean to slowly release its scent and flavor into the sugar. My method is for those bakers who don't always think ahead, and gives a stronger vanilla flavor.

∎ ∎ ∎

COOKIES
2 cups all-purpose flour
I cup (3½ ounces) natural sliced almonds
Pinch of salt
I cup (2 sticks) unsalted butter,
at cool room temperature
¾ cup confectioners' sugar
½ vanilla bean, split lengthwise
I large egg yolk, or more as needed

VANILLA SUGAR
½ cup granulated sugar
½ vanilla bean

∎ ∎ ∎

1. To make the cookies: Process the flour, almonds, and salt in a food processor fitted with the metal blade until the almonds are very finely chopped, almost a powder. Beat the butter in the bowl of a heavy-duty mixer fitted with the paddle blade on high speed until smooth, about 1 minute. On low speed, gradually beat in the confectioners' sugar, then return the speed to high and beat until the mixture is very light in color and texture, scraping down the sides of the bowl often, about 2 minutes. Using the tip of a small knife, scrape in the seeds from the vanilla bean, reserving the pod.

Add the yolk to the dough and mix. Remove the bowl from the stand. Using a spoon, stir in the flour mixture to make a stiff dough that holds together when pressed. (If the dough is crumbly, add a bit more beaten egg yolk.) Gather the dough up into a thick disk, wrap in plastic wrap, and refrigerate for at least 1 hour.

2. Meanwhile, make the vanilla sugar: Process the sugar, vanilla bean, and reserved vanilla pod in a blender until the bean is very finely chopped (it won't be completely pulverized) and the sugar is ground to a powder. Sift through a wire sieve into a medium bowl to remove any large pieces of vanilla.

3. Position racks in the center and top third of the oven and heat to 350°F. Line two baking sheets with parchment paper.

4. Using about 2 teaspoons of dough for each, roll the dough between your palms to soften (it will be crumbly at first, but will come together with the heat of your hands). Roll into a 3-inch rope with tapered ends, form into a crescent, and place on the sheets.

5. Bake until the cookies are a light golden brown around the edges, 15 to 17 minutes. Cool for 2 minutes on the sheets. Roll the warm cookies in the vanilla sugar to coat. Reserve any remaining vanilla sugar. Cool completely. If necessary before serving, give the cookies another toss in the reserved vanilla sugar.

MAKE AHEAD

The dough can be prepared up to 2 days ahead, or frozen up to 1 month and thawed overnight in the refrigerator before using. The cookies can be baked up to 5 days ahead and stored in an airtight container at room temperature.

WALNUT CRESCENT COOKIES FROM POZSONY
POZSONY KIPFLI
Makes 48 cookies

When I was writing this book, I often heard, "I hope you have a recipe for Pozsony kipfli!" which are a favorite Christmas cookie. Pozsony, originally on the Hungarian side of the Austrian border, was called Pressburg in Germany and Austria, and today it is known as Bratislava and is the capital of Slovakia. The local walnut-filled crescents were so wonderful that they took on the city's name (in Vienna, they're known as *Pressburger Kipfeln*). They can be made as large as regular croissants, but this bite-size version, reminiscent of rugalach cookies, is equally popular. Thanks to Sarabeth Levine, owner of Sarabeth's Bakery in Manhattan, for sharing her recipe, an heirloom from her former mother-in-law, a formidable Hungarian baker.

■ ■ ■

DOUGH
1 teaspoon active dry yeast
½ cup warm milk (105° to 115°F.)
1 cup (2 sticks) unsalted butter, at cool room temperature
2 large eggs, at room temperature
1 tablespoon granulated sugar
1 teaspoon vanilla extract
½ teaspoon salt
3½ cups all-purpose flour, as needed

FILLING
2 cups coarsely chopped walnuts
¼ cup granulated sugar
⅓ cup brewed coffee

1 large egg yolk beaten with 1 teaspoon water, for glaze
Confectioners' sugar, for serving

■ ■ ■

1. To make the dough: Sprinkle the yeast over the milk in a small bowl. Let stand 5 minutes, then stir to dissolve. In a standing heavy-duty mixer fitted with the paddle blade, beat the butter on high speed until light in color, occasionally scraping down the bowl, about 3 minutes. One at a time, beat in the eggs, then the yeast, sugar, vanilla, and salt. Reduce the speed to low. Gradually beat in enough of the flour to make a soft, slightly sticky dough that cleans the sides of the bowl. Gather up the dough into a ball. Return to the machine and beat with the paddle blade (not the dough hook) on medium-low speed until the dough is shiny, about 3 minutes. Knead briefly on an unfloured work surface and form into a ball. The dough will look rough. Wrap the dough in plastic wrap and refrigerate for 30 to 60 minutes. (The dough should barely rise.)

2. Make the filling: Process the walnuts and sugar in a food processor fitted with the metal blade until the nuts are very finely chopped into a paste. Add the coffee and pulse to moisten. Transfer to a bowl.

3. Line two baking sheets with parchment paper. Cut the dough into 4 portions and form into flat disks. Working with one disk at a time, roll out on a lightly floured surface into a 14-inch round. Spread one fourth of the filling on the dough, leaving a 1-inch border around the edges and a 2-inch-diameter circle empty in the center. Using a pizza wheel or sharp knife, cut the round into quarters, then each quarter into thirds, to make twelve triangles. Starting at a long end, roll up each triangle and place 1 inch apart on the baking sheets. Cover each sheet loosely with plastic wrap and let stand in a warm place while the oven heats. (The cookies should barely rise.)

4. Position racks in the center and top third of the oven and heat to 350°F. Brush the tops of the cookies with the egg glaze. Bake, switching the positions of the sheets from top to bottom and front to back halfway during baking, until golden brown, about 20 minutes. Some of the filling may melt out of the cookies, but the parchment will prevent scorching. Transfer to wire racks to cool completely. Sift the confectioners' sugar over the cookies before serving.

MAKE AHEAD

The cookies are best when served the day they are made.

THUMBPRINT COOKIES
HUSSAREN
Makes 36 cookies

Looking like the bright buttons on a Hussar's uniform, these melt-in-your-mouth treats can be filled with a variety of preserves to add color to your cookie selection. Apricot, raspberry, strawberry, or even pineapple are all good choices. Most versions call for filling the cookies after baking, but the sticky preserves make the cookies difficult to store. Filling them about halfway through the baking period sets the preserves and solves the problem.

■ ■ ■

¾ cup (1½ sticks) unsalted butter,
at cool room temperature
1 cup confectioners' sugar, plus more
for sifting
2 large egg yolks, at room temperature
1 teaspoon vanilla extract
1½ cups coarsely chopped walnuts or
toasted, peeled hazelnuts
1½ cups all-purpose flour, divided
Pinch of salt
½ cup fruit preserves (see suggestions above)

■ ■ ■

1. Position racks in the center and top third of the oven and heat to 350°F. Line 2 large baking sheets with parchment paper.

2. Beat the butter with an electric handheld mixer on high speed just until smooth. On low speed, add the confectioners' sugar, just to combine. Beat in the yolks and vanilla.

3. Process the nuts with ½ cup of the flour until the nuts are ground into a powder. Add the remaining 1 cup flour and the salt and pulse to combine. Add the nut flour to the butter mixture and stir to make a stiff dough.

4. Using a level tablespoon of dough for each cookie, roll into walnut-size balls and place 1 inch apart on the sheets. Using the end of a wooden spoon or your little finger, made a ¼-inch deep indentation in the center of each cookie.

5. Bake until the cookies are set, about 12 minutes. Remove the sheets of cookies from the oven. Place the preserves in a large plastic storage bag. Squeeze the preserves into the corner of the bag, and snip off the corner with scissors to make a ½-inch-wide opening. Pipe the preserves into the indentations in the cookies. Return to the oven, switching the positions of the sheets from top to bottom, and continue baking until the cookies are lightly browned, 7 to 10 minutes.

6. Transfer the cookies to a wire rack and cool completely. Before serving, sift confectioners' sugar over the cookies.

MAKE AHEAD

The cookies can be made up to 5 days ahead and stored in layers separated by wax paper in an airtight container at room temperature.

MARDIS GRAS DOUGHNUTS
FASCHINGKRAPFEN
Makes 12 doughnuts

These feather-light doughnuts are filled with various goodies (apricot preserves, prune butter, chocolate, cooked apples) and stenciled in vanilla-flavored confectioners' sugar to identify the filling (an M for *Marillen*, or apricot, and so on). They are sometimes called "ribbon doughnuts," because the perfectly made ones have a pale band around their equator (the doughnuts are purposely cooked in a shallow depth of oil so it doesn't reach the center, leaving a belt that is cooked by the residual heat). Don't be concerned if yours lack this mark and are completely golden brown—they'll still be delicious.

To cut out the dough, you'll need two round biscuit cutters, 2¾ inches and 2½ inches in diameter. The first cuts out the dough, and the second seals the two sandwiched rounds together—an important step to keep the preserves from seeping out during frying.

● ● ●

SPONGE
⅔ ounce (⅓ cube) fresh compressed yeast or
2¼ teaspoons (1 envelope) dry yeast
½ cup milk (heated to 105° to 115°F.
if using dry yeast)
½ cup all-purpose flour
1 teaspoon sugar

DOUGH
½ cup lukewarm milk
4 tablespoons unsalted butter, melted
2 tablespoons granulated sugar
1 tablespoon golden rum
Grated zest of 1 lemon
½ teaspoon salt
4 large egg yolks, at room temperature
3¼ cups all-purpose flour, as needed

Approximately ¼ cup apricot preserves
1 large egg white, beaten until foamy
Vegetable oil, for deep-frying
Confectioners' sugar, for dusting, optional

■ ■ ■

1. To make the sponge: Crumble the yeast into the milk in a small bowl, let stand for 3 minutes, and whisk to dissolve the yeast. Add the flour and sugar and whisk until smooth. Cover tightly with plastic wrap and let stand until doubled in volume, about 30 minutes.

2. To make the dough: Whisk the milk, butter, sugar, rum, zest, and salt in the bowl of a heavy-duty standing mixer. Whisk in the yolks, then the sponge. Attach to the mixer and fit with the paddle blade. With the mixer on low speed, gradually add enough of the flour to make a soft, sticky dough that barely cleans the sides of the bowl. Increase the speed to medium and beat the dough with the paddle blade (don't use the dough hook) for 2 minutes.

3. Gather up the dough into a ball and knead briefly until smooth. Place the dough in a large buttered bowl, turn to coat with butter, and cover tightly with plastic wrap. Let stand in a warm place until doubled in volume, 45 to 60 minutes. (The warm ingredients make this dough rise more quickly than others.)

4. On a very lightly floured work surface, roll

out the dough to ¼ inch thick. Using a 2¾-inch round biscuit cutter, cut out rounds of dough, set aside on a baking sheet lined with a lightly floured kitchen towel, and cover loosely with plastic wrap (you can stack the rounds). Kneading the scraps until smooth, roll and cut out to make a total of 24 rounds, discarding any excess dough.

5. Place a heaping ½ teaspoon of preserves in the center of a round. Moisten the circumference of the round with the egg white. Cover with a second round, pinching the edges together with your fingertips (the seal should end up in the middle of the two rounds, forming a "belt"). Place a 2½-inch round biscuit cutter over the sandwiched rounds, and press down to cut out a doughnut, discarding the trimmings. Double check to be sure the doughnut is sealed. Transfer to a baking sheet lined with a lightly floured

kitchen towel. Cover loosely with plastic wrap and let stand in a warm place until the doughnuts have barely risen, about 15 minutes. Do not let the doughnuts rise until puffy or doubled, or they will expand too much during frying.

6. Pour oil into a large heavy skillet or electric skillet just to a depth of ½ inch and heat over high heat to 350°F. Place a wire rack over a jelly-roll pan to drain the doughnuts (this works much more efficiently than paper towels).

7. Place 3 or 4 doughnuts in the oil and cover. (Covering doughnuts during frying goes against deep-frying convention, but this contains the heat and helps cook the exposed side of the dough.) Fry until the undersides are golden brown, about 1½ minutes. Turn and fry uncovered until the other sides are golden brown, about 1 minute. There should be a white ribbon around the center of each doughnut where the

▪ THE STORY BEHIND ▪
FASCHINGKRAPFEN

In the Danube region, many foods are related to the season, but probably none as much so as the filled doughnuts known as Faschingkrapfen. They were traditionally served only in the carnival season period between Epiphany and Ash Wednesday, with huge Faschingkrapfen feasts on Mardi Gras. Even though bakeries now offer them year-round, old-timers consider this a sacrilege.

This is another Viennese recipe that is filled with myth and legend. For a while, Faschingkrapfen were called *Cillikrapfen*, as they were the specialty of a baker named Cecile (Cilli was her nickname). It was claimed that Cilli invented the doughnut when she angrily threw a piece of dough at her husband and it landed in a pot of cooking fat. This story isn't likely, as Faschingkrapfen are intricately made, and not just tossed in oil.

Regardless of their pedigree, the Viennese love Faschingkrapfen. How much? It is said that during the pre-Lenten celebrations of the Congress of Vienna, the royal bakers made more than fifteen million Faschingkrapfen to meet the demand.

I was once in Vienna on Fat Tuesday and went on a Faschingkrapfen crawl with my friend Karitas at the Naschmarkt, Vienna's outdoor market. Not only did every bakery in the complex sell Faschingkrapfen, they had temporary tables set up with heaping mountains of doughnuts, sold by staff bedecked in Mardi Gras costumes. We bought a selection of about two dozen and, armed with a plastic knife to cut them into bite-size pieces, we went to a local coffeehouse to evaluate them. We expected some resistance from the waiter (after all, they sell food at the café and probably wouldn't want any brought in from the outside), so we prepared ourselves for an argument. None came. As a Viennese, he understood that two people and two dozen Faschingkrapfen was the most natural thing in the world, especially on Mardi Gras.

oil did not reach. Using a wire skimmer, transfer the doughnuts to the rack to drain and cool. Sift the confectioners' sugar over the warm doughnuts. Reheat the oil between batches. Cool the doughnuts completely.

APPLE DOUGHNUTS
Substitute canned apple pie filling for the apricot preserves.

CHOCOLATE DOUGHNUTS
Substitute chocolate-nut spread (such as Nutella brand) for the apricot preserves.

PRUNE DOUGHNUTS
Substitute prune butter (lekvar) for the apricot preserves.

MAKE AHEAD
The doughnuts are best served the same day they are made.

CRULLERS WITH RUM GLAZE
SPRITZKRAPFEN
Makes 14 crullers

Egg-rich doughnuts with curly edges, Spritz-krapfen are prepared from cream puff dough piped through a star-tipped pastry bag. You can substitute another alcoholic beverage for the rum (applejack is good), or use fruit juice (orange juice would be delicious).

■ ■ ■

Cream Puff Dough (page 14)
Vegetable oil, for deep-frying

RUM GLAZE
2 cups confectioners' sugar
2 tablespoons golden rum
1 tablespoon water, approximately

■ ■ ■

1. Cut out fourteen 4-inch squares of parchment paper. Place a large wire rack over a jelly-roll pan for draining the crullers.

2. Fit a large pastry bag with a ⁹⁄₁₆-inch-wide open star tip (such as Ateco Number 825), and fill with the cream puff dough. On each piece of parchment paper, pipe a 3-inch-diameter circle of dough.

3. Meanwhile, fill a Dutch oven or large saucepan with enough oil to come 3 inches up the sides. Heat the oil over high heat to 360°F.

4. In batches, without crowding, place the dough circles (still on their papers) upside-down in the hot oil. Cook for about 15 seconds, then use kitchen tongs to pull off and discard the papers. Cook on high heat, trying to keep the temperature as close to 360°F. as possible, turning once, until golden brown on both sides, about 4 minutes. Using a wire skimmer, transfer the crullers to the rack to drain and cool. Reheat the oil between batches.

5. To make the glaze: Sift the confectioners' sugar into a medium bowl. Whisk in the rum and enough water to make a glaze with the consistency of heavy cream. Dip each cruller, upside down, in the glaze, and let the excess glaze drip off. Place the crullers, right side up, on the rack to dry and set the glaze.

MAKE AHEAD
The crullers are best the day they are made.

·PANCAKES· &·SWEET· ·OMELETS·

Warm desserts have a special place in the collective culinary consciousness of the old empire. Pancakes, which can be as thin as crêpes or thick and cakelike, are considered national treasures and are enjoyed throughout the day, not just for dessert. For American tables, these dishes are perfect for the leisurely Sunday brunch.

The Fall and Rebirth of the Kaffeehaus

After World War I, and the fall of the empire, a new literary coffeehouse was a necessity: Art cannot exist without change. In Vienna the torch was passed to the Café Herrenhof, near both the Griensteidl and the Central. In spite of the presence of future Nobel Prize winner Elias Canetti (he won for literature in 1981), movie-star-to-be Peter Lorre, and Franz Werfel (whose book *The Song of Bernadette* was an enormous international best-seller), its vogue lasted only until the 1938 Anschluss, when Adolf Hitler annexed Austria. It struggled along through the war and fizzled out in the 1950s. The war decimated Vienna's Jewish population, and tragically, there were simply fewer people to return to the tables. The establishment that now stands in its place is an espresso bar.

Espresso was another reason for the long fallow period of the coffeehouse. In the early 1950s, Italian espresso trickled upward into Austria. Instead of meditating over their Melange (coffee with hot milk), the Viennese started downing their tiny piping-hot demitasses of espresso Italian-style, in a few quick sips. Even though many coffeehouses fought to maintain tradition for drip-brewed coffee, popular taste ran to Vienna Roast coffee pressure-brewed in a steaming espresso machine, a habit that remains.

The Viennese were working hard to rebuild their city, and leisure time was at a premium. In prewar Vienna, there had been scores of newspapers, magazines, and brochures to be written, and writers had worked feverishly at their coffeehouse tables to supply fresh copy. Many a writer's imagination had been fueled by a cup of coffee and the conversation of friends. Now the job of freelance writer was an endangered species. The atmosphere of the espresso bars reflected the clientele's new attitude: They were people who didn't need an attractive interior to drink their coffee. Stools replaced comfortable chairs, pegs on a wall took over for wrought-iron coat racks. Like other generations before them, this one rejected the values of their fathers and sought new places to gather with their friends and solve the problems of the world.

Without the customers to support them, many coffeehouses closed. The spacious, elegant cafés of the Ringstrasse were perfunctorily turned into banks, automobile showrooms, and fast-food outlets. In fact, café owners refer to the 1960s as *Kaffehaussterben:* the death of the coffeehouse. After the postwar dust finally settled, and the Austrians regained a sense of place in the European community, many leaders believed that coffeehouses could be a great civic tool for restoring Viennese pride. In 1983, the government gave landmark status to four cafés: Landtmann (the favorite of the city leaders, near the Rathaus, and Freud's café of choice), Goldegg (a working-class café near the Belvedere with a rare furnace imported from America), Sperl (built in the classic L shape), and Prückel (even though little of its original design remains, it housed a famous cabaret).

Perhaps the renovation of the Sperl is a good way to show the loving care that was lavished on these landmarks. Under the direction of architect Joerg Nairz, the old fabric designs were carefully copied and woven. The wooden floor was repaired and refinished, and the marble-topped tables, Thonet chairs, and heavy iron coat racks were refurbished. Discrete air filters were installed to recirculate the chronically tobacco-smoke-laden air. Coffeehouses once again became places to see and be seen.

As usual, the fates of coffeehouses in Budapest and Prague mirrored that of the Viennese, and you could glean the former life of many a drab state office building by its crumbling bas-relief decorations and huge, if grimy, windows. Both of these cities had boasted thousands of coffeehouses in their golden years.

In Hungary, an entire revolution had sprung from a coffeehouse in 1848. News of the Viennese uprising had spread from the Café Pilvax throughout Budapest, giving rise to a homegrown insurrection against Hapsburg rule. Such famous Hungarian patriots as Lajos Kossuth; Lajos, Count Batthyány; István, Count Széchenyi; and Ferenc Deák, whose names grace many streets and squares in Budapest, plotted revolution over countless cups of Café Pilvax's brew. The revolution was brutally squelched by the Hapsburg forces, with help from the Russians, and many of these patriots became martyrs as well. Budapest also sported a Café Central, which, along with the Café New York, was a hothouse of Hungarian literary thought. With the spread of Communism, many coffeehouses closed, or their names were changed to downplay any unpleasant associations (the luxurious Café New York became Café Hungaria).

In Prague, the art-deco Café Slavia managed to stay open for a while even under Communism. It was home to Václav Havel and his associates as they planted the seeds for the Velvet Revolution. With the rise of democracy, many of the old places reopened. Budapest has a Café Central once again, Prague's Kavárna Obecní dům (Municipal House Café) is one of the most beautiful in all of Europe, and after a long hiatus complicated by a real-estate snafu, the Slavia is back full force.

Almost every restaurant in Hungary offers crêpes in sweet and savory forms. Historians believe that the flat pancake goes back to Roman times. Roman soldiers stationed in present-day Romania may have been the ones to perfect these pancakes, which they called *placenta* (from Latin meaning flat cake). All of the words for crêpe— the Austrian-German (*Palatschinken*), the Hungarian (*palacsinta*), and the Czech (*palačinky*) —derive from this root. The pancakes were originally made from corn and other grains; wheat is a relatively recent development.

Sweet omelets came into favor during the initial exchange of French and Austrian cuisines in the early eighteenth century. The Viennese always looked at the omelet as a French invention, and even though some old cookbooks referred to them as *Eierkuchen* ("egg cakes"), they were also known as *französische Strudelflecken* (loosely translated as "French strudel squares"). When the French diplomats and their attendant chefs made such an impression on the Viennese palate during the Congress of Vienna, the sweet omelet rose to new heights and its fluffy texture delighted many a gourmet. During the subsequent years, omelets were named for many famous persons, such as Johann Strauss the younger (served with an orange sauce), the French author George Sand (garnished with

chestnut purée and served with a vanilla sauce), and the Austro-Hungarian Crown Princess Stephanie (filled with apricots or preserves).

The crêpes in this chapter were made with a standard 8-inch nonstick skillet, measured across the bottom of the pan. Authentic steel crêpe pans are available at some kitchenware stores, but they need to be seasoned with oil before use, and they lose their seasoning easily unless used often. If you use one, never wash it with hot soap and water, or you will remove the cooked-on seasoning and need to reseason. Just wipe it with a moist paper towel and coarse salt, which will remove the cooking residue.

The larger pancakes like Kaiserschmarren and Stephanie Omelet were tested in a heavy 12-inch nonstick skillet. This pan should be standard equipment in everyone's kitchen; it's equally useful for savory cooking. It can be used to sauté an entire cut-up chicken, which is difficult to fit into a smaller skillet. Most brands are made for the professional kitchen, so the handle is ovenproof. If you have a model with a plastic handle, protect it in the oven with a double-thick wrapping of aluminum foil.

BASIC CRÊPES
PALATSCHINKEN
Makes 16 to 18 crêpes

Central European crêpe recipes rarely include butter, as the cooks believe that the filling and sauce will be rich enough, and they are right. To allow the flour time to absorb the liquid and strengthen the batter, make it at least one hour before cooking the pancakes. Sparkling water gives the crêpes a light texture without chemical leavenings.

This recipe makes a few more crêpes than you may need. Cooks who are inexperienced crêpemakers will need to practice, and even master crêpemakers know that the first crêpe is usually tossed out, having served to test and modulate the heat under the skillet. You will have enough crêpes for up to nine guests, if you adjust the fillings. Or, if you have more than you need, freeze them. A stash of frozen crêpes is very useful: For an impromptu breakfast or dessert, just defrost the crêpes at room temperature, fill with your favorite jam, brush with melted butter, and bake in a toaster oven until sizzling.

■ ■ ■

1½ cups milk
3 large eggs
1½ teaspoons sugar
Pinch of salt
1½ cups all-purpose flour
½ cup club soda
Nonstick vegetable oil spray, for cooking

■ ■ ■

1. Whisk the milk, eggs, sugar, and salt in a medium bowl to combine. Add the flour and whisk until smooth. Cover and set aside at room temperature for 1 to 2 hours. Just before making the pancakes, stir in the soda.

2. Over medium-high heat, heat a nonstick skillet that measures 7½ to 8 inches in diameter (measured across the bottom) until the skillet is hot, about 1½ minutes. Spray lightly with the oil. Pour a scant ¼ cup of batter into the bottom of the skillet and immediately tilt and swirl the skillet so the batter coats the bottom in a thin layer. Fill in any holes with dribbles of batter from the measuring cup. Cook until the edges look dry and the top is set, about 1 minute. Using a spatula, lift and turn the crêpe. Cook until the other side is splotched with golden brown spots, about 30 seconds. Transfer to a plate. Repeat with the remaining batter, separating the crêpes with pieces of wax paper.

MAKE AHEAD
The crêpes can be prepared up to 1 day ahead, cooled, covered tightly with plastic wrap, and refrigerated. Or freeze the crêpes for up to 1 month.

GUNDEL-STYLE CRÊPES
PALACSINTA GUNDEL MÓDRA
Makes 6 servings

Gundel, nestled on the outskirts of Budapest's City Park, is the most respected and luxurious restaurant in the city. Although it isn't a café or bakery, many of Gundel's dishes have become so famous in Hungary that they have found their way onto the menus of more modest establishments. This is one of their most enduring creations: crêpes filled with a walnut paste, served with a thin chocolate sauce.

■ ■ ■

FILLING
½ cup raisins
⅓ cup amber rum
1⅔ cups coarsely chopped walnuts
½ cup sugar
¾ cup heavy cream
Grated zest of ½ orange
Pinch of ground cinnamon

CHOCOLATE SYRUP
1 cup milk
¼ cup confectioners' sugar
3½ ounces bittersweet chocolate, finely chopped

2 tablespoons Dutch-processed cocoa powder
2 tablespoons amber rum
2 large egg yolks
1 tablespoon unsalted butter,
at room temperature
¼ teaspoon vanilla extract

12 Basic Crêpes (page 160)
2 tablespoons unsalted butter, melted,
for brushing
Confectioners' sugar, for garnish

■ ■ ■

1. To make the filling: Soak the raisins in the rum in a small bowl until plumped, about 1 hour. Or microwave on medium for 30 seconds, and cool.
2. Process the walnuts and sugar in a food processor until the nuts are very finely chopped. Combine the walnut mixture, heavy cream, orange zest, cinnamon, and the raisins with their liquid in a medium saucepan. Bring to a simmer over medium heat, stirring often. Cook, stirring constantly to avoid scorching, until thickened into a paste, about 5 minutes. Transfer to a bowl.
3. To make the chocolate syrup: Bring the milk and sugar to a simmer in a medium saucepan over medium heat. Place the chocolate in a heat-proof bowl, and pour the hot milk over it. Let stand 3 minutes, then whisk to melt the chocolate.
4. Briskly whisk the cocoa and rum in a medium bowl to dissolve the cocoa. Whisk in the egg yolks. Gradually whisk in the hot chocolate mixture. Return to the saucepan and stir over medium-low heat until thick enough to lightly coat a wooden spatula (about 185°F. on an instant-read thermometer), about 3 minutes. Stir in the butter and vanilla until smooth. Strain into a glass measuring cup and keep the sauce warm by placing it in a saucepan of very hot water.
5. Position a rack in the center of the oven and heat to 375°F. Lightly butter a 15½ × 10½-inch jelly-roll pan.
6. Place a crêpe on a work surface, spotted side up. Place a heaping tablespoon of the filling in the lower right quadrant of the crêpe. Fold the crêpe in quarters, enclosing the filling, and place on the jelly-roll pan. Repeat with the remaining

crêpes and filling, overlapping the crêpes. Brush with the melted butter and bake until heated through, about 10 minutes.
7. Transfer 2 crêpes to each serving plate, with their points facing the top of the plate and overlapping as needed. Cover one side of the crêpes with a sheet of wax paper. Sift the confectioners' sugar over the crêpes and remove the wax paper, leaving one side of the crêpes dusted with sugar. Mask the other side of the crêpes with the warm chocolate syrup. Serve immediately.

MAKE AHEAD

The walnut paste and chocolate syrup can be prepared up to 1 day ahead, covered, and refrigerated. Bring the walnut paste to room temperature, and thin with hot water, if necessary. Reheat the chocolate syrup in a double boiler over simmering heat, stirring constantly, until heated through. Take care not to overheat, or the egg yolks will curdle.

JAM-FILLED CRÊPES
OBST PALATSCHINKEN
Makes 12 crêpes

The sweet possibilities for filling crêpes are almost endless. Apricot preserves are a popular choice, not to mention prune butter, cherry preserves, or Nutella, the Italian hazelnut-chocolate paste. You can also use the poppy seed filling from kolacky (page 102), or the walnut filling on page 150. Sprinkle them with your choice of walnuts or confectioners' sugar, or serve them with a chocolate sauce, if the filling is compatible.

■ ■ ■

12 Basic Crêpes (page 160)
¾ cup apricot preserves, or see other
suggestions above
2 tablespoons unsalted butter, melted,
for brushing
Walnut Topping (recipe follows) or
confectioners' sugar, for garnish

1. Position a rack in the center of the oven and heat to 375°F. Lightly butter a 15½ × 10½-inch jelly-roll pan.

2. Place a crêpe on a work surface, spotted side up. Place a heaping tablespoon of the filling in the lower right quadrant of the crêpe. Fold the crêpe in quarters, enclosing the filling, and place on the pan. Repeat with the remaining crêpes and filling, overlapping the crêpes. Brush with the butter and bake until heated through, about 10 minutes.

3. To serve, transfer 2 crêpes to each serving plate. Sprinkle with walnut topping or sift with confectioners' sugar and serve immediately.

WALNUT TOPPING

Process ½ cup coarsely chopped walnuts with 2 tablespoons sugar until the walnuts are very finely chopped, almost a powder.

THE EMPEROR'S PANCAKE
KAISERSCHMARREN
Makes 2 to 4 servings

Kaiserschmarren is probably the most obvious example of Austrian *Mehlspeisen* (literally, a repast made from flour). This large pancake, torn into pieces to give it an appealing rustic look, is truly a "flour meal"—quickly prepared from basic ingredients, yet hearty enough for supper. The classic accompaniment is *Zwetschkenröster*, which mysteriously translates as "roasted plums," even though the plums are stewed. Two Austrians could readily polish off this amount of Kaiserschmarren, but for American tastes and appetites, it would more likely serve four as a hearty breakfast or brunch dish, served with any jam or warm fruit compote, with bacon or sausage on the side.

When making Kaiserschmarren, remember that part of its charm is its imperfect look. Most cooks would question quartering and flipping sections of an almost-raw pancake, but the batter will eventually cook through to make a light, fluffy pancake.

▪ THE STORY BEHIND ▪
KAISERSCHMARREN

In Austrian dialect, *Schmarren* means "a little nothing," or "nonsense," the kind of word that is said with a shrug. How did such an illustrious personage as the Kaiser get mixed up with this inconsequential (but delicious) dish?

Franz Joseph wanted to be seen as a benevolent emperor of the people. While he certainly ruled with an autocratic hand, he spent his down time hiking in the mountains near his estate in Bad Ischl, clad in lederhosen and a hunting cap complete with feather. He loved simple food; in fact, his favorite dinner was said to be *Tapfelspitz*, a very plain boiled beef dish. Legend says that the pancake was originally named for the Kaiserin, but since her taste ran to more extravagant fare, it was a simple step to delete two letters and rename it for the Kaiser.

Nice story, but like so many other Viennese tales, it is not easy to corroborate with fact. Actually, this kind of pancake had been a staple of farmhouse cooking for centuries. It's possible that the word *Schmarren* derives from the old German *Schmer*, another word for *Schmalz*, or melted fat, as these pancakes were always cooked in hot fat (butter is preferred by today's cooks). An early eighteenth-century cookbook has recipes for schmarren made with rice, semolina, or bread crumbs, among other "flours."

• • •

"ROASTED" PLUMS
1 pound Italian prune-plums, pitted and
quartered lengthwise
1/4 cup granulated sugar
1 tablespoon fresh lemon juice
Grated zest of 1/2 lemon
Pinch of cinnamon
Pinch of ground cloves

BATTER
1/3 cup raisins
2 tablespoons golden rum, apple juice,
or water
4 large eggs, separated, at room temperature
3 tablespoons granulated sugar
1 cup milk
4 tablespoons unsalted butter (2 tablespoons
melted, and 2 tablespoons for cooking)
1 cup all-purpose flour
Pinch of salt
Confectioners' sugar, for serving

■ ■ ■

1. To make the "roasted" plums: Combine the plums, sugar, lemon juice and zest, cinnamon, and cloves in a medium saucepan. Cover and bring to a simmer over medium heat. Cook, stirring occasionally, until the plums are tender and juicy, but still hold their shape, about 10 minutes. Remove from the heat and keep warm.

2. To make the batter: In a small saucepan, bring the raisins and rum to a simmer (or, combine the raisins and rum in a small microwave-safe bowl, and microwave on high for 30 seconds). Set aside until ready to cook the pancakes. Drain off the rum before using.

3. In a medium bowl, using a handheld electric mixer at high speed or a whisk, beat the yolks and sugar until very thick and light in color. Beat in the milk and the 2 tablespoons of melted butter, then the flour and salt. Do not overbeat.

4. In a medium bowl, using clean beaters, beat the whites on high speed just until soft peaks form. Stir in about one fourth of the whites to lighten the mixture, then fold in the remaining whites.

5. In a 12-inch nonstick skillet over medium-high heat, heat 1 tablespoon of butter until sizzling.

Pour half of the batter into the skillet, and sprinkle with half of the raisins. Reduce the heat to medium and cook, uncovered, until the underside is golden brown and the pancake is set around the edges, about 3 minutes. Even though the top batter will be uncooked, using a heat-proof pancake turner (a plastic one won't scratch the nonstick skillet), cut the pancake into quarters and flip each quarter over. Don't worry if they fall on each other—just slide them back into the skillet. Using the edge of the spatula, cut the pancake into largish bite-size pieces. Continue cooking, turning the pieces occasionally, until cooked through, about 3 more minutes.

6. Sift confectioners' sugar over the pancake and serve immediately from the skillet. Use the remaining ingredients to make a second pancake when you've finished the first one.

CHEESE-FILLED CRÊPES
TOPFENPALATSCHINKEN
Makes 6 servings

Like their close relative blintzes, these rolled crêpes are a fine addition to any brunch menu. If farmer's cheese isn't available, rub small-curd cottage cheese through a wire strainer. The crêpes come with their own baked-on sour cream sauce; cornstarch keeps the sour cream from curdling.

• • •

FILLING
1/3 cup golden raisins
2 tablespoons golden rum
1 pound farmer's cheese
1/3 cup plus 1 tablespoon confectioners' sugar
3 large eggs, separated, at room temperature
Grated zest of 1 lemon

12 Basic Crêpes (page 160)
1/2 cup plus 1 tablespoon milk
1 teaspoon cornstarch
1 1/2 cups sour cream
Confectioners' sugar, for sprinkling

1. To make the filling: Soak the raisins in the rum in a small bowl until plumped, about 1 hour. Or microwave on medium for 30 seconds, and cool.
2. Stir the cheese and confectioners' sugar in a medium bowl to break up the cheese. Stir in the yolks, lemon zest, and the raisins and their liquid. Beat the whites in a medium bowl until soft peaks form, and fold into the cheese mixture.
3. Position a rack in the center of the oven and heat to 350°F. Lightly butter a 15 × 10-inch baking dish.
4. Place a crêpe on a work surface, spotted side up. Spoon about 2 tablespoons of the filling in a strip, slightly to the left of the center of the crêpe. Roll up the crêpe and place in the dish. Repeat with the remaining crêpes and filling, fitting 10 crêpes crosswise and 2 crêpes lengthwise to fill the dish.
5. Pour the milk into a medium bowl, sprinkle with the cornstarch, and whisk to dissolve. Whisk in the sour cream. Pour over the crêpes. Bake until the filling is cooked through, 25 to 30 minutes. Serve hot, sprinkled with the confectioners' sugar.

order from Sweet Celebrations (see Mail-Order Sources, page 225). The truth is, you can also spoon tablespoons of the batter onto a conventional griddle and still have Dalken. This recipe is too good to be restricted for use with the "correct" pan.

Dalken can be leavened with yeast or baking powder, but I prefer these delicate sour cream pancakes lightened by no more than air. The recipe makes an odd number of pancakes, allowing for a few not-so-perfect specimens for the cook's treat.

••••

FRUIT FILLING
½ pint fresh raspberries, blueberries, blackberries, or hulled and sliced strawberries
1 to 2 tablespoons granulated sugar
1 tablespoon fresh lemon juice

PANCAKES
4 large eggs, separated, at room temperature
¾ cup all-purpose flour
½ cup sour cream
½ teaspoon vanilla
Pinch of salt
¼ cup granulated sugar
Melted butter, for greasing pan
Confectioners' sugar, for serving

••••

SOUR CREAM MINI-PANCAKES
DALKEN
Makes about 28 pancakes, about 4 servings

Dalken originally came from Bohemia, the part of today's Czech Republic that supplied Vienna with a virtual army of accomplished bakers in the late nineteenth century. Dalken are more than just small pancakes sandwiched together with preserves or fresh fruit: They are always cooked in a special pan with indentations to keep the batter in perfect rounds. A true Dalken pan is something you'll have to bring back with you from a trip to Vienna or Prague. You can also use a Swedish pancake pan (also called a Plätte Panna), available at many specialty kitchenware shops and Scandinavian grocers and by mail

1. To make the fruit filling: In a medium bowl, mix the berries, sugar to taste, and lemon juice. Crush a few of the berries to release their juice. Cover and let stand at room temperature for 30 to 60 minutes so the berries can lose their chill and release more juices.
2. To make the pancakes: Position a rack in the center of the oven and heat to 200°F. Line a baking sheet with a clean kitchen towel (be sure it doesn't have any residual perfumes from washing, or the pancakes will pick up the scent).
3. In a medium bowl, whisk the egg yolks, flour, sour cream, vanilla, and salt until combined. In another medium bowl, using an electric handheld mixer at high speed, beat the egg whites and granulated sugar until they form soft, shiny peaks. Stir about one fourth of the whites into

the batter, then carefully fold in the remainder.

4. Heat a Swedish pancake pan over medium heat. Wipe the indentations with a paper towel dipped in melted butter. Using 1 tablespoon of batter for each, fill the indentations. Cook until tiny bubbles appear on the surface and the undersides are golden brown, about 2 minutes. Using a dinner knife or a heat-proof rubber spatula, turn the pancakes (don't worry if you don't fit the turned pancakes exactly back into their indentations). Cook until the other sides are golden, about 1½ minutes. Transfer to the prepared baking sheet and keep warm while making the rest.

5. To serve, sandwich 2 pancakes with a spoonful of the fruit filling, and arrange on plates. Sift confectioners' sugar over the top and serve immediately.

SALZBURG DESSERT SOUFFLÉ
SALZBURGER NOCKERL
Makes 4 servings

The best restaurants in Austria have made a specialty of Salzburger Nockerl, which, of course, was born in the mountain town to Vienna's southwest. But the original recipe bore no resemblance to today's soufflé-like puff. Nockerln were balls of cream-puff dough, poached in milk. Somewhere along the line, they started being baked to give them a glaze. Later, as France began asserting its culinary influence throughout Europe and chefs in other countries adapted their local recipes to give them a more sophisticated edge (and as stoves became more reliable), the Nockerl combined with the soufflé to create the current hybrid. It is usually served without a sauce, but a vanilla or raspberry sauce would not go unappreciated.

■ ■ ■

2 tablespoons unsalted butter, softened
⅓ cup plus 2 tablespoons granulated sugar, divided

6 large eggs, separated, at room temperature
4 large egg whites, at room temperature
⅔ cup milk
¼ cup all-purpose flour
1 teaspoon vanilla extract

■ ■ ■

1. Position a rack in the center of the oven and heat to 425°F. Slather the inside of a 2-quart baking dish, preferably oval, with the softened butter. Sprinkle with the 2 tablespoons of sugar and tilt to coat the dish. Set aside.

2. Beat the 10 egg whites in a large bowl with a handheld electric mixer at high speed until soft peaks form. Gradually beat in the remaining ⅓ cup of sugar and beat until the peaks are very stiff and shiny, but not dry.

3. Pour the milk into the dish and bake for 2 to 3 minutes while beating the yolks. The dish and milk must be hot when adding the egg mixture in the next step.

4. Beat the yolks, flour, and vanilla in another large bowl at high speed until thickened and pale yellow, about 3 minutes. Stir one fourth of the whites into the yolks to lighten, then fold in the remaining whites. Remove the dish from the oven. Using a large serving spoon, make 4 large mounds in the hot milk.

5. Return the dish to the oven and bake until the mounds are golden brown, about 12 minutes. Serve immediately.

SWEET FRUIT OMELET
STEFÁNIA-OMELETTE
Makes 2 to 4 servings

In Viennese parlance, a dessert omelet is more closely related to a soufflé than to scrambled eggs. A bit of flour in the batter gives it a lovely texture similar to that of a light sponge cake. Stephanie omelet is always filled with some kind of apricot mixture—the simplest use apricot preserves—but in this version, fresh apricots are used, as befits a crown princess. Of course you can use any fruit in season, fresh or briefly sautéed, as long as it isn't chilled. Once you master this recipe, you'll turn to it often for a fast and easy dinner-party dessert or brunch entrée.

■ ■ ■

APRICOT FILLING
3 ripe apricots, cut into 1/2-inch dice
2 tablespoons granulated sugar, to taste
1 teaspoon fresh lemon juice
1 tablespoon apricot liqueur, optional

OMELET
4 large eggs, separated, at room temperature
1/3 cup granulated sugar
2 tablespoons unsalted butter, melted
2 tablespoons all-purpose flour
Grated zest of 1/2 orange
Pinch of salt

1 tablespoon unsalted butter, for the pan
Confectioners' sugar, for dusting

■ ■ ■

1. To make the filling: Mix the apricots, sugar, and lemon juice in a medium bowl, adding the liqueur, if using. Cover and let stand at room temperature for 30 to 60 minutes.

2. To make the omelet: Position a rack in the center of the oven and heat to 350°F.

3. Beat the egg whites in a medium bowl with a handheld electric mixer on high speed until soft peaks form. Gradually beat in the sugar to form stiff, shiny peaks. Beat the yolks, 2 tablespoons melted butter, flour, orange zest, and salt in another medium bowl on high speed until thickened and pale yellow. Stir one fourth of the whites into the yolks to lighten the mixture, then fold in the remainder.

4. Melt 1 tablespoon butter in a nonstick 10-inch skillet over medium-high heat, tilting the pan to coat with the melted butter. Do not let the butter brown. Add the egg mixture and immediately place in the oven. Bake until the omelet is puffed and springs back when pressed in the center, about 12 minutes.

5. Spread the apricots over one half of the omelet and fold the omelet to cover the filling. Slide the omelet out of the pan onto a serving platter (you will have to plump and shape the omelet when it comes out of the pan). Sift confectioners' sugar over the top and serve immediately.

MAKE AHEAD

The omelet must be served immediately, but if you have all of the ingredients measured and ready to go, the procedure will go very quickly.

▪ THE STORY BEHIND ▪
STEFÁNIA-OMELETTE

Crown Princess Stephanie is one of history's most tragic wives. When her husband, Crown Prince Rudolf, committed murder-suicide at Mayerling in 1889 with his young mistress, it set off a scandal that shook Austria and contributed to the decay of the Hapsburg Empire.

Of course, Stephanie immediately gained the sympathy of the Viennese. But she wasn't easy to like. She didn't much care for the city, for its citizens, or for the Hofburg's palace intrigues (understandable after what she went through), and she was constantly written up in newspapers for putting her bejeweled foot in her mouth. One of her most common complaints was that "the food in Vienna is coarse and unappetizing," fighting words to the Viennese. The local chefs responded by creating a number of dishes in her honor, including the Stephanie omelet, hoping to sway her opinion. Another of them, the Stefániatorte, is no less ornate than the Dobostorte, without its caramel topping.

SWEET DUMPLINGS & NOODLES

Of all the desserts served in Vienna, Budapest, and Prague, this category of sweetened dumplings and noodles is the most foreign to the American palate. Yet, whenever I spoke to American friends about this book, if they had any Austro-Hungarian or Czech heritage at all, they wanted to be sure that I was including dumpling recipes. They all fondly remembered their grandmothers serving fruit-stuffed dumplings in the summer, and none had eaten dumplings since. Cooks in the American south make fruit dumplings, but those dumplings are usually drops of dough cooked on top of a thick fruit sauce.

These dishes are created from a trio of basic doughs: potato, farmer's cheese, and yeast. Dumplings (*Knödeln*) and noodles (*Nudeln*) are comparatively new in Austro-Hungarian cooking, not having become established until the late 1600s. But when they gained ground, they really took over. For a few decades, almost anything that was made from flour was called a *Knödel*. Because potatoes and cheese were plentiful, they were used to make the dough. There was huge variety to these dumplings, but like other desserts, the more savory ones gave way to the sweet versions as sugar became less expensive. In the past, seasonal fruit played a large part in people's diets, and simple fruit dishes kept food on the table, especially during times of war. Candied fruit was a luxury, so covering a small amount of them with a generous amount of inexpensive dough was a simple way to indulge,

and for a time these dumplings enjoyed a vogue.

Sweet dumplings and noodles are an integral part of the Austro-Hungarian culinary heritage, and yet they are everything Torten are not: While Torten are sophisticated, dumplings are down-home and simple. These flour-based dishes are admittedly heavy, and they're supposed to be. In the past, they were most often served as a meatless meal, and rarely for dessert. Even today, when they're ordered at a Kaffeehaus they usually make a meal, unless they're shared as an after-dinner dessert. They are usually served without a lot of embellishment, with just a dusting of confectioners' sugar, ground walnuts, or fried bread crumbs. When I serve them to my guests in America, however, I can't resist adding a splash of raspberry or strawberry sauce, a drizzle of heavy cream, or a dollop of sour cream to make them a bit less stodgy.

Flour or Sugar? Hot or Cold?

There *is* an Austrian word for dessert, but no one ever uses it. It's too general to describe the endless parade of choices.

Desserts are separated into two main categories, *Mehlspeisen* and *Süßspeisen*. *Mehl* means "flour," and *Süß* means "sugar." *Speisen* means "meal" or "repast." Therefore, the former means a meal made from flour and the latter refers to a meal made from sugar, or meals with flour or sugar as the main ingredients. Anything baked is considered Mehlspeisen, and most cold desserts without flour, such as ice creams or custards, are Süßspeisen.

In Austria, rich desserts are ubiquitous, not just because they are delicious and good for the spirit, but because of their ability to fill the stomach. Meatless Fridays and Lenten seasons were a way of life for the Catholic population, so they devised a large repertoire of hearty dishes that could be served for dinner and not just at the end of the meal. While cheesecakes, strudels, sweet dumplings, and noodles are now considered desserts, they are also good examples of the *Fastenspeisen* (fasting meals). There is another reason these dishes are so well established. It wasn't so long ago that postwar rationing finally became unnecessary. During the years of rationing, people ate Fastenspeisen and Mehlspeisen because they required only inexpensive, more readily available ingredients like cheese, fresh fruit, and nuts. Many of my friends remember eating this way in childhood, and many still prefer it, because it centers on seasonal produce with little meat. Of course, the lifestyle was more active back then, and you walked or worked many of your calories away.

Within Mehlspeisen itself there are two more categories, *kalte* (cold) and *warme* (warm). Kalte Mehlspeisen encompasses anything that is served cold or at room temperature: baked goods such as tortes, yeasted sweet rolls, individual pastries, plain cakes, and cookies. Warme Mehlspeisen covers desserts that are served warm: strudel; sweet dumplings and noodles; steamed or baked puddings; soufflés or their Viennese counterpart, Auflauf; pancakes, thick or thin; sweet omelets; doughnuts; and deep-fried fruits in batter. (Battered fruits are very popular but are not standard coffeehouse fare, so they aren't included in this book.) If you are browsing through an Austrian cookbook for fruit desserts (salads, compotes, or flambléed fruits), you'll find them in their own chapter, designated to Viennese culinary limbo, neither hot nor cold.

FARMER'S CHEESE AND STRAWBERRY DUMPLINGS
ERDBEERKNÖDEL
Makes 4 to 6 servings

Americans will find these golden brown dumplings intriguing to look at as well as delicious to eat. Few Austrians would serve them with fresh strawberry sauce, but it makes sense to today's palates.

■ ■ ■

FARMER'S CHEESE DUMPLING DOUGH
8 ounces farmer's cheese
3/4 cup all-purpose flour, plus additional
for kneading
1 large egg, at room temperature
2 tablespoons granulated sugar
2 tablespoons unsalted butter,
at room temperature
1 teaspoon vanilla extract
Grated zest of 1 lemon
Pinch of salt

1 pint fresh strawberries, hulled
3 tablespoons granulated sugar
1 tablespoon fresh lemon juice
12 small sugar cubes (cut large cubes in half,
if necessary), or substitute 1 tablespoon
granulated sugar
4 tablespoons unsalted butter
1 1/2 cups fresh bread crumbs
Confectioners' sugar, for serving

■ ■ ■

1. To make the dough: Using a rubber spatula, press the cheese through a coarse-meshed wire sieve into a medium bowl. Add the flour, egg, sugar, butter, vanilla, zest, and salt. Using a handheld electric mixer on medium speed, beat to form a soft dough. Cover and let stand at room temperature for 30 minutes.

2. Cut 6 strawberries lengthwise into quarters and set aside. Purée the remaining strawberries with the 3 tablespoons granulated sugar and the lemon juice. Pour the sauce into a bowl, cover, and set aside at room temperature.

3. On a lightly floured work surface, knead the dough into a thick log, kneading in more flour as

needed to make a dough that doesn't stick to the surface. Cut the log into 12 pieces. Working with one piece of dough at a time, pat into a 3½-inch-diameter disk. Place 2 strawberry quarters and a sugar cube (or ¼ teaspoon sugar) in the center of the disk. Wrap the dough around the fruit and sugar to enclose, and roll between your palms to form a ball. Place on a lightly floured kitchen towel on a baking sheet. Repeat with the remaining dough, strawberries, and sugar cubes.

4. Meanwhile, bring a large pot of lightly salted water to a boil over high heat. One at a time, add the dumplings and reduce the heat to medium-low. Cook at a steady simmer until the dough is cooked through, 8 to 10 minutes. Using a slotted spoon, transfer the dumplings to a baking sheet lined with a clean kitchen towel to drain briefly.

5. While the dumplings are cooking, melt the butter in a skillet over medium heat. Add the bread crumbs and cook, stirring often, until crisp and golden, about 5 minutes. Set aside until ready to serve.

6. When ready to serve, place the dumplings in the skillet of crumbs and turn to completely coat the dumplings. Cook over medium heat, turning occasionally, until the crumbs have recrisped, 3 to 5 minutes. Transfer 2 or 3 dumplings to dessert bowls, drizzle with the strawberry sauce, sift with confectioners' sugar, and serve immediately.

MAKE AHEAD
The dumplings are best served immediately. The dumplings, strawberry sauce, and crumbs can also be prepared up to 2 hours ahead and stored at room temperature. Just before serving, roll the dumplings in the crumbs in the skillet and cook for 3 to 5 minutes to reheat.

FARMER'S CHEESE DUMPLINGS WITH "ROASTED" PLUMS
TOPFENKNÖDEL MIT ZWETSCHKENRÖSTER
Makes 4 to 6 servings

Serve these simple dumplings with the plum compote, or any warm fruit compote that strikes your fancy.

■ ■ ■

Farmer's Cheese Dumpling Dough (page 172)
3 tablespoons unsalted butter, melted
½ cup ground walnuts or hazelnuts
Confectioners' sugar, for garnish
"Roasted" Plums (page 163),
at room temperature

■ ■ ■

1. Form the dough into a thick log on a lightly floured surface and cut into 12 equal pieces. Flour your hands, and roll each piece between your palms into a ball. Set aside on a lightly floured kitchen towel on a baking sheet.
2. Bring a large pot of lightly salted water to a boil over high heat. One at a time, place the dumplings in the water. Cover the pot to return the water to the boil. Reduce the heat to medium. Simmer, uncovered, until the dumplings are cooked through, about 10 minutes. Using a slotted spoon or wire skimmer, transfer the dumplings to a clean kitchen towel to drain.
3. Place 2 or 3 dumplings in each bowl, drizzle with the butter, and sprinkle with the nuts. Sift confectioners' sugar over the top and serve hot, with the plums passed on the side.

POTATO NOODLES WITH SWEET POPPY SEEDS
MOHNNUDELN
Makes 4 to 6 servings

Mention this dish to just about anyone in Vienna, Budapest, or Prague, and you'll immediately become involved in a discussion of favorite recipes. You'll also receive a firm warning that those recipes are never to be made with packaged egg noodles. The first time I had these potato noodles was at the talented hands of Mrs. Bleuel at the Berghotel Tulbingerkogel in the Vienna Woods. Potato dough is still considered a basic dough for bakers to master, as it is used to make many different noodle and dumpling dishes. The amount of flour needed depends on the relative starchiness of the potatoes. I've made two batches on the same day, and one batch needed only a few tablespoons of flour but the next batch (with different potatoes) took almost ½ cup. Be flexible.

I've never seen these noodles served with sour cream at a coffeehouse or restaurant, but at my house, a dollop certainly doesn't hurt.

■ ■ ■

POTATO DOUGH
1¼ pounds (about 2 large) baking potatoes,
such as russet, Idaho, or Burbank,
peeled and cut into 2-inch chunks
2 tablespoons unsalted butter,
at cool room temperature
¾ cup all-purpose flour, as needed, plus
additional for kneading
3 tablespoons semolina
Pinch of salt
2 large egg yolks, beaten

3 tablespoons unsalted butter
3 tablespoons poppy seeds, ground
(see page 212)
2 tablespoons confectioners' sugar
Sour cream, at room temperature, for serving
(optional)

■ ■ ■

1. Place the potatoes in a large saucepan and add enough lightly salted cold water to cover. Bring to a boil over high heat. Reduce the heat to low and cook until tender, about 20 minutes. Drain well. Return the potatoes to the pan and cook over medium heat, stirring constantly, until the potatoes begin to film the bottom of the pan, about 2 minutes. (This step removes excess moisture from the potatoes and makes the dough easier to handle.)

2. Put the potatoes through a ricer or rub them through a coarse wire sieve into a bowl. Add the butter and stir to melt. Stir in the flour, semolina, and salt, then the yolks to make a soft dough. Turn out onto a lightly floured work surface and knead in enough flour to make a soft, workable dough that doesn't stick to your hands or the work surface.

3. Pinch off a cherry-size piece of dough. Roll under your palms on the work surface into a 5-inch-long noodle about ½ inch wide with tapered tips. Transfer to a lightly floured kitchen towel on a baking sheet. Repeat with all of the dough.

4. Bring a large pot of lightly salted water to a boil over high heat. A few at a time, add the noodles to the water, stirring gently to keep the noodles from sticking to each other. Cover the pot and return to a boil. Uncover and cook until the noodles are cooked through, about 4 minutes. Drain well.

5. In a large skillet, melt the 3 tablespoons butter over medium heat. Add the poppy seeds and confectioners' sugar. Add the drained noodles and toss gently until the noodles are completely coated with the poppy-seed mixture. Transfer to bowls and serve hot, topped with a dollop of sour cream, if desired.

MAKE AHEAD

The noodles can be prepared up to 6 hours ahead of cooking, covered loosely with plastic wrap, and refrigerated.

PRUNE POCKETS
POWIDLTASCHERLN
Makes 4 to 6 servings

Dumplings don't always have to be round, as these turnover-shaped "pockets" illustrate. Use apricot preserves, if you wish.

■ ■ ■

Potato Dough (page 174)
⅓ cup prune butter (lekvar), as needed
3 tablespoons unsalted butter
½ cup fresh bread crumbs
Confectioners' sugar, for serving

■ ■ ■

1. On a well-floured work surface, roll out the dough to ¼ inch thick. Using a 3-inch round biscuit cutter, cut out rounds. Gather up the scraps and reroll until all the dough has been cut out. You should have about 30 rounds.

2. Place about ½ teaspoon prune butter in the center of each round. Brush water on the edges, then fold over into half-moons, pinch the edges closed, and press the seal with the tines of a fork. Place on a lightly floured kitchen towel on a baking sheet.

3. Bring a large pot of lightly salted water to a boil over high heat. A few at a time, add the dumplings to the water. Cover to return the water to a boil. Reduce the heat to medium and cook until the dumplings are cooked through, about 4 minutes. Drain well.

4. Meanwhile, melt the butter in a medium skillet over medium heat. Add the bread crumbs. Cook, stirring often, until the crumbs are golden and crisp, 3 to 5 minutes.

5. To serve, place 3 or 4 dumplings each in soup bowl, sprinkle with the bread crumbs, sift with the confectioners' sugar, and serve immediately.

MAKE AHEAD

The dumplings can be prepared up to 2 hours ahead of cooking, covered loosely with plastic wrap, and refrigerated.

HOT & COLD PUDDINGS

The largest cafés serve, hot or cold, comforting spoon desserts. We would call them all puddings, but there are subtle differences.

Koch are usually based on bread crumbs, stale bread, ground nuts, or some other flour substitute, bound with an egg custard. They are so characteristic of the Viennese kitchen that they are sometimes called *Wiener Koch*. The *Auflauf* is related to the dessert soufflé, made light with separated eggs. The English word *pudding* is used in Vienna to describe warm, unmolded desserts like the steamed chocolate

Mohr im Hemd ("Moor in a Shirt") or the walnut *Nußpudding.*

Also in this chapter are other soft desserts that defy categorization but are nonetheless best when eaten with a spoon, bite by creamy bite. I have not included one of the pillars of the coffeehouse, ice cream. While the very best Konditorein make their own, most cafés buy the ice creams and sorbets from outside vendors and turn them into the kind of desserts that are familiar wherever you live. This is not to say they're not good, but an ice cream sundae is an ice cream sundae whether you're in Vienna, Austria, or Vienna, Virginia.

CROISSANT AND APPLE PUDDING
KIPFERLKOCH
Makes 4 to 6 servings

To Viennese tastes, buttery Kipferl would be a much better starting point for a bread pudding than plain bread. So when a café has stale crescent rolls, it's natural to turn them into a refined bread pudding with a few simple additions. You certainly don't need homemade croissants for this; the supermarket variety will do.

■ ■ ■

3 cups milk, heated
6 egg yolks
½ cup plus I tablespoon granulated sugar,
divided
5 or 6 large croissants, torn into I-inch pieces
(10 to 12 ounces total)
2 Golden Delicious apples, peeled, cored,
and thinly sliced
⅓ cup raisins
¼ teaspoon ground cinnamon
Confectioners' sugar, for garnish

■ ■ ■

1. Position a rack in the center of the oven and heat to 350°F. Lightly butter an 8-inch square glass baking dish.

2. Make a custard by whisking the milk, yolks, and ½ cup of the sugar in a medium bowl to dissolve the sugar. Place the croissants in another medium bowl and toss with 2 cups of the custard. Let stand, giving the croissants a stir every few minutes, until they have absorbed most of the custard, about 15 minutes.

3. Spread half of the croissants in the baking dish. Top with the apples and raisins and sprinkle with the remaining I tablespoon of sugar and the cinnamon. Spread with the remaining croissants. Pour the remaining custard over the croissants. Place the dish on a baking dish.

4. Bake until golden brown and the center feels set when pressed gently, about 1 hour, 10 minutes. Cool for 5 minutes. Dust the top with confectioners' sugar and serve warm.

MAKE AHEAD

The pudding is best served warm, but leftovers can be covered and refrigerated for up to 2 days.

Coffee, Vienna-Style

Sipping a cup of coffee in a Kaffeehaus is more than just a way to get caffeine into your system (for that you can stand up in an espresso bar, of which there are plenty). From the first sip, you'll notice that the coffee tastes richer and fuller than an American cup of Joe, and no matter where you go, the quality is consistent and high.

To find out what makes Viennese coffee uniquely delicious, I asked the coffee experts at Julius Meinl. The Meinl name is well known throughout Austria, Poland, Hungary, and the Czech Republic as a supermarket chain (including a spectacular new gourmet market on the Graben in Vienna), but they started out as a small coffee importer. The flavor of their Vienna roast coffee is the standard to which all Vienna roasts aspire. Herr Meinl opened his first store in 1862. At that time, coffee beans were sold green and were roasted at home, a time-consuming and exacting chore. Meinl decided to offer freshly roasted coffee beans to his customers, and that convenience turned his few stores into an empire.

Ever since the Turks brought it to Austria, the Viennese have preferred to mellow coffee's bitterness with milk or cream. To allow for this, the coffee beans are roasted to a point at which the flavor will blend well with the customer's dairy product of choice. The roasting temperature is one component, as Vienna roast is just a shade lighter than espresso. But the length of the roasting time is even more important: Vienna-roasted coffee beans lose only eighteen percent of their weight, whereas beans roasted to the espresso stage lose twenty percent. The result: rich roasted flavor without espresso's burnt edge. While the exact blend of beans remains a secret, the Meinl people did tell me that Guatemalan beans have the correct flavor for Vienna roast, while the Brazilian beans are favored for Italian espresso.

To further my Viennese coffee education, I spoke with Gert Gerersdorfer, the owner of Café Dommayer, one of the most traditional of cafés in this city where history lives on in every cup of melange. Along with the special roast, Herr Gerersdorfer feels that the clear Viennese water from the mountain springs of the Rax, Hochschwab, and Schneeberg ("snow mountain") also contribute to the special flavor.

But when I took my first sip of Dommayer's coffee, I immediately sensed there was something more. Herr Gerersdorfer explained that his café's blend of coffee was flavored with minuscule amounts of Feigenkaffee ("fig coffee") and Malzkaffee ("malt coffee"). During Austria's battle-scarred history, good coffee beans were often not to be had. To stretch what coffee was available, or to substitute for it altogether, ground dried figs or roasted malt were used to such an extent that the Viennese actually acquired a taste for the substitutes. The majority of people who like their coffee this way are probably older coffeehouse customers, and they can truly say that Dommayer's brew tastes just like they used to make it in the old days.

On my way home from Dommayer, I stopped in at the neighborhood Julius Meinl and picked up some Feigenkaffee and Malzkaffee. At a friend's house, we added a bit of each to our pot of Vienna roast coffee and evaluated the results. The figs did add a bit of sweetness, and the malt increased the creamy head on the coffee. They may not have actually improved a good thing, but we could discern a difference. Will I be carrying bags of dried figs and malt back on my next trip to add to my stateside morning coffee? Probably not. Like sipping Provençal wine in the South of France, the ephemeral pleasures of a Viennese melange are probably best savored at the source.

CHOCOLATE-CREAM "DUMPLINGS"
SOMLÓI GALUSKA
Makes 12 servings

Peter, my Hungarian translator, had met me at a neighborhood café near my hotel and was taking me on a personal tour of the café's glass dessert case, giving his picks and pans of the display. When he arrived at a bowl filled with scooped cake "dumplings," layered with vanilla cream and topped with chocolate sauce and whipped-cream rosettes, he paused in reverence. It was Somlói Galuska ("Somló Dumplings"), named for a wine town near Lake Balaton, but a big-city dessert that is on the top of almost every Budapester's short list of favorites.

This extravaganza originated at Gundel, the famous restaurant, but it isn't difficult to prepare at home. A restaurant pastry chef would have a battery of baking pans to easily bake the three required layers, dividing a basic biscuit dough into thirds and flavoring one part with ground walnuts and one with cocoa. I do not assume that a home cook will have three baking pans, so this recipes bakes them separately one after the other in the same pan. The layers are thin, so they bake and cool quickly, and the other components are quick to prepare. Make the cake at least eight hours ahead so the layers have time to soak.

■ ■ ■

PLAIN LAYER
3 large eggs, at room temperature
⅓ cup sugar
½ cup cake flour
Pinch of salt

WALNUT LAYER
⅓ cup cake flour
⅓ cup finely chopped walnuts
Pinch of salt
3 large eggs, at room temperature
⅓ cup sugar

COCOA LAYER
⅓ cup plus 1 tablespoon cake flour
2 tablespoons Dutch-processed cocoa powder
Pinch of salt
3 large eggs, at room temperature
⅓ cup sugar

RUM SYRUP
³/₄ cup sugar
³/₄ cup water
1 3-inch strip of orange zest, removed
with a vegetable peeler
1 3-inch strip of lemon zest, removed
with a vegetable peeler
¹/₃ cup golden rum

PASTRY CREAM
4 cups milk, divided
¹/₃ cup cornstarch
6 large egg yolks
²/₃ cup sugar
1¹/₂ teaspoons vanilla extract

ASSEMBLY
¹/₂ cup raisins
¹/₂ cup finely chopped walnuts
¹/₃ cup apricot preserves
1 tablespoon Dutch-processed cocoa powder,
for garnish
Sweetened Whipped Cream (page 19),
for serving
Rum Chocolate Sauce (page 18), for serving

■ ■ ■

1. Position a rack in the center of the oven and heat to 350°F. Lightly butter the bottom only of a 13 × 9-inch baking pan, and line the bottom with parchment or wax paper.

2. To make the plain layer: Combine the eggs and sugar in the bowl of a heavy-duty electric mixer or a stainless-steel medium bowl. Fit into a medium saucepan of simmering water (the water should not touch the bowl) on medium heat. Whisk constantly until the eggs are warm to the touch and the sugar has dissolved, about 1 minute. Using the whisk attachment or a hand-held electric mixer on high speed, beat until the mixture is tripled in volume, about 3 minutes. Combine the flour and salt. In two additions, sift the flour into the egg mixture, and fold in. Spread evenly in the pan, using an offset metal spatula to fill the corners.

3. Bake until the center springs back when pressed lightly with a finger, about 12 minutes. Cool for 3 minutes. Run a knife around the edge of the cake to release. Cover the pan with a sheet

of wax or parchment paper, then with a baking sheet. Invert the cake, and carefully peel off the top paper. (The bottom layer of paper will help transport the cooled cake layer.) Cool the baking pan before making the other layers, then repeat the buttering and lining process.

4. To make the walnut layer: Process the flour, walnuts, and salt in a food processor fitted with the metal blade until the walnuts are chopped into a fine powder. Following the procedure and baking time for the plain layer, make the walnut layer, substituting the walnut mixture for the cake flour and salt, but fold the walnut mixture into the eggs without sifting (the nuts will not pass through the sieve).

5. To make the cocoa layer: Sift the flour, cocoa, and salt together. Following the procedure and baking time for the plain layer, make the cocoa layer, substituting the cocoa mixture for the cake flour and salt.

6. To make the rum syrup: Stir the sugar, water, and the orange and lemon zests in a small saucepan over medium heat until boiling. Boil without stirring until the syrup has reduced slightly, about 5 minutes. Cool completely. Stir in the rum, and remove the zests.

7. To make the pastry cream: In a saucepan or a microwave oven, heat 3 cups of the milk until simmering. Pour the remaining 1 cup milk into a heavy-bottomed, medium saucepan. Sprinkle the cornstarch over the cold milk and whisk until dissolved. Add the yolks and sugar and whisk until combined. Gradually whisk in the hot milk. Cook over medium heat, whisking often, until the mixture comes to a full boil. Remove from the heat and stir in the vanilla. Transfer to a medium bowl set in a larger bowl of ice water. Let stand until cooled, stirring occasionally.

8. To assemble: Mix the raisins and walnuts in a bowl. Bring the preserves to a boil over medium heat, stirring often; keep warm.

9. Place the walnut layer in a 13 × 9-inch baking or serving dish. Brush with one third of the syrup, spread with the apricot preserves, then spread with one third of the pastry cream. Sprinkle half of the raisin-walnut mixture on top. Top with the cocoa layer, brush with half of the remaining syrup, and spread with half of the remaining pastry cream. Sprinkle with the remaining raisin-walnut mixture. Add the plain layer, brush with the remaining syrup, and spread with the remaining pastry cream. Sift the cocoa over the top. Cover with plastic wrap and refrigerate for at least 8 hours or overnight.

10. For each serving, using a 2-inch diameter ice-cream scoop or large dessert spoon, scoop 2 or 3 "dumplings" from the cake and stack in a soup bowl or on a plate. Transfer the whipped cream to a pastry bag fitted with a ⁹⁄₁₆-inch-wide open-star tip, such as Ateco Number 825. Pipe whipped cream rosettes on top, and drizzle the rum chocolate sauce over all. Serve chilled.

MAKE AHEAD

The dessert can be prepared up to 2 days ahead, covered with plastic wrap, and refrigerated. Spoon into dumplings just before serving.

MOLDED RICE PUDDING WITH RASPBERRIES
REIS TRAUTTMANSDORFF
Makes 8 servings

French cuisine has its regal rice pudding (*riz à l'impératice*), but the Austrians, never to be outdone by the French, have their Reis Trauttmansdorff. A molded extravaganza of creamy rice and fresh berries (most recipes prefer raspberries, but fraises de bois or blueberries are also wonderful), it is truly a dish for the emperor's table, and it was served often at the Hofburg palace.

There are a few tricks to making it well. First, use medium-grain rice (see page 185 for suggestions), as its high starch content will help thicken the sauce; long-grain rice won't do. Do not rinse the rice, as you want its surface starch to remain intact. Also, be sure that the rice is cooked until very soft; you will probably consider it overdone for most purposes. Rice firms up when chilled,

and unless it is very tender, it will refrigerate into hard little pellets. While Maraschino is the traditional flavoring, you can substitute any colorless fruit liqueur.

■ ■ ■

1 cup (6 ounces) fresh raspberries
2 tablespoons Maraschino, kirsch, framboise, or Triple Sec, divided
³⁄₄ cup sugar, divided
1 teaspoon fresh lemon juice
3¹⁄₂ cups milk, or more as needed
²⁄₃ cup (4³⁄₄ ounces) rice for risotto, such as Arborio
Grated zest of ¹⁄₂ lemon
¹⁄₄ cup cold water
1 envelope plain powdered gelatin
¹⁄₂ teaspoon vanilla extract
1 cup heavy cream, chilled

Raspberry Sauce (recipe follows), for serving

■ ■ ■

1. Gently combine the raspberries with 1 tablespoon of the Maraschino, 1 tablespoon of the sugar, and the lemon juice in a small bowl. Set aside to macerate while you prepare the pudding.

2. Bring the milk, rice, and lemon zest to a boil in a heavy-bottomed medium saucepan over medium heat, stirring often to avoid sticking. Reduce the heat to low and simmer, stirring often, until the rice is very tender and has absorbed much of the milk to create a thick paste, 25 to 30 minutes. If the milk is absorbed before the rice is tender, stir in ¹⁄₃ cup milk and continue cooking. The finished rice should be slightly loose and very tender.

3. Meanwhile, pour the ¹⁄₄ cup of water into a small bowl and sprinkle the gelatin on top. Let stand until the gelatin absorbs the water, about 5 minutes. Stir the soaked gelatin and 7 tablespoons of the sugar into the rice and stir until the gelatin is completely dissolved, about 1 minute.

4. Transfer to a large bowl set in a larger bowl of ice water. Stir in the remaining 1 tablespoon of Maraschino and the vanilla. Cool, stirring often, until the rice mixture is cool, but not set, about 20 minutes.

The Trauttmansdorff family is a very old noble line that goes back to the fourteenth century. One count in particular, Ferdinand Trauttmansdorff (1749-1827), was a career diplomat who was dispatched as president of the governorship of the Netherlands (then under Hapsburg rule) when its residents became rebellious. He returned to the court as lord steward to Franz I during the Congress of Vienna. If the Congress of Vienna hadn't occurred, the Viennese dessert table could look much different, or at least many of the dishes would have different names. Even if it isn't clearly documented, rice pudding must have been one Count Ferdinand's favorite desserts.

5. In a chilled medium bowl, beat the cream and the remaining ¼ cup of sugar until the cream is stiff. Fold into the rice.

6. Drain the raspberries. (If you wish, reserve the juices and add to the raspberry sauce.) Fold about ½ cup of the rice mixture into the raspberries.

7. Lightly oil a 7-cup tubed steamed pudding mold. Spoon about half of the pudding into the mold and smooth the top. Spoon the raspberry mixture into the mold. Spread the remaining rice pudding in the mold. Cover tightly with plastic wrap and refrigerate until firm and chilled, at least 2 hours and up to 1 day.

8. To serve, run a sharp knife around the inside of the mold and the tube. Dip the mold in a large bowl of warm water for 10 seconds. Dry the outside of the mold and invert the pudding onto a platter. Cut into wedges and serve chilled, with the raspberry sauce.

RASPBERRY SAUCE

Purée 2 half-pints fresh raspberries, ¼ cup confectioners' sugar, and 1 teaspoon fresh lemon juice in a food processor. If you wish, add the juices from the strained raspberries used in the pudding. Strain the sauce through a fine wire sieve to remove the seeds. Taste and add more sugar or lemon juice as needed. Makes about 1 cup.

MAKE AHEAD

The pudding can be stored for up to 2 days, covered and refrigerated.

STEAMED CHOCOLATE PUDDING
MOHR IM HEMD
Makes 8 servings

This comforting warm dessert translates as "Moor in a shirt," a reference to its appearance: dark chocolate steamed pudding cloaked with a white meringue cream. While you can serve *Mohr im Hemd* with plain sweetened whipped cream, the addition of the meringue cleverly discourages the cream from melting in contact with the warm pudding. The pudding is traditionally made in a tubed steamed pudding mold. You can substitute an 8-inch fluted tube cake pan, well covered with a lid of buttered aluminum foil. Allow about 45 minutes to cook the pudding.

Be sure the eggs are at room temperature. If the yolks or whites are chilled, they cause the butter-chocolate mixture to firm up and make the batter difficult to fold.

■ ■ ■

PUDDING
4 ounces high-quality bittersweet chocolate, finely chopped
1¼ cups (4 ounces) sliced blanched almonds
½ cup plus 2 tablespoons granulated sugar, divided
½ cup (1 stick) unsalted butter, at room temperature
5 large eggs, separated, at room temperature
Confectioners' sugar, for garnish
Meringue Cream (page 18)
Warm Chocolate Sauce (page 18), optional

■ ■ ■

1. Butter the inside of a 7-cup tubed steamed pudding mold, including the lid. Sprinkle the inside of the mold with dried bread crumbs and turn to coat, tapping out the excess (no need to "crumb" the lid).

2. In the top part of a double boiler over hot, not simmering, water, melt the chocolate. Remove from the heat and cool until tepid, stirring occasionally.

3. Process the almonds and 2 tablespoons of the sugar in a food processor fitted with the metal blade until very finely chopped but not oily. Set aside.

4. In a medium bowl, using a handheld electric mixer on high speed, beat the butter until shiny and light in color, about 1 minute. One at a time, beat in the egg yolks. Beat in the melted chocolate, then the chopped almonds.

5. In another medium bowl, using very clean beaters, beat the egg whites until soft peaks form. Gradually add the remaining ½ cup of sugar and beat to form stiff, shiny peaks. Stir about one fourth of the whites into the chocolate mixture to lighten it, then fold in the remainder.

6. Spoon the batter into the mold, smooth the top, and attach the lid. Place on a rack in a tall kettle. Pour enough hot water into the kettle to reach the bottom of the mold. Bring to a boil over high heat. Cover tightly and adjust the heat to medium-low, keeping a good head of steam. Cook, adding more boiling water to the kettle if needed, until a toothpick inserted in the pudding comes out clean, about 1 hour. Remove the mold from the kettle and cool for 5 minutes (the pudding will deflate).

7. To serve, unmold the pudding onto a warmed serving platter. Sprinkle the top with confectioners' sugar. Cut into wedges and serve on dessert plates, each wedge topped with a large dollop of the meringue cream, and a spoonful of the chocolate sauce, if desired.

MAKE AHEAD

The pudding is best served immediately. If you wish, make it 2 hours ahead, cool in the mold, and keep at room temperature. Reheat the pudding in the mold on a rack in a covered pot of boiling water for 15 minutes, then unmold and serve.

WARM RICE PUDDING WITH CHERRIES
REISAUFLAUF MIT KIRSCHEN
Makes 4 to 6 servings

This is a far cry from the standard rice pudding. It is served warm and has a soufflé-like texture, and fresh cherries give it a distinction that the familiar raisins in common rice puddings lack. Other fruits can be substituted for the cherries: Austrians love this with sliced apples, but berries are excellent, too. The pudding can be served by itself, or with a pitcher of Vanilla Sauce (page 18) or room-temperature heavy cream for pouring on top.

Because of their shared border with Italy, Austrians cook most often with Italian medium-grain rice, which has more starch than our popular long-grain rice and gives the pudding its special creaminess. Be sure to use Arborio rice or another variety that is appropriate for risotto. Other possibilities include Vialone Nano, Carnaroli, Baldo, Spanish Valencia rice, or even a supermarket medium-grain brand, such as Goya, which can be found in the Latino section of the market.

■ ■ ■

3½ cups milk, or more as needed
⅔ cup (5 ounces) rice for risotto
(see suggestions above)
Pinch of salt
3 tablespoons unsalted butter,
at room temperature
I teaspoon vanilla extract
Grated zest of I lemon
3 large eggs, separated, at room temperature
⅔ cup granulated sugar, divided
8 ounces fresh sweet cherries, pitted
and halved
Confectioners' sugar, for garnish

■ ■ ■

1. Combine the milk, rice, and salt in a heavy-bottomed medium saucepan. Bring to a simmer over medium heat, stirring often to discourage the milk from boiling over. Reduce the heat to medium low. Simmer, uncovered, stirring often to avoid scorching, until the rice is tender and most of the milk has been absorbed, about 25 minutes. Don't simmer the rice too quickly or it will absorb the milk before it becomes tender. If necessary, add ⅓ cup milk to the rice; the final rice–milk mixture should be slightly loose. Remove from the heat and add the butter, vanilla, and lemon zest. Stir to melt the butter.

2. Meanwhile, position a rack in the center of the oven and heat to 350°F. Butter an 11 × 8-inch glass baking dish, dust with dried bread crumbs, and tap out the excess crumbs.

3. Beat the egg whites in a medium bowl with a handheld electric mixer until soft peaks form, then gradually add ⅓ cup of the sugar and beat until the mixture forms stiff, shiny peaks.

4. In another medium bowl with the mixer on high speed, beat the egg yolks and the remaining ⅓ cup of sugar until they are thick and pale yellow, about 2 minutes. Gradually stir the hot rice mixture into the yolks. Stir in one fourth of the whites to lighten the mixture, then fold in the remaining whites.

5. Spread half of the rice into the pan. Sprinkle with the cherries and spread with the remaining rice. Bake until the pudding is puffed and golden brown and the center feels set when pressed, about 30 minutes. Dust the top of the pudding with confectioners' sugar and serve immediately.

MAKE AHEAD

The pudding is best served warm, but leftovers can be refrigerated for up to 2 days.

WARM WALNUT PUDDINGS
NUßPUDDINGS
Makes 6 puddings

This is another delicious, old-fashioned recipe from Mrs. Bleuel, proprietress of the Berghotel Tulbingerkogel in the Vienna Woods. After we had already enjoyed a hearty game supper, Mrs. Bleuel presented these warm, comforting puddings, along with her famous "milk-cream" strudel and her noodles with poppy seeds (see pages 84 and 174). Walnut puddings are now a favorite dinner-party dessert at my table, because they can be made ahead and reheated. If you wish, substitute sliced natural almonds or skinned hazelnuts for the walnuts, or any combination of these three nuts.

■ ■ ■

I cup (2½ ounces) fresh bread crumbs
½ cup milk
½ cup (1 stick) unsalted butter,
at room temperature
4 large eggs, separated, at room temperature
2 large egg whites, at room temperature
½ cup sugar, divided
I cup (4 ounces) finely chopped walnuts

Warm Chocolate Sauce (page 18),
for serving

■ ■ ■

1. Position a rack in the center of the oven and heat to 350°F. Butter six 5-ounce pots-de-crème cups or ramekins. Sprinkle the cups with dried bread crumbs, tilt to coat, and tap out the excess crumbs.

2. In a small bowl, soak the fresh bread crumbs in the milk for 5 minutes. Drain in a wire sieve. Press the excess milk out of the crumbs, discarding the milk. The bread crumbs should be pasty, but not too dry.

3. In a medium bowl, using a handheld electric mixer on high speed, beat the butter until shiny and light in color, about 1 minute.

4. In another bowl, beat the egg yolks and ¼ cup of the sugar on high speed until very thick and light in color, 2 to 3 minutes. Beat into the butter. Mix in the bread crumbs, then the walnuts.

5. In a third bowl, using very clean beaters on low speed, beat the 6 egg whites until foamy. Increase the speed to high. Still beating, gradually add the remaining ¼ cup of sugar and beat until the whites form shiny, stiff peaks. Stir about one fourth of the whites into the walnut mixture, then fold in the remainder.

6. Spoon into the cups and arrange the cups in a baking dish. Place in the oven and add enough hot water to the baking dish to come ½ inch up the sides of the cups. Bake until the puddings are puffed and a toothpick inserted in the center of a pudding comes out clean, about 30 minutes.

7. Remove the cups from the baking dish and let stand at room temperature to cool slightly, 5 to 10 minutes. To serve, run a knife around the inside of each cup and invert the puddings onto dessert plates. Serve warm, with some warm chocolate sauce poured over each pudding.

MAKE AHEAD

The puddings are best served immediately after baking. However, you can make them 2 hours ahead, cool them in their molds, and keep them at room temperature. Cover each pudding with aluminum foil and reheat in the water bath in a 350°F. oven for about 15 minutes.

VIENNESE-STYLE ZABAGLIONE WITH RASPBERRIES
WEINCHAUDEAU
Makes 4 to 6 servings as a dessert, 8 servings as a sauce

Certainly descended from the Italian zabaglione, the Viennese version is different from its ancestor in many ways. Weinchaudeau is always made from a fruity white wine, not Marsala. And while zabaglione uses egg yolks only, Weinchaudeau includes an egg to give the froth a lighter consistency. Otherwise the cooking procedure remains the same, requiring constant whisking over simmering water and immediate serving. It's imperative that the ingredients be at room temperature before you begin. Weinchaudeau is a popular sauce for strudel, especially for the grape and hazelnut version on page 82.

■ ■ ■

I pint fresh raspberries, blackberries, or hulled, sliced strawberries
5 large egg yolks, at room temperature
I large egg, at room temperature
½ cup semidry, fruity white wine, such as Riesling, at room temperature
⅓ cup plus I tablespoon sugar

■ ■ ■

1. Divide the raspberries among wine glasses and set aside.

2. Combine the yolks, egg, wine, and sugar in a large heat-proof bowl. Place over a medium saucepan of briskly simmering water (the water should not touch the bottom of the bowl). Whisking constantly with a large balloon whisk (or mixing with a handheld electric mixer on high speed), cook until the Weinchaudeau is tripled in volume and very light and fluffy, about 5 minutes. Immediately spoon over the berries and serve.

MAKE AHEAD

Weinchaudeau must be served immediately after making.

·HOT·&·COLD· BEVERAGES

When you go to a coffeehouse, you never just ask for a cup of coffee. Do you want a big cup or a small cup? Espresso or drip? Black or with milk? If you take milk, what color would you like it to be? A melange of half milk and half coffee? Or perhaps a Franziskaner, in which the milk has been added to the coffee until it is the color of the robes of a Franciscan monk.

Of course, other beverages are available. Tea has its fans. And while a coffeehouse is not a bar, alcoholic beverages are for sale, so why not slip a little rum into your coffee? Fruit juices, soft drinks, beer, and wine—the larger the coffeehouse, the larger the selection.

Much attention is paid to serving the right beverage in its season. Winters can be brutally cold, and warm punches and hot chocolate fend off the chill. When serving them, fill the cup with boiling water and let it stand for a minute or two to warm before tossing the water out and adding the beverage; the warm cup will keep the beverage hot much longer. During the warmer months, ice-cold drinks, many based on coffee, are just as important. A coffeehouse worth its salt would never pour hot coffee over ice; the coffee for iced drinks is chilled.

Vienna is a wine city—in fact, there are more productive vines within its limits than those of any other city in the world—and the Viennese are always looking for ways to use their local product. *Glühwein* and *Bowle* are at the opposite ends of the spectrum. Christmas is the time for Glühwein, the Austro-Hungarian version of mulled red wine. But when summer's fruits appear, they are used to flavor a refreshing (if potent) white wine punch called Bowle. Hot punches are best served from an electric slow cooker (such as a Crock-Pot), because they shouldn't boil. When serving cold punch, the Viennese advise to never chill it with a block of ice, or the punch will become watered down. Instead, place the punch bowl in a larger container filled with crushed ice to keep it cold.

• THE STORY BEHIND •
MARIA THERESIA

Maria Theresia ruled for forty years, but she almost didn't make it to the throne. The Hapsburg line ascended through male heirs, and her father, Charles VI, left no son. Before his death, he instituted the Pragmatic Sanction, which assured his female heir's ascension in 1740. This did not stop a faction from contesting her rule, and the War of Austrian Succession raged for eight years. When the dust cleared, Maria Theresia was still empress, although with her husband, Franz Stephan, as male co-regent.

During most of her very active reign, Austria was at war, mainly trying to fend off the advances of Frederick of Prussia, which kept her subjects fervently patriotic. Under her patronage, the arts thrived, especially in church architecture and music. (Maria Theresia was very religious and Frederick's fervent Protestantism didn't help their relationship.) She was a maternal ruler, revered as her country's *Landesmutter,* or "mother of the people."

Maria Theresia was maternal in other meanings of the word as well. She had sixteen children, which certainly ensured the continuation of the Hapsburg line. (One of her daughters was Marie-Antoinette, the ill-fated empress of France. And Maria Theresia's successor, her son Joseph II, was much more liberal than the character portrayed in the play and movie *Amadeus.*) By all accounts, the royal children were very spoiled and extremely well fed. Like any good Viennese mother, Maria Theresia indulged her children's sweet tooth. In fact, one staircase at the Hofburg palace was so well used by the bakeries making deliveries that it is still called the *Zuckerbäckerstiege,* or Sugar-Baker's Staircase.

HOT COFFEE WITH ORANGE LIQUEUR
MARIA THERESIA
Makes 1 serving

Any time a food is named for the beloved empress Maria Theresia, you can be sure it includes the most refined blend of ingredients. (Chicken Maria Theresia has poached chicken breasts with sliced ox tongue masked with a creamy poultry sauce—over the top to some tastes, but the height of luxury cooking in earlier times.) You'll find this hot coffee drink on almost every Viennese coffeehouse menu. It's often made with a clear orange liqueur like Triple Sec or Curaçao, but Cognac-based Grand Marnier stands up to the strong coffee with more authority. By substituting rum for the orange liqueur, you'll get a Fiaker, named for the horse-carriage drivers, who needed something warming to keep themselves going. Fiaker is traditionally served in a glass with a handle, as carriage drivers would need to keep one hand free for holding the reins.

■ ■ ■

Boiling water, for heating the glass
3 tablespoons orange-flavored liqueur, such as Grand Marnier
1 teaspoon superfine sugar
1 cup hot, brewed coffee, preferably Vienna roast
A dollop of Sweetened Whipped Cream (page 19)
Freshly grated orange zest, to taste, for garnish

■ ■ ■

Fill a coffee cup with boiling water and let stand for 1 minute to heat the glass. Pour out the water. Pour the liqueur into the cup and stir in the sugar. Add the coffee. Top with the whipped cream, then grate the orange zest over the top. Serve immediately.

FIAKER
Substitute golden rum for the liqueur, and omit the orange zest.

Coffee, Tea, and Chocolate

The European explorers who ventured to the Americas found a cornucopia of new foods to bring back to their homelands. Tomatoes, sweet potatoes, turkey, corn, beans, and other edibles that are taken for granted today were then considered exotic, if not downright dangerous, to consume. The foods that had the most impact weren't foods at all, but beans and leaves that were turned into beverages.

Coffee, tea, and chocolate radically changed the way people ate and drank. (Although coffee originally came to Europe from interaction with Turkey, it wasn't until coffee plantations were established in the tropical regions of the Americas and other newly discovered regions, such as the Dutch colonies in Indonesia, that the Turkish monopoly was broken and a reliable supply of beans was ensured.) During the popularization of coffee, tea, and chocolate in the sixteenth and seventeenth centuries, alcohol abuse was threatening to destroy the lower classes. Wine, beer, and gin flowed through the great cities of Europe, leaving destitution in their wake. Beer, in particular, made from grains and ostensibly more nutritious than wine, was often served at breakfast, lunch, and dinner, so one could go through the day in a state of drunkenness. Coffee was touted as an alcohol replacement that revived without intoxicating and provided stimulation without hallucination. Tea slowly usurped coffee in Britain, but never in Austria. While chocolate does not have as strong an effect on the nervous system as its more caffeinated cousins, it satisfied in other ways, being more filling than other hot beverages.

In spite of the effects of caffeine, a typical coffeehouse had a relaxed atmosphere, a direct contrast to the raucous beerhall. At first, only men were allowed in them, and it took some time before women became customers as well. This did not stop women from serving coffee at home. In seventeenth-century Germany, ladies formed afternoon coffee clubs called *Kaffeekränzchen* (coffee circles), the forerunner of the *Kaffeeklatsch* (coffee-gossip). In Vienna, this became the Jause.

Improved trade routes brought a constant flow of tea from the East. Coffee remained the favorite drink in the German-speaking countries, but it eventually lost favor in Britain. No one knows exactly why the dramatic change occurred. Certainly the British East India Company, which had a monopoly on tea trade, had something to do with it. One uses less tea than coffee to make the same amount of beverage, so the cost factor could have played a part in coffee's demise in Britain.

Another stalwart of the Austro-Hungarian coffeehouse, chocolate became known early on not only as a beverage, but as an aphrodisiac in the court of the Aztec kings. When the Spanish conquistadores took it home to their royal sponsors, it was touted as a medicine. For its first hundred years in Europe, only the Spanish knew about chocolate, which they flavored with honey and spices. According to tradition, chocolate started its conquest over the rest of the continent in 1613, when the Hapsburg Anne of Austria, who was raised in Spain, married French King Louis XIII. It seems more likely that it first entered France as a medicine. Regardless, the French defined chocolate drinking as an aristocratic art, one that was adapted by the Viennese court.

Chocolate is ground cocoa beans, usually processed with sweeteners or flavorings. Until the early nineteenth century, most people knew it only as a drink, dissolved in hot water, sometimes with wine. It was difficult to use chocolate in cooking because of the high fat content of the beans, which tended to separate out of the beans when heated. Also, chocolate was highly acidic and didn't combine well with other ingredients. In 1828, a Dutch chemist named Coenraad Van Houten patented a new process to separate the cocoa solids from the cocoa butter. The solids could be pulverized to make cocoa powder, the ingredient that we know today. He also treated the cocoa solids with an alkalai wash to reduce their acidity. To the delight of bakers and candymakers, chocolate became easier to work with, and it paved the way for new chocolate creations such as Sachertorte. To this day, alkalized cocoa powder is called Dutch-processed in commemoration of Van Houten's discovery.

HOT RUM PUNCH
PUNSCH VON RUM
Makes 1 serving

If you are fortunate enough to be visiting a European coffeehouse, this is a drink to savor on a cold winter afternoon after settling into your favorite booth with a stack of newspapers. At home, nestle into your most comfortable chair with a good book. Of the many Austro-Hungarian recipes for tea-based punch, I like this one best. It's easy to multiply the ingredients for a large party, and I have served it as a substitute for the familiar mulled wine at holiday gatherings with great success.

■ ■ ■

⅔ cup water
⅓ cup fresh orange juice
1 tablespoon fresh lemon juice
2 tablespoons sugar
1 teaspoon loose-leaf black tea
2 to 3 tablespoons golden rum, to taste

■ ■ ■

Bring the water, orange juice, lemon juice, and sugar to a boil over medium heat. Remove from the heat, stir in the tea, and cover. Let steep for 3 minutes. Strain into a warmed cup and serve immediately.

MULLED "GLOW" WINE
GLÜHWEIN
Makes 10 to 14 servings

The bitter cold winter weather makes mulled wine a coffeehouse staple that stays on the menu until springtime warmth is well established. It is served from stands at the outdoor Christmas markets throughout Vienna—a necessary evil if ever there was one. The hint of vanilla in this version makes it extraordinary.

There are a few caveats to making great Glühwein. First, start with a fruity wine that's not too dry or full-bodied. Be sure to use a non-reactive pot (stainless steel or enameled iron), because the wine will react with unlined aluminum and acquire a metallic taste. Never let the wine come to a boil. If you're serving from the kitchen, a heat diffuser under the pot will be helpful; but I've seen many a Viennese corner Glühwein stand that serves its product from an electric slow cooker, and that's the best way because it eliminates the danger of boiling. Because mulled wine is such a popular party drink, I've given crowd-size proportions.

■ ■ ■

2 750-ml bottles of fruity red wine,
such as merlot
⅔ cup fresh orange juice
2 4-inch strips of orange zest, removed with
a vegetable peeler
⅔ cup honey
2 3-inch-long cinnamon sticks
1 vanilla bean, split lengthwise

■ ■ ■

Heat the ingredients in a large nonreactive pot over very low heat until hot, but not simmering. Keep warm (an electric slow cooker is the perfect appliance) and serve hot.

FRUIT AND WINE PUNCH
BOWLE
Makes 10 to 14 servings

Bowle is the standard hot-weather punch, but watch out—it's so delicious you'll find yourself quaffing it down. The most popular fruits are peaches or strawberries, but I like to use both. If you want to reduce its potency a bit, simply omit the brandy and toss the fruit with just the sugar. A semidry white wine, such as Riesling, is the perfect partner for the fruit.

■ ■ ■

1 pint strawberries, cut into 3/4-inch dice
2 ripe peaches, pitted and cut into 3/4-inch dice
1/2 cup sugar
2 tablespoons fresh lemon juice
1 cup brandy
2 750-ml bottles of semidry white wine, such as Riesling, chilled
Fresh mint sprigs, for garnish, optional

■ ■ ■

1. Mix the strawberries, peaches, sugar, and lemon juice in a medium bowl. Stir in the brandy. Cover tightly with plastic wrap and refrigerate at least 4 hours or overnight.
2. Combine the fruit and its liquid with the wine in a punch bowl. Serve chilled, spooning some of the fruit into each serving, with the optional mint sprigs.

MAKE AHEAD
The fruit mixture can be prepared 1 day ahead. The punch is best served the day it is made.

REAL HOT CHOCOLATE
HEIßE SCHOKOLADE MIT SCHLAGOBERS
Makes 1 serving

For a intensely chocolate liquid experience, use high-quality bittersweet chocolate. Hot water helps the flavor blossom. And whipped cream is not an option, but a must.

■ ■ ■

2 ounces bittersweet chocolate, finely chopped
1/4 cup hot water
2 teaspoons sugar
1 cup hot milk
A dollop of Sweetened Whipped Cream
(page 19), for garnish

■ ■ ■

Melt the chocolate in the water in the top part of a double boiler over simmering water. Transfer to a blender, add the sugar, and turn on the machine. Slowly add the hot milk through the feed tube. Pour into a warmed cup and serve hot, with a dollop of whipped cream.

HOT SPICED TEA
GEWÜRZTEE
Makes 1 serving

True, coffeelovers have countless places to indulge in their passion in Vienna, Budapest, and Prague, but tea enthusiasts have their temples, too. Many of these establishments brew pots of their own signature spiced blends like this one with star anise, cloves, and lemon peel—both invigorating and soothing at the same time. Let the water come to a boil very slowly so the flavorings release gently.

■ ■ ■

1 cup water
2 3-inch strips of lemon zest, removed with a vegetable peeler
1 whole star anise, broken into points
6 whole cloves
2 teaspoons loose-leaf oolong or other black tea
1 teaspoon honey

■ ■ ■

Slowly bring the water, lemon zest, anise, and cloves to a boil in a small saucepan over medium-low heat. Remove from the heat and stir in the tea and honey. Cover and let stand for 3 minutes. Strain into a warmed cup and serve immediately.

The Coffee Menu

A complex coffee menu has developed over the years, attaching names to the many nuances that a cup of coffee can hold. At one café in the early 1900s, one waiter even went to the trouble of carrying a card with twenty paint chips to show the entire range of possibilities from very dark brown to very pale beige with increasing additions of milk.

Here's a list of the different coffees you're likely to find in today's Viennese café (and keep in mind that many of them have house coffee drinks worth trying). Coffee choices aren't as extensive in Budapest and Prague. Where they are served with regularity, the Czech (C) and Hungarian (H) equivalents are listed.

Kleiner Schwarzer
Káva espresso (C)
Eszpresszó (H) — Demitasse of espresso

Kleiner Brauner — Demitasse of espresso with a dash of milk

Großer Schwarzer
Dupla Eszpresszó (H) — Double shot of espresso

Großer Brauner — A large Kleiner Brauner

Verlängerter Schwazer
Hosszú kávé (H) — Espresso "stretched" with hot water

Mokka
Káva Mocca (C) — Very strong black drip coffee

Franziskaner — Coffee with enough milk to resemble the color of a Franciscan monk's robes

Kapuziner
Kapucíner (H) — Coffee with a little less milk than above to resemble the color of a Capuchin monk's robes; not to be confused with a cappuccino

Nußbraun — "Nut-brown," a little lighter than the above

Nußgold — "Nut-gold," two shades even lighter than a Kapuziner

Gold — Very light coffee and milk

Eidotter	The cure for post-Carnival party hangovers: a glass of coffee with an egg yolk
Portion or Kännchen Kaffee	A pot of coffee (usually for 2 people), with milk served separately
Melange Vídeňská káva (C) Melange (H)	*The* Viennese coffee: half Vienna-roast coffee and half steamed milk, sometimes with a dollop of whipped cream
Milchkaffee Tejeskávé (H)	Half coffee, half milk
Cappuccino Kapučíno (C) Cappuccino (H)	Espresso with steamed milk froth
Einspänner	A tall espresso and milk, with generous whipped cream topping
Fiaker	Hot coffee with rum or brandy, often with whipped cream on top; sometimes called a Pharisäer
Türkischer Káva turecká (C) Török kávé (H)	Coffee boiled in the Turkish style, served in copper cups; curiously, not easy to find in Budapest
Eiskaffee Švycarská káva (C) Jeges kávé (H)	Iced coffee with vanilla ice cream and whipped cream
Maria Theresia	Hot coffee with orange liqueur and whipped cream
Mazagran	Iced coffee with Maraschino liqueur
Koffeinfrei/Haag Káva bez kofeinu (C) Koffeinmentes (H)	Decaffeinated coffee; not easy to find, and often prepared from Haag brand insant coffee.

GLOSSARY OF INGREDIENTS, EQUIPMENT & TECHNIQUES

Biscuit Cutters

Round biscuit or cookie cutters (they're the same thing, really) come with plain edges or fluted, in groups of seven to twelve cutters, graduating in size from about 3½ inches to ¾ inch in diameter. For variety's sake, it's good to have both plain and fluted cutters. The classic cutters are made of heavy-weight tinned steel, and newer versions are available in hard plastic. Because the cutters should be sharp (dull edges compress the layers of dough and reduce the rise), the steel version has the edge over plastic. Replace your cutters whenever you think they might be getting dull; the sharpness won't last forever.

Brushes, Pastry

You really need a variety of brushes to do different jobs. For glazing small pastries, a 1-inch-wide brush is perfect. Larger pastries require a 3- to 4-inch brush. To butter cake pans, a brush with bristles bound into a cylinder reaches best into crevices. A feather pastry brush is an option for coating delicate filo with melted butter, as heavier brushes can tear the pastry. Natural bristles are actually more durable than synthetic ones and easier to clean. After each use, "shampoo" the bristles with a drop of detergent, rinse well, and air-dry.

Butter

All of the recipes in this book were tested with Grade AA unsalted butter. During the postwar period in Vienna and the Communist regimes in Budapest and Prague, margarine necessarily was used in baking, but butter has been welcomed back. Butter is preferred not only for taste but for texture; margarine makes greasy pastries and cakes. Unsalted butter also allows the baker to control the amount of salt in the recipe, and as salt can cover up any off flavors in rancid butter, unsalted butter is usually fresher.

For creaming with a handheld electric mixer, butter should be softened to *cool* room temperature until malleable, and not squishy and shiny. (If you are using a standing heavy-duty mixer, you can use cold butter cut into thin slices.) To soften butter at room temperature, cut the butter into thin slices or ½-inch cubes and let stand for about 15 minutes. (Use this time to complete other steps in the recipe, like measuring the other ingredients and greasing the pans.)

One of my favorite tricks, which I learned from the late, great food writer Richard Sax, is to grate a cube of chilled butter on the large holes of a cheese grater; it will be the perfect consistency for creaming. If you have a heavy-duty standing mixer, you can use chilled butter straight from the refrigerator, cut into thin slices, beating for about 1 minute at high speed until smooth and light colored. After the butter is smooth, add the sugar and continue creaming. Some cooks soften butter in a microwave, but it's not worth the risk of melting.

Buttering Cake Pans

After trying every spray coating under the sun, both plain and with flour, I've come to the conclusion that nothing beats good old-fashioned butter with a dusting of either flour or dried bread crumbs. This is especially true of fluted tube pans, which usually strike fear into the hearts of bakers: will the cake unmold without breaking?

To butter cake pans, use well-softened (but not melted) butter and a round-bristled brush. Be sure that the pan is evenly coated, particularly in the grooves of a Gugelhupf or fluted tube mold. Sprinkle the inside of the pan with about 3 tablespoons of all-purpose flour or dried unflavored bread crumbs, turning the pan to give an even coating. Rap the pan over a garbage can to remove the excess flour or crumbs. After the cake is baked, let it cool on a wire rack for 5 minutes (10 minutes for a tube pan), so the cake can cool and contract away from the pan, making it easier to unmold.

Cake Dome

Many tortes have decorations that would be marred if covered with plastic wrap. A clear plastic or hard rubber cake dome will cover the cake in the refrigerator, keeping out unwanted odors.

Cardboard Cake Rounds

Made from strong cardboard with a white paper covering, these support the cake during icing and serving. To hide the rim and give the cake a cleaner look, trim the round with scissors about 1 inch smaller than the cake's diameter—this also allows you to ice the cake more evenly at the base. If you wish, you can cut a round from any sturdy cardboard, or simply use the bottom of the springform pan.

Cherries and Cherry Pitters

Bing cherries are delicious to eat out of hand, but for baking, search out sour (sometimes called pie) cherries. Sour cherries have a tart flavor and firm texture that stand up to baking. They are light red and sometimes have a translucent cast. You'll find them during their short season (mid-July to early August on the east coast) at farmstands and farmers' markets and some gourmet produce markets. You can substitute sweet Bing cherries, reducing the sugar in the recipe by one third.

If you cook with a lot of cherries (and when they're in season I seem to make nothing but cherry desserts), you'll need a good cherry pitter. The handheld models that look like a paper punch are adequate, but it still takes a lot of time to pit a couple of pounds of cherries. The best cherry pitter is a plastic box with a hopper and a plunger. The cherries are fed into the hopper and the plunger punches out the pits in a fraction of the time it takes with a handheld pitter. There is also a model without the box that attaches to the work counter with a clamp. The plunge-style cherry pitter is available at well-stocked kitchenware shops or by mail order from A Cook's Wares and Sur La Table (Tools for the Cook). See Sources.

Chestnuts and Chestnut Purée

Chestnuts have a sweet flavor all their own and are a beloved dessert ingredient all over Europe. During their season, which coincides with the cold weather, every bakery serves chestnut specialties. Nonetheless, I have restricted the number of chestnut recipes in the book for a few reasons. They are not all that popular in America as a dessert and it can be difficult to find plump, fresh chestnuts, even in season. Look for firm, shiny chestnuts; avoid any nuts with tiny holes, which indicate insect infestation. Always buy a few more chestnuts than you need because there are always stubborn ones that refuse to let go of their skin during peeling or some that are just not up to snuff. (Chestnuts are often roasted, but some recipes boil them.) The earlier in the season, the fresher the chestnuts. You may find chestnuts in the market in February, but ask the produce manager to be sure they aren't left over from Thanksgiving. Chestnut purée in 1-pound cans comes in sweetened and unsweetened varieties, so be sure to buy the right one for the recipe.

Chocolate and Cocoa Powder

There are literally hundreds of chocolates available to the consumer at gourmet stores, supermarkets, and Web sites. Unfortunately, you often can't tell much about the chocolate by a glance at the label. Pick a chocolate that is too bitter and your dessert may not be as sweet as you like. In central Europe, the chocolate choices for cooking are mostly limited to bittersweet chocolate or unsweetened Dutch-processed cocoa powder. (When milk chocolate is used, it is as a garnish, never as an ingredient in a cake batter.)

Roasted and ground cocoa beans form a pasty mass called chocolate liquor, the basic ingredient in chocolate manufacturing. Each manufacturer sweetens and flavors it to a specific formulation. The chocolate liquor also can be pressed hydraulically, which will extract most of the ivory-colored cocoa butter. The cocoa butter can be processed separately or used later in the chocolate-manufacturing procedure. The chocolate mass that has most of the cocoa butter removed is dried and ground into cocoa powder.

Each type of chocolate in a brand is made from the manufacturer's own proprietary formula. The United States Food and Drug Administration (USFDA) has set Standards of Identification for the various types of chocolate (milk, dark sweet chocolate, and so on). These standards state the different ingredients that must be present in chocolate and cocoa products and the range of percentages for each. For example, semisweet chocolate can contain anywhere from 35 to over 70 percent chocolate. One brand's bittersweet is another's semisweet. Even though only a couple of chocolate products are used in this book, it's important to know the differences between all of the varieties so you don't accidentally buy the wrong thing.

Unsweetened chocolate is chocolate liquor that has been cooled and molded into blocks. It is also known as baking or bitter chocolate. It is not a common ingredient in central Europe. *Sweet chocolate* (also known by its brand name, Baker's German's), has a very high sugar content and is not interchangeable with semisweet or bittersweet chocolate. It is reserved for American desserts like German Chocolate Cake. *Milk chocolate* is delicious as a snack, but it is a poor choice for baking, as its high content of milk solids and sugar seriously impairs the true

chocolate flavor. *White chocolate* isn't chocolate at all, but vanilla-flavored cocoa butter (some brands use hydrogenated vegetable oils to replace the cocoa butter and are generally considered inferior). None of the above chocolates is used in this book.

Bittersweet chocolate and *semisweet chocolate* can have a very similar ratio of chocolate liquor to sugar. Many chocolate manufacturers now state the percentage of chocolate liquor in their product on the label (you may have to look closely, but it could be there). Some brands are 70 percent chocolate liquor or even higher. The more chocolate, the less sugar, and some of these chocolates can be quite bitter. In my experience, it takes a very particular recipe to support a chocolate with a very high liquor content. Also, some chocolates with a high liquor content can affect the viscosity of the icing.

Most of the bakers I worked with in central Europe preferred a much sweeter and more versatile chocolate with a 40- to 42-percent liquor content, which is quite sweet for American tastes. I take the middle ground with a high-quality European bittersweet chocolate with a moderate ratio of liquor to sugar. All of the recipes in this book were tested with Lindt Swiss Bittersweet, a reliably delicious brand that is available at most supermarkets. Lindt Bittersweet used to come in 3-ounce bars, but lately my supplier has been carrying 3½-ounce bars, so look carefully at the label to check the weight. Other brands with approximately the same ratio are Lindt Surfin, Valrhôna Extra Noir, and Tobler Tradition.

Couverture chocolate has a high cocoa-butter content that is perfect for candy coatings but is not necessary for cake batters.

The main difference between European and American chocolates is the length of conching, a grinding procedure that activates the many enzymes in the chocolate liquor. (The original rollers had grooves like conch shells.) The longer the conching, the smoother the chocolate, and most European brands are conched for the maximum period. Many fine American chocolates are on the market, but my philosophy is, when baking European desserts, use European chocolate. When I am baking American desserts like devil's-food cake or brownies, however, I use American chocolates.

Cocoa powder is chocolate liquor with some of the cocoa butter removed. The amount of cocoa butter varies from brand to brand, but this is of little concern to most home bakers. You should, however, understand the difference between nonalkalized and alkalized (Dutch-processed) cocoa powder, as the packages may not indicate the variety on the label.

Nonalkalized (natural) cocoa powder is familiar as Hershey's cocoa in the brown box. Natural cocoa is a highly acidic product. In the American baking tradition, this kind of cocoa is often mixed with an alkali (such as baking soda), and the two react to create carbon dioxide, making the batter rise.

Alkalized (Dutch-processed) cocoa powder has been treated with an alkali solution to reduce the cocoa's acidity, which gives it a darker color and mellower flavor. (The alkalizing procedure was developed in the Netherlands by chemist Coenraad Van Houten, hence the term "Dutch-processed.") European bakers use it because it's the type that's most readily available in their markets; and it also gives their baked goods a richer, darker color. The most common brand is Droste. Hershey's also makes a "European-style" (i.e., "Dutch-processed") cocoa, which is sold in a silver box. If you look closely at the labels of ingredients of other brands, you may be surprised to find the words "alkalized" or "Dutch-processed" in the fine print.

The reduced acidity of Dutch-processed cocoa powder does not affect most European recipes for baked goods, because they don't usually include chemical leaveners like baking powder or baking soda. But if you're making a traditional American recipe with baking soda, don't substitute Dutch-processed cocoa for regular, or you might not have enough acid in the recipe to make the cake rise.

Chopping Chocolate

Properly chopped chocolate will ensure smooth and speedy melting. As a rule of thumb, remem-

ber that the greater the surface area, the more uniform the melt. Therefore, it is easier to control the melting of finely chopped chocolate in the top of a double boiler than in a small bowl in the microwave oven.

Chocolate should be chopped with a large chef's knife into ¼-inch squares, as uniformly as possible. Use a dry, odor-free cutting surface. (You really should have at least two cutting boards in your kitchen—one reserved for chopping chocolate, dried fruit, and nuts for baking, and the other for savory ingredients like garlic and herbs.) Do not chop chocolate in the food processor, as it may melt from the resulting friction between blade and bowl.

Melting Chocolate

There are two ways to melt chocolate—in a double boiler or in a microwave oven—and both are equally proficient.

In either procedure, chocolate is very susceptible to heat and moisture. Avoid overheating chocolate. Whenever chocolate is exposed to temperatures above 125°F., it may scorch, lose flavor, and "seize" (tighten and become grainy).

Unless called for in a recipe, never let any liquid get into melting chocolate or it will "bind" and thicken. It only takes a drop or two of liquid to bind chocolate, but if the recipe includes about 1 tablespoon of liquid or more for every ounce of chocolate, you've passed the binding threshold, and the chocolate will melt smoothly.

Double Boiler Method Heat the finely chopped chocolate in the top part of an uncovered double boiler (or use a heat-proof bowl) over very hot, not simmering, water. The insert should be above, not in, the water. Melt chocolate uncovered; collected condensation on the lid could drip down into the chocolate. Stir occasionally until the chocolate is melted.

Microwave Method Place the finely chopped chocolate in a microwave-safe bowl and microwave at 50-percent power for 2 to 4 minutes, interrupting the procedure every 30 seconds to stir. The chocolate may not always appear melted and must be stirred occasionally to gauge its progress.

Piping Melted Chocolate from a Paper Cone

For piping decorations, melted chocolate is often transferred to a cone created from parchment or wax paper. It cannot be piped from a pastry bag with a metal tip, because the melted chocolate tends to harden as soon as it comes into contact with the cool metal.

To start, melt the chocolate, but let it cool for a few minutes so it is slightly less viscous. If the chocolate is too warm, it will be too liquid and not hold its design when piped.

To make a paper cone, cut a large triangle from the corner of a piece of parchment or wax paper. The base should be at least 12 inches long. Consider the top of the triangle as point A, with the left corner B, and the right corner C. Hold the triangle at B and C, with A pointing up. Bring B diagonally up to the right, and C diagonally up to the left, and the paper will start to form a cone, with the tip directly across from A (1). Continue tightening the cone, keeping the tip as sharp as possible, until B and C meet at A. Fold all three points down into the cone to secure it (2). Stand the cone up in a tall glass (3). Pour the melted chocolate into the cone (the tip should be tight enough that the chocolate doesn't leak). Close the cone, and fold over the right and left corners to enclose the chocolate (4). Snip the tip of the cone with scissors to make a small opening, about 1⁄16-inch wide, just large enough to allow the chocolate to flow freely.

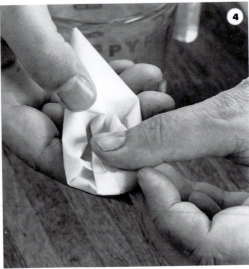

Making Chocolate Curls

One of the easiest and most effective chocolate decorations, chocolate curls are made from block chocolate, available at gourmet markets and some supermarkets. Cut a 3- to 4-ounce chunk from the chocolate. The chocolate must be slightly warm before curling. One way to warm it is to place the chocolate in your apron pocket (if it has one) for about 30 minutes to heat from your body's warmth. Or, place the chocolate in a warm place (near a turned-on oven or stove) for about 30 minutes. Another alternative is to microwave the chocolate on low power at 10-second intervals. Or blow warm air from a hair dryer over the chocolate. The chocolate should be warmed, but not melting.

Line a baking sheet with wax or parchment paper. Working over the baking sheet, use a vegetable peeler to shave chocolate curls from a flat side of the chocolate. The harder you press, the thicker the curls. If the chocolate breaks into shavings, the chocolate is too cold; warm the chocolate. If the curls don't hold their shape, the chocolate is too warm; let the block of chocolate cool at room temperature (don't refrigerate). Refrigerate the chocolate curls until ready to use. Don't touch the curls with your fingers, or they could melt.

Storing Chocolate

If chocolate is exposed to high temperatures during storage, the cocoa butter will separate from the solids, collecting and hardening on the surface. This unattractive streaking is called bloom. Bloomed chocolate is harmless enough in recipes where the chocolate will be melted to reincorporate the cocoa butter. But if the chocolate is crumbly and grainy, the chocolate is the victim of sugar bloom, a sign that the chocolate was stored in a moist environment. The chocolate will never melt smoothly, so discard it.

Chocolate should be stored in a cool, dry place (which eliminates a humid refrigerator). Ideal storage is about 70°F. If buying bars, keep them in their original wrapping. If buying chocolate in blocks, wrap in aluminum foil after opening.

Cream, Heavy

The best *heavy cream* has a high butterfat content (36 to 40 percent), with a discernibly thick body for whipping into clouds of Schlagobers. Many natural food stores, farmers' markets, and supermarkets now carry organic, high-butterfat heavy cream without additives. Use it whenever possible. *Whipping cream* usually has a lower butterfat content of 30 to 36 percent, and emulsifiers are often added to compensate. *Ultrapasteurized cream,* unfortunately the most commonly available cream suitable for whipping, has been briefly heated to about 300°F. to prolong its shelf life, which adds a slightly boiled taste and decreases its whipping ability. It works, but once you've tasted high-butterfat whipped cream, it's quite a compromise to use anything else.

Crumbs, Bread and Cake

Many central European recipes call for bread or cake crumbs as a batter ingredient or as a garnish. The use of crumbs in a batter goes back to when cooks were especially frugal and needed ways to use up stale baked goods. Both types of fresh crumbs can be made in a food processor or blender. Dried unflavored bread crumbs are easily purchased.

Fresh bread crumbs should be made from sturdy white bread with a tender crust. White sandwich bread or soft-crusted French bread are perfect. If you don't want to buy a whole loaf, buy a dinner roll or two. I never trim the crust when making bread crumbs. Get in the habit of turning day-old bread into bread crumbs and storing them in a self-sealing plastic bag in the freezer for up to three months.

Dried bread crumbs, so easy to purchase at the supermarket, aren't worth the trouble to make from scratch. I used to balk at recipes that asked to coat the pans with bread crumbs because I didn't always have them in the cupboard. But the bakers I worked with in central Europe convinced me that a coating of butter and bread crumbs is the best coating for fluted tube pans like Gugelhupf molds. If you are concerned about using up the entire box before it goes rancid (although the crumbs seem to last forever when airtight), store it in the freezer. Of course, be sure you buy the unseasoned variety.

In bakeries, there is a constant supply of cake crumbs created from trimmings. In a home kitchen, this isn't the case, although you could save up a stash of trimmings in the freezer (not likely). If you need a small amount (less than ½ cup) of crumbs as a garnish, these can usually be culled by trimming off a very thin layer from the top of the cake. Or, purchase an inexpensive pound cake or even a muffin. If you do a lot of this kind of baking, you may want to store a pound cake in the freezer just for the purpose of having cake crumbs handy. When needed, slice off a piece; it will defrost quickly. For the Burgtheatertorte on page 30, you will probably have to bake a separate chocolate cake to acquire the necessary 4 cups of crumbs, but it is worth the effort.

Cutting Cakes in Layers

A long serrated knife (at least 12 inches) is the best tool for slicing cakes into layers. The ideal way calls for making a series of deep horizontal cuts around the outside edge of the cake; eventually all of the cuts will meet in the center, and the layer can be lifted off.

Hold the serrated knife level at the point where you want to slice the cake into halves or thirds. (If you want absolutely perfect layers and are nervous, you can measure the height of the cake to find the exact point, but usually estimating the point by eye works just as well.) Hold the knife as level as possible, make a horizontal cut about 2 to 3 inches deep into the cake; keep the knife in the cake. Rotate the cake about one quarter turn. Make another deep horizontal cut at the exact same level as the first one. Repeat the procedure, rotating the cake and cutting around the sides until you have cut a deep horizontal ring around the center of the cake. Rotating the cake, cutting horizontally at the ring, cut deeply into the center of the cake to cut all the way through. Lift off the layer, using a cardboard cake round or the bottom of a springform pan as an aide, if needed. If cutting into thirds, repeat the procedure.

Here's another method: Wrap a long piece of dental floss around the equator of the cake, crossing the two ends. Pull the two ends in opposite directions to draw the floss taut, pulling through the cake at the same time.

Decorating Comb

A useful triangle-shaped tool for marking the buttercream on cakes in a pattern of closely spaced lines. Each side of the triangle has a border with jagged teeth allowing for three different gradations: the closer the teeth, the closer the lines on the buttercream.

To use a decorating comb, place the frosted cake on a decorating stand; the frosting should be about ⅛ inch thick. Place the teeth of the comb against the buttercream, just deep enough to make an indentation. Holding the comb steady, turn the cake on the stand until the decorative lines meet in a full circle.

Decorating Stand

A pivoted table on a pedestal that can be rotated 360 degrees, allowing the baker to frost or decorate a cake without holding it. Using a pedestal is a matter of preference; placing the cake on a wide coffee can and rotating it as needed works quite well.

Ebelskiver Pan

Originally used in Scandinavian cooking to make ebelskiver (apple dumplings cooked in the pan's round molds on top of the stove), this is the best pan to use for baking the small, round Indianerkrapfen cakes on page 127. If the pan has a plastic handle, remove it (they usually are attached with a screw), or wrap it well in a double thickness of foil to protect it from the oven's heat. If cast iron, the pan needs to be seasoned before use. Wash the pan well in hot, soapy water, then dry. Using a paper towel dipped in flavorless vegetable oil, rub the pan's indentations with oil. Bake in a preheated 350°F. oven for 30 minutes. Let the pan cool, then repeat the process. To keep the pan seasoned, don't wash it in soapy water. After using the pan, clean it with a wet paper towel and salt (gritty kosher salt works best). The salt will loosen any cooked dough without removing the natural nonstick coating created by the oil.

Eggs

Use large Grade A eggs for baking. Substituting another size will cause trouble. Size variations with eggs may not be apparent to the eye, but the difference in volume between six large eggs and six jumbo (or small) is enormous.

Eggs brought to room temperature will beat well because they incorporate the most air. On the other hand, chilled eggs separate most easily. (In recipes in which the eggs will be heated over hot water, as in Biskuittorten [sponge cakes], the temperature is immaterial, so use chilled eggs if you wish.) For room-temperature whites, separate the cold eggs, opening the eggs over a heatproof bowl so the whites can fall into it. Place the bowl in a larger bowl of hot tap water and let stand, stirring occasionally, until they lose their chill, about 2 minutes.

Fat inhibits the aeration of egg whites, so when beating whites, be sure that not a speck of fat comes in contact with the whites. The beaters and bowl must be absolutely clean, so wash them in soapy water and dry well. Never use a plastic or rubber bowl for beating whites, as they retain grease, even after washing. If I am using a bowl that has been washed already, I pour a splash of vinegar into the bowl and wipe it out with paper towels. This will cut through and remove any grease, and the tiny amount of residual vinegar will help beat the whites, replacing or complementing the acidic cream of tartar or lemon juice that you will find in some recipes.

To beat egg whites to their optimum height, they need to be gradually inflated. In most cases, a handheld electric mixer is best because it allows you to observe the process; it's easy to overbeat with a standing mixer. Start beating at low speed and beat until the whites are foamy. (If the recipe uses cream of tartar, add it now.) Increase the speed to high and beat until the whites form soft peaks. (When the beaters are lifted, the peaks of whites will bend at the tips). If beating to the stiff stage, keep beating, gradually adding sugar if the recipe directs, just until the whites stand in pointed peaks when the beaters are lifted. Don't overbeat the whites. If they are beaten past the stiff peak stage, they will look clumpy, and there's no way to save them.

Egg whites can be frozen for up to 3 months, so save them in an airtight container to use for meringues and desserts. (Egg yolks do not freeze well.) One large egg white equals 2 tablespoons. Allow the egg whites to defrost overnight in the refrigerator, but bring them to room temperature before beating.

A Note of Caution

Some classic recipes call for uncooked eggs. Wherever possible, I have altered the recipe to cook the eggs to kill any harmful bacteria, but in a couple of cases, this wasn't possible. Please keep the tips below in mind whenever cooking with eggs. None of them is a guarantee against ingesting salmonella, but they will reduce the risk.

Look closely at the expiration date on the carton and buy the freshest eggs. Store eggs in their carton in the coolest part of the refrigera-

tor. Never store them in the egg holders on the door, as this is really one of the warmest places in the appliance. The carton helps keep out unwanted odors that can seep into the eggs through the porous shells. Never use cracked eggs. Wash your hands, utensils, and any work surface that may have come into contact with raw eggs with hot, soapy water and rinse well. Raw eggs should not be served to the very young, very old, or those whose immune systems are compromised.

Electric Mixers

Every serious baker really needs two electric mixers—one heavy-duty model and one handheld mixer.

For recipes requiring a heavy-duty mixer, I used a 5-quart KitchenAid. The paddle blade creams chilled butter beautifully, the whisk whips eggs for Biskuitmasse (sponge cake batter) in no time, and the dough hook does a fine job of kneading bread. One caveat: Be sure to stop the machine and occasionally scrape down the sides of the bowl during mixing, bringing up the batter from the bottom at the same time, as some ingredients have a tendency to sink to the bottom of the bowl and stay there. I reserve my heavy-duty mixer for recipes with a large volume of batter. It doesn't do a good job with small amounts of ingredients.

When whipping egg whites separately for a dough, beating a small amount of heavy cream, or mixing a small amount of a light batter, a handheld electric mixer works best. Don't choose a hand mixer by motor capacity alone; but do judge a mixer by the size of its beaters. Large beaters incorporate more air into the ingredients. Smaller beaters, even on a high-wattage mixer, take too long and make chores out of the simplest kitchen jobs.

Farmer's Cheese

A fresh, moist cheese with very small curds pressed into blocks (*Topfen* in German), it's the basis for many central European desserts. For the best results, use whole-milk cheese and not the low-fat variety. It is available at well-stocked cheese stores. If necessary, substitute small-curd cottage cheese (not creamy- or California-style, which are too liquid), rubbed through a coarse-meshed sieve.

Flour

In central Europe, the consumer is not confronted with the dizzying array of flours that greet the American baker. Most markets there carry three white flours: *Universal* variety (similar to our all-purpose flour, and sometimes called *Typpe 480* in Austria), *Glattes* (literally "smooth," with a moderate gluten content), and *Griffiges* ("bulky," or high-gluten). In Hungary, there also is a gritty white flour called *réteslişt* for making strudel dough.

When testing my recipes for the American kitchen, I followed the European fashion and kept it simple by using only cake, all-purpose, and unbleached flours. The amount of gluten in wheat flour affects the tenderness of the baked goods. When moistened, gluten forms strands of proteins that strengthen with mixing and kneading. The lower the gluten content, the more tender the final result. Bleaching also reduces the gluten content. Wheat is the only grain with gluten, although rye contains small amounts. *Cornstarch,* which has no gluten, is sometimes combined with wheat flour to reduce the gluten content even more and give baked goods an especially delicate texture.

Most of the desserts in this book are made with *bleached all-purpose flour,* the moderate gluten content of which mimics the most commonly used European flour. *Unbleached all-purpose flour* has a high gluten content and works best with yeast-leavened recipes. All of the national brands are similar enough to use them interchangeably. *Cake flour* is a bleached, low-gluten flour that gives cake layers a fine crumb. Be sure to buy unleavened cake flour such as Softasilk or Swans Down, and not a self-rising brand with baking powder (Presto).

Measuring Flour

I measure flour by the dip-and-sweep method because it is the most efficient method for American home bakers. The rival measuring method, spoon-and-sweep, has the cook spoon the flour into a measuring cup, then sweep off the excess, which gets all over the place. Yes, weighing is best, but asking American cooks to weigh their ingredients is a pie-in-the-sky request because no matter how many proponents they have, kitchen scales just aren't standard equipment in our kitchens.

Always use a metal or plastic dry-volume measuring cup. Dry ingredients will mound in a glass cup and the measurement will be inaccurate. Conversely, always use a liquid measuring cup for measuring liquids.

To measure by the dip-and-sweep method, stir the flour to loosen it. Dip the cup into the flour to fill it without packing. Using a knife or your finger, sweep off the excess flour to level the top with the edge of the cup.

Cake flour will incorporate best into batters if sifted first. Sift a generous amount of cake flour (about twice as much as the recipe's measurement) into a deep bowl. Then measure the flour by the dip-and-sweep method.

Fruit, Dried and Candied

Raisins, golden raisins, and currants are used profusely in the Austro-Hungarian kitchen. Dried fruit should be plump and soft; stale, hard fruit will lack flavor, even if it is softened by soaking in a liquid, as most recipes require. The soaking step is to infuse the fruit with flavor, not to cover up any staleness. The best place to buy dried fruit is natural food stores, where it is visible in large storage bins or plastic containers, as you want to check it for any signs of dryness or crystallization. Store dried fruit in a tightly covered container in a cool, dark place.

The most common *dark raisin* is the seedless Thompson, and it will certainly do. But for special-occasion baking, look for especially plump and flavorful Monukka raisins, available at many natural food stores or in the self-service bins at large supermarkets. Both raisins are processed from green grapes, which darken during the drying process. Dark raisins can pose a problem in batters—if they touch the cake's hot metal pan during baking, they have a tendency to burn. For this reason (as well as for their availability and a simple preference for their color), *golden raisins* are often preferred by many central European bakers. American golden raisins are also Thompson grapes, treated with sulfites to retain their color during drying. While some bakers generically refer to all golden raisins as Sultanas, these are made from a particular Turkish grape, and are usually imported. *Dried currants* are a misnomer; they are not dried fresh currants, but tiny Corinth grapes, from whence they get their name (they are also called Zante currants).

Candied fruit is also a popular flavoring in cakes and yeast breads. Candied cherries, orange and lemon peel, and citron (a large, hard lemon-like citrus whose skin candies well) have a bad reputation in our country, thanks to mediocre commercial holiday fruitcakes, which tend to be made from hard, flavorless candied fruit. Adventures in Cooking and La Cuisine are two excellent sources for moist, tasty candied fruit, which more often than not, is imported.

Gelatin

European bakers use gelatin sheets, which are soaked in water to soften, wrung to remove the water, then dissolved in hot liquid. Even though gelatin leaves are now available at some specialty grocers and through mail order, I used commonly available gelatin powder for these recipes.

Gelatin must be dissolved carefully before using. Sprinkle the gelatin over a small amount of liquid in a small heat-proof bowl (large amounts do not absorb the gelatin properly) and let stand until the gelatin softens and absorbs the liquid, about 5 minutes. Place the bowl in a skillet with about ½ inch of barely simmering water over low heat, and stir with a small rubber spatula, scraping down any undissolved gelatin from the sides of the bowl, until the powder is completely dissolved. This will take 1 or 2 minutes of constant stirring, so don't be in a hurry. The gelatin can also be heated in the microwave on medium power at 10-second intervals, stirring well after each period until dissolved. Try not to boil the gelatin.

Gugelhupf Pan

At a glance, these will remind you of the typical American fluted tube cake pan (sometimes called a Bundt pan). However, a Gugelhupf pan is more narrow and a bit taller. They're usually made of heavy, unlined metal with their diameter designated in metric measurements on the box or stamped somewhere on the pan. Kaiser is a very reliable brand. The Gugelhupf pan I've used most often is the common 9-inch/22-centimeter (12-cup capacity) size, but some recipes (such as Sandtorte) bake best in the smaller 8-inch/20-centimeter (8-cup capacity) pan. If you buy a pan with a nonstick surface, reduce the oven temperature by 25°F., as the dark surface of the pan holds the oven heat, and can make the exterior of the cake brown too quickly. Don't be concerned about the lack of a nonstick surface in a traditional Gugelhupf pan. The heavy metal construction encourages even baking, and if the pan is buttered and floured properly, you won't have any problem unmolding the cake. You can substitute the American fluted cake pan for a Gugelhupf pan—do not fill the pan more than two-thirds full. The cake in the wider American pan will probably bake in less time, so check it often toward the end of baking to avoid overcooking.

Icing Cakes

A properly iced cake has smooth surfaces and an even top. An offset metal icing spatula is easier to work with than a straight spatula because it lets you work at a more comfortable angle.

For easy access to all sides, place the cake on a decorating stand (or on top of a wide coffee can). Start with the top of the cake. Spoon about 1 cup of the icing on the top of the cake and smooth it with the spatula just until it reaches the top perimeter. Now frost the sides of the cake, using large dabs of the icing to gradually work your way around the cake, turning the stand as needed (or, turn the cake on the can). Use the spatula to sweep the ridge of icing around the top edge toward the center of the cake, leveling the top at the same time.

Kitchen Scale

American cooks don't rely on kitchen scales, but every kitchen should have one. Even if we don't routinely weigh our dry ingredients, there are still many times when a scale comes in handy. I use it to measure portions of yeast dough for uniformly sized baked goods, and to weigh pastry dough for recipes that call for dividing it into equal amounts. It's indispensable to double-check the weight of produce and is the best way to measure nuts and chocolate.

Digital electronic scales are more accurate than those with spring mechanisms, and weighted scales are too complicated to use. Because working with European bakers has forced me to master the metric system (the decimal-based system is just easier to work with), I prefer scales that easily switch back and forth between metric and ounce measurements. Automatic switch-offs and large measuring baskets are other plusses.

Liquors and Liqueurs

Austro-Hungarian bakeries are liberal in their use of alcoholic beverages as flavorings. The alcohol also helps to heighten the flavors of the other ingredients. *Liquors* are alcoholic beverages distilled from grains and other plants. *Eau-de-vie* is a clear alcoholic beverage distilled from fruit juice, sweetened only by the residual sugars in the fruits. Highly perfumed and not especially sweet, they are quite expensive, as it takes pounds of fruit to make a bottle of eau-de-vie. *Liqueurs* are sweet alcoholic beverages, usually made from an infusion of an ingredient (fruit, herbs, or seeds, as examples) with a spirit (such as brandy). When cooking with any liquor, the rule of thumb is to always use what you would happily drink by itself. Invest in the best you can possibly afford, as it will keep for years. If you get too budget-minded, the flavor of the dessert will be compromised.

If you don't want to cook with alcoholic beverages, you can substitute appropriate fruit juices or syrups. Apple juice or brewed coffee are good substitutes in tortes that use Cognac, rum, or brandy. In cream desserts, you can use any of the above suggestions or simply substitute an equal amount of heavy cream for the liquor. Here are the most common alcoholic beverages used to make Austro-Hungarian pastries:

Cognac and Brandy

These liquors are both distilled from wine. Cognac, from a specific region in France, is considered the finest of all brandies. In cooking, the two are interchangeable.

Golden Rum

Distilled from fermented sugarcane juice or molasses, rum brings its distinctive flavor to many pastries. A golden or amber rum, such as Bacardi, is best for baking, as dark rum often has a deep caramel flavor that isn't right with every recipe. I prefer Bacardi Gold for its full, but not aggressive, flavor and light color.

Cherry-Flavored Liqueurs

Maraschino is a mildly sweetened liqueur made from wild *marasca* cherries and their stones. Originally from what is now Croatia, it is now most often available in Italian brands, and is most easily found at liquor stores in Italian neighborhoods. Kirsch (also known as kirschwasser) is a clear cherry eau-de-vie. I once accidentally purchased a bottle of crème de kirsch, which turned out to be a sweetened kirsch, perfect for baking but not so great in savory recipes. Don't be tempted to substitute inexpensive products such as artifically flavored kirsch, which is harsh-tasting, or cherry schnapps, which has an artificial lollipop flavor.

Orange-Flavored Liqueurs

Grand Marnier, made with bitter oranges and Cognac, is my favorite. Triple Sec or Curaçao are fine substitutes.

Raspberry-Flavored Liqueurs

Framboise is an eau-de-vie distilled from raspberries, and Chambord is a dark-red, sweet black-raspberry liqueur. When you don't want to tint your dessert red or pink, use framboise; otherwise, Chambord is a wonderful liqueur and flavoring.

Nuts

Hazelnuts (also called filberts), walnuts, and almonds are a veritable triumvirate in the Austro-Hungarian pastry kitchen. They're sprinkled over dumplings, turned into fillings for buns, and used to create the base for many tortes. Buy them in bulk from a reliable source, such as a natural foods store. Store nuts in self-sealing plastic bags in the refrigerator for up to 3 months or freeze them for up to 6 months.

Toasting Nuts

Toasting enhances the flavor of nuts. Spread them in an even layer on a jelly-roll pan, and bake in a preheated 350°F. oven, stirring occasionally, until fragrant, about 10 minutes.

Peeling Hazelnuts

Hazelnuts must be peeled. Bake the hazelnuts as directed in "Toasting Nuts" until the dark skins are cracked and pulling away from the nuts. Wrap the warm nuts in a kitchen towel and cool for about 20 minutes. Rub the nuts in the towel to remove the skins. Don't worry about removing every last bit of skin, because a little will add color and flavor. If you insist on removing every remnant of skin, transfer the hazelnuts to a wire sieve, and rub the recalcitrant brown skin against the sieve to rasp it away. Some markets now carry peeled hazelnuts, a true boon, but if needed, toast them until light golden brown to add color and flavor.

Grinding Nuts

Many of these recipes call for ground nuts. A rotary nut grinder is a standard tool in central European kitchens, but is not considered a must in the States. The grinder can also be used to grate hard or semi-hard cheeses, so it's not a one-job gadget. Adventures in Cooking, Bridge Kitchenware, and Sur La Table (Tools for the Cook) are all good sources for Mouli or Zylis nut grinders (see Sources).

I have given instructions for grinding nuts in a food processor in the recipes where this isn't a compromise, even though hand-ground nuts do have a lighter texture that combines well in bat-

ters. (In the Walnut Torte on page 66, the nuts *must* be ground with a hand grinder.) Processor-ground nuts tend to release their oils; too much grinding and you'll have nut butter. To protect against this, grind the nuts with a portion of the recipe's flour or sugar, which acts as a buffer. The texture is not quite as fine as hand-ground nuts, but a food processor is very fast and convenient. If you prefer to grind the nuts by hand in a recipe with processor instructions, simply return the flour or sugar that would have been used to grind the nuts in the processor to the balance of the ingredients in the recipe.

Parchment Paper and Silicone Baking Pads

Once you get used to the ease and convenience of parchment paper, there's no turning back. You won't have to worry about sticking pastries or cakes again. Buy the largest sheets you can find so they can be cut to size without patching. Whenver possible, buy parchment paper that is packaged flat, and not rolled—the rolled paper curls up on the pan. The only way to fix this problem is to grease the pan to glue the paper in place.

Wax paper starts to scorch at 300°F., so while it can be used for lining the bottoms of cake pans (where it is covered and protected by the batter), it can't substitute for parchment paper in applications where it will be exposed to the oven heat.

Baking pads are flexible sheets of silicone that can be reused hundreds of times before they lose their nonstick quality. Some brands can be trimmed with scissors to fit your pans. It's worth having a few of them to fit the baking pans you use most often.

Parchment paper and baking pads are available at most kitchenware stores. *The Baker's Catalogue* from King Arthur Flour is a good mail-order source for flat parchment paper (see Sources).

Pastry Bags and Tips

Some frostings and batters are piped from pastry bags. Buy large cloth pastry bags (at least 14 inches long) with plastic linings. Small bags don't hold much and it's a nuisance to have to refill them, and plastic bags don't have enough flexibility for most jobs. Have two or three bags handy, as some recipes require piping from multiple bags.

Filling a large pastry bag can be awkward. Here's an efficient method. Start by fitting the bag with the tip. Place the bag inside a tall glass, folding the top of the bag back over the lip of the glass to form a cuff. With the bag opened and standing, it will be much easier to fill.

Unless you are decorating a wedding cake with frosting, there is little need for a full contingency of pastry tips. You can do many decorating and piping jobs with just a few tips. Ateco is the main manufacturer, and the various widths, from 5/32- to 11/16-inch diameter, are numbered from 0 to 9, with the relative size number found at the end of the model's sequence. I use moderately sized Number 5 tips (approximately ½ inch wide) to do almost every decorating and piping job in this book. A 7/16-inch-wide plain tip (Ateco Number 805) is used for piping out ladyfingers and cream puffs. For decorating, use a 7/16-inch open star tip (Number 825) or 7/16-inch French star tip (Number 865, which has smaller teeth than the regular star tip and makes a slightly fancier swirl). The eclairs on page 123 use an 11/16-inch plain tip (Ateco Number 809). Adventures in Cooking, Sweet Celebrations, and Sur La Table (Tools for the Cook) all mail-order pastry tips and bags (see Sources).

Poppy Seeds

One of the most distinctive flavors of the central European kitchen, poppy seeds have a mildly nutty flavor. When central European cooks talk about a poppy seed cake, they don't just mean one with a couple of tablespoons: Their cakes are black from the amount of seeds used. And there are almost a million poppy seeds to a pound!

The tiny, gray-black, ripe seeds of *Papaver somniferum* are used in baking. Unripe poppy seeds have narcotic qualities, and opium is extracted from the unripe seed capsules. Not surprisingly, the cultivation of these poppies is prohibited in the United States, so any poppy seeds you buy here will be imported. Poppy seeds have a high oil content that makes them susceptible to rancidity, and when you add this factor to the shipping time, freshness can be a problem.

Buy poppy seeds in bulk from a purveyor with a steady turnover, such as a central European delicatessen or Middle East or Indian grocer (poppy seeds are used in the cuisines of the East, too). Poppy seeds in tiny jars from the supermarket are likely to be prohibitively expensive and rancid. Store poppy seeds in an airtight container in the refrigerator or freeze them for up to 6 months. Always give poppy seeds a good sniff before using to check for any hint of rancidity. Otto's European Import Store is a great place to buy reasonably priced poppy seeds by mail order (see Sources).

Poppy seeds are usually ground before use to crack their tough hulls, which releases their flavor and moisture. In Europe, bakers use a special crank-operated poppy seed grinder. However, buy from a trustworthy source. The ones that are imported to this country are unreliable, and are often missing an irreplaceable washer or bolt, rendering them useless. Never mind; an electric coffee grinder or blender does a fine job. Grind the seeds in ¼-cup batches until they look smaller than whole seeds and begin to clump together. A blender takes longer than a grinder, about 1 minute, and be sure to stop the blender occasionally to loosen the ground seeds that collect arount the blade.

Preserves

Apricot and red currant preserves are used again and again in Austro-Hungarian desserts. Be sure to use preserves, which are less sweet than jams and jellies and have fruit pieces. Traditional preserves made with sugar are preferred over spreads sweetened with fruit juice. The preserves are usually boiled briefly (to evaporate a bit of moisture so they dry into a firm set), then strained to remove the fruit. Use any brand you like.

Prune Butter

We also know these dark, tart preserves by their eastern European name, lekvar. They're called

Powidl in Austria, from *powidlen*, the high German word for "made in Bohemia," the region where the preserves are especially fine. To give prune butter the typical central European flavor, stir in a generous pinch each of ground cinnamon and cloves to each cup of prune butter, and, if desired, add 1 tablespoon of golden rum. Refrigerate the prune butter after opening, and it will keep indefinitely.

Pudding Molds

Steamed pudding requires a special mold, which is easy to find at specialty kitchenware stores during the Christmas holiday season. Steamed pudding molds are made from metal, with tight-fitting lids (to keep out the steam) and central tubes (to encourage even baking of the thick, moist batter). They stand about 5 inches tall, and have a capacity of about 7 cups. You can use an 8-inch Gugelhupf pan (covered tightly with buttered aluminum foil) as a substitute, allowing about one quarter less steaming time.

Rehrücken Pan

A fluted baking pan in a half-cylinder shape, about 12 inches long. The pan is used to bake a cake that is supposed to resemble a cooked saddle of venison. It usually has a nonstick surface.

Rolling Pin

Surprisingly, there aren't many tarts in the Austro-Hungarian dessert lexicon, but a rolling pin still gets a workout from rolling out sweet yeast doughs and puff pastry. A long wood rolling pin (about 20 inches long) with tapered ends will allow you to control the amount of pressure needed for the particular dough. The tapered ends are perfect for rolling out edges of dough that may be a bit too thick. Never wash your rolling pin or it will warp. Just scrape off the dough (use something dull so you don't nick the wood) and wipe it clean with a moistened paper towel.

Ruler

This may seem like a silly suggestion, but you should always have a ruler in the kitchen. When a recipe asks for a dough to be rolled out to a certain dimension or thickness, don't guess—take out the ruler! Plastic rulers are easy to keep clean.

Salt

Central European bakers do not use salt as a flavor enhancer in batters and doughs, except in yeast dough, where the salt inhibits yeast activity so the dough won't rise too fast. However, a small amount of salt brings out the flavors of the ingredients, so I include it in my versions of Austro-Hungarian recipes for the American kitchen. By a pinch, I mean about ⅛ teaspoon.

In my opinion, iodized or plain salt is best for baking because its fine texture makes for easy dissolving. Kosher or fine-grained sea salt are coarser, so you get a different volume measurement and could need about fifty percent more than iodized or plain to get the same level of seasoning. Because Europeans rarely use salt in their desserts anyway, if I am in a kitchen with kosher or sea salt, I don't bother with increasing the amounts, except for yeast doughs.

Serrated Knife

To cut a cake into even layers, use a serrated knife with a blade 12 to 16 inches long. Knives with shorter blades aren't as easy to control and don't reach as well to the center of the cake layer.

Thermometers

Every good baker relies on accurate thermometers to identify the correct cooking temperatures. An *oven thermometer* is essential—very few ovens are exactly calibrated, and a free-standing thermometer is a great backup. You'll need a *candy/deep-frying thermometer* (from 0° to 400°F.) for heating fat for doughnuts and checking the temperature of syrups. An *instant-read thermometer* (0° to 220°F.) comes in handy for testing the temperature of liquids for dissolving yeasts.

You used to need all three of the aforementioned thermometers, but there is one great new tool that does the job of all three. *Probe thermometers* were originally used for roasting. The probe, which is inserted into the meat or poultry, is attached to a cord that connects by a flexible cable to the read-out unit, but it measures the temperature of anything from 0° to 392°F. It is especially great when measuring shallow amounts of syrup (an instant-read thermometer usually needs to be submerged ½ inch or more to reach the tiny notch on the stem). One drawback: If you run out of batteries, you're stuck, so you may want to keep your old thermometers around as backups.

Spatulas

Icing spatulas have thin, flexible metal blades. They come in two styles, straight and offset. I prefer the angled blade of an offset spatula because it fits best into jelly-roll pans when spreading batters into corners, and makes it easier to apply icing in a level horizontal layer.

Rubber spatulas come in many sizes. Look for the heat-proof models, which are sturdier than the old versions and fight off odors and stains. I use a small spatula for scraping chocolate into a piping cone or stiring gelatin as it melts, and a medium-size one for stirring certain liquids that need to be scraped from the sides of the bowl while cooking. But my large, spoon-shaped spatula (sometimes called a "spoonula") really gets a workout, transfering batter to pastry bags and cake pans and doing other chores.

Springform Pans

European bakeries use round metal cake rings to create their tortes. However, they aren't easy to find in America. Sur La Table (Tools for the Cook) is the only mail-order source I could find. And, because many of the cream-filled tortes need to be unmolded, regular cake pans with bottoms are not an option.

Springform pans with removable bottoms are a happy compromise. In only a few cases will the indentation from the pan's clip show in the filling, and that can be fixed with a coating of finely chopped nuts or cake crumbs. Buy the best pan you can afford. Inexpensive pans made from thin metal have clips that fall off and bottoms that warp. Try to purchase pans with a true 9-inch diameter. European pans with 22- and 24-centimeter diameters are really a little smaller or larger than 9 inches, but they will work.

In some recipes, even if the bottom of your pan fits snugly into the ring, butter will run out of the pan and burn in the oven. To prevent this, tightly wrap the bottom of the pan in aluminum foil to catch any drips.

Wire Racks

Cakes should be unmolded onto a wire rack so the air can freely circulate around the cake to cool quickly. (If cakes are cooled completely in their pans, they become soggy from the trapped steam.) Some simple cakes are meant to cool in the pan, but the pan should still sit on a rack to speed up the cooling. Round wire racks are fine for round cake layers, but a large rectangular rack is more versatile. Bakers with restricted counter space should look for the tiered model that has three stacked racks. *The Baker's Catalogue* from King Arthur Flour (see Sources) has a big selection of racks.

Yeast

Most European bakers and American baking professionals prefer compressed (also called fresh or cake) yeast. It dissolves easily in cool water, and it has a bit more rising power than dry yeast, as well as a milder, less "yeasty" flavor. My market carries the 2-ounce cubes, and I use that as my standard, but fresh yeast is also available in smaller 0.6-ounce cubes. When the measurement is one-third cube, it means one third of a 2-ounce, not a 0.6-ounce, cube. It should be smooth and evenly pale; discard any hard, discolored fresh yeast. It isn't available in every store, so I give substitute measurements for active dry yeast.

Active dry yeast is available in ¼-ounce envelopes, usually in strips of three, and in tinted jars. You can buy dry yeast (do not confuse it with nutritional or brewer's yeast) in bulk at natural food stores, but unless it is stored in the refrigerated section or freezer, pass it up. Dry yeast should be dissolved in warm (105° to 115°F.) liquid to dissolve the protective coating on the tiny capsules of yeast. Use an instant-read thermometer to gauge the temperature until you get used to testing by touch.

If you want to use instant yeast (which is really the same thing as fast-acting or bread machine yeast), there are a few caveats. Instant yeast is stronger than active dry yeast. If used in equal quantities, it will make the bread rise more quickly, but at the expense of flavor. Therefore, use one-quarter less instant yeast than active dry. Also, instant yeast does not need to be dissolved in liquid before using; simply add it to the dry ingredients and disregard any disregard any instructions on the package to use hot liquid in the dough.

No matter what yeast you use, keep the temperature of the liquid in mind. If the water is ice-cold, the capsules won't dissolve as well, and temperatures above 140°F. will kill any baking yeast.

To proof yeast (test its potency), dissolve a pinch of yeast with a pinch of sugar in ¼ cup of warm liquid. Let stand 5 minutes; if there is discernible action, either a fizzing sound or bubbling (not all yeast will foam when active), the yeast is potent. You can use this liquid in the recipe, if you wish. Frankly, I never proof my yeast, because I buy it fresh as needed, store it properly, and pay strict attention to the expiration date.

Store yeast in the refrigerator or freezer. Active dry yeast can be frozen for up to a year (fresh yeast doesn't freeze well). However, pay attention to the use-by date on the package, as refrigerated yeast, especially fresh yeast, quickly loses its strength after that date. Leftover dry yeast should be stored in an airtight container, and fresh yeast should be tightly wrapped in plastic, with the expiration date marked on the wrapping.

Here are some common equivalents for fresh and dry yeast:

- One ¼-ounce envelope of active dry yeast equals 2¼ teaspoons
- One 2-ounce cube of fresh yeast equals three ¼-ounce envelopes of active dry yeast
- One third of a 2-ounce cube of fresh yeast equals one ¼-ounce envelope of active dry yeast
- One 0.6-ounce cube of fresh yeast equals one ¼-ounce envelope of active dry yeast

Zest, Lemon and Orange

Freshly grated zest adds flavor to many baked goods. Because the dyes on mass-harvested oranges and lemons aren't completely nontoxic (the dyes aren't harmful in the small amounts used in baking, however), it's probably best to use organic citrus for zesting. Wash and dry the fruit well before zesting.

There are a few options for getting the zest off the fruit. No matter what tool you use, remove only the colored zest (which contains the flavorful essential oils) and avoid digging into the pale, bitter pith. Among bakers, the microplane zester, a long metal utensil that resembles a wood rasp, has become *the* kitchen tool of the past decade. It effortlessly removes the zest in very fine shreds. Before I bought my new zester, I happily used the small holes on a box cheese grater or Parmesan cheese grater; just be sure the grater holes aren't jagged, or you'll dig into the pith instead of removing the zest. I don't like the small zesters with four or five small holes, as they create long strips of zest that must be chopped before using, making another step in the process.

If your supply of fresh fruit is depleted, substitute pure lemon or orange oil for the zest. Boyajian brand is excellent, and can be found at kitchenware shops and by mail order. Depending on whether the citrus flavor should be subtle or strong, use ¼ to one ½ teaspoon of pure lemon or orange oil for the zest of one fruit. I always have some on hand.

A PERSONAL COFFEE-HOUSE GUIDE

It would be impossible to visit every one of the thousands of coffeehouses in Vienna, Budapest, and Prague, but I did visit those with biggest impact on each city's history and culture. This list compiles personal favorites and is not meant to be a complete catalogue. Not every coffeehouse is steeped in nostalgia. Sparkling new coffeehouses open regularly, often with admirable individuality and a sense of style that brings the comfortable home-away-from-home into this century. I've included a few of my favorite "new-style" cafés here along with the established classics. For ease of alphabetization, the word *Café* is ignored in the list.

I have provided a landmark and the closest subway stop in each city to provide a sense of direction. I've also concentrated on cafés in areas that a traveler is most likely to visit, and I didn't include too many places in the far reaches of the cities. An important word of advice about how to get where you want to go: The subways in each city are very efficient, and are worth getting to know. In Prague and Budapest, taxis are a problem (not so in Vienna, but they aren't cheap). To be blunt, don't ever take a taxi unless your hotel has booked one from an honest company. Never hail a taxi on the street, or you could be overcharged. The newspapers are constantly filled with complaints from hustled tourists, and as hard as the local governments are trying, the problem persists.

Vienna

Vienna is divided into twenty-three districts, generating out from the First District, home to St. Stephen's Cathedral and the Hofburg. The café's district or a landmark follows the name. The hours for establishments with live music are also listed.

A number of coffeehouses have their own web sites, but they are not always in English. Use this link to hook up to some of the most best-known cafés: www.tourist-net.co.at/coffee. By American standards,

it is virtually impossible to have a seriously lackluster dessert at any of the establishments below, but the places that make their own are highly recommended.

Blaue Café (near Museum of Art and History)
Eschenbachgasse 7 (corner of Nibelungengasse)
587-63-08
HOURS: Monday through Friday, 4 P.M. to 2 A.M.;
Saturday and Sunday, 6 P.M. to 2 A.M.
U-BAHN: Babenbergerstrasse
Look for the blue door (there's no sign), and go downstairs into Vienna's funkiest café. It has a dimly lit, lived-in bohemian atmosphere that is miles away from the gilt and mirrors of the Ringstrasse cafés.

Café Bräunerhof (near the Dorotheum)
Stallburggasse 2
512-38-93
HOURS: Monday through Friday, 7:30 A.M. to 7:30 P.M.; Saturday, 7:30 A.M. to 6 P.M.; Sunday, 10 A.M. to 6 P.M.
MUSIC: Saturday and Sunday, 3 P.M. to 6 P.M.
U-BAHN: Stephansplatz
Located near the Dorotheum (the premier auction house in Vienna), this is a jewel box of a café. The resident chamber music trio is wonderful, so this is the perfect spot to enjoy live Schubert with your coffee.

Café Central (near the Hofburg)
Herrengasse 14 (corner of Strauchgasse)
533-37-63
HOURS: Monday through Saturday, 8 A.M. to 10 P.M.; closed Sunday and holidays.
U-BAHN: Herrengasse
Famous as the center of the early twentieth-century Austrian literary world, the spacious quarters complete with vaulted ceiling gives you the feeling you're sitting in a castle rather than a coffeehouse. They offer a good selection of Warme Mehlspeisen. If you're in a hurry, try their small bakery-café across the street.

Café Diglas (near St. Stephen's Cathedral)
Wollzeile 10
512-57-65
HOURS: Monday through Wednesday, 7 A.M. to 11:30 P.M.; Thursday through Saturday, 7 A.M. to 2 A.M.; Sunday, 9 A.M. to 11 P.M.
MUSIC: Friday and Saturday, 10 A.M. to 12:30 A.M.
U-BAHN: Stubentor

One of the few coffeehouses in Vienna with full menus for breakfast, lunch, and dinner. Hans Diglas, whose family has been in the restaurant business for many years, knows the importance of making his customers feel that his coffeehouse is their second home. The décor keeps many original touches from its opening in 1923. The desserts are baked on the premises (actually down the street, but close enough), and are excellent. Try the Schaumschnitten.

Café Dommayer (Hietzing, near Schönbrunn)
Dommayergasse 1
877-54-65
HOURS: Daily, 7 A.M. to midnight
MUSIC: May 1 to October 31, Saturday and Sunday, 2 to 4 P.M.
U-BAHN: Schönbrunn

On a relaxing weekend afternoon, there are few experiences more Viennese than coffee at Café Dommayer, listening to the straw-hatted, all-women orchestra, Die Walzermädchen, "The Waltz Maidens." (The worldwide waltz craze started at the original Dommayer, which was around the corner.) The café is at the forefront of reviving old traditions, and it keeps up the connection between the coffeehouse and culture by offering theatrical and musical entertainment and literary readings. In the summer, you can see productions in their gazebo theater. If you are already visiting Schönbrunn, Dommayer is the place to go, although coffee lovers will find it's worth a special trip.

Café Frauenhuber (near St. Stephen's Cathedral)
Himmelpfortgasse 6
512-83-83
HOURS: Daily, 8 A.M. to 11 P.M.
U-BAHN: Stephansplatz

This is the oldest Viennese café in continuous operation. Music lovers will want to drop in, as both Mozart and Beethoven played here.

Café Goldegg (Fourth District, near Belvedere)
Argentinierstrasse 49
505-91-62
HOURS: Monday through Friday, 8 A.M. to 10 P.M., Saturday, 8 A.M. to 3 P.M.
U-BAHN: Südtirolerplatz

Dating from 1910, this landmark café is on a quiet side street on the way to the Belvedere Palace. It has a quiet charm with details like inlaid wood paneling and a free-standing American-made furnace, quite a conversation piece in its time. This is a good example of a café that has changed little over the years and remains a viable part of its neighborhood without any sign of trying to attract tourists or other outsiders.

Café Griensteidl (across from Hofburg)
Michaelerplatz 2
535-26-92
HOURS: Daily, 8 A.M. to midnight
U-BAHN: Herrengasse

The first Café Griensteidl was the home to Young Vienna, a group of upstart artists who influenced thought in the last decades of the nineteenth century. When it was demolished in 1897, the regulars packed up and moved across the street to Café Central. Almost a hundred years later, this reproduction opened on the same site. It lacks the original's literary connection, but it is a mellow place to sit and watch the world go by, framed by the enormous hulk of the imperial palace known as the Hofburg, right outside the window.

Habig (near Karlsplatz and the Opera)
Wiedner Haupstrasse 14
502-80-33
HOURS: Daily, 9 A.M. to midnight
U-BAHN: Karlsplatz

One of my favorite new café-restaurants artfully combines the old and the new. Formerly a haberdashery that catered to royalty, Habig has been transformed into a café-restaurant. Many of the original hand-carved wood fixtures remain, and you half expect the clientele to walk through the door looking for the perfect hat for a court ball rather than a coffee. This is a great place to come for a meal before or after the opera, which is a few minutes' walk away.

Café Hawelka (near the Dorotheum)

Dorotheergasse 6

512-82-30

HOURS: Monday, Wednesday through Saturday, 8 A.M. to 2 A.M.; Sunday, 4 P.M. to 2 A.M. Closed Tuesday.

U-BAHN: Stephansplatz

The night-owl's café. The legendary owners, Leopold and Josefine Hawelka, now both in their late eighties, have nurtured their café into the closest thing Vienna has to a bohemian hangout. The art on the walls, donated by famous Austrian artists who sustained themselves on Hawelka's coffee and sweet rolls, is probably worth a small fortune. Nobel laureate Elias Canetti was a frequent customer in his youth. Be sure to try the Buchteln, which are baked fresh in small batches in their tiny kitchen and are served after 10 P.M. or so every night.

Café Imperial (near Musikverein)

Kärntner Ring 16

501-10-389

HOURS: Daily, 7 A.M. to 11 P.M.

Music: Saturday and Sunday, 3:30 to 6:30 P.M.

U-BAHN: Karlsplatz

In 1873, just in time for the jubilee celebrating Franz Joseph's twenty-fifth anniversary of rule, the Hotel Imperial opened in the former Palace Württemberg, and the café immediately established itself as being a favorite of the Ringstrasse's fashionable denizens. Near the concert hall of the Vienna Philharmonic, the café has played host to many musical greats. It was also the pulpit from which Karl Kraus, one of Vienna's most eccentric and egocentric literary critics, pontificated, after he left his former roost, Café Central, in a huff.

Café Im KunstHausWien (in the KunstHausWien/Hundertwasser Museum)

Weißgerberlände 14

712-04-97

HOURS: Daily, 10 A.M. to midnight

MUSIC: Wednesday and Saturday, 7 to 10 P.M.

TRAM: N

Friedensreich Hundertwasser is one of Austria's love-him-or-hate-him artists. His bright colors, shiny tiles, and irregular, undulating lines are shocking to the architectural consciousness of a city that most often looks like a concrete wedding cake. The café is part of the gift shop for the KunstHausWien, the museum he built to showcase his art, and it is a lively place to partake of apple strudel surrounded by lush live foliage.

Kleines Café (near St. Stephen's Cathedral)

Franziskanerplatz 3

No telephone

HOURS: Monday through Saturday, 10 A.M. to 2 A.M.; Sunday, 1 P.M. to 2 A.M.

U-BAHN: Stephansplatz

When seeing the sights of the First District near St. Stephen's Cathedral, you might want to duck into Kleines Café (The Little Café), which lives up to its name. Two tiny rooms (it used to be only one room!) make this the antithesis of the wide-open spaces of the classic cafés. This is another jewel by architect Hermann Czech (see the MAK Café).

Café Landtmann (near Rathaus)

Dr. Karl Lueger Ring 4

532-06-21

HOURS: Daily, 8 A.M. to midnight

Music: Wednesday and Sunday, 2:30 to 5:30 P.M.

U-BAHN: Rathausplatz

This was Freud's favorite café, and it is said that he was not above holding a session with a patient here instead of in his office. Now it is the haunt of politicians from City Hall across the street and actors from the Burgtheater next door. In the small front room, you'll find relief figures of ladies sipping their coffee, a reminder of the time when the room was closed to men and their cigars. The savory food is good here, too; try the goulash with spaetzle.

MAK Café (in the Museum of Applied Arts)

Stubenring 5

714-01-21

HOURS: Tuesday through Sunday, 8:30 A.M. to midnight; closed Monday

U-BAHN: Stubentor

At the Museum für Angewandte Kunst (known by its initials MAK, or Museum of Applied Arts), this is Vienna's sleekest café. The problem of how to design a modern space that showed respect for the one-

hundred-year-old coffered ceilings was overcome by architect Hermann Czech, who rose to the occasion with functional industrial lighting that didn't cover up the existing space. The MAK is more than just a place to grab a coffee while visiting the museum; it has become a destination of its own that is packed with the students from the nearby design school. The museum is a treasure house of artistically created useful objects, from fabric to jewelry. Coffeehouse lovers will want to catch the exhibit of Vienna-made Thonet bentwood furniture, which, fittingly, is one of the definitive features of the classic café.

Das Möbel (Spittelberg)

Burggasse 10
524-94-97
U-BAHN: Burggase-Stadthalle

Ultra-modern Das Möbel ("The Furniture") is around the corner from a cobblestoned street. Nonetheless, it is surely one of the most cutting-edge and quirky coffeehouses in the world, much less Vienna. Don't fall in love with any of the furnishings —they're all for sale and your favorite chair could be gone by your next visit. Das Möbel is a crafty mix of furniture showroom and coffeehouse, and the tables, chairs, standing lamps, and other fixtures are changed every six weeks or so. Instead of a museum piece atmosphere, the neighborhood locals get a constantly evolving canvas for their comings and goings. As hip as can be, Das Möbel still exists for those daily customers, and not just for the youngsters in black clothing looking to move on to the next cool place in a month or so.

Café Mozart (near Albertina)

Albertinaplatz 2
513-08-81
HOURS: Daily, 8 A.M. to midnight
Music: Wednesday and Sunday, 2:30 to 5:30 P.M.
U-BAHN: Karlsplatz

Remember the café in the movie The Third Man *where Holly Martins (Joseph Cotten) meets the gangster? Well, you wouldn't recognize it today, all spiffed up to attract the tourists. Owned by the same family as Café Landtmann, Café Mozart is a chocophile's paradise, with five varieties of hot chocolate.*

Café Museum (near the Opera)

Friedrichstrasse 6
586-52-02
HOURS: Daily, 7 A.M. to 11 P.M.
U-BAHN: Karlsplatz

This stark café was one of the first major works of the Viennese architect Adolf Loos. Loos derided ornamentation, so the café is all about function over form. You can see some of Loos's buildings Vienna, and while they seem tame today, they were shocking when they were first built. This edifice, opened in 1899, must have stuck out like a sore thumb in the middle of all the frilly buildings on the Ringstrasse. Its detractors dubbed it "Café Nihilismus." It attracted many of the top creative talent of pre-1916 Vienna, artists like Klimt, Schiele, and Kokoschka, and Loos's fellow architects Joseph Hoffman, Otto Wagner, and Joseph Maria Olbrich, designer of the Secession Pavilion across the streeet from the café.

Café Prückel (across from MAK)

Stubenring 24
512-61-15
HOURS: Daily, 9 A.M. to 10 P.M.
Music: Monday, Wednesday, Friday, 7 P.M. to 10 P.M.
U-BAHN: Subentor

Built at the turn of the century, the café did not make it through World War Two unscathed, and in 1955, the owners gave the place a makeover in the latest style. The Sputnik-style interior is as stylistically recognizable as a nineteenth-century café's gilt and mirrors.

Sacher (near the Opera)

Philharmonikerstrasse 4
512-14-87
HOURS: Daily, 6:30 A.M. to 11:30 P.M.
U-BAHN: Karlsplatz

Sacher is on the short list of any chocolate lover's stops in Vienna. The red velvet walls of the café give a rosy glow to the proceedings. The Sacher has a shop that sells the famous Sacher cake in wooden boxes for transport.

Café Savoy (near Naschmarkt)

Linke Wienzeille 36

586-73-48

HOURS: Monday through Friday, 5 P.M. to 2 A.M.; Saturday, 9 A.M. to 6 P.M., then 9 P.M. to 2 A.M.

U-BAHN: Kettenbrückengasse

Does the Café Savoy have the biggest mirrors of any coffeehouse in Vienna? It must have had the heaviest chandeliers, as a hole in the ceiling shows. As the evening proceeds, the clientele becomes mostly gay. This café is right near the Naschmarkt, Vienna's outdoor market and a must-see for food lovers.

Café Sperl (near Theater an der Wien)

Gumpendorferstrasse 11

586-41-58

HOURS: Monday to Saturday, 7 A.M. to 11 P.M.; Sunday, 3 P.M. to 11 P.M.

U-BAHN: Kettenbrückengasse

Café Sperl is perhaps the most classic of the classic coffeehouses. The owners really never had any extra money to refurbish the place, so when it was chosen as a landmark coffeehouse in 1983, much of the original work was in place. It has been gloriously returned to its cozy atmosphere, with huge booths, a frou-frou service counter, and a parquet floor. You'll see all of the components of the traditional Kaffeehaus here: the L-shaped design with one room reserved for billiards; marble tables; and wrought-iron coat stands. If you're here during the fall, try the plum cake.

Café Stein (near Votivekirche)

Währingerstrasse 6-8

319-72-41

HOURS: Daily, 7 A.M. to 2 A.M.

U-BAHN: Schottentor-Universität

Ladies of a certain age with their pet doggies in tow do not frequent Café Stein. This is the ultimate student café, situated in the streets behind the university. It's nothing like the small, dark holes posing as cafés that I frequented in college, except for the walls plastered with posters for poetry readings and political rallies; it's big and sprawling and choked with cigarette smoke. Be ready to talk loudly, as the rock and roll on the sound system is never at low volume. Don't miss the bathrooms, which seem to be purposely designed for chance encounters with the opposite sex

(it will take more than a few seconds to figure out what door is the portal to which gender's toilet). Café Stein also has a cybercafé tucked away upstairs.

Café Tirolerhof (near Albertina)

Tegetthoffstrasse 8

512-78-33

HOURS: Monday to Saturday, 7 A.M. to 9 P.M.; Sunday, 9:30 A.M. to 8 P.M.

U-BAHN: Karlsplatz

Even though it's in the heart of Vienna, you won't see many tourists in this coffeehouse. It's not the most luxurious café, but it has soul. The apple strudel is as good as Grandma's (if your grandma was Viennese).

Viennese Bakeries with Tables

Aida (throughout Vienna)

Locations throughout Vienna

587-25-85

HOURS: Usually Monday through Saturday, 7 A.M. to 7 P.M.; Sundays 9 A.M. to 7 P.M.

No need to give the addresses to the twenty-eight locations, as you'll hardly walk in any neighborhood without coming across an Aida. Stop in and be served by one of their pink-and-white-clad waitresses.

Demel (near the Hofburg)

Kohlmarkt 14

533-55-16

HOURS: Daily, 10 A.M. to 7 P.M.

U-BAHN: Herrengasse

To me, and to any true dessert-lover, it is unthinkable to visit Vienna without at least one stop at Demel. It is impossible to have a less-than-perfect dessert here, as their attention to detail is legendary. Making a selection from the array of desserts on the marble counter is a mix of frustration and hedonism. Go for one of their house specialties, such as Annatorte (a truffle torte wrapped in chocolate-hazelnut gianduja) or Burgtheatertorte (an unglazed chocolate torte with hints of orange). There are dining rooms for lunch and dinner, as well as the front café with its marble-topped tables. You'll be served by a woman in a plain black aproned frock, a copy of a local convent uniform from back in the days when girls from the school were hired as waitresses.

Gerstner (near the Opera)
Kärtnerstrasse 11-14
512-49-63
HOURS: Monday through Saturday, 8:30 A.M. to
7:30 P.M.
U-BAHN: Stephansplatz
*Walking down the pedestrian-only Kärtnerstrasse, it
is hard to miss Gerstner and harder to walk by without stopping and taking a table. They have outdoor
seating in the summer.*

L. Heiner (near St. Stephen's Cathedral)
Wollzeile 9
512-48-38-0
HOURS: Monday through Saturday, 8:30 A.M. to
7:00 P.M.; Sunday 10 A.M. to 7:30 P.M.
U-BAHN: Stephansplatz
*It is pointless to talk about which of the Inner City
pastry shops is better. Heiner has been in business for
160 years and serves all the classics in impeccable
style. Their ice cream desserts are especially refreshing on a hot day. There is another shop at Kärtnerstrasse 21-23 that has outdoor seating in warm
weather.*

Lehman (near St. Stephen's Cathedral)
Graben 12
512-18-15
HOURS: Monday through Saturday, 9 A.M. to 7 P.M.
U-BAHN: Stephansplatz
*Another of the venerable institutions near St.
Stephen's Cathedral, right in the middle of Vienna's
most exclusive shopping street.*

Oberlaa (near Dorotheum)
Neuer Markt 16
512-29-36
HOURS: Monday through Friday, 8 A.M. to 7 P.M.;
Saturday, 8 A.M. to 6 P.M.; Sunday, 10 A.M. to 6 P.M.
U-BAHN: Stephansplatz
*Oberlaa is the new kid on the block, and they are
making waves with their modern renditions of the old
favorites. During the Christmas holidays, try their
panettone, studded with marzipan as well as their own
candied fruit. They have three other locations; the
Neuer Markt is the one that you're most likely to come
across in the center of the city. Their flagship café, at*

*the Oberlaa spa, is sparkling with modern glass and
brass, but it requires a long tram trip and the spa isn't
set up for American visitors. But if you speak German, it's a trip in more ways than one.*

Sluka (near Rathaus)
Rathausplatz 8
406-88-96
HOURS: Monday through Friday, 8 A.M. to 7 P.M.;
Saturday, 8 A.M. to 5:30 P.M.
U-BAHN: Rathaus
*Tucked in an arcade by the Rathaus (City Hall),
Sluka has meant top-quality pastry for over a hundred
years (there is a gold medal on their door from the
1898 Vienna Culinary Arts Competition). During the
cold weather, it is the place to go for chestnut desserts.*

Budapest

Budapest is divided by the Danube and has three distinct districts: Buda (with Castle Hill) on the right
bank, Pest (the business center) on the left bank,
and the hills of Óbuda to the northwest of Buda.
The Roman numeral at the beginning of each
address refers to the postal codes; the first district is
I, and so on.

   The quality of desserts in Budapest can be hit or
miss. After the world-class pastries at Gerbeaud, other
bakeries can suffer in comparison. In fact, some of the
garnishes can be quite garish. Concentrate on the local
specialties and don't judge by Viennese standards, and
you'll have a wonderful experience. Also, the cafés in
Budapest are gorgeous, and the atmosphere makes up
for any maraschino cherries you might see sitting on
top of your cake.

Angelika Cukrászda (Buda)
I. Batthyány tér 7
201-48-47 or 212-37-84
HOURS: Daily, 10 A.M. to 10 P.M.
METRO: Batthyány tér
*In a historic vaulted building situated next to Buda's
St. Anne's Church, Angelika has a good selection of
tea, which is hard to find in Budapest.*

Astoria Kávéház (Inner Pest)
V. Kossuth Lajos utca 19-21
01/318-67-98
HOURS: Daily, 7 A.M. to midnight
METRO: Astoria

The Astoria is an ornate, grand old hotel from the turn of the twentieth century. Its enormous café with high ceilings—and with tables big enough to hold the largest open newspaper—also has big windows that look out on a busy intersection. If you don't feel like reading, you'll have the best people-watching in town.

Central Kávéház (Inner Pest, near Food Hall)
V. Károlyi Mihály út 9
266-21-10
HOURS: Daily, 7 A.M. to 1 A.M.
METRO: Ferenciek tér

Along with Café New York, this was one of the most important hangouts for the literati of Old Hungary. After decades of hibernation, the Central reopened in the fall of 1999, having been elegantly refurbished. This café easily accommodates tourists from the nearby pedestrian area of Vaci utca and Budapesters wanting to check out the hot new place in town. It's not far from the Market Hall, where food vendors ply their wares in a gorgeous 1897 structure, a place that must be on the list of every food-loving tourist.

Fiori (Inner Pest)
V. Oktober 6 út 6
267-11-64
HOURS: Daily, 10 A.M. to 7 P.M.
METRO: Vörösmarty tér

Not really a café, but a strudel (rétes in Hungarian) shop, where they stretch and roll up the dough right before your eyes. They make four to six kinds of strudel, sweet and savory. Just point to the one that you want, perch on a stool, and enjoy it at the counter.

Frolich Cukrászda (near Old Synagogue)
Dob út 22
276-28-51
HOURS: Monday through Friday, 8 A.M. to 6 P.M.; (closed last two weeks in August)
METRO: Astoria

The only kosher bakery in Budapest, and very good by any standards. It's best for one of the homestyle Jewish pastries, such as flòdni or almas pitéks. Also, don't miss the beautiful, unusual memorial to Charles Lutz, about a half block down on the same side of the street, which projects out of an old wall.

Gerbeaud Cukrászda (Inner Pest)
V. Vörösmarty tér 7
118-13-11
HOURS: Daily, 9 A.M. to 9 P.M.
METRO: Vörösmarty tér

For world-class pastries in Budapest, go to Gerbeaud. The specialty is the Gerbeaud slice, thin layers of a sweet dough layered with jam and nuts with a chocolate icing. It's totally unlike anything you'll ever have in the U.S. Chestnuts, especially beloved by Hungarians, are turned into some very fine desserts here. They have a smaller café around the corner for a quick bite.

Lukács Cukrászda (Embassy District)
Andrássy utca 70
302-87-47
HOURS: Daily, 9 A.M. to 8 P.M.
METRO: Vörösmarty utca

Another favorite of the teatime set, with sophisticated fin-de-siècle fittings. The café was originally built as part of a bank, so expect to walk through a pretty businesslike lobby to reach your destination. The ice creams here are especially good. Fine for a stop after taking in Heroes' Square or one of its adjacent museums.

Mellis István Cukrászda (Inner Pest)
V. Oktober 6 út 17
331-32-74
HOURS: Monday through Saturday, 8 A.M. to 6 P.M.
METRO: Deák Ferenc tér

It's easy to miss one of the most charming bakeries in Budapest, a place where neighborhood folks buy their goodies to take home. Look for the old etched-glass sign with Sütemények (baked goods). Choose your pastry from the case and tell them what kind of coffee you like, and head upstairs to the small salon. Your selection will be sent to you via an electric dumbwaiter. If you need something to read while you relax with your coffee, almost next door is Bestseller's Bookshop, one of the few English-language bookshops in town.

Mûvész Kávéház (Inner Pest)

VI. Andrássy út 29

353-13-37 or 351-39-42

HOURS: Daily, 9 a.m. to midnight

METRO: Opera

Decaffeinated cappuccino served here! Another place steeped in Old World ambiance, but expect crowded quarters to dampen the experience. A good place for a coffee after the Opera, which is right across the street.

Café New York (Elizabeth Town)

VII. Erzsébet körút 9-11

322-38-49 or 322-16-48

HOURS: Daily, 9 A.M. to midnight

METRO: Blaha Lujza tér

The setting of the imposing Café New York will make you feel like royalty, even if some of the other components fall short. It's as grand as a grand café can get. The prix fixe dinner is excellent.

Pierrot (Castle Hill)

I. Fortuna utca 14

375-65-71

HOURS: Daily, 11 A.M. to 1 A.M.

BUS: Castle Line bus from Moszkva tér

A very attractive modern coffeehouse that nonetheless accomplishes a warm, comfortable setting. The charming Museum of Commerce and Catering, one of the quirkiest museums in the world (but incredible fun for foodies), is right down the street.

Ruszwurm Cukrászda (Castle Hill)

I. Szentháromság utca 7

375-52-84

HOURS: Daily, 10 A.M. to 7 P.M.

FUNICULAR: From Clark Ádám tér to Castle Hill

Since 1838, this tiny coffeehouse/bakery near the royal castle has been serving delicious pastries to royalty and commoner alike. You will wonder how the owners have managed to save the unique Empire-period interior during the ravages of almost countless wars and revolutions. (Actually, the fittings and bric-a-brac are now protected by the state, and are maintained by the nearby Museum of Commerce and Catering.) Just about any of the Hungarian-style pastries here is worth the calories.

Prague

Central Prague consists of five quarters: Hradčany (near the castle), Little Quarter (the hills leading up to the castle on the west bank of the Vltava River), Josefov (the old Jewish Quarter), Old Town (with most of the popular Gothic sights like the Old Clock), and New Town. Most of the classic cafés are in the Old Town and New Town sections.

The outdoor markets in Prague are limited, and not very special. To pick up goodies to bring back to the hotel, visit Dům Lahůdek, a food emporium located at Malé náměstí 3), a four-story food emporium in Old Town.

As in Budapest, die-hard dessert lovers will sometimes prefer the café's atmosphere and architectural appointments to the pastry. Make a careful selection from what looks good in the dessert case, and don't blindly order your favorite, as Czech bakers need a little more time to get back on their feet after decades of Communist suppression. What the cafés lack in culinary finesse, they make up for in architectural splendor.

Café Evropa (New Town, on Wenceslas Square)

Václavské nám. 25

02/2422-8117

HOURS: Daily, 7 A.M. to midnight

METRO: Mústek

When visiting this, the epitome of faded Old World elegance, on Wenceslas Square, it's not difficult to glean how beautiful it must have been in its glory. A balcony wraps around the dining room, and it's fun to imagine the intrigues that must have developed in some of its darker corners.

The Globe Bookstore (North of Town Center)

Janovského 14

02/6671-2610

HOURS: Daily, 10 A.M. to midnight

METRO: Vltavská

This used-books store carries mostly American and British titles and sports a thriving café in the back room. Well off the beaten tourist track, this is where many American ex-pats come for their brownies and carrot cake.

Café Imperial (Old Town)
Na porici 15
02/2481-6607
HOURS: Daily, 9 A.M. to midnight
E-MAIL: info@hotelimperial.cz
On a recent trip to Prague, I stumbled across this newly renovated beauty, not far from the Municipal House. The interior is stunningly decorated with magnificent ceramic tiles. The menu is disconcertingly eclectic—it may be best to enjoy something to drink, but save your serious dessert eating for elsewhere.

Café Milena (Old Town, near Astrological Clock)
Staroměstské nám. 22
02/2163-2609
HOURS: Daily, 10 A.M. to 10 P.M.
METRO: Staroměstská
Named after Kafka's mistress, Milena Jesenska, this is a pretty ordinary modern café. But it has a second-floor location that can't be beat, with a clear view of the famous Orloj clock, so time your visit to coincide with the clock's hourly performance.

Kavárna Obecní dům (Old Town, near Powder Tower)
Náměstí Republiky
01/2200-2100
HOURS: Daily, 7:30 A.M. to 11 P.M.
METRO: Náměstí Republiky
An Art Nouveau masterpiece in the Municipal House building, this is bound to be one of the most beautiful places you'll ever have a cup of coffee in. While you're there, take a tour of the entire building, an architectural jewel of central Europe.

Kavárna Slavia (New Town, near National Theater)
Národní 1 and Smetanovo nábřeží
02/6155-2579
HOURS: Daily, 8 A.M. to midnight
METRO: Národní Třida
Right across from the National Theater, with a beautiful view of the Vltava River, this Art Deco treasure has a lot to offer the café aficionado. They have a full menu in addition to the regular coffeehouse fare. Try an absinthe, if you dare.

Mail-Order Sources

Adventures in Cooking
12 Legion Place
Wayne, NJ 07470
(973) 305-1114
www.AdventuresInCooking.com
A very fine all-around cookware shop with personalized service. You can give them a call and talk to a friendly, efficient person who will see if they have what you're looking for—and they usually do.

The Baker's Catalogue
P.O. Box 876
Norwich, VT 05055-0876
(800) 827-6836
www.KingArthurFlour.com
This excellent catalogue from King Arthur Flour has everything for the baker from flour to pans to flavorings.

Bridge Kitchenware
214 East 52nd Street
New York, NY 10022
(212) 688-4220
www.BridgeKitchenware.com
Before the days when every mall had a kitchenware store, Manhattan's Bridge Kitchenware supplied discerning cooks with high-quality goods. They're still at the top of the heap. Their website is especially helpful.

The Broadway Panhandler
477 Broome Street
New York, NY 10013
(212) 966-3434
Another soup-to-nuts kitchenware shop with an especially strong baking section.

A Cook's Wares
211 37th Street
Beaver Falls, PA 15010-2103
(800) 915-9788
No-frills mail-order shopping for utensils, pots, and pans.

La Cuisine

323 Cameron Street

Alexandria, VA 22314

(800) 521-1176

La Cuisine has a wide selection of wares, including edibles like pearl sugar. Everything is of the highest quality.

New York Chocolate and Baking Distributors

56 West 22nd Street

New York, NY 10010

(212) 675-2253, (800) 942-2539

www.NYCakeSupplies.com

Agent source for bakeware, cooking utensils and equipment, edible decorations, food colorings and flavorings, chocolate and candy supplies, and more. Their web site is worth visiting.

Otto's European Import Store and Deli

2320 West Clark Avenue

Burbank, CA 91506

Phone: (818) 845-0433

Fax: (818) 845-8656

http://members.aol.com/HungaryHu

An excellent and authentic source for the freshest poppy seeds and walnuts, both available ground; nut grinders; canned chestnut purée; and many other Hungarian groceries.

Sur La Table (Tools for the Cook)

Catalog Division

1765 Sixth Avenue South

Seattle, WA 98134-1608

(800) 243-0852

www.SurLaTable.com

This chain is quickly gaining a reputation as one of the best kitchenware shops. Call or check their website for a location near you.

Sweet Celebrations

P.O. Box 39426

Edina, MN 55436-0426

(800) 328-6722

www.SweetC.com

Formerly Maid of Scandinavia, this has long been a source for serious bakers. They carry about every cake pan or dessert mold under the sun, including the ebelskiver and Swedish pancake pans that can be used for Indianerkrapfen and Dahlken.

E-Commerce Sites

www.chocosphere.com

High-quality chocolate from all over the world.

www.demel.at

An excellent site with many of Demel's most famous products available by mail order, including Burgtheatertorte, Gugelhupf, Stollen, and Schokoladentorte.

www.meinl.com

The official site of Julius Meinl grocers. Authentic Viennese-roast coffees and accessories for the coffee lover.

jenkins@netway.at

Irene Jenkins is a certified tourist guide and can arrange personalized walking tours of any of Vienna's sights, but she excels at showing her city's classic cafés.

www.sacher.com

When you must have an "Original Sacher Torte," order it directly from the Sacher Hotel itself.

LShafton@earthlink.com

Lori Shafton is the author of the self-published book The Coffeehouses of Prague, *a guidebook to the more recent additions to the coffeehouse scene.*

BIBLIOGRAPHY

Auinger-Pfund, Edith, et al., *Lehrbuch der Konditorei*. Linz: Trauner Schulbuch Verlag, 1997.

Balázs, Mester. *Történeteck Terített Asztalokról És Környékükről*. Budapest: Pallas Stúdió, 1999.

Beer, Gretel. *Classic Austrian Cooking*. London: Andre Deutsch, 1993.

Beranbaum, Rose Levy. *The Pie and Pastry Bible*. New York: Scribner, 1998.

Beyreder, Adelheid. *Wiener Mehlspeisen*. Munich: Gräfe und Unzer Verlag, 1993.

Břízová, Joza. *The Czechoslovak Cookbook*. New York: Crown Publishers, 1965.

Brook-Shepherd, Gordon. *The Austrians*. London: HarperCollins, 1997.

Coe, Sophie D., and Michael D. Coe. *The True History of Chocolate*. New York: Thames and Hudson, 1996.

Demetz, Peter. *Prague in Black and Gold*. New York: Hill and Wang, 1997.

Derecskey, Susan. *The Hungarian Cookbook*. New York: Harper & Row, 1972.

Gajdostíková, Hana. *Czech National Cookbook*. Václavská: Jan Kanzelsberger Publishing House, 1998.

Gergely, Anikó. *Culinaria Hungary*. Cologne: Könemann Verlagsgesellschaft Gmbh, 1999.

Hargitai, György. *Konyha Magyar Édességek*. Budapest: Média Nova, 1998.

Heise, Ulla. *Coffee and Coffee-Houses*. West Chester: Schiffer Publishing Ltd., 1987.

Hess, O., and A. Hess. *Viennese Cooking*. New York: Crown Publishers, 1952.

Hofmann, Paul. *The Viennese: Splendor, Twilight, and Exile*. New York: Doubleday, 1988.

Holub, Karel. *Velká Kavárna Slavia*. Prague: Ars Bohemica, Holub & Artner, 1998.

Kellerman, Monica. *Das Große Sacher Backbuch*. Weyarn: Seehammer Verlag, 1994.

Langseth-Christensen, Lillian. *Gourmet's Old Vienna Cookbook: A Viennese Memoir*. New York: Gourmet Distributing Corporation, 1959.

Linton, Douglas. *To the Coffee House! An Insider's Guide to Vienna's Cafés*. Vienna: Glattau & Schear, 1998.

Lukacs, John. *Budapest 1900: A Historical Portrait of a City and Its Culture*. New York: Grove Press, 1988.

Maier-Bruck, Franz. *Das Große Sacher Kochbuch: Die österreichische Küche*. Weyarn: Seehammer Verlag Gmbh, ca. 1980.

Mayer, Eduard. *Wiener Süßspeisen*. Linz: Trauner Verlag, 1993.

Mayer-Bahl, Eva. *Das große Buch der österreichischen Mehlspeisen*. Munich: BLV, 1999.

Morton, Frederic. *A Nervous Splendor: Vienna 1888/1889*. New York: Penguin Books, 1980.

———. *Thunder at Twilight: Vienna 1913/1914*. New York: Charles Scribner's Sons, 1989.

Morton, Marcia Colman. *The Art of Viennese Pastry*. New York: Doubleday, 1969.

Neumann, Petra. *Wien und seine Kaffeehäuser: Ein literarischer Streifzug durch die berühmtesten Cafés der Donaumetropole*. München: Heyne Verlag, 1997.

Oberleithner, Peter. *Süßes Bäcken: Weltberühmte Mehlspeistradition aus Wein*. Vienna: Michael Lechner Verlag, 1989.

Pasternak, Joseph. *Cooking with Love and Paprika: A Treasury of Continental Cookery*. New York: Bernard Geiss & Associates, 1966.

Pendergrast, Mark. *Uncommon Grounds: The History of Coffee and How It Transformed Our World*. New York: Basic Books, 1999.

Péter, Jánosné. *Sütemények és Egyéb Édességek*. Budapest: Esély Mozaik Kiadó & Holding KFT, 1998.

Polvay, Marina. *All Along the Danube*. New York: Hippocrene Books, Inc., 1996.

Reich, Lilly Joss. *The Viennese Pastry Cookbook*. New York: Macmillan Publishing, 1970.

Riegl, Andrea, and Andreas Augustin. *Das Café Central Treasury*. London: The Most Famous Hotels in the World, 1998.

Schivelbusch, Wolfgang. *Tastes of Paradise*. New York: Vintage Books, 1993.

Schorske, Carl E. *Fin-De-Siècle Vienna: Politics and Culture*. New York: Vintage Books, 1981.

Schratt, Katharina. *To Set Before the King: Katharina Schratt's Festive Recipes*. Iowa City: University of Iowa Press, 1996.

Segel, Harold B. *The Vienna Coffeehouse Wits, 1890–1938*. West Lafayette, Ind.: Purdue University Press, 1993.

Shenton, James P., et al. *American Cooking: The Melting Pot*. New York: Time-Life Books, 1971.

Wagner, Christoph. *Die Wiener Küche*. Frankfurt am Main: Insel Verlag, 1998.

Wechsberg, Joseph. *The Cooking of Vienna's Empire*. New York: Time-Life Books, 1968.

Weismüller, Maria. *Austrian Pastries and Desserts*. Innsbruck: Kompass, 1999.

Witzelberger, Richard. *Das Wiener Zuckerbäcker Handwerk*. Wien: Mayer & Comp., 1947.

INDEX

Note: Page references in *italics* indicate photographs.

Almás Pites (Apple Squares), 118–19
Almond(s)
  Bishop's Fruit-and-Chocolate Tea
    Cake (*Bischifsbrot*), 36
  -Cherry Coffee Cake (*Meggyes
    Piskóta*), 27
  -Chocolate Macaroons (*Schokolade
    Busserln*), 145–46
  Chocolate "Saddle of Venison"
    Cake (*Rehrücken*), 28, *29*
  -Chocolate Torte (*Panamatorte*),
    69–70
  Chocolate-Orange Cake
    (*Burgtheatertorte*), 30–31
  Christmas Sweet Bread (*Stollen*),
    108–10
  Nut Meringue Slices
    (*Esterházyschnitten*), 130–31
  Vanilla Crescents (*Vanillen
    Kipferln*), 149–50
Apfel im Schlafrock (Apples in Pastry
  Robes), 119
Apfelstrudel (Apple Strudel), 80
Apple, Walnut, and Poppy Seed Bars
  (*Flódni*), 116–17
Apple and Croissant Pudding
  (*Kipferlkoch*), 178
Apple Doughnuts, 154
Apple Squares (*Almás Pites*), 118–19
Apple Strudel (*Apfelstrudel*), 80
Apples in Pastry Robes (*Apfel im
  Schlafrock*), 119
Apricot preserves
  Apricot Glaze (*Marillenglasur*), 16
  Dalmatian Four-Flavor Kolacky
    (*Domažlicé Koláče*), 100–102
  Gerbaud Slices (*Gerbaud-Szelet*),
    132, 133–34
  Jam-Filled Crêpes (*Obst
    Palatschinken*), 161–62
  Mardis Gras Doughnuts
    (*Faschingkrapfen*), 152–54
  Meringue and Ladyfinger Slices
    (*Kardinalschnitten*), 136, *137*
  Viennese Jam Rolls (*Buchteln*),
    95–96
Apricot(s). *See also* Apricot preserves
  Christmas Sweet Bread (*Stollen*),
    108–10
  Coffee Cake (*Marillenfleck*),
    26–27
  Sweet Fruit Omelet (*Stefánia
    Omelette*), 166–67
  Tart (*Marillenkuchen*), 26
Aranygaluska (Golden Dumplings),
  99–100

Babka (Walnut Crown Cake), 46–47
Bacon *Pogácsa*, 139
Banana Gugelhupf
  (*Bananengugelhupf*), 33–34
Banana-Chocolate Slices (*Schokolade-
  Bananenschnitten*), 124–26
Bananengugelhupf (Banana
  Gugelhupf), 33–34
Beerenschaumschnitten (Berry
  Meringue Slices), *120*, 121
Beigli (Hungarian Walnut Roulades),
  110–11
Berries. *See specific berries*
Beverages
  Fiaker, 192
  Fruit and Wine Punch (*Bowle*), 197
  Hot Coffee with Orange Liqueur
    (*Maria Theresia*), 192
  Hot Rum Punch (*Punsch von
    Rum*), 195
  Hot Spiced Tea (*Gewürztee*), 197
  Mulled "Glow" Wine (*Glühwein*),
    195
  Real Hot Chocolate (*Heiße
    Schokolade mit Schlagobers*), 197
Birnenstrudel aus Butterteig (Pear
  Strudel with Puff Pastry), 86–87
Bischifsbrot (Bishop's Fruit-and-
  Chocolate Tea Cake), 36
Bishop's Fruit-and-Chocolate Tea
  Cake (*Bischifsbrot*), 36
Biskuitmasse (sponge cake batter), 4
Blueberry(ies)
  Berry Meringue Slices (*Beeren-
    schaumschnitten*), *120*, 121
  Cream Roulade
    (*Heidelbeerroulade*), 40–41
  Sour Cream Mini-Pancakes
    (*Dalken*), 164–66
Bowle (Fruit and Wine Punch), 197
Brandteig (Cream Puff Dough), 14
Bread crumbs, 205
Breads and rolls. *See* Rolls; Sweet
  yeast breads
Brioche Braid (*Briochestriezel*), 92–93
Briochestriezel (Brioche Braid), 92–93
Buchteln (Viennese Jam Rolls), 95–96
Buchty (Cheese-Filled Sweet Rolls),
  94–95
Burgtheatertorte (Chocolate-Orange
  Cake), 30–31
Butter, in recipes, 200
Butterteig (Puff Pastry), 4
  recipe, 13–14

Cake(s)
  cooling, 214
  crumbs, in recipes, 205
  cutting into layers, 205–6
  pans and equipment, 200–201, 206,
    209, 213, 214
Cakes, simple and fancy, 24–75
  listing of recipes, vii
Cheese. *See also* Farmer's Cheese
  Pogácsa, 139

Cheesecake, Farmer's (*Topfentorte*),
  24–25
Cherry(ies), 201
  -Almond Coffee Cake (*Meggyes
    Piskóta*), 27
  -Chocolate Mousse Cake
    (*Lúdlábtorta* [Hungarian]), *48*,
    74–75
  -Chocolate Roulade (*Schokolade-
    Kirschenroulade*), 42–43
  Christmas Sweet Bread (*Stollen*),
    108–10
  Sour, Strudel (*Kirschstrudel*), 82
  Warm Rice Pudding with
    (*Reisauflauf mit Kirschen*),
    185–86
Chestnut(s), 201
  "Potatoes" (*Kaštanové Brambůrky*),
    147
  Slices (*Gesztenyeszelet*), 35
Chocolate, 201–5
  -Almond Macaroons (*Schokolade
    Busserln*), 145–46
  -Almond Torte (*Panamatorte*),
    69–70
  -and-Fruit Tea Cake, Bishop's
    (*Bischifsbrot*), 36
  -Banana Slices (*Schokolade-
    Bananenschnitten*), 124–26
  -Cherry Mousse Cake (*Lúdlábtorta*
    [Hungarian]), *48*, 74–75
  -Cherry Roulade (*Schokolade-
    Kirschenroulade*), 42–43
  chopping, 203
  -Covered "Indian" Cupcakes
    (*Indianerkrapfen*), 127–29
  -Cream "Dumplings" (*Somlói
    Galuska*), 180–82
  curls, creating, 204–5
  Dobos Torte (*Dobos Torta*), *72*,
    73–74
  Doughnuts, 154
  Gerbaud Slices (*Gerbaud-Szelet*),
    132, 133–34
  Glaze (*Schokoladeglasur*), 16
  Gundel-Style Crêpes (*Palacsinta
    Gundel Módra*), 160–61
  Hazelnut Roulade with Mocha
    Cream (*Haselnußroulade mit
    Mokkacreme*), 44–46
  Hot, Real (*Heiße Schokolade mit
    Schlagobers*), 197
  Ischl Tartlets (*Ischler Törtchen*),
    142–45
  Leschanz's Sachertorte (*Leschanz-
    Sachertorte*), 62–63
  Marble Gugelhupf
    (*Marmorgugelhupf*), 34
  melting, 203
  Mousse Cake, Leschanz's
    (*Leschanztorte*), 58–59
  Mousse Squares, Hungarian (*Rigó
    Jancsi*), 122–23
  -Orange Cake (*Burgtheatertorte*),
    30–31

piping from paper cone, 204
Pudding, Steamed *(Mohr im Hemd)*, 183–85
Sachertorte *(Sachertorte)*, 59–62
"Saddle of Venison" Cake *(Rehrücken)*, 28, *29*
Sauce, Rum, 18
Sauce, Warm *(Schokoladesauce)*, 18
Sponge Cake *(Schokolade Biskuittorte)*, 8
storing, 205
types of, 201–3
Christmas Sweet Bread *(Stollen)*, 108–10
Cocoa powder, types of, 203
Coconut Macaroons *(Kokobusserln)*, 146–47
Coffee
  Eclairs *(Moka Eclairs)*, 123–24
  Faux Fondant Icing, 15
  Fiaker, 192
  Hot, with Orange Liqueur *(Maria Theresia)*, 192
Coffee Cake, Apricot *(Marillenfleck)*, 26–27
Coffee Cake, Cherry-Almond *(Meggyes Piskóta)*, 27
Cookies
  Chestnut "Potatoes" *(Kaštanové Brambůrky)*, 147
  Chocolate-Almond Macaroons *(Schokolade Busserln)*, 145–46
  Coconut Macaroons *(Kokobusserln)*, 146–47
  Ischl Tartlets *(Ischler Törtchen)*, 142–45
  Linzer "Eyes" *(Linzer Augen)*, 148
  Thumbprint *(Hussaren)*, 151
  Vanilla Crescents *(Vanillen Kipferln)*, 149–50
  Walnut Crescent, from Pozsony *(Pozsony Kipfli)*, *140*, 150–51
Cream, in recipes, 205
Cream Puff Dough *(Brandteig)*, 14
Crêpes
  Basic *(Palatschinken)*, 160
  Cheese-Filled *(Topfenpalatschinken)*, 163–64
  Gundel-Style *(Palacsinta Gundel Módra)*, 160–61
  Jam-Filled *(Obst Palatschinken)*, 161–62
Croissant and Apple Pudding *(Kipferlkoch)*, 178
Crullers with Rum Glaze *(Spritzkrapfen)*, 155
Crumbs, bread and cake, 205
Cupcakes, Chocolate-Covered "Indian" *(Indianerkrapfen)*, 127–29
Currant(s), 209
  Bishop's Fruit-and-Chocolate Tea Cake *(Bischifsbrot)*, 36
  and Hazelnut Snails *(Schnecken)*, *88*, 98

Dalken (Sour Cream Mini-Pancakes), 164–66
Dalmatian Four-Flavor Kolacky *(Domažlicé Kolače)*, 100–102
Decorating comb and stand, 206
Diostorte (Walnut Torte with Walnut-Custard Buttercream), 66–67
Dobos Torte *(Dobos Torta)*, 71, *72*
  recipe, 73–74
Domažlicé Kolače (Dalmatian Four-Flavor Kolacky), 100–102
Dommayerschnitten (Zucchini Slices with Chocolate Glaze), 47
Dough
  Cream Puff *(Brandteig)*, 14
  filo, working with, 83
  Short Crust *(Mürbteig)*, 4, 15
  Strudel *(Strudelteig* [German]), 78–80
  Viennese Sweet Yeast *(Plunderteig)*, 4, 8–11
  Yeast *(Germteig)*, 4
Doughnuts
  Crullers with Rum Glaze *(Spritzkrapfen)*, 155
  Mardis Gras; var. *(Faschingkrapfen)*, 152–54
Dumplings
  Farmer's Cheese, with "Roasted" Plums *(Topfenknödel mit Zwetschkenröster)*, 174
  Farmer's Cheese and Strawberry *(Erdbeerknödel)*, *168*, *172*, *173*
  Prune Pockets *(Powidltascherln)*, 175
"Dumplings," Chocolate-Cream *(Somlói Galuska)*, 180–82

Ebelskiver pan, 206
Eclairs, Coffee *(Moka Eclairs)*, 123–24
Eggs, 206–7
  Salzburg Dessert Soufflé *(Salzburger Nockerl)*, 166
  Sweet Fruit Omelet *(Stefánia Omelette)*, 166–67
The Emperor's Pancake *(Kaiserschmarren)*, *156*, 162–63
Equipment, baking, 200–215
Erdbeerknödel (Farmer's Cheese and Strawberry Dumplings), *168*, *172*, *173*
Erdbeeroberstorte (Strawberry Cream Torte), 67–68
Esterházyschnitten (Nut Meringue Slices), 130–31

Farmer's Cheese, 207–8
  Cheese-Filled Crêpes *(Topfenpalatschinken)*, 163–64
  Cheese-Filled Sweet Rolls *(Buchty)*, 94–95
  Dalmatian Four-Flavor Kolacky *(Domažlicé Kolače)*, 100–102

Dumplings with "Roasted" Plums *(Topfenknödel mit Zwetschkenröster)*, 174
Farmer's Cheesecake *(Topfentorte)*, 24–25
  and Raisin Filo Strudel *(Topfenstrudel)*, 86
  and Strawberry Dumplings *(Erdbeerknödel)*, *168*, *172*, *173*
  Warm "Milk Cream" Strudel with Vanilla Sauce *(Milchrahmstrudel)*, *76*, 84–86
Faschingkrapfen (Mardi Gras Doughnuts), 152–54
Fiaker, 192
Filo dough, working with, 83
Flódni (Apple, Walnut, and Poppy Seed Bars), 116–17
Flour, buying and measuring, 208
Francia Krémes (Puff Pastry Cream Slices with Coffee Icing), 134–35
Fruit. *See also* Fruit preserves; *specific fruits*
  -and-Chocolate Tea Cake, Bishop's *(Bischifsbrot)*, 36
  dried and candied, 208–9
  Omelet, Sweet *(Stefánia-Omelette)*, 166–67
  Sour Cream Mini-Pancakes *(Dalken)*, 164–66
  and Wine Punch *(Bowle)*, 197
Fruit preserves, 212. *See also* Apricot preserves
  Brown Linzertorte *(Linzertorte Braun)*, 52–53, *53*
  Ischl Tartlets *(Ischler Törtchen)*, 142–45
  Jam-Filled Crêpes *(Obst Palatschinken)*, 161–62
  Linzer "Eyes" *(Linzer Augen)*, 148
  Red Currant Glaze, 16
  Thumbprint Cookies *(Hussaren)*, 151

Gelatin, in recipes, 209
Gerbaud Slices *(Gerbaud-Szelet)*, *132*, 133–34
Gerbaud-Szelet (Gerbaud Slices), *132*, 133–34
Germgugelhupf (Yeast Gugelhupf), 102–3
Germteig (Yeast Dough), 4
Germzwetschkenfleck (Yeast Plum Squares), 104–7
Gesztenyeszelet (Chestnut Slices), 35
Gewürztee (Hot Spiced Tea), 197
Glaze, Apricot *(Marillenglasur)*, 16
Glaze, Chocolate *(Schokoladeglasur)*, 16
Glaze, Red Currant, 16
Glühwein (Mulled "Glow" Wine), 195
Grape Strudel with Weinchaudeau *(Weintraubenstrudel mit Weinchaudeau)*, *81*, 82–83

Gugelhupf, 103
    Banana *(Bananengugelhupf)*, 33–34
    Marble *(Marmorgugelhupf)*, 34
    pans, 209
    Poppy Seed *(Mohngugelhupf)*, 32,
        33
    Yeast *(Germgugelhupf)*, 102–3
Gundel-Style Crêpes *(Palacsinta
    Gundel Módra)*, 160–61

Haselnußroulade mit Mokkacreme
    (Hazelnut Roulade with Mocha
    Cream), 44–46
Hazelnut(s), 211
    Brown Linzertorte *(Linzertorte
        Braun)*, 52–53, *53*
    and Currant Snails *(Schnecken)*, *88*,
        98
    Dobos Torte *(Dobos Torta)*, *72*,
        73–74
    Nut Meringue Slices
        (Esterházyschnitten), 130–31
    Roulade with Mocha Cream
        *(Haselnußroulade mit
        Mokkacreme)*, 44–46
Heidelbeerroulade (Blueberry Cream
    Roulade), 40–41
Heiße Schokolade mit Schlagobers (Real
    Hot Chocolate), 197
Himbeerjoghurttorte (Raspberry Yogurt
    Torte), 70–71
Hungarian Chocolate Mousse Squares
    (Rigó Jancsi), 122–23
Hungarian Flaky Scones *(Pogácsa)*,
    112, 138–39
Hungarian Walnut Roulades *(Beigli)*,
    110–11
Hussaren (Thumbprint Cookies), 151

Icing, applying, 209
Icing, Faux Fondant; var.
    (Wasserglasur), 15
Indianerkrapfen (Chocolate-Covered
    "Indian" Cupcakes), 127–29
Individual desserts
    Apple Squares *(Almás Pites)*,
        118–19
    Apples in Pastry Robes *(Apfel im
        Schlafrock)*, 119
    Bacon *Pogácsa*, 139
    Berry Meringue Slices
        (Beerenschaumschnitten),
        120, 121
    Cheese *Pogácsa*, 139
    Chocolate-Banana Slices
        (Schokolade-Bananenschnitten),
        124–26
    Chocolate-Covered "Indian" Cup-
        cakes *(Indianerkrapfen)*, 127–29
    Coffee Eclairs *(Moka Eclairs)*,
        123–24
    Gerbaud Slices *(Gerbaud-Szelet)*,
        132, 133–34
    Hungarian Chocolate Mousse
        Squares *(Rigó Jancsi)*, 122–23

Hungarian Flaky Scones *(Pogácsa)*,
    112, 138–39
Meringue and Ladyfinger Slices
    (Kardinalschnitten), 136, *137*
Nut Meringue Slices
    (Esterházyschnitten), 130–31
Puff Pastry Cornets with Whipped
    Cream *(Schaumrollen)*, 126–27
Puff Pastry Cream Slices with
    Coffee Icing *(Francia Krémes)*,
    134–35
Raspberry Slices, 121
Red Currant Slices, 121
Whipped-Cream Puff Pastry
    Slices, 135
Ingredients, for recipes, 200–215
Ischl Tartlets *(Ischler Törtchen)*,
    142–45
Ischler Törtchen (Ischl Tartlets),
    142–45

Jams, fruit. *See* Fruit preserves

Kaiserschmarren (The Emperor's
    Pancake), *156*, 162–63
Kalte Biskuittorte (Cold-Method
    Sponge Cake), 7–8
Kardinalschnitten (Meringue and
    Ladyfinger Slices), 136, *137*
Kaštanové Bramb̊urky (Chestnut
    "Potatoes"), 147
Kipferlkoch (Croissant and Apple
    Pudding), 178
Kipferln (Viennese Crescent Rolls),
    96–98
Kirschstrudel (Sour Cherry Strudel),
    82
Kokobusserln (Coconut Macaroons),
    146–47
Kolacky, Dalmatian Four-Flavor
    (Domažlicé Kolače), 100–102

Ladyfinger Slices, Meringue and
    (Kardinalschnitten), 136, *137*
Ladyfinger Torte with Rum Cream
    (Malakofftorte), 54–56
Leschanz's Chocolate Mousse Cake
    (Leschanztorte), 58–59
Leschanz's Sachertorte *(Leschanz-
    Sachertorte)*, 62–63
Leschanz-Sachertorte (Leschanz's
    Sachertorte), 62–63
Leschanztorte (Leschanz's Chocolate
    Mousse Cake), 58–59
Linzer Augen (Linzer "Eyes"), 148
Linzer "Eyes" *(Linzer Augen)*, 148
Linzertorte, Brown *(Linzertorte
    Braun)*, 52–53, *53*
Linzertorte, history of, 54
Linzertorte Braun (Brown Linzertorte),
    52–53, *53*
Liquors and liqueurs, in recipes, 210
Lúdlábtorta (Hungarian) (Chocolate-
    Cherry Mousse Cake), *48*,
    74–75

Macaroons, Chocolate-Almond
    (Schokolade Busserln), 145–46
Macaroons, Coconut *(Kokobusserln)*,
    146–47
Malakofftorte (Ladyfinger Torte with
    Rum Cream), 54–56
Marble Gugelhupf
    (Marmorgugelhupf), 34
Mardis Gras Doughnuts; var.
    (Faschingkrapfen), 152–54
Maria Theresia (Hot Coffee with
    Orange Liqueur), 192
Marillenfleck (Apricot Coffee Cake),
    26–27
Marillenglasur (Apricot Glaze), 16
Marillenkuchen (Apricot Tart), 26
Marmorgugelhupf (Marble
    Gugelhupf), 34
Meggyes Piskóta (Cherry-Almond
    Coffee Cake), 27
Meringue
    Cream *(Schaumobers)*, 18–19
    and Ladyfinger Slices
        (Kardinalschnitten), 136, *137*
    Shell with Strawberries and Cream
        (Spanische Windtorte), 64–65
    Slices, Berry *(Beerenschaum-
        schnitten)*, *120*, 121
    Slices, Nut *(Esterházyschnitten)*,
        130–31
Milchrahmstrudel (Warm "Milk
    Cream" Strudel with Vanilla
    Sauce), *76*, 84–86
Mohngugelhupf (Poppy Seed
    Gugelhupf), *32*, 33
Mohnkuchen (Flourless Poppy Seed
    Cake), 39
Mohnnudeln (Potato Noodles with
    Sweet Poppy Seeds), 174–75
Mohr im Hemd (Steamed Chocolate
    Pudding), 183–85
Moka Eclairs (Coffee Eclairs), 123–24
Mürbteig (Short Crust Dough), 4
    recipe, 15

Noodles, Potato, with Sweet Poppy
    Seeds *(Mohnnudeln)*, 174–75
Nußpuddings (Warm Walnut
    Pudding), 186–87
Nut(s). *See also* Almond(s);
    Chestnut(s); Hazelnut(s);
    Walnut(s)
    -Filled Crescents, 98
    grinding and toasting, 211
    Meringue Slices
        (Esterházyschnitten), 130–31

Obst Palatschinken (Jam-Filled
    Crêpes), 161–62
Omelet, Sweet Fruit *(Stefánia-
    Omelette)*, 166–67
Orange Torte with Orange Cream
    Frosting *(Orangentorte)*, 57–58
Orange-Chocolate Cake
    (Burgtheatertorte), 30–31

Orangentorte (Orange Torte with Orange Cream Frosting), 57–58

Palatschinken (Basic Crêpes), 160
Panamatorte (Chocolate-Almond Torte), 69–70
Pancake(s). *See also* Crêpes
    The Emperor's *(Kaiserschmarren)*, *156*, 162–63
    Mini, Sour Cream *(Dalken)*, 164–66
Pear Strudel with Puff Pastry *(Birnenstrudel aus Butterteig)*, 86–87
Pink Faux Fondant Icing, 15
Plum(s)
    The Emperor's Pancake *(Kaiserschmarren)*, *156*, 162–63
    "Roasted," 163
    "Roasted," Farmer's Cheese Dumplings with *(Topfenknödel mit Zwetschkenröster)*, 174
    Squares, Yeast *(Germzwetschkenfleck)*, 104–7
    Squares *(Zwetschkenflecken)*, 38–39
Plunderteig (Viennese Sweet Yeast Dough), 4
    recipe, 8–11
Pogácsa (Hungarian Flaky Scones), *112*, 138–39
Poppy Seed(s), 212
    Apple, and Walnut Bars *(Flódni)*, 116–17
    Cake, Flourless *(Mohnkuchen)*, 39
    Dalmatian Four-Flavor Kolacky *(Domažlicé Kolače)*, 100–102
    Gugelhupf *(Mohngugelhupf)*, *32*, 33
    Sweet, Potato Noodles with *(Mohnnudeln)*, 174–75
Potato Noodles with Sweet Poppy Seeds *(Mohnnudeln)*, 174–75
Pound Cake, Viennese *(Sandtorte)*, 38
Powidltascherln (Prune Pockets), 175
Pozsony Kipfli (Walnut Crescent Cookies from Pozsony), *140*, 150–51
Preserves. *See* Fruit preserves
Prune butter, 212–13
    Dalmatian Four-Flavor Kolacky *(Domažlicé Kolače)*, 100–102
    Prune Doughnuts, 154
    Prune Pockets *(Powidltascherln)*, 175
    Viennese Jam Rolls *(Buchteln)*, 95–96
Pudding
    Chocolate-Cream "Dumplings" *(Somlói Galuska)*, 180–82
    Croissant and Apple *(Kipferlkoch)*, 178
    Molded Rice, with Raspberries *(Reis Trauttmansdorff)*, *176*, 182–83
    molds, 213

Steamed Chocolate *(Mohr im Hemd)*, 183–85
Viennese-Style Zabaglione with Raspberries *(Weinchaudeau)*, 187
Warm Rice, with Cherries *(Reisauflauf mit Kirschen)*, 185–86
Warm Walnut *(Nußpuddings)*, 186–87
Puff Pastry *(Butterteig)*, 4
recipe, 13–14
Puff Pastry Cornets with Whipped Cream *(Schaumrollen)*, 126–27
Puff Pastry Cream Slices with Coffee Icing; var. *(Francia Krémes)*, 134–35
Punch, Fruit and Wine *(Bowle)*, 197
Punch, Hot Rum *(Punsch von Rum)*, 195
Punch Cake *(Punschtorte)*, 56–57
Punsch von Rum (Hot Rum Punch), 195
Punschtorte (Punch Cake), 56–57

Raisin(s), 208–9
    and Farmer's Cheese Filo Strudel *(Topfenstrudel)*, 86
    Yeast Gugelhupf *(Germgugelhupf)*, 102–3
Raspberry(ies)
    Molded Rice Pudding with *(Reis Trauttmansdorff)*, *176*, 182–83
    Sauce, 183
    Slices, 121
    Sour Cream Mini-Pancakes *(Dalken)*, 164–66
    Viennese-Style Zabaglione with *(Weinchaudeau)*, 187
    Yogurt Torte *(Himbeerjoghurttorte)*, 70–71
Red Currant Glaze, 16
Red Currant Slices, 121
Rehrücken (Chocolate "Saddle of Venison" Cake), 28, *29*
Rehrücken pan, 213
Reis Trauttmansdorff (Molded Rice Pudding with Raspberries), *176*, 182–83
Reisauflauf mit Kirschen (Warm Rice Pudding with Cherries), 185–86
Rice Pudding, Molded, with Raspberries *(Reis Trauttmansdorff)*, *176*, 182–83
Rice Pudding, Warm, with Cherries *(Reisauflauf mit Kirschen)*, 185–86
Rigó Jancsi (Hungarian Chocolate Mousse Squares), 122–23
Rolls
    Crescent, Viennese *(Kipferln)*, 96–98
    Currant and Hazelnut Snails *(Schnecken)*, *88*, 98

Dalmatian Four-Flavor Kolacky *(Domažlicé Kolače)*, 100–102
Golden Dumplings *(Aranygaluska)*, 99–100
Hungarian Walnut Roulades *(Beigli)*, 110–11
Jam, Viennese *(Buchteln)*, 95–96
Nut-Filled Crescents, 98
Sweet, Cheese-Filled *(Buchty)*, 94–95
Roulade
    Blueberry Cream *(Heidelbeerroulade)*, 40–41
    Chocolate-Cherry *(Schokolade-Kirschenroulade)*, 42–43
    Hazelnut, with Mocha Cream *(Haselnußroulade mit Mokkacreme)*, 44–46
Rum, 210
    Chocolate Sauce, 18
    Chocolate-Cream "Dumplings" *(Somlói Galuska)*, 180–82
    Cream, Ladyfinger Torte with *(Malakofftorte)*, 54–56
    Punch, Hot *(Punsch von Rum)*, 195
    Punch Cake *(Punschtorte)*, 56–57

Sachertorte, Leschanz's *(Leschanz-Sachertorte)*, 62–63
Sachertorte *(Sachertorte)*, 59–62
Salt, in recipes, 213
Salzburg Dessert Soufflé *(Salzburger Nockerl)*, 166
Salzburger Nockerl (Salzburg Dessert Soufflé), 166
Sandtorte (Viennese Pound Cake), 38
Sauce
    Chocolate, Rum, 18
    Chocolate, Warm *(Schokoladesauce)*, 18
    Raspberry, 183
    Vanilla *(Vanillesauce)*, 18
    Weinchaudeau, 187
Schaumobers (Meringue Cream), 18–19
Schaumrollen (Puff Pastry Cornets with Whipped Cream), 126–27
Schlagobers (Sweetened Whipped Cream), 19
Schnecken (Currant and Hazelnut Snails), *88*, 98
Schokolade Biskuittorte (Chocolate Sponge Cake), 8
Schokolade Busserln (Chocolate-Almond Macaroons), 145–46
Schokolade-Bananenschnitten (Chocolate-Banana Slices), 124–26
Schokoladeglasur (Chocolate Glaze), 16
Schokolade-Kirschenroulade (Chocolate-Cherry Roulade), 42–43